THE
EVERYTHING®
GUIDE TO
ONLINE GENEALOGY
3RD EDITION

Dear Reader,

Tracing your family tree is exciting enough, but the wealth of records now available online exponentially heightens the adventure. When I first began researching my family tree about thirty years ago as part of a class project, I wrote letters to my grandparents, looked at my baby book, walked through a few family cemeteries, and created a family tree. As I gained knowledge and experience, I learned how to load a roll of microfilm onto a reader and encountered a world of census records and land deeds. I also discovered the courthouse, where I still love to research—full of big, heavy books of often handwritten historical records.

Genealogy finally started gaining ground online during the mid-1990s, but there were initially very few records available. The Internet was primarily a tool for connecting with fellow genealogists—and that was pretty exciting at the time! Now you can find your ancestors in marriage records, census enumerations, ship passenger lists, passport and social security applications, Revolutionary War pension files, Civil War service records, land grants, and a wealth of other digital documents, all without leaving home. Even those still necessary visits to the courthouse, library, or cemetery are made easier because you can use the Internet to do advance scouting, ask questions, or request record copies online. Online software tools make it easy to easily build your family tree online. You can also connect with hundreds of fellow genealogists online through blogs, Facebook, Twitter, Google+, and other social media—I think you'll find us a helpful and welcoming group.

I appreciate this opportunity to introduce you to the fascinating and exhilarating field of genealogy. It's a wonderful journey, and I'm honored that you've chosen to begin it here.

Happy hunting,

Kimberly Powell

Colfax Public **Library**
613 Main P.O. **Box 525**
Colfax, WI 54730
715-962-4334

Welcome to the EVERYTHING. Series!

These handy, accessible books give you all you need to tackle a difficult project, gain a new hobby, comprehend a fascinating topic, prepare for an exam, or even brush up on something you learned back in school but have since forgotten.

You can choose to read an Everything® book from cover to cover or just pick out the information you want from our four useful boxes: e-questions, e-links, e-alerts, and e-ssentials.

We give you everything you need to know on the subject, but throw in a lot of fun stuff along the way, too.

We now have more than 400 Everything® books in print, spanning such wide-ranging categories as weddings, pregnancy, cooking, music instruction, foreign language, crafts, pets, New Age, and so much more. When you're done reading them all, you can finally say you know Everything®!

QUESTION

Answers to
common questions

LINK

Important
websites

ALERT

Urgent
warnings

ESSENTIAL

Quick
handy tips

PUBLISHER Karen Cooper

MANAGING EDITOR, EVERYTHING® SERIES Lisa Laing

COPY CHIEF Casey Ebert

ASSISTANT PRODUCTION EDITOR Alex Guarco

ACQUISITIONS EDITOR Pamela Wissman

SENIOR DEVELOPMENT EDITOR Eileen Mullan

EVERYTHING® SERIES COVER DESIGNER Erin Alexander

Visit the entire Everything® series at *www.everything.com*

THE
EVERYTHING®
GUIDE TO ONLINE GENEALOGY

3RD EDITION

Trace your roots, share your history,
and create your family tree

Kimberly Powell

The About.com Expert to Genealogy

Avon, Massachusetts

To Albrecht, my incredible husband who fills my life with passion, inspiration, purpose, and love. Thank you for bringing your parents and our children into my world, and for being my best friend.

An Everything® Series Book.
Everything® and everything.com® are registered trademarks of F+W Media, Inc.

Published by Adams Media, a division of F+W Media, Inc.
57 Littlefield Street, Avon, MA 02322. U.S.A.
www.adamsmedia.com

ISBN 10: 1-4405-7068-X
ISBN 13: 978-1-4405-7068-1
eISBN 10: 1-4405-7069-8
eISBN 13: 978-1-4405-7069-8

Printed in the United States of America.

12 11 10 9 8 7 6 5 4 3

Library of Congress Cataloging-in-Publication Data
Powell, Kimberly.
  The everything guide to online genealogy : trace your roots, share your history, and create an online family tree / Kimberly Powell. -- 3rd edition.
      pages cm. -- (Everything series)
  Includes bibliographical references and indexes.
  ISBN 978-1-4405-7068-1 (alk. paper) -- ISBN 1-4405-7068-X (alk. paper) -- ISBN 978-1-4405-7069-8 (eISBN) -- ISBN 1-4405-7069-8 (eISBN)
  1. Genealogy--Computer network resources. I. Title. II. Title: Online genealogy.
  CS21.5.P69 2014
  929.10285--dc23

                              2013033378

Cover image © istockphoto/John Woodcock.

This book is available at quantity discounts for bulk purchases.
For information, please call 1-800-289-0963.

Contents

Introduction **11**

01

Click Into Your Past / 13

Family Tree Basics **14**

Plan Your Project **14**

Collect Information **18**

Evaluate Your Evidence **21**

Organize the Search **22**

Record Your Progress **27**

Document Your Findings **31**

02

Begin Backward / 35

Interview Yourself **36**

Rummage Through the Attic **38**

Question Your Family Members **40**

Has It Already Been Done? **44**

From One Generation to the Next **47**

03

Learn How to Search / 49

Search Engine Basics **50**

Database Search Strategies **53**

Get Creative with Names **56**

Connect with Living Kin **58**

More Search Tools and Tactics **59**

Find the Right Tree in the Forest **61**

Spread the Wealth **62**

04

Online Starting Points / 65

What Is and Is Not Online **66**

Find Family at FamilySearch **66**

Explore More Free Databases **70**

Seek Out Subscription Sites **73**

Discover History at the National Archives **76**

Look at the Library of Congress **78**

Search State Libraries and Archives **79**

05 Dig Into Death Records / 81

A Good Place to Begin 82

Search for Obituaries 82

Social Security Death Index 86

Death Certificates and
Online Indexes 88

Visit Virtual Cemeteries and
Funeral Homes 90

Put It Into Practice 94

06 Check the Census / 97

The U.S. Federal Census 98

Access Census Images and
Indexes Online 100

Census Research Tips
and Caveats 104

Follow Census Clues to
New Records 106

Special and State Censuses 109

Utilize Census Alternatives 112

Put It Into Practice 114

07 Hunt Down Family Connections / 117

Marriage and Divorce Records 118

Birth and Baptismal Records 120

Unearth Wills and Estate Records 122

Chase Down Court Records 125

Identify Adoptions and Orphans 127

08 Look Local / 131

Maps and Geography 132

Land and Property Records 134

Historical Newspapers 142

Libraries and Societies 146

Churches and Schools 149

09 Mine the Web for Military Records / 155

Find Clues to Military Service 156

Compiled Military Service Records 157

Pensions and Bounty Land
Warrants 160

Discover Revolutionary and
Civil War Ancestors 163

Research Twentieth-Century
Conflicts 168

Bone Up on Military History 172

10 A Nation of Immigrants / 175

Find the Birthplace of Your
Immigrant Ancestor 176

Plunge Into Passenger Lists 177

Naturalization Records 186

Ethnic Research 191

Put It Into Practice 192

11 Reach Out to Others / 195

Make the Most of Boards and Lists **196**

Ferret Out Family Trees **199**

Ask the Right Way **203**

Share Your Research **206**

Take a Class **207**

Connect with the Pros **210**

12 Dig Deeper / 215

Books, Magazines, and Blogs **216**

Occupational Records **218**

Membership Organizations **221**

Photos and Postcards **223**

DNA and Genetic Genealogy **228**

13 Locate Records Abroad / 235

A Nation of Immigrants **236**

Canada **236**

Mexico, Central America, and South America **239**

British Isles **240**

The Rest of Europe **247**

Australia and New Zealand **255**

Asia and Africa **256**

14 Putting It All Together / 259

Evaluate What You've Found **260**

Protect Your Family History from Disaster **266**

Publish Your Family History **268**

Dos and Don'ts of Online Genealogy **272**

See It in Action **275**

Appendix A: Further Readings / 277

Appendix B: Examples of Family Trees / 285

Appendix C: Genealogical Standards / 289

Index / 295

Acknowledgments

There are many people to whom I owe a tremendous debt of gratitude, and I'm blessed that the list continues to grow longer with each passing year. My children, Kelsey, Garrett, and Kira, have to come first—I am so proud and blessed to be your mother. Thank you for warming up leftovers and holding down the fort to give me time to work, and inspiring me every day to be a better mother, writer, and person. Thank you also to Albrecht, for always supporting my dreams and challenging me to spread my wings a little further than I otherwise would.

I probably would have never taken that first step into writing if it weren't for my mother, Roselyne Thomas. Thank you for nurturing my continual curiosity, and inspiring my love of reading, learning, and, yes, teaching! Daddy (Larry Thomas), thank you for your constant love and encouragement. I'm so glad that you are finally getting to follow your dreams. And, of course, thank you to my two grandmothers, Gisele Owens and Lucile Thomas, for their constant love, and for being the foundation on which my passion for family history was built.

I would also like to express my appreciation to all the wonderful people I've worked with in my thirteen years at About.com, as well as my many loyal readers. Thank you for helping me find my voice and giving me the opportunity to share my passion for genealogy with the world. Thank you to my editors at Adams Media, Eileen Mullan and Pam Wissman, for giving me this opportunity to share my love of family history with the world, and for keeping me focused on the journey. Thank you to Harold Henderson, for always being available when I need some last-minute writing or editing advice, and to all of my friends and colleagues in the genealogy community who keep me challenged and make me feel loved.

Introduction

IT SEEMS AS IF almost everyone is at least mildly interested in discovering his or her roots. Maybe you're curious about the origin of your last name or why Grandpa never spoke about his family. Perhaps you hope for a famous relative or a bit of scandal in your background. Or maybe you're tired of people asking you where your red hair and freckles came from and want to find out for yourself. Ten years ago, your curiosity may have ended with asking your parents a few questions about your ancestors or looking in the library for a book on your family. Today, the Internet has revolutionized the search for family history and heritage, allowing anyone with a consuming curiosity and a passion for answers to trace his or her ancestry and make connections with long-lost relatives.

Remote Internet access to historical documents and records has dramatically increased the number of people interested in researching the past. Following the release of the 1940 U.S. census on April 2, 2012, the National Archives reported that 1.9 million users hit its census servers in the first four hours after the data went public, with requests coming in as fast as 100,000 per second. Documents that once required extensive travel to view are now instantly available to anyone around the world at the click of a mouse. This tremendous growth of online source material means that time and distance are no longer the constraints to research that they once were. Genealogy really has become accessible to anyone.

While the Internet is a valuable tool for anyone researching a family tree, don't expect to be able to conduct your research solely online. Some of the information you seek will only be found in the files of the state archives or county courthouse, or on the tombstone concealed in the middle of a North Carolina cornfield. Even in these cases, however, the Internet can provide clues to the location of such records and connect you to other genealogists who may be able to help you access them. You can also use the Internet to build a family tree and share it with your extended family, take a class to expand your knowledge, collaborate with fellow researchers on puzzling problems, explore the history that your ancestors once lived, and connect with previously unknown cousins.

Beyond the Internet, technology has also advanced genealogy research in other ways. Specialized software makes it easy to keep track of hundreds or thousands of tangled family connections. DNA testing can tell you if you share common ancestry with another individual, or help you confirm descent from a particular ethnic or geographical population. Satellite images help you visualize the places where your ancestors once lived. Constructing a medical family tree can possibly even save your life!

Real-life examples of genealogy research on the Internet are a special feature of this book. In most cases, well-known individuals such as Laura Ingalls Wilder and J.K. Rowling are used to illustrate the research process, but while there is more information available about these famous figures online than you'll find for most people, the biographies and media accolades are ignored, and the search for records that chronicle the lives of their ancestors is conducted in the same databases and websites you would examine for your own relatives. By seeing how the research techniques discussed in this book can be used to research their family trees, you'll hopefully gain a better understanding of how to apply the same techniques to your own family history search.

You are about to embark on a fascinating trip into your own past. You'll make many discoveries along the way, both about your ancestors and about yourself. You may find that ancestors who led quiet, ordinary lives can be fascinating in their own special ways, and that history is much more interesting when you know that your ancestors were participants. Before long, you'll be addicted for life. Genealogy is an extremely rewarding pastime. I hope you enjoy the journey!

CHAPTER 1

Click Into Your Past

This is a fantastic time to start your journey into genealogy. Paper is the past and digital is now. New technologies, ranging from the Internet to digital photography, have spawned an explosion in the popularity of genealogy. New software simplifies storing, organizing, and retrieving family tree data. Images of original records long locked away in archives can be viewed online. Research guides, databases, and the expertise of other genealogists are all readily available at the click of a mouse. In short, research can be conducted more quickly, and data is more readily available to anyone with an interest in his or her past. So jump right in!

Family Tree Basics

Thanks to new technological advances, information on your ancestors is just a click of the mouse away. Millions of digitized images, from marriage certificates to military service records, can be viewed online. Published genealogies allow budding family historians to extend their family tree by generations in just a few minutes. There is even free online software available to help you record the information you find and build your family tree. It sounds so easy, right?

As valuable as the Internet is for family history research, it does have its limitations. Most important, don't expect to find your family tree already done for you. The Internet is just one of many research tools and resources you'll utilize in the discovery of your past. For every genealogical record that you find online, thousands more are still only available in libraries, archives, courthouses, and other repositories.

Much of the genealogy information published online comes in the form of indexes or transcriptions, which point to more likely reliable original records. And, of course, not everything located online is correct, necessitating research in additional sources to prove your family connections. Yes, the Internet will simplify and enhance your quest for your roots, but it should be considered a valuable supplement to more traditional methods of research, not the sole tool for tracing your family tree.

Before using the Internet to plug into your past, you first need to learn a few tools of the trade—the symbols, terminology, and conventions used by genealogists to collect, record, and communicate the relationships in a family tree. Some of the information presented in this introductory chapter may seem a bit complex if you are new to genealogy, but after you spend a little time tracing your family tree it will all start to come together.

Plan Your Project

Why are you interested in your family history? Are you curious about the origin of your last name? Do you want to learn more about great-grandpa's Polish roots? Are you hoping to identify as many of your ancestors as possible? Has an interesting story been handed down in your family that you want to pursue? Defining what you hope to learn on this journey is an important first step.

Even if your goal is to trace your entire family tree, it is practical to begin with one family line at a time. Otherwise, your research will quickly lead you into a bewildering maze of branching lineages. Go back just three generations in your own family tree, and you'll find yourself faced with researching the genealogy of eight great-grandparents. One family tree has now branched into eight, and it continues to multiply from there. By the time you've worked your way through ten generations of your family, you'll have discovered more than 1,000 ancestors!

LINK

As you research your family tree you may encounter numerous unfamiliar words—terminology specific to family history, as well as acronyms, and legal and Latin terms commonly encountered in genealogical records. Look them up in online genealogy glossaries such as the ones listed under "Specialized Dictionaries for Genealogists" (*http://genealogy.about.com/od/glossaries*) at About.com Genealogy.

What Is a Family Tree?

There are several different approaches you can take when beginning a family tree. A few of the more popular examples are detailed next, but pretty much anything related to researching something in the history of your family qualifies as genealogy. The format you choose to follow should be based on your individual research goals.

Direct Lineage

A direct lineage, alternately called a *pedigree* or ascendant tree, typically begins with you, a parent, or grandparent, and then follows a single surname or bloodline back through several generations in a direct line. This can also be expanded to include multiple direct lines, both of your parents, both of their parents, and so on. This is what most people think of when they refer to a family tree, and where many people begin.

Family Lineage

Take the direct lineage family tree and throw in siblings—the siblings of your parents (your aunts and uncles), the siblings of your grandparents (your great-aunts and -uncles), and so on. This type of genealogy provides a more complete picture of the "family" going back through generations, rather than focusing only on the individuals from whom you directly descend.

Descendant Tree

A descendant tree is the reverse of the traditional family tree. It usually starts with an ancestral couple pretty far back in the family tree and works forward to the present, attempting to account for all known descendants in all lines, both male and female. This is a popular approach for published family histories and for those looking to find relatives to plan a family reunion. It is also used for DNA testing.

Collateral Genealogy

Basically an extension of the direct lineage, a collateral genealogy includes additional relatives who descend from the same common ancestor through lines other than your direct line, such as the spouses and children of siblings. This is similar to the descendant tree, except that most people use collateral genealogy as a type of "cluster" research approach to get around a brick wall in certain areas of their family tree, rather than because they are trying to document all descendants of a particular couple.

What Next? Basic Research Steps

The typical family tree often ends up incorporating elements of most of the approaches discussed in the previous section, so just consider these as a starting point for your research. The point is to begin by selecting a particular individual, couple, or family line that you want to research. Once you've selected this starting point, genealogy research follows a fairly standard set of steps.

1. **What do you want to know first?** Review the information that you have collected to determine what you already know about your ancestor and what you still have left to learn. From there, select a fact that you want to uncover.

2. **Identify a possible record or source for the information.** If you want to learn a death date, you might want to search for a death record or obituary. If you're looking for the names of a couple's children, you may want to begin by searching for the family in the census. Learn what records are available for the time and place in which you are researching, and then begin with the ones most likely to answer your question.

3. **Locate and search the record or source.** Determine where and how you can access the record or source. Then search for your ancestor in the record. If you have trouble locating him or her, use the search strategies discussed later in this book.

4. **Record what you find (or don't find).** Transcribe and/or abstract the important details from each document or source that you examine, and make a copy, whether paper or digital. If a source contains no information on your ancestor, make a note to that effect. Attach a full citation for the document or record to your research notes, as well as on any document copies.

5. **Did you find what you were looking for?** If you found the information you were looking for, move on to the next step. If not, go back to Step 2 and identify another source that may offer the information you hope to find. Since you can't always expect to find what you're looking for the first time, and because a single source is not really credible enough for "proof" on its own, be prepared to cycle through Steps 2 through 5 several times.

6. **Analyze and evaluate the new information.** Look at how the information you uncovered relates to what you already know. Does it answer your question? Does the new information match up with everything else you know about the individual? Is the source credible? Does it suggest another record that might provide confirmation? Use this new information to decide what you need to research next.

7. **Organize and write as you go.** If you don't write down where you found a particular piece of information, you'll eventually find yourself asking the same questions over again and repeating the same searches. Your brain just can't hold it all. Most genealogists use a research log or some type of software to keep track of the sources they've searched and the information they've found—and even the information they don't find. You'll especially appreciate this approach when you pick back up your research after a few weeks or months away from it.

If you've answered the question you formulated in Step 1, select a new goal and begin the genealogical research process over again. If you haven't yet met your research goal, or feel that you need further evidence to support your findings, return to Step 2 and select a new record or source. If you've tried every source you can think of and still haven't found the answer you seek, don't get discouraged. At least you've learned where the answer isn't, and, as your knowledge continues to grow, new approaches will likely present themselves.

Collect Information

Written records are the foundation of genealogy research, documenting the vital events in an individual's life, from birth to marriage to burial. They also provide data on property ownership, military service, occupation, taxation, school attendance, association memberships, and other important aspects of day-to-day life. These records, whether created by governments, organizations, or private institutions, are where you'll find many of the details about your ancestors. Documentary evidence of your relatives may also be found in other less "official" sources, including newspapers, photographs, tombstones, family Bibles, school yearbooks, church membership lists, and even oral family histories.

ALERT

Genealogists generally consider a digital image that has been scanned or created from an original record as equivalent to the original as long as no evidence suggests that the image has been manipulated, other than to enhance readability. Thus, there is generally no need to view both the original and digitized version of the same record, unless there's a legibility issue or something appears to be missing or altered.

The sources you'll encounter in your genealogy research can generally be classified, according to the Board for Certification of Genealogists (BCG), as either *original* or *derivative records*, or as an *authored narrative*. These are a little different than the terms "primary source" and "secondary source" that you may be used to, because they refer to the physical form and provenance of a document or record, not the information that it contains.

- An **original record** is one that exists as it was originally recorded. Examples might include an oral recorded history, a handwritten will, a baptism recorded in the church records, a diary, or a photograph.
- A **derivative record** is created by reproducing some or all of the content contained in an original record. Abstracts, extracts, transcriptions, databases, indexes, and online family trees are generally considered to be derivative sources. Examples include a transcript of an obituary, a database of marriage records, or a published genealogy.
- Outside of the framework of traditional records, **authored narratives** represent a third source classification, created from information gathered from a variety of sources (original or derivative) enriched by the author's analysis, interpretations, and conclusions.

Whenever possible, it is best to view an original record. Each time a record is transcribed, copied, or manipulated in some way there is a chance for errors to creep in. Handwriting can be difficult to interpret. Typographical errors are easy to make. Vital information can easily be skipped by accident or left out because it isn't considered important. Original records are generally more likely to be accurate than derivative records, but even original records can be wrong.

QUESTION

How reliable is information found on the Internet?
Many of the records you'll encounter online will be derivative sources, but this doesn't necessarily mean they are unreliable. It is best, however, to consider such information as a clue for further research and not a statement of absolute fact. Look for a citation to the original record from which the information was derived so you can evaluate the source for yourself.

Most genealogists use the terms "primary" and "secondary" to classify *information*, rather than *sources*. This is because any single source may include both primary information and secondary information. There are also situations in which the source of the information cannot be determined. In this case the information can be classified as "indeterminable."

- **Primary information** is generally provided close to the time of an event, by someone with firsthand knowledge of the reported assertion(s). A birth date recorded on the birth certificate by a doctor or parent present at the birth is an example of primary information.
- **Secondary information** is provided by someone with secondhand knowledge of the reported fact(s) or is information that was recorded long after the event occurred. A birth date recorded on a death certificate by a child of the deceased is an example of secondary information. This doesn't mean the information is incorrect, just that there is a greater chance that it could be.
- Information can also be classified as **indeterminable** in cases where the informant cannot be determined, or it is unclear where the identified informant acquired the information.

Each assertion or piece of information found within a source needs to be evaluated separately to determine whether it is primary, secondary, or indeterminable. This classification doesn't refer to the accuracy of the information—it refers to the likelihood of its accuracy. The quality or weight of the information should also be further assessed based on who provided the information, knowledge of the informant, and how closely the information correlates with information provided by other sources. Secondhand information is often correct. And firsthand information can sometimes be wrong. A group of people who experienced a car accident firsthand, for example, will often tell slightly different versions of the story. Or a couple may have moved back their marriage date by a few months when they recorded it in the family Bible to cover up a pre-marriage conception. The information found in sources can't really be considered "facts" in the pure sense of the word. Instead, genealogists treat them as "assertions."

Evaluate Your Evidence

Now that you have found information about your family, what does it really tell you? Sources provide information. From this information you identify *evidence*. Evidence is the interpretation of information as it relates to a particular research question and is classified by genealogists in three ways: direct, indirect, and negative. In its most basic form, direct evidence is obvious, and any combination of indirect or negative evidence could be called circumstantial.

- If evidence answers a research question all by itself, then it is **direct evidence**. A marriage record that lists the date of marriage directly answers the question of when the couple got married, as well as if they were married.
- If a piece of evidence needs to be combined with other evidence to answer the research question, then it is referred to as **indirect evidence**. An 1873 marriage record for Jeremiah Jones to Susannah Applegate, when combined with an 1880 census in the same county for Jeremiah Jones with Susannah (listed as wife) and three children born between 1873 and 1880, provides indirect evidence that the mother of these children is Susannah Applegate. Because neither of these sources directly states the relationship between Susannah and the children, the evidence is indirect.
- A third category of evidence—known as **negative evidence**—describes interpretations or conclusions derived from the absence of expected information. An individual's absence from the 1870 census in a particular locality, after being consistently enumerated between 1830 and 1860, suggests that he may have died or moved from the area.

The terms *direct*, *indirect*, and *negative* apply only to the ability of the evidence to answer a specific research question, not to the likelihood that it is correct. Indirect evidence may be highly compelling and direct evidence may be wrong. All three types of evidence can be used alone or in combination to support a particular statement or argument. However, when possible, *at least* two independently created pieces of evidence should be used to support each point critical to your research. The body of evidence on which you build your research conclusions is the basis for genealogical *proof.*

Organize the Search

As your tree starts to bear fruit, you'll find that a computer can be of tremendous help in organizing your research and presenting your results. Some traditional organization of paper files and documents will still likely be necessary, but organization of your overall research is much more important, and this is where the computer can really shine. Not only does it take up much less space than piles of papers and boxes of documents, but a computer also makes it easier to search and sort through your family tree.

ESSENTIAL

GEDCOM, an acronym for GEnealogical Data COMmunication, is a special file format that can be read by most genealogy programs, allowing easy transfer of your family tree file from one program to the other. Learn how to open and read a GEDCOM file, as well as how to use your family tree program to create and share your own, in "Genealogy GEDCOM 101" (*http://genealogy.about.com/od/family_tree_software/a/Genealogy-Gedcom.htm*).

Download or Purchase a Genealogy Program

Family tree software is much easier to use than pencil and paper once your family tree begins to grow. Computer software allows you to type in the name, date, and other information on each individual just once; easily move back and forth between generations in your family tree; view and print a variety of reports on your ancestors; and exchange information with family members and other researchers.

For those of you wondering which genealogy software is the best, there really isn't a clear-cut answer. Most genealogy programs today offer good, basic functionality, so your choice should really depend upon your individual goals and preferences. Some family tree software excels at publishing books or charts. Other programs do a better job at helping you organize and document your data. Some genealogists even prefer to forego traditional genealogy software entirely, opting instead to use a word processing program or other writing software, such as Scrivener (*www.literatureandlatte.com*), to keep track of their research and their writing.

The best option is to try before you buy. Most companies that sell genealogy software have a website where you can download a free trial or demo version. Some programs, such as the standard/basic versions of Ancestral Quest, Legacy Family Tree, Family Tree Builder, and RootsMagic, are free. If you need more advanced features, you can easily upgrade to the full-featured version at a later date.

There are dozens of genealogy software programs available, but the following are some of the ones most widely used by genealogists and still kept current with new versions and updates:

- Ancestral Quest (*www.ancquest.com*)
- Brother's Keeper (*www.bkwin.org*)
- DoroTree Jewish Genealogy Software (*www.dorotree.com*)
- Family Historian (*www.family-historian.co.uk*)
- Family Tree Builder (*www.myheritage.com/family-tree-builder*)
- Family Tree Maker (*www.familytreemaker.com*)
- Heredis for Windows (*www.heredis.com*)
- Legacy Family Tree (*www.legacyfamilytree.com*)
- RootsMagic (*www.rootsmagic.com*)
- The Master Genealogist (*www.whollygenes.com*)

There are some excellent options for Macintosh users as well, including:

- Family Tree Maker for Mac 2 (*www.familytreemaker.com*)
- Heredis for Mac (*www.myheredis.com*)
- MacFamilyTree (*www.syniumsoftware.com/macfamilytree/*)
- Reunion (*www.leisterpro.com*)

A number of Internet-based family tree offerings allow you to create, view, and edit your family tree entirely online—an alternative to traditional, standalone computer software. This is an excellent option for families or groups who are collaborating on a genealogy, as well as for individuals who like to work on more than one computer. The most full-featured, standalone option is Ancestry Member Trees (*http://trees.ancestry.com*), which allows you to build your family tree online from scratch (or GEDCOM upload), include notes and sources, and even attach documents (either records found on Ancestry.com or documents/photos uploaded from your own computer). Other online tools for building and sharing a family tree on someone else's website include MyHeritage's Web Family Tree (*www.myheritage.com/family-tree*), GeneaNet (*www.geneanet.org*), and Family Pursuit (*www.familypursuit.com*). Most require some type of membership fee for full-feature use (e.g., ability to search and add historical records to your tree), and none currently offer the tools, power, and flexibility of the best computer-based genealogy software programs.

LINK

For assistance with choosing genealogy software, GenSoftReviews (*www.gensoftreviews.com*) publishes user reviews of over 175 different genealogy programs. Read the actual reviews—especially those that provide specific details beyond just "great" or "lousy" program—instead of relying solely on the star ratings, as this will provide better insight into how a particular program may or may not meet your needs. Additional reviews and comparison charts can be found on Modern Software Experience (*www.tamurajones.net/reviews.xhtml*) and Genealogy Tools (*www.genealogytools.com*).

A Research Log Is Essential

Whether you keep it on paper or on your computer, a research log is a method for tracking your research, from the planning stage through completion—essentially a journal of your research process. You use it to record what you are planning to look for and where you plan to look for it. After you search a source, you add information about when you searched, what names and name variations you searched for, and what you did and did not find. You may also choose to include a record of any correspondence (e-mails, letters, and so on) in your research log, although some genealogists choose to maintain a separate correspondence log. You can track all of your research in one big research log or maintain separate research logs for each individual, family group, or surname.

Right now, as you're just setting out on your family tree journey, a research log may seem like a waste of time. But chances are that after you've spent a few weeks and months researching online, you'll end up visiting the same places again and again. That's not to say that you shouldn't revisit websites. Most are continually adding new information, and you'll also keep discovering new ancestors to research. But unless you keep track of where you've been and who and what you've searched for, you can end up wasting a lot of time and effort retracing your previous trail.

You can find a variety of research log forms online for free download, or you can easily design your own. Many genealogy software programs also offer a simple to-do list or research log feature. The goal is to keep track of the research you've done and plan to do, and whatever format is the easiest for you to use and maintain is the one you should use.

ALERT

Clooz is an electronic filing cabinet and research tool designed just for genealogists who prefer computer organization to paper files. It includes more than 100 templates for recording information found in a wide variety of different genealogical records, along with blank templates, source templates, and other methods of analyzing, organizing, and storing the clues you come across when researching your family tree. You can download a free trial at *www.clooz.com*.

Taking Good Notes Will Improve Results

You don't want to have to rely on your memory for vital details, so consider using your computer or a notebook to take notes. Most genealogical software has a special space for notes on each individual, and some include a notes field for each individual event as well. Always label your notes with the date and place where they were taken, as well as a complete reference, or citation, to the source you consulted.

Part of taking good notes is learning how to copy the information you find in documents and other source materials. This copying can take a number of forms, but the three most common are transcripts, abstracts, and extracts.

- A **transcript** (**transcription**) is a complete, word-for-word copy of the original document. Everything is copied exactly as it appears, including any errors, misspellings, abbreviations, and punctuation.

If something needs clarification, or you want to include your interpretation of something, comments can be added in square brackets [like this], not in parentheses. This convention tells other readers that you have added the information contained within the brackets, and that it was not found in the original.

- An **abstract** is a summary of a document's essential details, including names, dates, places, and events, in the same order that they appear in the original record. Nonessential words, "boilerplate" legal terminology, and punctuation are omitted. As with transcriptions, copy all names, dates, and abbreviations exactly as they appear in the original.
- **Extracts** are similar to abstracts in that they include only portions of the original document text. Instead of summarizing, however, an extract is an exact word-for-word copy of a selected portion of text, set off by quotation marks. Extracts can stand alone, but you'll more commonly find them included as part of an abstract to highlight essential portions of the text.

Even if you keep both digital and paper copies of original documents such as wills and land deeds, it is very useful to make a full transcription and include it in the notes section of your genealogy software, or with your research, for easy reference. A transcription is much easier to review quickly than old, faded handwriting, and the process of transcribing forces you to look at every single word, making it easier to identify and analyze each item of information contained within the document—including small details you might have otherwise missed. If you save most of your research digitally, then a transcription is also every-word searchable.

Tame the Paper Monster

Even if you keep almost all of your genealogy research on the computer, you'll probably still have boxes and files of certificates, photocopies, photos, and other paper records generated during the course of your search. You can scan important documents and photos into your computer, of course, but even then you may not want to throw away the originals. Genealogists use a number of different systems for organizing their files, including folders, binders, and notebooks. You can find an overview of several common filing systems online—just type *genealogy organization* into your favorite search engine. The books *Organizing Your Family History Search* by Sharon DeBartolo Carmack and *The Organized Family Historian* by Ann Carter Fleming, CG, CGL, offer additional organization examples and advice.

ESSENTIAL

While transcribing a document, if you feel the need to insert a comment, correction, interpretation, or clarification, include it in square brackets [like this], not parentheses, to avoid confusion. Bracketed question marks [?] can be substituted for letters or words that can't be interpreted or for interpretations that are questionable.

Record Your Progress

A family tree is basically one big puzzle. If you don't put the puzzle pieces together in just the right way, you'll never get to see the final picture. To help fit all of the puzzling clues together, genealogists use a variety of charts and forms to record their research data. The chart most people begin with is the pedigree chart, or ancestor chart. This chart begins with you, or the individual whose ancestry you're tracing, and then branches with each generation to display the line of your direct ancestors. Pedigree charts come in a wide variety of shapes, sizes, and styles. The most common is a four-generation chart on standard 8½" × 11" paper. Some charts squeeze five or six generations into the same space but necessarily include less room for information about each ancestor. Large, wall-sized ancestor charts can be printed from many genealogy software programs and then cut and pasted together, or you can order a specially printed wall chart of your family tree from a chart-printing service (great for family reunions).

The other commonly encountered genealogy form is the family group sheet. This form focuses on a family unit, with space for recording a couple and their children, including birth, death, and marriage events for each individual. Generally, these two forms work in conjunction. The pedigree chart provides the overall picture of the family tree, with links between generations, while the family group sheet records additional family details for each couple or marriage recorded on the pedigree chart.

Most genealogists follow certain standard conventions when recording data, whether on a paper chart or in their genealogy software program. By following these conventions, you help to ensure that the information you record is as complete as possible, easy to understand, and not open to misinterpretation.

Record Names in Their Natural Order

Enter the first name (also referred to as a given name or forename), followed by the middle name and surname or last name. Married women are recorded under the last name they were born with—their maiden name—not the last name they took when they got married. In situations where you wish to include both last names (such as in a written family history), you can enclose the maiden name in parentheses prior to the married name.

While it is not necessary, some genealogists record surnames in capital letters (e.g., THOMAS). This makes it easy to distinguish surnames at a glance when scanning pedigree charts or genealogy queries. If you're using genealogy software, it is usually better not to enter the surname in all capital letters, as most programs will allow you to choose how you want the names printed in charts or reports. Entering last names in the usual format of initial capital letter followed by lowercase (e.g., Thomas) allows for greater flexibility.

Naming conventions also exist for certain special situations. Again, if you're using genealogy software, you won't need to worry about most of these.

- When a woman has married several times, enter her given name followed by her maiden name in parentheses, followed by the last name of her husbands in order of marriage. (Don't do this if you are using genealogy software, as you'll enter each marriage and husband separately and record the wife only under her maiden name.) Example: Linda Michelle (Koth) GARDNER MITCHELL.
- Enter nicknames in quotes, not parentheses, following the given name. Genealogy software generally offers a special field in which to enter nicknames. Example: Mary "Polly" JENNINGS.
- If an individual was known by more than one name because of adoption or name change, include the alternate name in parentheses following the surname. Precede the alternate name with "aka" for "also known as." If you're using a genealogy program, look for a special alternate name field. Example: William Maxwell MILLS (aka William Maxwell CRISP).
- If the surname spelling has been changed, you can record the earlier surname first, followed by the more current usage. Alternately, you can just record the surname for each individual as he or she commonly spelled it. Example: Stanislaw TOMAN/THOMAS.

Record Dates Carefully to Avoid Confusion

In the United States, dates are written differently than in most other parts of the world. Americans are used to dates with the month first, followed by the day and year—as in July 9, 1971. In most other countries, the same date would be written as 9 July 1971 with the day first. Both dates are easy to understand when they are written out as in the previous examples, but when you see a date written 7/9/71 do you interpret it as July 9, 1971 or September 7, 1971? Or could the year be 1871 or 1771? To avoid confusion in family histories, genealogists conventionally follow the day, month, and year format (9 July 1971) for all dates, with the year written out in full. Months are generally written out in full as well, although some genealogists choose to use standard three-letter abbreviations.

There will be plenty of occasions in your research when you will only have an approximate date for an event. In such situations you can specify the date as "about" (abt. 1890) or "circa" (c. 1890). If you are able to narrow a date down to a specific time span (e.g., your ancestor most likely died between the date he signed his will and the date the will was admitted into probate), record the time span using the abbreviation "bet." (between), followed by the two dates separated by a hyphen, as in bet. 23 May 1789–3 June 1789. You can also record an event as occurring before or after a specific date— for example, (bef. 18 Jan 1892) or (aft. 11 Sep 2001).

Record Places from the Smallest Jurisdiction to the Largest

In general this would mean the name of the place (town, village, or city), followed by the county or parish in which it was located, and then the state or province. The county or parish can be set off by commas or included in parentheses, as in Pittsburgh, Allegheny County, Pennsylvania, or Tarboro (Edgecombe), North Carolina.

ALERT

When recording a location in your family history, be sure to use the correct county or other entity that had jurisdiction over the town or city at the time the event occurred, not as it currently exists. Geographical and political boundaries may have changed over time.

The specific geographical divisions will be different in different countries and regions, but just apply the "smallest to largest" convention and you'll have it right. If your research is predominantly in one country, such as the United States, you don't need to record the name of that country, although you might want to record the country for locations outside of your predominant country of research to avoid confusion.

Document Your Findings

Gathering data about your family and assembling it into a family tree is quite an accomplishment, but it is thorough research, accurate interpretations, and documentation that give your research credibility. Keeping track of where you found each piece of information or assertion is important for assessing its reliability and ensuring a thorough understanding of the source and the evidence it provides. It also demonstrates to others that your conclusions are supported by the least error-prone sources available. To do this, genealogists use what is called a source citation. The source is the document, database, photograph, interview, or other "container" in which the specific assertion or information was found. The citation is the formal reference to that source, including all details necessary for someone to identify and locate the source material.

Source citations in genealogy generally follow standard bibliographic citation standards, similar to those found in *The Chicago Manual of Style*. In the most basic sense, citations include the following components:

- Author, creator, or informant (if known)
- Title of the source (book, website, etc.)
- Date of publication or creation
- Specific details needed to locate the information within the source (page number, chapter, entry, search terms, etc.)
- Publication details (place, publisher, etc.) for published sources; repository information (name, location, etc.) for unpublished sources.

An excellent guide to understanding the why, what, and how of genealogical source citations can be found in chapter 4, "GPS Element 2: Source Citations" of *Mastering Genealogical Proof* by Thomas W. Jones. A reference note citation to this source might appear as follows:

Thomas W. Jones, *Mastering Genealogical Proof* (Arlington, Va.: National Genealogical Society, 2013), pp. 33–52.

Internet sources generally follow the same format as traditional published materials. A website title, for example, is equivalent to a book title. A database contained within a specific website can be treated as a book chapter. The publisher is the entity that owns or created the website, although this can be omitted if it duplicates the name of the website, as it does with Ancestry.com. In place of traditional publication place and date, you cite the URL of the website and the date on which you accessed or viewed the site. The additional details necessary for a footnote citation would include the information necessary to find the actual record, such as the individual's name and location and the entry number. When it can be determined, the original source of the online record or database is also generally included.

A reference note source citation for a World War I Draft Registration Card found online at Ancestry.com might appear as follows:

> "*World War I Draft Registration Cards, 1917–1918*," digital images, Ancestry.com (*www.ancestry.com*: accessed 13 July 2013), card for Claude Mancil Crisp, no. 2927, Edgecombe County, North Carolina; citing World War I Selective Service System Draft Registration Cards, 1917–1918, National Archives microfilm publication M1509; imaged from Family History Library film roll 1,765,639.

Sources will use slightly different punctuation and arrangement depending on how they are used—as reference notes (footnotes), or in source lists (bibliographies). Periods, for example, are used to separate each major element of a citation in a *source list* entry, or bibliography, while commas are used to divide most major sections in *reference notes*. More complex reference note citations, such as the World War I Draft Card example, may require semicolons to separate major parts, with commas used to separate smaller items within each major part.

ESSENTIAL

Learn more about how to structure source citations in Elizabeth Shown Mills's *Evidence Explained: Citing History Sources from Artifacts to Cyberspace, 2nd Edition*. For quick reference help, check out her "QuickSheet" citation guides, as well as the citation help forums on the author's website, Evidence Explained (*www.evidenceexplained.com*). Both the book and QuickSheets are available from the publisher, Genealogical.com, as well as other booksellers. Electronic versions of Evidence Explained and the QuickSheets can also be purchased from the Evidence Explained website.

Cite what you see! Many of the sources you'll be using online, such as indexes, pedigree charts, and cemetery transcriptions, have been created or "derived" from a previously existing source. While such a derivative record may include a citation to the original source of the information, you must cite what you actually "see" or use—the derivative record, not the original from which it was created. Derivative records are prone to human error, including typing mistakes and misinterpreted handwriting. If such a mistake exists and you cite the original record without reference to the online derivative record where you actually found your information, you may not realize that you still need to examine the original if you encounter conflicting information.

Consider a situation where you locate your great-grandmother's birth date from a transcription made and posted online by the local genealogical society. In this case, you would not cite her tombstone and/ or the cemetery as your source because you have not personally seen her grave marker. Instead, you would cite the online transcription created by the genealogical society.

Many people don't take the time to cite sources when they first begin researching their family tree. It's just so easy to assume that all of your data is accurate, so why does it matter where it came from? It's also easy to get caught up in the excitement of the search and tell yourself that you'll go back and do it later. Problems arise, however, when you find new information that contradicts your previous "accurate" data. Without sources, you have no way to know where you found the earlier information, which makes it difficult to resolve the discrepancy. Documenting sources for all information as it is uncovered can save many, many hours of backtracking. Source citations really are worth the extra time and effort!

CHAPTER 2

Begin Backward

Many people begin their family tree search knowing next to nothing about their own grandparents and great-grandparents. Sure, you know their names, and perhaps their date of birth, but do you know when they were married? What they did for a living? Where they lived when they were growing up? Do you know the names of their siblings? Without at least some basic knowledge of your family tree, you're likely to quickly find yourself spinning your wheels online. That's why a good genealogy search should always begin at home.

Interview Yourself

Why not? You probably know more about your own history than you think you do. You're impatient to jump right on to the Internet to find everything you can on your family, but your search will almost always bring more success if you begin at home—with yourself and your living relatives. Surfing the Internet for information on an average name will bring up somewhere in the neighborhood of 1 million plus sites that may shelter tidbits about your family, and who has time to wade through all of that? The more details you have about your family before you hit the web, the more easily you'll be able to distinguish your ancestors from others with the same name and the less frustrating the search will be.

ESSENTIAL

A journal or notebook can be a handy tool for recording your progress during this information-gathering stage. Write down the people you talk to, the questions you ask, the information you collect, and the stories you're told. If you have family members who prefer to write rather than talk, a special memory book full of thought-provoking family history questions may provide just the inspiration they need.

Begin your family tree by writing down as much basic information as you can remember about your relatives. This might include dates and locations of birth, marriage, and death; names of spouses and children; wars in which relatives served; where they went to school; their occupation; their church and/or religion; and any other details that you can recall. Start with yourself or your children and then work backward through the generations to your parents and grandparents—as far back as you can go. If you can, extend the information to aunts, uncles, siblings, and other family members. Try to remember full names, including middle names, nicknames, and the maiden names for married women. If you know the exact date of an event, write it down. If you only know that it was about 1952 or sometime during World War II, write that down. Everything doesn't have to be perfect. The goal here is just to get something down on paper so that you have somewhere to start.

Create Your First Family Tree

Once you've pulled together every scrap of knowledge from your head and your home, it's time to enter the information into your computer software or a pedigree chart. This helps you see at a glance where you have gaps in your family history knowledge, which in turn can lead to questions to ask your relatives or details to look up online. Be sure to include a source for each piece of information, whether you learned it from a birth certificate or your great uncle. This may seem like a waste of time right now, but you'll appreciate it down the road when you find conflicting information—which you will. Memories are faulty, stories get embellished, and you'll probably find at least one female relative who fudged her age.

Record Your Personal Story

While you're busy reflecting on the past, it's worth taking some time to record your own story, or at least some of the major events, feelings, and experiences from your own life. It doesn't necessarily need to be done before you dig into your family history, but it's also likely to mean more to your descendants than any family tree you create ever could. It's hard to express how wonderful it is to find a journal or diary written by long-dead ancestors. Even a simple letter in their handwriting is a treasure. To be able to read about their life in their own words, to learn how the major events experienced only through history books impacted them, to see how the names and dates discovered during research really fit into their life—that is true family history.

A personal history doesn't need to be an entire autobiography. Begin small, with some basics about yourself. Then add more stories over time. Eventually, the plan would be to cover every stage of your life: birth and childhood, family life, school years, courtship and marriage, and raising your own family. Touch on all the major points—your job(s), your beliefs, your travels, your hobbies, your favorite foods—asking yourself who, what, when, where, why, and how questions about each. And don't use the excuse that your life is boring! No matter how mundane it may seem to you, a hundred years from now your stories will fascinate your descendants.

What do I write about?

The Internet is a great source for prompts and inspiration for writing a personal family history, as well as journal-keeping software and services. Subscription services, such as LifeBio (*www.lifebio.com*), offer online questions and templates to help you write your own story. At MyLifeHereOnEarth.com (*www.mylifehereonearth.com*) you can create a free personal online diary, journal, or autobiography to record your story, either day by day or as you have time. Links to these and similar resources can be found in the "Writing Your Life Story" section of About.com Genealogy (*http://genealogy.about.com/od/autobiography*).

If you don't want to do your own writing, there are personal historians who will interview you, and your family members if you wish, and then use the collected stories plus photographs to create a video, book, or family website to publish your personal history. The Association of Personal Historians (*www.personalhistorians.org*) can help you locate a professional near you. You can also locate many through a simple web search for "personal historian."

Rummage Through the Attic

Genealogy is all about clues, and many of the best clues can be found without leaving home. Generations of family "stuff" await your discovery in attics, basements, drawers, and closets. Take a good look through your house. Most people have at least a few official documents in their home, such as birth certificates, passports, report cards, military discharge papers, or marriage certificates. Look for these and other records that might provide names, dates, and locations. But don't stop there! Pull out your family photo albums and scrapbooks. Look for old letters, newspaper clippings, and family memorabilia. Anything from your past is fair game. Label everything you recognize, and add any new information to your research notes.

LINK

Family memorabilia that has escaped the family home can sometimes be found online. The National Genealogical Society (*www.ngsgenealogy.org*) maintains an online database of more than 3,100 Bibles for its members. Family records, photos, and heirlooms can often be found on auction sites such as eBay (*www.ebay.com*) or on lost-and-found sites (*http://genealogy.about.com/od/orphan_photos*) where people post family items they have rescued from flea markets and antique stores.

Even if you can find no real genealogical treasures in your own home, you might be surprised what lurks in the homes of your relatives. They may be surprised, too! Family history can be found in unusual places—the hem of a quilt, the back of a photo, a locket inscription. Photos and albums help match names with faces. If pictures aren't labeled, ask your relatives to help you with identification. Family Bibles often contain information about marriages, births, baptisms, deaths, and other important family events. Letters and postcards may be filled with family news and stories, and the date and postmark may provide clues as to where your family lived at a given time. If your family has been in the same home for generations, even the walls can talk. You may find notes recorded on the inside of closet doors, growth charts penciled on the walls, or old newspapers used for insulation in the attic. Ask your relative if he or she will agree to go through the house with you, as this allows you to easily ask questions about anything you find. If this isn't possible, however, here are some things you might ask your relative to look for:

- Important papers (birth certificates, wills, naturalization documents, titles, and deeds)
- Pictures, photo albums, scrapbooks, baby books
- Newspaper clippings
- Bibles
- Letters and postcards
- Diaries and journals
- Books (check for inscriptions)
- Funeral and Mass cards
- Family trees

- School papers, including report cards and yearbooks
- Awards and certificates
- Quilts, samplers, or other needlework
- Jewelry (check for inscriptions)

Your relatives may be understandably reluctant to let precious family records or mementos out of their possession, so consider bringing a portable scanner and a laptop with you on your attic hunt. A good digital camera can also do the trick. This way you'll have digital copies of everything for your records and to easily share with the rest of the family. Take good notes, and transcribe any documents in case your pictures or scans don't turn out as well as expected.

Question Your Family Members

There's nothing quite as deflating as calling your grandmother to share your latest genealogy "find" only to have her reply, "I could have told you that." Your family members represent a vast source of untapped knowledge about your family history, and questioning them will likely turn up countless interesting details. Contact everyone you can think of, from your ninety-eight-year-old great-grandma to the second cousin you haven't seen since you were kids. Even friends of the family can provide useful details. Everyone, both old and the young, will have different memories and perspectives. They may recall the same event in a different way, have interacted with different family members, or be able to provide details that no one else can. You probably won't get to them all before the urge to jump on the Internet finally gets the better of you, but try to talk to as many as you can.

Talking to your family members can mean anything from a formal recorded interview to a casual conversation over the dinner table, or even an occasional question asked by e-mail. The casual conversation approach works especially well, as it seems to put family members more at ease. The downside, however, is that you don't always get the chance to take notes right away, and have no recording to fall back on. A nice compromise is to set up a video camera on a tripod in the corner of the dining room or other room where the interviewee feels comfortable, and then start a casual conversation about family events and memories. Your subject will often forget the camera is running (or at least stop worrying about it). If you can get two or more family members together at once, the informal conversation and memory sharing pretty much take care of themselves. Either way, ask a few questions to get the conversation started, but don't be afraid after that point to let your relative(s) wander from one memory to the next.

ALERT

StoryCorps (*www.storycorps.com*) brings trained facilitators and high-quality recording equipment to locations around the country to help record interviews between friends and family, in which one person interviews the other. The recorded interviews are added to the Story-Corps Archive, housed at the American Folklife Center at the Library of Congress, and participants receive a broadcast-quality copy of their interview on CD.

Decide Who to Interview First

Begin by talking to the oldest living family members, when possible, because they are the ones whose memories are most at risk of being lost forever, and they usually know the most about the family. It helps to think about what you're hoping to learn and who is most likely to have that information. If your goal is to learn your great-grandmother's maiden name, you might want to start with your grandmother, if she is still living, or one of her siblings. Or you may just want to start with the people who are most willing or interested in the information you are gathering.

Most families also have at least one person known to be the keeper of the family history—the one who has spent some time researching the family tree, who has the largest collection of family photos and memorabilia, or is just the "busybody" sort who knows everything about everyone. This is someone you're definitely going to want to talk to. He or she may not always be someone in your direct line, however, so it may take some detective work on your part. If your great-grandfather, for example, had several siblings, then descendants of any of those other children are just as likely as your grandfather to have family photos, letters, and other items that have been saved.

What questions should I ask my relatives?
Begin by using the family tree chart you've started to create a basic list of questions. Next, add additional questions based on major life events, such as going to school and getting married—focusing not just on facts, but also on how, why, where, and with what results. Open-ended questions that require more than just a "yes" or "no" answer help encourage personal commentary.

Prepare for a Successful Interview

There are many online tutorials and guides to help you prepare for and conduct a successful oral history interview, covering such matters as what to bring with you and which questions to ask for the best results. More important than all these little details, however, is actually sitting down and talking to your relatives. To get you started, here are a few basic principles to keep in mind:

- Don't interrupt. The best way to keep your interviewee involved is to listen to what she has to say. You can ask follow-up questions to get more details, but don't worry too much about your interview getting off track as long as your relative is still talking about the family. Sometimes those little "tangents" reveal the most interesting clues.
- Be respectful, not pushy. If your relative appears reluctant to give details about a particular event or person, don't press. There may be a "secret" or a painful memory, and pushing too hard can mean an end to her willingness to talk to you. Save it for a future conversation, or as something to ask other relatives about.
- Make note of any names, places, and events mentioned during the interview. After the interview, ask your relative to go through this list with you to add full names with correct spellings.

While you're busy digging for information to fill in the blanks of your genealogy software or family tree chart, don't forget to ask for and record the stories as well. Every family has them. Some are well rehearsed—like the stories Grandpa likes to tell just about every time the family gets together. Others may have never been told because no one ever thought to ask. Both are an important part of the family history and deserve to be written down.

Don't Believe Every Story You Hear

Almost all family stories have a kernel of truth, but sometimes that's about all that's true. You may hear stories of being related to a famous individual, such as Abraham Lincoln or Napoleon Bonaparte. You may be told that your great-great-grandmother was a Cherokee princess. Or you may encounter the common tradition that your family tree goes back to "three brothers" who came to America. It's possible, of course, that these stories are true. It's much more likely, however, that such stories are more myth than fact.

There's a game you may have played as a child known as "Chinese whispers" or "Telephone." A sentence or phrase is whispered into the ear of the first participant, who then whispers what he hears to the next person in line. By the time the sentence reaches the end of the line, it is often unrecognizable from the one uttered at the beginning. In the same way, family stories are often changed or embellished as they are passed down through successive generations. For this reason, all family stories and traditions should be verified through careful genealogy research before you accept them as fact. Don't laugh at the stories, however, no matter how ridiculous they may sound. Respect the feelings of those who believe them and wait to correct any misconceptions until you have evidence that disproves the family tradition.

ESSENTIAL

Even if you've been asking your family members questions for years, they will still manage to surprise you with new information. Don't expect to learn everything the first time you ask, and don't listen when a family member tells you he or she doesn't know anything. It may take time, patience, and creativity, but you can generally learn something useful from every living relative in your family tree.

Family Interviews Aren't a One-Time Deal

Look at every family gathering as a potential source for information. If you're getting together for a family reunion or the holidays, e-mail your family members in advance and ask them to bring their favorite family photographs or heirlooms to share. You can even scan the collection and create a CD for everyone to take home. E-mail offers a great medium for asking a quick question about something that comes up in your research. Alternatively, you may want to try an e-mail question of the week or month—sort of an ongoing family history conversation. You can also create a private family website that allows your relatives to post recipes, share stories and photos, and keep up-to-date on your research. Some family sites even offer private family chat rooms, blogs, and message boards, which can be a great way to collect and preserve your family's stories. See "Top 10 Places to Put Your Family History Online" (*http://genealogy.about.com/od/publishing/tp/web_sites.htm*) for suggestions.

Has It Already Been Done?

Even if you can't locate someone in your immediate family who has researched the family history, it doesn't mean it hasn't already been done. Most family trees have many, many branches that have spread far and wide through successive generations. This means that records that detail your family may not always be found in the possession of your relatives or even in the area where your ancestors lived. A written family history, a collection of old family letters, or a scrapbook of ancestral photographs may have been donated to a library or repository on the other side of the country, but how do you find it?

Look for Published Family Histories

In reality, only a small percentage of families have published genealogies. It is, however, always worth a look to see if someone has compiled and published a genealogy on your family, or the family in which you're interested.

One of the best places to search for published genealogies online is the Library of Congress, which has one of the world's premier collections of genealogical and local historical publications from the United States and around the world. To find published family histories that may relate to your family, search the library's online catalog (*http://catalog.loc.gov*) for your surname plus the term "family," such as *powell family*. You can also search by location, such as *kennedy family westmoreland co* or *church records virginia*.

ALERT

Remember the old adage that just because it's in print doesn't make it true? Family histories, both published and unpublished, vary in scope and quality. Authored narratives can be invaluable for presenting interpretations and theories that may not exist elsewhere or sources you may not have thought to examine, but you must also consider the possibility that the author may have misinterpreted certain information or reached erroneous conclusions. Always use original records, when possible, to verify information from published family histories.

The Family History Library also maintains a large collection of published family histories. Use the surname search in the Family History Library Catalog to locate catalog entries for family histories and other compiled works that include a specific surname. More than 80,000 family history books, biographies, and diaries from the Family History Library in Salt Lake City, and other major genealogical libraries, have also been scanned and placed online in digital format by FamilySearch (*http://books.familysearch.org*).

Genealogy and local history books can also be freely accessed online through a number of digital archives. In some cases, entire books can be downloaded free of charge. For books still protected by copyright, you may be able to view the index, table of contents, and selected portions of the text, or at least confirm the presence of certain names or keywords. You may already be familiar with Google Books (*http://books.google.com*), which offers free online access to millions of digitized books, including thousands of published biographies, local histories, and family genealogies. HathiTrust Digital Library (*www.hathitrust.org*), a partnership of over 70 libraries and research institutions, encompasses over 10.5 million total volumes, of which over 3.25 million are in the public domain and freely accessible online. The nonprofit Internet Archive (*www.archive.org/details/texts*), known best for its Wayback Machine, also hosts a rich text archive of books and other texts available for free searching, viewing, downloading, and printing. Their American Libraries, Canadian Libraries, and U.S. Library of Congress collections include over 1,000 family histories, as well as city directories and other published resources of interest to genealogists. Additional sources for online family histories, as well as tips for using them to find genealogical content, can be found in "10 Fabulous Sources for Family History Books Online" (*http://genealogy.about.com/od/ digital_documents/tp/family_histories.htm*).

ESSENTIAL

More than 30 percent of published material related to genealogy and history, including family genealogies, can be found in genealogical and historical magazines and journals. The Periodical Source Index (PERSI), which indexes more than 11,000 such periodicals by surname and locality, can be accessed through Find My Post (*www.findmypost.com*), a database available in many major libraries, or through a personal subscription. Eventually digitized versions of individual genealogical periodicals will be linked to the index.

If you locate a reference to a published family history that isn't available online, you'll often be able to find a copy in the collection of the local public library or genealogical society library that serves the area where your ancestors lived. Check their online catalog, if available, or e-mail them to ask if they have a copy. If they do, you can generally request copies of selected pages for a fee.

Seek Out Manuscript Collections

More than 1,400 American institutions actively collect family and personal papers and make them available to the public for research. Each body of archival records created by an individual or organization is normally kept together in a collection referred to as a manuscript collection. A manuscript is basically a handwritten or typed document, as distinguished from a printed, published record, and may include such items as personal letters and diaries, photographs, coroner's inquests, prison records, church records, voter registration records, and unpublished family histories.

The major difficulty with using manuscript collections often lies in locating a manuscript that may be useful to you, as papers that pertain to your ancestor may exist in collections and locations you wouldn't normally think to explore. One very handy tool for this is the National Union Catalog of Manuscript Collections (NUCMC), an index of mostly unpublished materials in both well-known and obscure repositories across the United States. NUCMC records created since 1986 can be freely searched on the Library of Congress website through the OCLC WorldCat Catalog (*www.worldcat.org*). NUCMC records created from 1959 to 1985 are available in printed volumes that can be found at major research libraries throughout the country. Archive Finder (*http://archives.chadwyck.com*), available at most major research libraries and other institutions, makes all of NUCMC (1959 to the present) fully searchable online. A free online service, ArchiveGrid (*www.archivegrid .org*), includes over 1 million descriptions of archival collections held by repositories worldwide, drawing from many of the collections indexed in NUCMC, as well as online finding aids (detailed collection descriptions) from participating institutions. Manuscript collections should also be explored at the repository level for institutions that may hold collections from areas or specialties in which you research, as not all collections are included in the databases mentioned previously.

ALERT

Don't let the dates fool you! Dates in the National Union Catalog of Manuscript Collections (NUCMC) refer to the date the records were catalogued, not when they were created. Many older records have been added to the collection since 1986 and are available in the free version available on the Library of Congress website.

From One Generation to the Next

It is very tempting when you're researching your family tree to jump ahead of yourself and skip a generation or two. Imagine that you discover a census record for your grandmother living with her husband and children. But wait! You look further down and find her father living in the same household. Just think, you've learned your grandmother's maiden name and her father's name in one fell swoop. You're probably already typing his name into a search box to see what else you can learn. And then there's the tale your grandfather told of his father arriving at Ellis Island as a young man of eighteen with nothing more than the clothes on his back. One of the first things you're going to want to do online is search for him in the Ellis Island database, right?

ESSENTIAL

Naming patterns can sometimes help identify links between generations of a family. You may find names of grandparents, parents, aunts, and uncles repeated in succeeding generations. Occasionally you'll even find an unusual name that has survived in the family for decades. Sometimes an unusual middle name may indicate the maiden name of the mother or grandmother.

Jumping ahead of oneself is human nature. But in genealogy it can also mean disaster. By skipping a generation or two, you run the risk of identifying the wrong people as your ancestors and becoming tangled forever in someone else's family tree. It happens more frequently than you may think. This doesn't mean you can't pursue a new lead when it smacks you in the face, but after you've done some searching to satisfy your curiosity, go back and finish your research on the previous generation(s) to ensure that everything does indeed match up as you believe.

Don't just rely on your grandmother's name and the name of her father. Identify as much as you can about your grandmother, checking all of the available records for any details you can tease from them. Just learning something as simple as where and when she was born can help distinguish her from others of the same name. Additional research may also provide you with the names of siblings, the birthplace of her parents, her mother's name, and other clues. This way, when you locate records for her parents, you can feel confident that you have correctly identified the next branch in your family tree.

CHAPTER 3

Learn How to Search

One of the first things many would-be family historians do when they decide to peek into their family's past is type the name of their ancestor into a major search engine or genealogy database. After sifting through thousands of irrelevant results, they throw up their hands in frustration, convinced that nothing exists online about their family. The problem with this scenario, however, isn't the lack of information; it's the technique. Strong search skills are an essential tool for successful online genealogy research.

Search Engine Basics

You wouldn't wander aimlessly through the stacks at a large city library looking for a book on your family. In the same way, you shouldn't approach a family history hunt on the Internet without a plan. Whether you're using a search engine like Google or searching for your ancestors in the Ellis Island database, an important part of online genealogy research is learning how to search. The sheer magnitude of information available online makes locating information on a particular individual a bit more complicated than just typing a name into a search engine. There are three simple ways to improve your search results: (1) choose your search terms carefully, (2) learn how to use special search operators, and (3) restrict your search with special commands.

Distinguishing Details Help Narrow the Search

It's always a good idea to think about your search before you begin. What do you know about your great-grandfather Jack Smith that can help you distinguish him from all the other Jack Smiths of the world? Perhaps you know that he was born in Monongahela, Pennsylvania. You also know that he married your great-grandmother, Cornelia, and that he was a blacksmith. Use these distinguishing details as keywords to help narrow down your search. A search for *jack smith blacksmith monongahela* or *jack smith cornelia monongahela* is much more likely to yield something relevant about your great-grandfather than a search for just *jack smith*.

QUESTION

Which search engine is best for genealogy?
Most genealogists prefer Google (*www.google.com*) or Bing (*www.bing.com*), but widening your net improves discoverability. Genealogy-specific search engines like Mocavo (*www.mocavo.com*) return more relevant results but often miss items on nongenealogy websites. Cluster search engines, such as Yippy! (*www.yippy.com*) and Gigablast (*www.gigablast.com*), combine searches from various sources, then narrow things further with categorized results. For something factual, give the "computational knowledge engine" WolframAlpha (*www.wolframalpha.com*) a try. You can learn more about these and other search options in Wendy Boswell's "The Perfect Search Engine: How to Pick the Right Tool for the Job" (*http://websearch.about.com/od/enginesanddirectories/p/websearch101.htm*).

For more general results, you might try adding the word "genealogy" or "family" to your surname, as in *powell genealogy* or *owens family*. This type of search will often bring up family history information that other researchers have posted online. To be honest, this type of search technique lends itself better to names more unique than Powell or Owens. In the previous example, better results were achieved when at least one more identifying keyword was added to the search, such as *archibald powell genealogy* or *owens family edgecombe nc*.

Along these same lines, consider what you want to find. If you're looking for death information, you'll want to try the word "death" or "died" in your search. You could also try adding the word "cemetery" or "obituary" to your search query to bring up death information about your ancestor. Add a street name if you're looking for ancestors in a particular city. Think about the types of words that might appear in the information you're looking for, and use these as keywords to help focus your search.

Use Search Operators to Focus Results

Most major search engines, including Google, Bing, and Yahoo!, allow you to use special search operators to focus results. These operators allow you to search for specific phrases, exclude certain words, or otherwise fashion a search query that will help you find exactly what you want:

- **Use quotation marks to find complete phrases.** Regular searches look for all keywords to appear on the same page, but don't pay any attention to their proximity to one another. A search for *jebediah smith* would turn up a page that contained Jebediah Brazelton and Bob Smith, neither of which are your Jebediah Smith. By enclosing specific search phrases in quotes, you force the search engine to find documents that contain the exact phrase, as in *"jebediah smith"* or *"washburn cemetery."*

- **Include the Boolean operators AND or OR between words.** As it sounds, the Boolean operator AND used between two words tells the search engine that both terms must be present on the web page to be included in the search results. Most search engines assume an AND between keywords, or you can use the plus sign, so it isn't often necessary to use this command. The Boolean operator OR requires one term or the other to be present on a web page, but not both. This feature can be helpful when searching for name variations *powell AND archie OR archibald* or when searching for variations of the same term crisp AND tombstone OR gravestone. Boolean operators are generally entered as ALL CAPS.

- **Add a plus (+) to force certain words to be included in your search.** The plus sign is rarely needed but can serve as a substitute for AND to ensure that all of your keywords are included in the results. So, instead of using *crisp AND cemetery AND macclesfield* you could use *crisp +cemetery +macclesfield*. There are also some small words, called "stop words," that search engines commonly ignore when processing a search query. If you really need these to be a part of your search, add a plus (+) in front of them, as in *thomas jefferson +will*. It is important to note that Google discontinued its recognition of the plus (+) search operator after launching Google+, so to force a certain word to be included in a Google search exactly as you typed it, you'll need to enclose the word in quotation marks.

- **Add a minus (–) to exclude specific words from your search.** When your ancestor shares a name with a famous individual or a popular product, you can use this option to help direct the focus away from these irrelevant results. A search for *jimmy dean –sausage* will help eliminate results from the Jimmy Dean company, while *washington –dc –george –president* will help eliminate at least some of the clutter caused by the millions of results for President George Washington.

Restrict Your Search with Special Commands

As you get more comfortable with simple searches, you might want to try your hand at more advanced techniques. Most major search engines include special commands that allow you to restrict your search in some way—to a specific site or date range, for example. The list of available search commands varies by search engine, but one of the most useful for genealogy purposes is the *site:* command, which restricts your search results to a specific website or domain. The search command *"james brown" site: www.archives.gov*, for example, would restrict the results for the phrase "james brown" to return only pages from the website of the

National Archives. You can also use this command to restrict your searches to sites with a specific domain extension—a search for *vital records site:.gov* will return matches for vital records only on sites in the .gov, or government, domain. Check your favorite search engine's help page to learn what commands are available and become familiar with them.

LINK

Specialized genealogy directories and search engines can help you locate genealogy-specific sites without wading through as many irrelevant results. Cyndi's List (*www.cyndislist.com*) is a popular starting point with more than 320,000 links to online genealogical resources, organized into more than 199 categories. Cyndi Howells has maintained this site since 1996. Linkpendium (*www.linkpendium.com*), developed by Karen Isaacson and Brian Leverich, is another genealogy directory, with more than 10 million links to resources organized by locality and surname.

To eliminate the need to remember all of these search options, you can also use the search engine's advanced search page. Most allow you to use all of the features discussed previously by selecting variables from a drop-down list or clicking a check box. Look for a link to "advanced search" on the search engine's home page.

Database Search Strategies

When faced with a search page full of empty boxes, many genealogists begin by typing in a name and, perhaps, a date and location. But what do you do when this doesn't work? Use more than one search engine. Search with wildcards. Try searching the record collection or database via a different website, if available. Search without the surname. Browse the records page by page. Search each database individually. You can't employ the same search techniques time after time and expect a different outcome. Shake up your research!

Read the Database Descriptions

Most online genealogical databases provide a description. Often these descriptions will include information necessary for citing the database, but, more importantly, they also provide information that may be helpful in determining the best way to search, use, and evaluate the source. Does the database contain all extant records in that collection? Are all relevant locations (towns/counties) and time periods represented? Are records still being added? Was the database created from original or derivative sources? Begin a search of any new database by understanding why, how, and from what it was created. Then follow up with a review of the database itself for both composition and arrangement.

Identify What Makes Your Ancestor Unique

Locating an ancestor in a particular database is not always the most difficult part of the search. Sometimes the hardest thing to do is recognize your ancestor when you do find him. Learn to focus on what makes your ancestor unique. How can you identify him from all of the other John Smiths in the world? This might include attributes such as his age, occupation, birthplace, middle name or initial, family members (especially those with more unusual names), associates, religion, military status, physical description, and even signature. This strategy is especially vital when dealing with individuals with common names.

Make Use of Wildcards

Many major genealogical websites, such as *www.FamilySearch.com* and *www.Ancestry.com*, allow the use of wildcards when searching their databases.

- **An asterisk * represents multiple characters.** Depending on the specific website, it can generally be used at the beginning or end of a word, or even in the middle, as long as combined with a minimum number (usually three) of letters. A search for *john** returns John, Johnson, Johnsen, Johnathon, and Johns. A search for *b*ers* finds Bauers, Bowers, and Byers, as well as Backers, Benders, etc. A search for *owen* can find both Rowen and Bowen.

- **A single character is represented by a question mark "?"** Thus, a search for sm?th will return both Smith and Smyth, and a search for *peters?n* will find both Petersen and Peterson. A search for ?andy will help locate names with initial letters prone to being misread by transcribers such as Sandy, Tandy, Landy, and Handy.
- **The * and ? wildcards can be used together as long as three non-wildcard characters are also included.** For example, a search for *w?s*ska* will find names such as Winoska, Wisnienska, Woskowioska, and Wysynska.

Wildcard searches help to overcome misspelled and misread names in a lot of different situations. Since vowels are often substituted when spelling names, try replacing every vowel in a name with wildcard characters. Eastern European names with their hard-to-pronounce consonant clusters can be especially tricky to locate, but replacing a consonant cluster most likely to affect an Americanized spelling with a wildcard can be an effective tool.

ALERT

Turn the page! Discovering a record of your ancestor online is exciting, but don't stop there. Click the "previous" and "next" buttons to be sure there aren't additional pages or other clues that you might be missing. That next digital image may contain another paper from your grandfather's naturalization packet or the back of his marriage license with the names of his parents. It's also good to explore both the beginning and end of the record series to learn more about the records or view addendums.

Don't Depend on Search

It's very handy to be able to search across a website's many collections at one time, and this strategy can often turn up ancestral clues in places you might not expect. However, making the most from genealogical databases also requires searching with a plan. Become well acquainted with the "Card Catalog" or "Collections List" for each site you use regularly, and learn how to use them effectively to find the specific databases or collections most likely to provide an answer to your research question. Search each relevant database individually, as you may achieve different results than with a broad search.

Dig Deeper

No matter how much experience you have with online research, there is always more to learn, and new records are coming online every day. Some websites maintain a special page where they post news of new updates, while others provide the option to sort their collections list by the date each collection was last updated. Many offer the option to sign up for new collection updates via e-mail as well. Search out new resources focused on the places, surnames, ethnicities, time periods, and religions associated with the people you are researching. Dig into the finding aids and catalogs of state archives, university libraries, historical societies, etc. to see what they have available online.

Get Creative with Names

It's important for genealogists to have an open mind when it comes to names. Your family's surname, for example, was not likely always spelled the same way that it is now. It may have been "Americanized" by your ancestors in order to help them assimilate into their new country and culture. An unusual spelling or non-Latin characters may have begged for simplification. A name change may have also arisen from a desire to conceal nationality or religious orientation for fear of reprisal or discrimination. Or your branch of the family may have just decided to change the spelling to make it easier to spell or because they liked the new name better. Some are simple spelling changes—the German surname Heyer has become Hyer, Hier, Hire, Hires, and Hiers. Other changes are more obscure, such as the surname Toman being "Americanized" to Thomas.

Misspelled names are also extremely common. Most of the records in which you'll find your ancestors were recorded by someone else—a court clerk, a priest, an immigration official—who may not have known how it was spelled. Your ancestor probably even spelled his own name in different ways at different times. Names are also often just written down wrong by people who spelled them phonetically or by individuals trying to transcribe messy handwriting or blurred records for an index.

ESSENTIAL

Many genealogy databases offer a search feature called Soundex, a special type of indexing system created for use with the U.S. census and other records, which groups last names based on the way they sound, so that similar names will be found together regardless of how they are spelled (e.g., Smith, Smyth, or Smythe). Learn more in the article "Soundex Explained" (*http://genealogy.about.com/od/ census/a/soundex.htm*).

When searching for your family in online databases, get creative with surname spellings. If your name is plural, such as Owens, search for both Owen and Owens. Use a wildcard in databases that allow it (many genealogy databases do, although Internet search engines generally do not) to help search for several options at once. Examples of this include *owen** to search for owen or owens and *john** to return surnames such as john, johnson, johnsen, johnathon, and johns.

For each database you search, read the instructions or look for an advanced search page to see what search options are available to you. First names or given names are also candidates for variation. Your grandmother Elizabeth may also appear in records as Liz, Lizzie, Lisa, Beth, Eliza, Betty, or Bessie. You might also find her listed by her initial, as in E. Martin or E.R. Martin. Some people also go by their middle name; in this case she may be listed as Roberta Martin. These people can sometimes be the most tricky to find, because they'll often choose to use their given name in official records and use their middle name in more informal situations. There are families in which all of the children are enumerated in one census by their first names, in the next census by the middle names they more commonly used, and in yet a third census by their initials. The key is to keep an open mind when searching for your ancestors and to search for all possibilities before you give up.

Connect with Living Kin

Genealogy isn't just about locating people who have been dead for decades or centuries. It is also about connecting with living family members—to capture their stories and memories, collaborate on research, learn about new branches of the family tree, or plan a family reunion. Not surprisingly, you can apply many of the same search strategies to locate living people. There are, however, a few online tools and databases that can assist with your search.

One of the most obvious places to begin a search for living individuals is an online telephone directory. However, this may not be very fruitful if they have a common name or if you aren't even sure which state they are in. If you can't locate a husband, try searching under his wife's name, and vice versa. A search by just the last name and location may also help turn up listings under initials or other first-name variations. Popular online directories include WhitePages (*www.whitepages.com*) and Switchboard (*www.switchboard.com*). People search engines such as Zabasearch (*www.zabasearch.com*) and ZoomInfo (*www.zoominfo.com*) can often help in locating living people. Most of the information available on these sites is offered free of charge; however, you will often be presented with links for additional information, such as e-mail addresses and background checks, that take you to a paid search service.

Generally you do not need to pay for this type of information. Using a variety of different online search techniques and resources, such as those discussed in About.com's "Find People Online: How to Search for Someone on the Web" (*http://websearch.about.com/od/searchingtheweb/u/search tools.htm*), you can often locate the same information yourself.

QUESTION

How can I locate information on someone who is recently deceased?
The best place to begin is the Social Security Death Index (SSDI), a database of more than 92 million Americans whose deaths have been reported to the Social Security Administration. From this free index you can learn the date of death and location where the final benefit was sent, which you might then use to locate an obituary notice.

Since the Internet is all about connecting the world, it's not a surprise to find so many websites dedicated to helping people reunite with one another. If you're searching for a military buddy, Wendy Boswell's "Free Military People Search" (*http://websearch.about.com/od/peoplesearch/a/militarysearch.htm*) may be of some assistance. Want to connect with an old classmate? Then search or sign up with an alumni reunion site such as Classmates.com (*www.classmates.com*) or Reunions.com (*www.reunions.com*). Adoption search is a bit beyond the scope of this book, but if you're looking for a birth parent or child, there are many online resources to assist you—enter *adoption search* or *adoption reunion* in your favorite search engine.

Facebook (*www.facebook.com*), with more than 1 billion active users worldwide, is probably the best place online for reconnecting with the people from your past. Register and create a basic page for the option to search by name, school, organization, society, and so on to locate and connect with old classmates, friends, or military buddies. Add details to your Facebook page, such as your occupation, organizations you've belonged to, birthday, schools you attended, and so forth, to make it easier for old acquaintances to find you as well. Be sure to include your maiden name if you're a married female! Other popular social media sites, such as Google+ (*http://plus.google.com*), should also be explored when searching for living people.

More Search Tools and Tactics

A good online genealogist knows how to work the search engines or databases to find what he or she seeks. However, knowing how to search is not enough by itself. You also need to know where to search and what to do with the results. To help you with this, several key search tools and strategies are outlined below.

Bring Back Sites from the Dead

How many times have you discovered a link to a promising website, only to find that it leads to a File Not Found page? Websites are in a state of constant flux, with webmasters changing file names, switching ISPs, taking down the site, or letting the domain name lapse, because they no longer have the time or interest to maintain it. As frustrating as this is, a File Not Found, or 404, error does not always mean the content is gone forever.

- **Trim back the URL.** Perhaps someone just moved that particular page into a new folder, or otherwise rearranged or renamed some of the files on the site. Try trimming the URL of the page you're trying to access back to the root domain (the root domain being everything between the http:// and the next backslash) to see if the site exists. If it does, use the Search feature or click on likely links or tabs to find the page you want.
- **Try Google Cache.** When you follow a link from Google that comes up 404, or missing, hit the Back button to return to Google and click on the little down arrow next to the URL in the Google listing and select the "Cached" option. If available, this will bring up a copy of the page as it appeared at the time that Google last indexed the page.
- **Visit the Internet Archive.** Sometimes sites really are taken offline. Even that doesn't mean the information is necessarily lost forever. The Wayback Machine at Internet Archive preserves websites for posterity by taking regular "snapshots" of web pages at various points in time. Type a URL into the Wayback Machine search box (*www.archive.org*), then select a date from the available archives, and you can begin surfing an archived version of the web page.

Use the Find Feature in Your Browser

Many genealogy transcriptions and records appear online as long scrolling pages of text. To quickly search these pages for a particular name or other piece of information, use the Find feature in your browser. To access the Find feature, press CTRL+F for PCs, or COMMAND+F for Macs.

LINK

For further help with understanding and using search engines to effectively find what you need, check out The Spider's Apprentice (*www.monash.com/spidap.html*). The site rates the various search engines based on their effectiveness, offers a variety of search strategies for finding various types of information on the web, and also explains how to improve your own search engine ranking if you maintain a blog or website.

Use the Stephen P. Morse One-Step Search Tools

The One-Step website (*www.stevemorse.org*) created by Stephen P. Morse offers enhanced search options for popular genealogical databases such as Ellis Island Records, Ancestry.com, and the Social Security Death Index. In almost every case, the One-Step search offers more flexibility than the original database's search engine. Use these One-Step tools as a back door when you're unsuccessful at searching popular databases directly.

Find the Right Tree in the Forest

Individuals are unique. Names are not. When searching for your ancestors on the Internet, you'll quickly find that there are numerous people with the same name. Even unusual names may not be as uncommon as you think. Dempsey and Kinchen Owens may sound like somewhat unusual names, but there were actually several men sporting those monikers living in mid-nineteenth-century North Carolina!

ALERT

One popular method for locating ancestors with common surnames, such as Smith or Powell, is to search for other less-common names from your ancestor's family. If your John Smith has a son named Elias, try searching for Elias Smith. Also look for sisters who married men with more unusual names.

To avoid the pitfall of merging two people with the same name into one, certified genealogist Marsha Hoffman Rising, author of *The Family Tree Problem Solver*, always assumed that two people of the same name lived in the same community. This reminds you not to attach a piece of data to a specific individual until you're sure that you have the right person. Search for *all* available records, and use them to identify the distinguishing characteristics of your ancestor. Two men with the same name will have different wives, different children, and perhaps a different occupation. Most importantly, they won't usually occupy the same piece of property, so be sure to include land and property records in your search.

It's not unusual to find two men of the same name living in the same community identified as Sr. and Jr. in local records, causing many researchers to mistakenly connect them as father and son. In reality, they could have a different family relationship, such as uncle and nephew, or even no relationship at all—with "junior" and "senior" used solely to distinguish between an elder and a younger man with the same name living in the area. These and other relationship terms such as "aunt" and "cousin" were often used very loosely in earlier times—and still are, even today. The lesson? It's important not to jump to hasty conclusions. Take time to research multiple sources of information for each individual and event in your family tree so you can be sure you have the correct individual identified as your ancestor.

Spread the Wealth

As mentioned earlier, a "cluster" approach to family history research requires you to branch out your genealogy search to include records of extended family members, neighbors, friends, or other individuals with whom your ancestors interacted in some fashion. Certified genealogist Elizabeth Shown Mills memorably refers to this group of individuals as your ancestor's "FAN club" (Family, Associates, and Neighbors). Cluster genealogy is generally used as a workaround approach when records on your own ancestors are lacking, but some people actually choose to focus their research on a group of unrelated but connected people, such as members of a particular town or school.

In its most simple form, cluster genealogy might mean ordering the death certificate for each of your grandmother's siblings when her death certificate turns up with "unknown" in the blank for mother's maiden name. The hope is that at least one of the siblings' informants knew the mother's maiden name and ensured that it was recorded correctly on their death certificate.

A cluster approach is frequently used to track down the family of a female ancestor. Individuals generally married someone who lived nearby or was otherwise in their social circle, such as the sibling of a classmate. Expand your research to include the records for individuals named as witnesses on your ancestor's land deeds, bondsmen on marriage records, or neighbors identified through census or tax lists, and you just might identify your great-great-grandmother's family!

Another, slightly more complex, example of the cluster approach is acquiring copies of and platting (mapping) the land grants for all of the individuals who owned land in the vicinity of your North Carolina ancestor around 1725, in an effort to distinguish him from another man of the same name who also owned land in the area.

The next time a previously unknown name pops up in a record that relates to your ancestor, spend some time researching him or her. At the very least, be sure to record the name in your research notes in case it pops up again. There may just be a connection there!

CHAPTER 4

Online Starting Points

The Internet is overflowing with tens of thousands of sites with family history information. With just a few clicks of your mouse, you can learn how to get started researching your family history, explore historical databases for your ancestors, share your discoveries with family and friends, and network with other genealogists. It's exciting and addicting, but without a road map, you may quickly find yourself lost.

What Is and Is Not Online

To help acquaint you with genealogy research online, this chapter presents some of the largest and most popular online sites to begin your family history search. Most of these will include sources in the form of indexes, transcriptions and abstracts, or digital images:

- **Indexes**—An index is a list of names, possibly including other relevant details such as date or location of an event, that directs you to the original documents in which the names appear.
- **Transcriptions and abstracts**—In a transcription, the full text of a document is copied out and placed online as text. Sometimes information is "abstracted," which means that only the most relevant details are pulled out.
- **Images**—The original document is scanned and may be presented online as an image file, a PDF file, or a document that you must view through a special viewer that you'll download to your computer.

Originally, most online data appeared in the form of indexes, because they are the least time-consuming and least costly to prepare and place online. This has important implications for genealogists, as it means you cannot do all of your research online. More and more indexes are now being linked to digital scans of the original documents, however. In cases where these scans aren't available online, all information you obtain from indexes and transcriptions should generally be checked against the original record for accuracy and completeness—often necessitating a letter, call, or visit to a courthouse, archives, or other records repository.

Find Family at FamilySearch

The Family History Library (FHL) in Salt Lake City has the largest collection of genealogical materials in the world, thanks to the diligent work of members of The Church of Jesus Christ of Latter-day Saints (LDS). Their online presence at FamilySearch (*www.familysearch.org*) features more than 3.5 billion names in searchable databases—all of them free.

ESSENTIAL

FamilySearch is currently in the process of digitizing the 6.875 billion historic records preserved on microfilm in its Granite Mountain Records Vault, for the purpose of allowing free online access to the public. In addition, they have partnered with other entities, such as the National Archives, to digitally capture, preserve, and publish other important genealogical records online. Over 35 million historic records are being added each month—visit the Historical Record Collections list (*http://familysearch.org/search/collection/list*) and click on the Last Updated column to see what's new!

Just Enter a Name

Over 1,500 record collections are available for searching on FamilySearch. Selecting "Search" from the home page will bring up a search form where you can enter a first and last name, as well as additional fields, such as the name of a spouse or parent or the date/location of a vital event. Clicking the "Search" button will bring up a list of results that match your criteria, along with options on the left-hand side of the screen for further narrowing and refining your search results. From the main search page, a variety of other options are also available, accessed through the tabs across the top of the page:

- **Records** (*http://familysearch.org/search*)—This tab (the main one) includes a search box at the top, plus links to browse genealogical records below, organized by country. This is where you'll find the true "meat" of the FamilySearch website, with digitized images and tran-scribed indexes for millions of family history records from countries all over the world. The biggest focus is on vital record collections, including baptismal records, marriage licenses, death certificates, and even burial records. This collection also includes census, pro-bate, emigration, and even school and workhouse records.
- **Genealogies** (*http://familysearch.org/family-trees*)—Select "Search" from the home page, followed by the Genealogies tab, to bring up a search screen specifically for searching user-submitted family trees. This large database includes lineage-linked family trees submitted

to Ancestral File and Pedigree Resource File by FamilySearch users worldwide.

- **Catalog** (*http://familysearch.org/catalog-search*)—The FamilySearch Catalog makes it easy to learn what is available in the world's largest collection of genealogical records. See more on this in the next section.
- **Books** (*http://books.familysearch.org*)—More than 80,000 digitized family history publications can be searched and viewed here, including family histories, county and local histories, genealogy magazines, how-to books, and gazetteers.
- **Wiki** (*www.familysearch.org/learn/wiki/*)—More than 74,000 articles provide research guidance on records and research methodologies for countries around the world. Browse by country or topic.

Make Use of the Family History Library Catalog

For a small fee, almost every microfilm in the vast Family History Library collection can be borrowed through your local Family History Center. Use the Family History Library Catalog (FHLC) to peruse available records, plan your research strategy, access digitized records online, and order nondigitized records to be sent to your local Family History Center. This virtual catalog of the vast holdings of the Family History Library can be searched by place, surname, title, author, subject, call number, film/fiche number, or keyword. The default Place Search is the most useful search for most genealogy purposes because it will return a list of all available records, from the area where your ancestor lived, that have been filmed and are available at the Family History Library, along with links if the records have been digitized and are available online.

Borrow Microfilm

Once you find a record of interest in the FHLC, scroll down to the Film Notes to locate call numbers for microfilms that contain the record you seek. With the name of the record and the call number for the film, you can submit a loan request through your local Family History Center, or click directly on the call number to order online. They charge a fee per microfilm to cover shipping and handling to and from the Family History Library in Salt Lake City. Most films will be available for viewing at your local FHC within a few weeks of your order. Books are generally not available for loan.

ALERT

The LDS Church operates more than 4,600 Family History Centers (FHC) in more than 130 countries around the world. These branch facilities of the Family History Library in Salt Lake City offer access to the library's vast genealogical holdings, through electronic databases and microfilm loan. While these centers are usually located inside buildings belonging to the church, everyone is welcome regardless of their religious beliefs. Visit their website (*www.familysearch.org/locations/centerlocator*) to find a Family History Center near you.

Even if you don't plan to borrow microfilms, the FHLC is a great way to view the types of records that are available for your area and time period you are interested in. A place search in the catalog for *Edgecombe County, North Carolina*, for example, displays a wide variety of records, from Bible records to voting registers. By selecting "Court, Land, Wills & Financial" and then "Land Records" from the Category List, you learn that deed records are available dating back to 1732, and indexes from 1759.

Access Helpful Research Tools and Guidance

Another thing that FamilySearch does well is to teach newcomers about genealogy. Select the Get Started section of FamilySearch from the navigation bar at the bottom of the home page to access learning articles in the previously mentioned Wiki, as well as over 600 online genealogy courses in the Learning Center. The free, self-paced courses can be browsed by locality or topic, and are available for individuals of all research levels, from beginner to advanced.

Help Index Records

FamilySearch Worldwide Indexing (*www.familysearch.org/volunteer/indexing*) is a big part of the reason that FamilySearch is able to make so many records available online for free to all researchers. Tens of thousands of volunteers from all over the world donate their time to help extract data from digitized records using FamilySearch's free online indexing tool. This user-extracted data is then used to create and provide free searchable indexes to digitized historical records on FamilySearch.org. Take the two-minute interactive test drive, accessible from the main Indexing page, to see how it works.

Explore More Free Databases

Thanks to the efforts of hundreds of thousands of volunteer genealogists and historians, there is a wealth of free genealogy data available online. Government agencies, libraries, and archives have also jumped on the digital bandwagon, offering free Internet access to some of the many public records under their domain. Here you'll learn about some of the largest, general-purpose sites for free genealogy research.

Root Around at RootsWeb

The oldest and largest free community genealogy site on the web, RootsWeb (*www.rootsweb.com*), offers hundreds of gigabytes of free genealogy data, including millions of records contributed by users. Search tabs at the top lead you to some of RootsWeb's most popular features:

- Click on "Searches" to access a variety of search engines and indexes. Here you'll find the RootsWeb Surname List (RSL), a registry of surnames along with information about how to contact the person who submitted the surname so you can share information and compare notes. This is also where you'll find links to the RootsWeb hosted genealogy records and databases, organized by location and/ or record type.
- The Family Trees tab takes you to the massive WorldConnect project, a lineage-linked database with more than 700 million names.
- The next two tabs take you to Mailing Lists and Message Boards, where you can connect with other researchers, ask questions about your family history, or search through more than a decade of archived posts.

- RootsWeb also hosts tens of thousands of websites for the genealogy community, including personal sites, surname sites, and major free genealogy projects. The Web Sites tab offers a good jumping-off point for exploring your roots.

Find Local Records at the USGenWeb Project

The goal of this large volunteer genealogy project is to maintain websites for genealogical research in every U.S. state and county. The databases, links, and information found at The USGenWeb Project (*www.usgenweb.org*) are all free, but because the sites are maintained entirely by volunteers, the quality and quantity of the information varies widely from site to site. Some are true gems, with a wealth of content not available elsewhere online. Whenever you're researching in a new locality, it's a good idea to include a visit to the local GenWeb site to check out the available databases, learn about the area's geography and changing boundaries, and identify local resources for research in the area.

Look in Lineage-Linked Databases

Lineage-linked databases offer family historians an easy way to search, contribute, view, or download family trees online. Instead of just a simple list or index of names, lineage-linked databases present family trees in a linked, pedigree format. Because these compiled databases offer access to millions of names and multiple generations of a family tree, they are a favorite of many online genealogists.

LINK

In addition to the large lineage-linked databases available through Ancestry.com, RootsWeb.com, MyHeritage, and FamilySearch, other large pedigree sites (some free and some subscription) include GeneaNet (*www.geneanet.org*), MyTrees.com (*www.mytrees.com*), and OneGreatFamily (*www.onegreatfamily.org*).

The Internet's largest collection of user-submitted family trees can be found at Ancestry.com, a collection of more than 46 million family trees containing more than 4 billion names, known as Ancestry Member Trees (*http://trees.ancestry.com*).

Another huge collection of family tree files can be found in the combined Ancestry World Tree/RootsWeb WorldConnect database. The database, containing more than 712 million names in over 430 million family trees, can be searched through RootsWeb as RootsWeb WorldConnect (*http://wc.rootsweb.ancestry.com*). Advanced search options, easy submission of your own family tree, contact information for submitters, and the ability to add electronic notes make this lineage-linked database a favorite with online genealogists.

At FamilySearch.org, the FamilySearch Family Tree (accessible from the Family Tree tab at *www.familysearch.org*) is another good lineage-linked collection of family trees with more than 900 million names submitted by FamilySearch users. The tool offers you the option to enter your own family tree information, but searching other user-submitted pedigree information is also available via the Find tab.

More than 27 million family trees and 1.5 billion profiles are available in the MyHeritage family trees database at MyHeritage (*www.myheritage.com/research/collection-1/myheritage-family-trees*). This site, based in Israel, boasts a large international audience, increasing the chance of making a connection for those whose ancestors were fairly recent immigrants to the United States. Searching is free, but access to the full family trees requires a subscription.

Despite the convenience of being able to download a big chunk of your family history in one place, lineage-linked or pedigree databases have one huge drawback: They are only as reliable as the research of the individual who posted them. The first option for evaluating a family tree's reliability is to look for good documentation of sources and conclusions, but to find such well-documented pedigrees online is rare. To ensure that the information you have found is correct, follow up all assertions found in online family trees through original records.

Seek Out Subscription Sites

Commercial sites generally offer the greatest wealth of genealogy data, drawn from records around the world. This information comes with a price tag, however, in the form of subscription or pay-per-view access. When evaluating a commercial genealogy site, consider whether the payment is worth the return in terms of the unique databases or records you will gain access to or the time you will save by being able to access them from your home.

Ancestry.com

The largest commercial online source for family history information, with more than 2.7 million subscribers across several branded websites, is Ancestry.com (*www.ancestry.com*). More than 11 billion historical records are available to subscribing members from over two dozen countries, including the United States, Great Britain, and Canada. As a subscriber to Ancestry.com, you can:

- **Search for historical records.** Ancestry.com has more than 11 billion records available online, including census records, immigration records, historical newspapers, military records, vital records, school yearbooks, and a variety of other resources. Advanced search features allow you to search across all databases at once.
- **View digital images of original records.** Ancestry.com places a focus on scanning and digitizing historical documents for online viewing. This organization's efforts made it the first site online to offer indexes and images of the complete U.S. census from 1790 to 1930. It also offers digitized passenger lists, British and Canadian census records, the England & Wales National Probate Calendar, a collection of more than 60 million school yearbooks, and U.S. military records such as Civil War pension application cards and WWI draft registration cards.
- **Connect with others researching the same ancestors.** The large genealogy community at Ancestry.com offers numerous chances to benefit from the research of others. The majority of the community features at Ancestry.com are free and available to even nonsubscribers, including user-submitted family trees and family history message boards.

Ancestry.com is a subscription-based site, offering unlimited access to records for a monthly or annual fee. A special subscription version for libraries, called Ancestry Library Edition, may be available to you for free through your local library, but you'll only have access from the library computers; this database is not available for remote access from home with a library card. Ancestry.com also offers free access to patrons at the Family History Library and select larger Family History Centers through a special arrangement with The Church of Jesus Christ of Latter-day Saints (the LDS or Mormon Church).

ESSENTIAL

Some databases at Ancestry.com and RootsWeb offer a special "Post-em Note" feature to help you connect with other researchers interested in the same family. This electronic equivalent of a yellow sticky note allows you to attach information such as your name and e-mail address or corrected data to a record. A slightly different version of the feature can be found listed in some Ancestry.com databases as Comments and Corrections.

MyHeritage

MyHeritage (*www.myheritage.com*) offers both free and paid family history content, searchable in over 40 languages. The company, based in Israel, is one of the fastest growing family history sites on the web with acquisitions of a number of other family history sites, including GenCircles (*www.gencircles.com*), WorldVitalRecords (*www.worldvitalrecords.com*), and Geni.com (*www.geni.com*). The bulk of its online content is found in its more than 27 million family trees, but it also offers a growing collection of genealogical records (most from WorldVitalRecords), plus free Family Tree Builder software and powerful search tools. Subscription options include a free Basic package, plus Premium and Premium Plus subscriptions.

GenealogyBank

NewsBank offers online access to millions of records from its digital vaults through a service geared specifically to genealogists. Known as

GenealogyBank (*www.genealogybank.com*), this subscription-based product offers access to more than 1 billion articles from more than 6,500 historical U.S. newspapers, plus historical documents and the Social Security Death Index. The biggest draw for genealogists is the historical newspaper collection dating back to 1690, plus the over 215 million obituaries and death records in its Historical Obituaries collection.

The Historical Documents collection includes the full-run of the American State Papers, plus the U.S. Congressional Serial Set. Unlimited access is available for a monthly or annual subscription, and there is a money-back guarantee if you're not satisfied. A similar service called America's GenealogyBank is available for library subscription, so check with your local or state library before you subscribe. You may already have access to this database through one of these sources.

ALERT

Digital images of original records found online are considered by most genealogists to offer a reasonable substitute for the original record in almost every research situation. In other words, if you've accessed a digital image of a census enumeration or military record from a reputable source, it's generally not necessary to also view the original record.

Fold3.com

Content at subscription-based Fold3.com (*www.fold3.com*), named for the third fold in the traditional flag-folding ceremony that honors and remembers veterans for their sacrifice, is a mix of historical documents and newspapers, with the bulk of the content digitized through a partnership with the National Archives. Fold3, now owned by Ancestry.com, is best known by genealogists for its U.S. military records collection, including Revolutionary War pension records, Civil War service records, and Army and Navy JAG case files. Other interesting collections among its more than 406 million images include FBI case files, records of the Southern Claims Commission, U.S. naturalization records, and interactive editions of the 1860 and 1900–1930 U.S. census, which allow users to create profile pages for any enumerated individual.

Fold3.com can be searched by name or keyword across all available records, or you can browse or search by collection or historical era. Results can be further narrowed by collection title, category, place, name, and year. The Flash-based site is beautiful and easy to navigate, but searching can be clunky at times. For the best results with more common names, browse directly to the collection/title of interest and then search within that collection. Fold3.com offers both monthly and annual subscription rates, as well as a seven-day free trial.

AmericanAncestors

The flagship website of the New England Historic Genealogical Society (*www.americanancestors.org*) hosts a large collection of online databases for individuals with New England ancestry, such as Massachusetts vital records and full text issues of the *New England Historical and Genealogical Register* (from 1847). There is also a growing collection of records for other areas, including resources for mid-Atlantic, Irish, and African American research. Annual membership includes access to more than 3,000 online genealogical and historical collections, plus subscriptions to *American Ancestors* magazine and the *New England Historical and Genealogical Register.*

Genealogy Today

This relatively inexpensive subscription-based site specializes in unique records of interest for social and family history. Databases available at Genealogy Today (*www.genealogytoday.com*) include school yearbooks, association membership rosters, orphanage records, church records, railroad seniority rosters, farm directories, donation lists, funeral cards, and insurance claims. Most of the information has been transcribed by hand from documents and books found in estate sales, used book stores, eBay, and so on. The content primarily spans 1830 to 1930 from U.S. sources.

Discover History at the National Archives

The U.S. National Archives and Records Administration (NARA) preserves a huge amount of information related to the history of our nation and its people—the paper documents alone would circle the earth more than fifty-seven times if laid end to end! Because the records at the National Archives (*www.archives.gov*) come from every branch of the federal government, almost all Americans can find themselves, their ancestors, or their community in the archival holdings.

The cost to digitize such a huge volume of materials is prohibitive, so only a small percentage of the National Archives records are available for research online. Instead, the greatest value of the site is in its research tools, such as microfilm indexes and finding aids, and articles on various record types and how to access them. There are, however, a few exceptions, such as Casualty Lists for the Korean and Vietnam Wars and Selected Chinese Exclusion Lists. Most of the rest of the available data on their website can be accessed through one of two NARA search engines.

- **Online Public Access** (*www.archives.gov/research/search/*) provides a streamlined method for searching and accessing multiple resources from the National Archives. This includes ARC (Archival Research Catalog), which describes about 50 percent of the holdings of the National Archives. Enter keywords in the basic search box, or use Advanced Search for even more options; see the Search Tips page (*www.archives.gov/research/search/help/search-tips .html*) for details. In some cases, an OPA search results in a direct link to an online record or database such as World War II Casualty Lists; indexes to several Native American census rolls, including the Guion-Miller Roll (a list of Eastern Cherokees who applied for money awarded in 1905 from a lawsuit in which they sued the U.S. for funds due them under treaties) and Dawes Rolls (tribal enrollment applications around the turn of the twentieth century); and fugitive slave case papers and petitions.
- **The Access to Archival Databases (AAD)** (*http://aad.archives.gov/ aad*) allows you to search for free through more than 85 million documents, including passenger lists for people who fled the Irish famine for the United States in the 1840s, photos of natural and manmade disasters, and the popular World War II army enlistment file. Be sure to check out the Search Values feature for any search field you use. In the World War II file, for example, you need to enter names as lastname,firstname (i.e., *owens,james*) and the year of birth as a two-digit number (such as *23*).

The National Archives has partnered with sites like Fold3.com and Ancestry.com to digitize additional records from its vast holdings, with tens of millions of pages digitized to date. Access to the digitized materials is available for no charge in the National Archives facilities and online with a subscription to the partnering website. National Archives content that is currently available on Fold3 (*www.fold3.com*) and/or Ancestry. com (*www.ancestry.com*) is highlighted in this list from the National Archives of "Microfilm Publications and Original Records Digitized by Our Digitization Partners" (*www.archives.gov/digitization/digitized-by-partners.html*).

Look at the Library of Congress

While many may not classify the Library of Congress (*www.loc.gov*) as a starting point for online genealogy research, it has a number of important features and collections that warrant its inclusion in this section.

The Library of Congress Online Catalog (*http://catalog.loc.gov*) is one of the best places to search online for published local and family histories. While the books themselves are not available online, you can easily see what books have been published that may relate to your research. With this information you can try contacting local libraries or historical societies to see if they have a copy of the book you can borrow, or have them make copies of the pages that concern your ancestors.

The American Memory collection (*http://memory.loc.gov*) presents a digital record of American history, chronicling historic events, people, places, and ideas through documents, maps, sheet music, moving images, sound recordings, and oral histories. A wide variety of collections cover topics such as narratives and life histories from the Works Progress Administration's Federal Writers' Project, U.S. Congressional documents and debates, and Civil War photographs. Enter your family name or hometown in the search box available at the top of each page to see if information about your ancestors or the community in which they lived is included in the online American Memory collection, or browse relevant collections individually (*http://memory.loc.gov/ammem/browse/index.html*).

Search State Libraries and Archives

The state library or archive can often be a genealogist's best friend—even online genealogists. Many are scanning, digitizing, and indexing the most popular records from their vast holdings and placing them online for free access by genealogists, historians, and other researchers. Budget shortages and other issues may dictate that new data isn't added as quickly as everyone might like, but these state resources often offer access to databases or indexes not available elsewhere online.

ESSENTIAL

Not all major libraries and archives yet offer online access to public records, but most maintain an online catalog of their holdings. Many will also allow you to request copies of records online—generally for a fee. Find links to digitized collections and online catalogs in "U.S. State Archives Online" (*http://genealogy.about.com/od/united_states/ tp/State-Archives-Online.htm*).

The Illinois State Archives (*www.cyberdriveillinois.com/departments/ archives/databases/home.html*), one of the first to provide online access to selected records, offers vital record indexes such as a Statewide Marriage Index, 1763–1900, and a Statewide Death Index, 1916–1950, along with public-domain land sales, emancipation records, military records, and several county-level probate and circuit court indexes. Another good example is the Missouri State Archives (*www.sos.mo.gov/archives/resources/ordb.asp*), where you can search a database of births and deaths prior to 1910, or view digital copies of death certificates from 1910 to 1962. They also have indexes and/or abstracts of coroner's inquest records, naturalization records, and digitized pre-1900 St. Louis City and County probate records. For those researching in Virginia, the website of the Library of Virginia (*www.virginiamemory.com/ collections*) offers eighty-plus databases, indexes, and finding aids of use to genealogists, including World War I history questionnaires; cohabitation registers; historical Virginia photographs; chancery records with an index and nearly 8 million images; and a database of Virginia Land Office patents, grants, and surveys from 1623 to 1992. Try a search for "*your state name*" *archives* or "*your state name*" *state library* to locate such sites.

CHAPTER 5

Dig Into Death Records

Since genealogy research begins with the present before moving back into the past, death records are a good place to start your search. They often provide enough detail to help verify that you have the correct individual and may include information that you don't already have to help you reach back to the previous generation. Death records are also among the easiest family history records to find online.

A Good Place to Begin

Why should you care when your grandfather died when what you really want to know is who your great-grandparents are? Death records—including death certificates, tombstone inscriptions, obituaries, and funeral home records—all provide important clues to an individual's past. Your grandfather's death certificate may list the maiden name of his mother, a significant little tidbit that living family members no longer recall. His obituary may mention a surviving sister, the great-aunt that you never knew existed. His tombstone may tell you that he was a member of the Sons of Confederate Veterans. Records from the funeral home may indicate his exact date of birth.

A second, but equally important, reason for beginning a search with death records is that they are among the most easily accessible records. The fact that the individual is deceased makes privacy less of a concern. Now all of this is not to say that you should always begin a genealogy search with death records. There's nothing wrong with beginning with your grandparents' marriage record, or their enumeration in the 1940 U.S. census. But once you've gathered as much information as you can from family members, death records generally make sense as the next good place to take your family history quest.

Search for Obituaries

Whenever you embark on a new family history project, it is often helpful to begin by searching for an obituary. This not only helps confirm the individual's date of death, but often provides extra family details that you may not have—the names of extended family members, place of birth, occupation, religious faith and/or place of worship, organization memberships, and any other particulars that people felt were important enough to mention in summing up the life of the deceased.

For example, biographies of soul singer James Brown repeatedly mention his being raised by his great-aunt Hansone Washington for a time, but offer few clues as to exactly how she was related. Was she a great-aunt on the mother's side or father's side? Was she an aunt or a great-aunt (the biographies don't agree)? Who were her parents? An online obituary for Mrs. Hansone Washington in the *Augusta Chronicle*, dated Saturday, June 18, 1977, provides some insight:

Mrs. Hansone Washington, 1029 Bennett Lane died Thursday in an Augusta hospital. Funeral arrangements will be announced by Blount Funeral Home. Survivors include two sisters, Mrs. Josephine Gilliam and Mrs. I Ganes; two brothers, Mansfield Scott and Willard Scott; and five sons, Stanley E. Figenson, Mike Jowery, Ella Figenson, William Glen, and Johney Washington. Friends may call at the residence or at Blount Funeral Home.

Armed with the names of her brothers and sisters from this obituary, you can identify the family of Hansone ("Handsome") Scott in the 1910 census of Barnwell County, S.C., prior to her marriage to William Washington and move to Augusta, Georgia. Obituaries for other family members, including the father of James Brown, help clarify her relationship to the singer.

When searching for an obituary, be sure to investigate all likely newspapers. Many cities have more than one paper, and an obituary for a specific individual could appear in more than one town. A thorough search should include the city where the person died and any locations where they lived for many years or still have family. You never know which paper is going to have the most detailed obituary, or turn up the one important clue that is omitted from the rest. Check the papers for at least a week after the individual's death, and up to several weeks if a specialized newspaper such as an ethnic or religious paper. Often a brief obituary or death notice will appear in the first day or two after the death and a longer, full obituary will follow a day or two later.

Obituaries of the past are often not as lengthy and detailed as more modern obituaries. Many of them are little more than a brief notice of the death and funeral arrangements. More recent obituaries are also much easier to locate online, while one from twenty or more years ago may require microfilm research or a request sent to the newspaper in which it was published. But for a genealogist, some information is better than no information at all, so don't assume that obituaries are only useful for people who died within the past few decades.

Look Online

There are many sources for locating obituaries online, such as major historical databases, volunteer obituary transcription sites, and the website of the newspaper itself. Google News Advanced Search (*http://news.google .com/news/advanced_news_search*) provides searchable access to more than 200 years of archived news content from individual publishers and news aggregators, making it a good place to begin your search. Use the "in archive" selection under "date added" to restrict your search to the archived content. Both free and fee-based content is included in Google News. Search results available for a fee are clearly labeled as "pay-per-view" or list a specific fee to access the content. Links from Google take you directly to the website of the publisher or aggregator where the content is hosted. When there are more than just a handful of results, use the "Archives" drop-down menu at the top to help you drill down into search results by decade or year. While some of the archived newspaper content is unique online to Google News, much could also be found through searching directly on the publishers' websites. However, Google's service makes it easy to search and navigate through multiple sources at once. If you end up with too many results for the individual's name, try adding search terms such as *obituary*, *funeral*, or *died* to help focus your results.

LINK

Searches for obituaries in Google Archive Search often yield results from the NewsBank service with a per-article access fee that varies by publisher. If you think you'll need to look at more than one or two articles or obituaries, you may get a better value through GenealogyBank (*www.genealogybank.com*). Its Recent Newspaper Obituaries collection contains more than 43 million obituaries from NewsBank, dating from 1977 to the present.

A variety of specialized search services can also help you locate an obituary online. The Obituary Daily Times (*www.rootsweb.com/~obituary*) offers a daily index of published obituaries compiled by volunteers and distributed freely via e-mail list. The entire database, going back to about 1999, is also searchable online. The Obituary Daily Times does not index all published obituaries, just the ones selected to be included by the volunteers. It also does not have the actual newspaper notices, just the name of the deceased, and the publication and date where the obituary appeared. With this information you can then request a copy of the obituary from the library or directly from the newspaper. ObitFinder (*www.obitfinder.com*) from Legacy.com (*www.legacy.com*) searches obituaries from more than 900 national and international newspapers. Some require a fee to access.

Subscription-based obituary and newspaper search sites, such as ObitsArchive.com (*www.obitsarchive.com*), Newspaper Archive (*http:// newspaperarchive.com*), and the National Obituary Archive (*www .arrangeonline.com*), can also be useful in locating obituaries. Many general genealogy subscription sites also get into the act; Ancestry.com, Archives .com, and Fold3 (*www.fold3.com*), for example, all offer online obituary and/or historic newspaper collections.

Locate Newspaper Websites

Use your favorite search engine to locate newspapers published in the area where your ancestor lived or died. A search for the town or county name and newspaper will usually turn up what you need. If you know the newspaper's title, you can search for that directly. Once you find the newspaper's website, visit the Obituaries section to see how far back in time these go. Look for an Archives section as well, where the newspaper offers access to older material. Some newspapers leave obituaries online forever, some for a year, and some for just a week or two. Some may charge for access to older articles and obituaries.

Look for a Library Website

The public library that serves the area in which your ancestor lived or died is often an excellent source for obituary and death notices. Many maintain obituary clipping files or, at the very least, have back issues of area newspapers available on microfilm. Numerous library websites even offer online indexes to obituary notices from their area. From there, it often takes no more than an e-mail or quick letter to get a copy of the actual obituary; some librarians will even e-mail a digitized copy. Many libraries don't charge for this service or request, only a minimal reimbursement for copying and postage. If you can't find anything on the website, contact the library via phone or e-mail to see how its staff handles such requests.

Use Your Local Library

Many libraries subscribe to a variety of helpful research databases for free use by their patrons. Subscriptions to databases such as NewsBank, GenealogyBank, ProQuest Obituaries, or Ancestry Library Edition can be useful for obituary searches. Contact your local or state library to see what databases are offered (most list them on their website) and whether you can connect from home with your library card number.

Social Security Death Index

When you're unsure of an individual's date of death, head straight for the Social Security Death Index (SSDI). This large database compiled by the U.S. Social Security Administration (SSA) contains vital information for more than 92 million people (primarily Americans) whose deaths have been reported to the SSA.

What You Will Find in the SSDI

Once you locate an individual in the Social Security Death Index, you may find some or all of the following information: first and last name, date of death, date of birth, social security number (SSN), the state where the SSN was issued, the last known residence of the deceased, and the location where the last SSA benefit was sent.

What You Won't Find in the SSDI

The biggest mistake that researchers make when using the SSDI is in assuming that it is an index to all deceased individuals who have held social security numbers. That is not the case. It is also not a database of all the deceased that have received social security benefits or whose families have received survivor benefits. Instead the Social Security Death Index (SSDI) indexes individuals whose deaths were reported to the Social Security Administration, the majority of them after 1962, when SSA first computerized its processing of benefits. If a relative of the deceased, the funeral director, or the state did not report the death to the SSA, or if the individual died prior to 1963, you probably won't find that person's name in the index.

How to Search the SSDI

The Social Security Death Index is available for free searching online on several different websites. Privacy concerns raised in 2011 by individuals incorrectly listed in the SSDI as deceased caused a big stir in the news and in Congress, resulting in many genealogy sites either removing their copy of the SSDI or removing information for individuals who had died within the past several years. Legislative maneuvering regarding public access to the Social Security Death Master File is still ongoing; however, you can still access this very important genealogical resource on several websites, although most have removed access to entries from the past year or so. A few sites require a fee for access, but their offerings are generally no better than the free versions.

A good place to start is the handy search form by Steve Morse titled "Searching the Social Security Death Index in One Step" (*www.stevemorse.org/ssdi/ssdi.html*). It combines all of the desirable search features from the various SSDI websites into one easy search. Other free SSDI search options include Mocavo (*www.mocavo.com/records/ssdi*) and GenealogyBank (*www.genealogybank.com/gbnk/ssdi/*), both of which require you to sign up for a free account, and American Ancestors (*www.americanancestors.org/free-databases/*).

Locating a particular individual in the large SSDI database, especially if you aren't sure when and where this person died, can be an exercise in frustration. Be sure to take advantage of all the search features available to you, and try different combinations of searches. For example:

- Search by last name or first name only, in combination with other known details such as date or year of birth and state of last residence. The first name in combination with the exact birth date, or month and year of birth, often produces results.
- Search for women under both their married name and their maiden name.
- Enter an initial in the given name field.
- Omit the zip code because this field does not exist for earlier records.
- Try alternate spellings in the name field, making use of wildcard operators when available.

Order a Copy of the Social Security Application

With the name and social security number from the SSDI, you can request a copy of your ancestor's original application for social security, otherwise known as Form SS-5. This form was completed by individuals applying for a social security number and asked for information that is of great value to genealogists, such as parents' names (including the mother's maiden name), date of birth, employer, and, later, the place of birth. The fee to receive the Social Security Application Form is a bit steep, but well worth it if you don't already know the information that the form often provides.

The Social Security Administration offers online ordering of photocopies of Social Security Number Application SS-5 forms. A link to the application form with current fees can be found in their guide to Freedom of Information Act (FOIA) requests (*www.socialsecurity.gov/foia/request.html*). Recent restrictions on access may affect the information you receive. For SS-5 requests for individuals who were born less than 120 years ago you are required to provide proof of death, such as a death certificate or newspaper obituary. The SSA will also generally not release the parents' names on an SS-5 for parents born less than 120 years ago unless you can prove that the parents are deceased (tough to do when the reason many genealogists request this record in the first place is to learn the parents' names).

Death Certificates and Online Indexes

A death certificate can provide important details about a person's life—date and cause of death, date and place of birth, parents' names (including mother's maiden name), funeral home, burial location, and name of the informant who provided the information. Since about 1967, most death certificates in the United States also list the deceased's social security number. Actual details included on a death certificate vary from state to state and by time period.

Death certificates in the United States are primarily a twentieth-century innovation. Most states did not officially register deaths until after 1900; some, such as Georgia and New Mexico, began as late as 1919! There are a few exceptions, namely in New York, New Jersey, and the New England states, where recording of deaths began in the mid- to late 1800s. In the United States, death certificates are generally maintained at the state level, usually through the Department of Health or Vital Records.

LINK

Vitalrec.com (*www.vitalrec.com*) offers current information for each U.S. state on the availability of death records, instructions and fees for ordering a death certificate copy, and a link to the state department that handles vital records. If you're in a hurry, VitalChek (*www.vitalchek.com*) processes online rush orders for each state, including online credit card payment—for an extra fee, of course.

Privacy laws may restrict access to death certificates for a certain period of time after the individual's death. A term of fifty years is fairly common. Some agencies will allow anyone to request a copy of a death certificate but will black out certain, more private information, such as the cause of death or social security number, unless you are a direct relative of the deceased. When requesting a death certificate from a vital records agency, be prepared to identify your relationship with the deceased and to provide a copy of a valid ID.

Death indexes are available online for many states, counties, and locations. Check first on the website of the state vital records office, state archives, and state library. The Ohio Historical Society, for example, includes an online Ohio Death Certificate Index, 1913–1944. The Illinois State Archives hosts the Illinois Statewide Death Index, 1913–1950. At the Minnesota State Archives website you can search an index for death certificates from 1908 to 2001. Genealogist and blogger Joe Beine organizes links to these and many other online death indexes at Online Searchable Death Indexes and Records (*www.deathindexes.com*).

The Historical Records collection at FamilySearch (*http://familysearch .org/search/collection/list*) offers the largest free online collection of death indexes and certificates for the United States as well as for many other countries around the globe, including indexed vital records from the former International Genealogical Index (IGI). Ancestry.com offers access to a wide variety of death indexes to its subscribers. Some of these are also available elsewhere on the web, and some are exclusive online to Ancestry.com.

Death indexes can also be found on a variety of other genealogy sites, both free and fee-based. The state and county sites at The USGenWeb Project (*www.usgenweb.org*) are a good place to find death record transcriptions and indexes, as well as links to offsite indexes. Genealogical society websites are another good place to try. Both the Italian Genealogical Group (*www.italiangen.org*) and German Genealogy Group (*www .germangenealogygroup.com*), for example, offer online searching of the New York City Death Index, 1862–1948. When all else fails, try a search for "death index" and the state name, such as *pennsylvania "death index,"* in your favorite search engine.

Visit Virtual Cemeteries and Funeral Homes

Cemetery tombstones or grave markers are good sources for death information, as well as providing evidence for date of birth, family relationships, military service, and membership in fraternal organizations or societies. A visit to the cemetery is a must for family tree projects, but not always easily done in person. While it can't quite match the special feeling you get standing before your ancestor's tombstone, online research in the form of tombstone transcriptions and photographs affords the opportunity for "virtually" traipsing through cemeteries around the world from the comfort of home.

ALERT

Tombstones often show the age of the individual when she died in place of either the date of birth or death. If this information is provided in the form *years, months, days,* such as "Age 22 Years, 11 Months, and 26 Days," then you can easily calculate the missing date with the help of a birth date calculator (just type *birth date calculator* into your favorite search engine).

Virtual Cemeteries Have Their Shortcomings

Convenient as it is to research cemetery records online, there are a few disadvantages over an in-person visit to the cemetery. Keep these in mind as you explore cemetery information online:

- Tombstone information may not always be read and transcribed correctly. Some grave markers can be very hard to read, or the transcriber may have mistyped the information when putting it online. He may also have missed information inscribed on the back of the stone (although the thorough ones won't).

- The arrangement of graves in the cemetery can be important because family members are often buried together or close to one another. That arrangement is not always preserved in the alphabetical listings you sometimes find online. Check to see if some type of placement information has also been transcribed, such as the cemetery section and row. This can at least help identify people buried in the same general area of the cemetery. If the site also includes individual tombstone photos, you can sometimes find clues in them to help identify a gravestone's relative position in the cemetery.

Find Online Cemetery Databases and Lists

Genealogical societies and volunteers are the greatest source for online cemetery transcriptions, so a good place to begin is on the website of an area genealogical society or the appropriate county site at USGenWeb. If that doesn't pan out, use a search engine to locate online cemeteries or transcriptions by entering a phrase such as *greene county virginia cemetery*. Or, visit ePodunk (*www.epodunk.com*) or the U.S. Board on Geographic Names information system (*http://geonames.usgs.gov*) to find the names of cemeteries in a given town or county and then search for the cemeteries directly by name. These sites won't usually pick up small family cemeteries, but they at least offer a place to start.

ESSENTIAL

The symbols and architecture you encounter in the cemetery can tell you a lot about your ancestors. *Stories in Stone*, by Douglas Keister, details many examples of funerary architecture and tombstone symbols, accompanied by photos. Alternatively, look online for information by searching for phrases such as *tombstone symbols* or *cemetery symbolism*.

In an effort to preserve the valuable information crumbling away in cemeteries, and to improve access to this information for genealogists, a variety of groups and organizations are collaborating to put cemetery data online. Best of all, these databases are all free!

- **Find A Grave**—Visit the well-organized Find A Grave site (*www.findagrave.com*) to search more than 101 million grave records for both the famous and the "nonfamous."
- **BillionGraves**—On BillionGraves (*http://billiongraves.com*), volunteers have contributed over 4 million GPS-tagged photos of headstones from cemeteries across the globe.
- **Interment.net**—Over 4 million cemetery records are available for searching or browsing on Interment.net (*www.interment.net*), representing more than 8,000 cemeteries around the world.
- **USGenWeb Tombstone Transcription Project**—Browse by state and county to view hundreds of thousands of cemetery transcriptions and photos contributed by volunteers to this special project at USGenWeb (*www.usgwtombstones.org*).
- **JewishGen Online Worldwide Burial Registry (JOWBR)**—Well over 1.9 million names are available for searching in this database of Jewish interments in cemeteries and other burial sites worldwide (*www.jewishgen.org/databases/cemetery*).
- **Veterans Affairs Nationwide Gravesite Locator**—Search for burial locations of veterans with the help of the U.S. Department of Veterans Affairs (*http://gravelocator.cem.va.gov*). The site includes information on veterans and their family members buried in veterans and military cemeteries, as well as those buried in private cemeteries where the grave is marked with a government grave marker.

Don't Disregard Funeral Home Records

Genealogists often overlook the records maintained by funeral homes. These can be a very valuable source of family history information. Depending on state or local laws, the funeral director may be the one responsible for filing the death certificate and placing the obituary with the news media, which means all of those valuable details collected from family members may reside in his files. A funeral home file may provide the deceased's date and place of birth, maiden name if a female, date and place of death, burial location, parents' names, veteran status, social security number, and, sometimes, names of surviving relatives.

It is important to realize, however, that a funeral home is a private business. Its primary responsibility is to the deceased and the grieving family, not to genealogists. You may find the funeral home to be reluctant about releasing private records. You may also find that older records are stored away in boxes in a basement or attic or have been thrown out to make room for more current records.

Some funeral home records may be found online in the form of transcribed data. Genealogical societies or volunteers, not the funeral homes, generally post these. There are exceptions, however. The records of the J.F. Bell Funeral Home in Charlottesville, Virginia, prior to 1970, have been placed online (*www.virginia.edu/woodson/projects/bell/intro.html*) in collaboration between the funeral home and the African American Genealogy Group of Charlottesville. To find funeral home records in your area of interest, do a search for *funeral records* and the location you are searching—for example, *funeral records missouri*. You can also use the Internet to locate funeral homes in the area in which you're researching, using an online funeral home directory such as FuneralNet (*www.funeralnet .com/funeral-home-search.html*). Death certificates, depending on the location and time frame, may include the name of the funeral home.

ALERT

Don't believe everything you see on a cemetery tombstone—even if it is carved in stone! This applies to funeral home records, death certificates, and other death records as well. The information is only as reliable as the memory or knowledge of the person who provided it.

If you're unable to find any funeral home records online, you may wish to contact the funeral home directly. For best results, address a written request to the manager of the funeral home. This gives them the opportunity to respond at their convenience. Be specific about what you're looking for, enclose a self-addressed stamped envelope, and offer to pay for any copying expenses.

Put It Into Practice

As previously discussed, most Internet searches for family information should generally begin with death records. If you know the date of death, look first for an obituary. If you're not sure of at least the year of death, and your subject died after 1962, begin with the Social Security Death Index. The order doesn't really matter too much, as you should eventually end up scouring all relevant sources of death information, just to make sure you don't overlook anything important.

For example, you have probably heard of Laura Ingalls Wilder, author of the famous Little House on the Prairie series. Since she's famous, you can find much more information about her online than you would for most people. Just ignore those biographies and other data for now, however, and search for her obituary using her name and year of death. Because it's free and indexes multiple newspaper databases, the archived newspaper collection in Google News is a good place to begin. A search for *laura ingalls wilder 1957* in subscription newspaper databases, such as Newspaper Archive (*http://newspaperarchive.com*) and GenealogyBank, turns up multiple articles on Mrs. Wilder; filtering by the year 1957 helps to narrow the results. This turns up about a dozen different obituary notices published in newspapers across the country.

If you subscribe to either news service, or have access through your local library, you'll be able to read the full obituary that includes a photograph and information on her life, including her work as a writer and editor. It also includes some family details, such as the full married name of her daughter, along with the name of her husband (Almanzo J. Wilder) and the year of their marriage and his death. There are also a few brief mentions of places that she lived—she was born in Wisconsin; she and her husband lived in De Smet, South Dakota when their daughter was born; they then moved to Florida and later to the Ozarks. Assuming that you knew little about Mrs. Wilder, this gives you approximate time frames, locations, and names of other family members, which will allow you to search for her in the census and other records.

The obituary also mentioned that Laura Ingalls Wilder died on her family farm, and a quick Internet search can tell you that this was Rocky Ridge Farm, in the Ozarks of Missouri. The next obvious step would be to use this information to locate a death certificate. The Missouri State Archives (*www.sos.mo.gov/archives*) has death records online, but if you weren't aware of this you would search for such a database using the search techniques and resources discussed in this chapter. The death certificate for Laura Ingalls Wilder is included in this free online database, which presently covers the years 1910 to 1962. A digital image of the certificate is linked, which tells us that she died on 10 February 1957 of "cerebral hemorrhage" and was buried in Mansfield Cemetery in Mansfield, Missouri. She is listed as an "author" and "widow," the daughter of Charles Ingalls and Carolyn Quiner. The informant who provided this information was her daughter, Rose Lane from Danbury, Connecticut.

A search of the database also turns up the death certificate for her husband, listed as Almanso [sic] James Wilder. His certificate tells us that Almanzo was born 13 February 1857 in Malone, New York, to James Wilder and Angeline Day; was a retired farmer; and lived about a mile east of the town of Mansfield in Wright County, Missouri. He is also listed as having being buried in the Mansfield Cemetery in Mansfield on 28 October 1949.

RECEIVED NOV 21 1949
District Health Office No. 6,
District File Number 1149-1260
Date Filed 11-28-49.

MAR 4 1951

STATEMENT BY LICENSED EMBALMER

I hereby certify that the body whose name is recorded on the reverse side of this certificate was embalmed by me, or by me

Student Embalmer No.

working under my personal supervision.

Student ....   Signed F.Q. Stiffe
        Student Embalmer   Licensed Embalmer No. 3221
                                               P. O. Address Mansfield

Note: The above MUST BE SIGNED BY THE LICENSED EMBALMER in his OWN HANDWRITING. (Failure to comply the above constitutes grounds for revocation of license.)

If this body is not embalmed, fact should be so stated above.

There is a lot of vital information on each of these death certificates that can lead you to additional records and the next generation of both family trees. Because the death certificates list Mansfield Cemetery as the burial location for both Laura and Almanzo, the next step is to search online for information on Mansfield Cemetery. A Google search for *"mansfield cemetery" missouri* turns up a result from Find A Grave. Clicking on this link leads to photos of the cemetery and the Wilder grave.

Granted, Laura and Almanzo are well-known, and there is more information available online for them than for most people because the family tree has already been well-researched. Obituaries can be found online for millions of everyday people, however. The Missouri death certificate database where you found Almanzo's death certificate includes everyone who died in Missouri during those years, not just the famous folk. And cemetery transcriptions and other death records are also fairly easy to find online. Just follow these same basic steps with your own ancestors, and you may be surprised at just how much you can find!

CHAPTER 6

Check the Census

Most people are familiar with the U.S. census, but did you know that federal census takers have been going door-to-door asking questions of American families since 1790? Though instituted and maintained primarily to track the population for government planning, a census is among the records genealogists refer to most frequently because it captures detailed information on an individual or family at a particular point in history—a once-per-decade snapshot. Begin with grandpa or great-grandma in the 1940 census, and you may be able to use the clues you find to track your family back through census records to 1850 or beyond!

The U.S. Federal Census

Census records are important tools for family history research. Using census records, you can learn who was living in a household at a given point in time, including spouses, siblings, and possibly even a mother-in-law. They can also tell you the approximate age of the individuals, where they were born, and what they did for a living. Some census records also provide details on an individual's immigrant status, including the year of immigration and whether the immigrant applied for U.S. citizenship. Best of all, every available U.S. federal census from 1790 to 1940 can be accessed online.

Exploring the U.S. Federal Census

The United States began to count its citizens in 1790, not long after its birth as a country. This first federal census, instituted by President George Washington, was intended to provide information on residents for the purpose of apportioning members of the House of Representatives and assessing federal tax. Since that first census, the U.S. government has conducted a federal census once every ten years, often referred to as a decennial census. However, data from more recent censuses are not available for public inspection because of a seventy-two-year restriction imposed by law to protect the privacy of living individuals. This means the most recent census currently open for public access is 1940 (released to great fanfare on April 1, 2012).

LINK

Census extraction forms offer a convenient method for extracting and recording the information that you find as you explore online census records, making it easy to see at a glance what information was collected for a specific census year. Download them for free online from sites such as Ancestry.com (*www.ancestry.com/download/forms#uscensus*), About .com Genealogy (*http://genealogy.about.com/od/free_charts/a/us_census.htm*), and CensusTools (*www.censustools.com*).

Before 1850, census schedules recorded only the name of the head of household and numbers and approximate ages of any other people living in the home. As the country's population grew, the government's need for additional information also grew and new questions were added to the census. The 1850 census is an important census document for researchers, as it was the first census to list names and ages for all individuals in a household, as well as include the place of birth. Another key year is 1880, as it marked the first federal census to document the relationship of household members to the head of household.

In 1900, the census asked for the month as well as year of birth, providing more detailed information on ages than any census before or since. It is also the first available census record to document immigration and citizenship data, asking whether an individual was foreign born, the year of immigration, the number of years in the United States, and the citizenship status of foreign-born individuals over the age of twenty-one. As the twentieth century progressed, additional questions were added to each census, while others were dropped. Most notable: the 1910 census recorded survivors of the Union or Confederate Army or Navy, the 1920 census asked for the year of naturalization for naturalized citizens, the 1930 census recorded whether the family owned a radio set, and the 1940 census included a question about the family's residence in 1935—essentially a mid-decade census!

What the Census Can Tell You about Your Ancestors

While the early censuses were little more than a head count of the population, more modern census records are filled with a wealth of valuable data. Most significantly, the 1850 to 1930 censuses can provide such details as:

- Names of family members
- Ages for each individual
- State or country of birth
- Parents' birthplaces
- Street address
- Estimated value of their home and personal belongings
- Marriage status and years of marriage
- Occupation
- When they came to the United States and from which country (if applicable)

What you can gain from census records is a wonderful snapshot in time for a particular family or place. You can learn whether your ancestors were literate or spoke English, where they and their parents came from, and even discover neighbors and nearby relatives. By locating your ancestors in multiple census years, you can watch the family grow, and the children move out and start families of their own. You can even use census records to discover whether your ancestors moved, changed jobs, or lost a child.

Access Census Images and Indexes Online

Traditionally, using census records to research your family tree involved wading through microfilm copies of the original handwritten pages produced by the U.S. government to preserve the records from decay. These microfilmed census records are generally available for viewing at Family History Centers, the National Archives, and libraries with large genealogy or local history sections.

ESSENTIAL

The better you understand the census recording process, the more information you can dig up from census records. The U.S. Census Bureau publication, "Measuring America: The Decennial Censuses from 1790 to 2000" (*www.census.gov/prod/2002pubs/pol02-ma.pdf*), contains instructions given to census takers on how to fill out the forms each year. Historical researcher Elizabeth Shown Mills, CG, offers examples of the importance of understanding these instructions in a series of articles including "Interpreting the Tick Marks on Federal Censuses" (*http://historicpathways.com/download/centickinterpret .pdf*) and "Census Tick Marks and Codes—Revisited Yet Again!" (*http://historicpathways.com/download/centickrevisitagain.pdf*).

Because census lists were typically recorded in order of visitation, searching for a particular family on a microfilmed record can be cumbersome and time-consuming. The U.S. government did create indexes for many census years to assist researchers in locating specific individuals or families in the microfilmed census records; however, not all census records were indexed and most were indexed only by the *head of household*—the individual identified to the census taker as the person responsible for the care of the home and/or family. With the recent advent of *every-name* computerized indexes, however, knowing the name of your ancestor or relative, and the state he or she resided in, is often enough to take you directly to the exact page and line where your ancestor is recorded.

Digitized images of original census pages are now readily available online, and every-name indexes allow you to click directly from your search results to a digital copy of the original census page where your ancestors were recorded—in the enumerator's own handwriting. Digital images are the best census records available online because they allow you to look directly at the record as it was originally created, without having to worry whether a modern-day transcriber misread the handwriting or mistyped the data. Digital images also allow you to look at *all* of the information included on the original census, while transcriptions usually only include details that someone felt were the most important.

ALERT

Free trials, available from most subscription genealogy sites, offer a great way to "try before you buy." Such trial periods are generally short, so make the most of your time by creating a list of the people and records you want to search before you sign up. This will help you better evaluate whether to continue or cancel the subscription.

This is where Internet genealogy research really provides a boost over more traditional microfilm research. The entire U.S. census, including complete every-name indexes and digital images of the microfilmed pages, is available for searching and viewing on the Internet. The most comprehensive collection of U.S. census records is available through a subscription to either Ancestry.com or MyHeritage.com (*www.myheritage.com*), which both offer the *complete* set of digitized images for the entire available U.S. census (1850–1940), as well as every-name indexes for each year. FamilySearch also hosts a large collection of U.S. federal and state census records with free access, including every-name indexes for all census years (1790–1940) and digital images for some years (certain years have the free index results linked to images on partner sites, which require a fee to view).

For 100 percent free access to the U.S. census from 1790–1930, you can use the free census indexes at FamilySearch.org in combination with the free digitized census images (not indexed) at Internet Archive (*www.archive .org/details/us_census*). The 1940 census is a special case due to agreements made at the time of its release, and it is available for free access on a number of sites, including Archives.com, Ancestry.com, FamilySearch, FindMyPast .com (*www.findmypast.com*), and MyHeritage.

Census indexes and images are also available online for other countries, including Canada, England, Scotland, Wales, Ireland, Australia, and France. FamilySearch is a good first stop when looking for international census records, followed by sites such as Ancestry.com, MyHeritage, and FindMyPast.com.

Check Census Gateway Sites

Census indexes, transcriptions, and abstracts that have been placed online by volunteers and organizations can be most easily found by using a census directory site such as Census Online (*www.census-online.com*). This gateway site has organized links to thousands of free census records from the United States and Canada. Just click on your state of interest, and then choose a county to view a list of census records from that area that have been transcribed or digitized. Links to census records at fee-based sites such as Ancestry.com are also included, but are separated from the free links at the bottom of the page and are clearly marked. While census directories are less useful now that the U.S. federal schedules are so easily found online, they can be a great resource for locating lesser-known state, local, and special censuses.

Other good census directories for locating free online census records include:

- Census Finder (*www.censusfinder.com*)
- African American Census Schedules Online (*www.afrigeneas.com/ aacensus*)

Search or Browse the USGenWeb Census Project

Two large volunteer census efforts, both using the USGenWeb name, are outgrowths of the official USGenWeb Project. Neither is formally affiliated with the USGenWeb any longer, although they both still bear its name. Both census projects, however, still display the same volunteer spirit, offering free access to U.S. census data transcribed and put online by volunteers.

The first USGenWeb Census Project (*www.us-census.org*) is hosted online by USGenNet. The navigation is very straightforward, making it easy to see at a glance what census records are available. Select On-Line Census Inventory to view available census records organized by state, then county. Then use your browser's find feature to search the page for your names of interest. In some cases a link to a scanned census image is also available. Alternatively, you can use the site's search engine to search across all census records.

QUESTION

Which census year should I search first?
It's generally a good idea to begin with the most current census year available and work backward. In most cases, this is the 1940 census. If your ancestor was deceased by 1940, begin your search with the most recent census taken while he was still living or the most recent census for which you know his location.

The second USGenWeb Census Project (*www.usgwcensus.org*) also offers straightforward navigation. Select a state from the right-hand column to view available census transcriptions. The data is displayed in a uniform text format, which can be easily searched by using your browser's find feature. This site does not link transcriptions to census images.

Access Census Records Online Through Your Local Library

Your library card could be your key to free census access. Hundreds of state, county, and local libraries offer free access to U.S. federal census indexes and images through subscriptions to Ancestry Library Edition or Heritage Quest Online. In the case of Heritage Quest Online, you can even save yourself a trip to the library and access the database remotely from home by logging in with your library card number (sometimes this requires signing up with your library first). Ask your local, state, or university library whether they subscribe to these databases, and if they offer remote access to library cardholders.

Census Research Tips and Caveats

Census enumerations are by no means the most reliable of records. At the time the census was recorded, the enumerator may have missed someone, written a name down wrong, or received inaccurate information. It's not uncommon to find someone who has aged less than five years in the decade between censuses, or whose birthplace changed with each successive decade. Throw in bad handwriting, changing county borders, and missing or illegible records, and there are plenty of opportunities for research frustration.

Because genealogists researching online typically use indexes to locate people in the census, there also exists the extra challenge of dealing with the misinterpretations, typographical errors, and other inaccuracies that often creep in during the census indexing process. This means that a name could actually have been butchered twice. Perhaps the census taker, tired at the end of a long, hot day, didn't take the time to ask Robert Stuart how his name was spelled, and recorded Stewart instead of Stuart. The individual later responsible for indexing the data was unable to accurately decipher the sloppy handwriting of that tired census taker and interpreted Stewart as Steward. Now, Robert Stuart is Robert Steward and much more difficult to find.

Don't let these caveats scare you away from census records. Census data provides a valuable look at your ancestors in a particular place and time. Census records are also easy to find and use and can yield a lot of information in a little time. Just keep in mind that census records and indexes are prone to inaccuracy, and the clues found within should always be corroborated with other records when possible.

Learn Creativity and Patience

When you're having trouble finding your ancestor in the census index, it's time to get creative. Her name may have been misspelled in the census enumeration or misread when it was indexed. Think about how the name *might* look instead of how it *should* look, and consider some of the following suggestions:

- Try alternate spellings for both the first name and last name.
- Search with just a first name and location.
- Don't count solely on Soundex; it doesn't pick up all spelling options for a surname.
- Try a nickname and/or middle name in the first name field.
- Substitute an initial for the first name.
- Be liberal with wildcards.
- Leave off the name entirely and use a variety of other descriptors (birth place, approximate age, etc.) to locate your ancestor.
- Search for other family members, or even neighbors, when you can't find your ancestor.

ALERT

Old handwriting is often a challenge to read, so it's no wonder census indexes are prone to inaccuracies. The surname CARTER, for example, might have been read as GARTER, or the name CRISP might be spelled as CHRISP or CRIPS. Create a list of alternative spellings for your ancestor's surnames and then try these name variations in every database you search.

Expect Little from the 1890 Federal Census

More than 99 percent of the 1890 census population schedules were damaged in a fire, and their remains were later destroyed by government order. The few fragments that survive include only about 6,000 names out of an original count of more than 62 million. Although most census sites allow you to search the 1890 census, and some have beefed up those names with alternative records from the time period, your chances of finding the person you're looking for are slim.

Explore the Community

A census enumeration is much more than a record of an individual family. It also tells the story of an entire community. After you get over the excitement of discovering your ancestor, take time to acquaint yourself with the people living nearby. Neighbors could turn out to be related, even if they don't share the same name. It's not uncommon to find a wife's parents living nearby, or an uncle or married sister. This is especially true in more rural communities. Becoming familiar with the neighbors also allows you to use their names as a search tool to help locate your ancestor in other census records. For best results, look at several households, if not several pages, on either side of your ancestor and add their names to your research notes.

Pay Attention to Penmanship

While you're exploring the community, it is also useful to spend time familiarizing yourself with the enumerator's handwriting. Each census taker will have a particular way of styling certain letters, such as a, f, h, j, p, and s. Scan the pages on either side of your ancestor for easily recognizable names, places, or occupations to learn how the enumerator wrote certain letters and letter combinations. This will help you to better judge the spelling of your own ancestor's name, as well as those of his family members.

Go to the Original Record When Possible

Census indexes and transcriptions can provide the information many genealogists want most to find—names, dates, and locations. The original census record, however, will almost always include more. By checking the original census image, you will often discover information that may have been misread or was left out of the transcription. And yes, digitized census images are generally considered an acceptable alternative to the original record.

Follow Census Clues to New Records

Census enumerations are packed with details, both large and small. Once you get past the names, ages, and relationships of the listed individuals, there are still many other clues to be found hidden among the census columns. Everything from the street address to the age of a mother at the time of her first marriage may hold a clue that leads to new records. Generally, you should look at every single piece of information contained in a census record (or any record for that matter) and ask yourself what it tells you about your ancestor. Does it fit what you know about him or her? If there is an anomaly, follow it up. It may be an error introduced during the census enumeration process, or it may just be the key to learning something new.

Many, many clues can be gleaned from a census record if you take enough time to fully explore the data recorded in each column, and compare the answers from one census to the next. To get you started, here are a few of the more obvious items to investigate in U.S. federal census records.

Number of Children

Column 11 of the 1900 census and Column 11 of the 1910 census asked for "mother of how many children." When combined with the "number of children living" indicated in the next column, much can be learned. First, compare the number of living children with the number of children listed in the household. Do they match up? If not, this may indicate children who were old enough to move out on their own (married or not) or were living elsewhere, such as in an institution, as an apprentice to another family, or with relatives. If there are more children listed in the household than born to the mother, this could possibly indicate a prior marriage of the father. Go back to previous census years to see if you can identify these children and then search for them again in 1900 or 1910 to learn where they are living.

A discrepancy between the number of children born and the number still living obviously indicates that one or more children have probably died. Again, go back to prior census years to identify as many children as possible and, hopefully, determine which ones are deceased prior to 1900 or 1910. Follow up with a search for death certificates, obituaries, and so on.

Marriage Age and Year

The 1900 and 1910 U.S. federal census both contain a column for "number of years in present marriage." Some simple subtraction gives you an approximate date of marriage—something easy to follow up in marriage records.

LINK

U.S. federal census records from 1790 through 1840 include only the name of each head of household, with statistical columns to group other household members by gender and age. This may seem like useless information, but by following patterns of age and gender in each household through successive census years, you can often glean more information than you might think. You can learn more in the article, "Digging Details from Pre-1850 U.S. Census Records" (*http://genealogy.about.com/od/census/a/pre_1850_us.htm*).

For ancestors who lived in 1930, pay special attention to Column 15, which asks for "age at first marriage." For married couples, compare that age with their "age at last birthday" from Column 13 to determine the approximate year that each was married. In many cases it will be the same, give or take a year or two, as you might expect for a married couple. But if this subtraction indicates that the husband was first married eighteen years ago and the wife only eight years ago, there is likely at least one other marriage in the picture. On the other hand, it could just be a recording error on the part of the census enumerator.

Year of Immigration and Naturalization

The 1900, 1910, 1920, and 1930 censuses each include a column that asked for the individual's year of immigration, which can obviously help narrow the time frame for passenger arrival manifests. It's not uncommon to find a wife immigrating a few years after her husband, as he came ahead to pave the way for his family. In the case of married couples, compare the year of immigration for both spouses with the date of marriage (actual or approximate) to learn if the couple was likely married before or after their arrival in the United States, which in turn narrows the search grid for the wife's parents.

Military Service

The 1910 census includes a column (30) to record whether the person was a "survivor of the Union or Confederate Army or Navy," indicated by "UA" for Union Army, "UN" for Union Navy, "CA" for Confederate Army, and "CN" for Confederate Navy. The 1930 census (Column 31) also asks about military service. A "CW" in this column indicates a Civil War veteran, "Sp" for Spanish-American War, "Phil" for Philippine Insurrection, "Box" for Boxer Rebellion, "Mex" for Mexican Expedition, and "WW" for World War I. Follow up these individuals in military service and pension records.

Street Address

Running vertically down the left-hand side of the 1880 and 1900 through 1930 censuses, you may find a street name indicated. This will vary depending on whether your ancestor lived in a city/town or a more rural area. Sometimes streets were just not recorded. If they were, however, the first column to the right of the street name includes the house number. With this information you can locate your ancestor in city directories or place their house on a historical or present-day map. The map can be used to place their neighbors as well, including those who lived behind them or across the street, as well as next-door.

Special and State Censuses

Special non-population schedules, including agricultural, manufacturing, and mortality schedules, can be an untapped gold mine for genealogists, providing information on recently deceased individuals, and little details of an ancestor's occupation. Other special censuses enumerated slaves, military veterans and their widows, Native Americans, and even deaf couples. A number of states and localities conducted censuses as well, often during the intervening years between federal census schedules. These are all records you may wish to explore once you've been through the federal census records.

ESSENTIAL

The states of Colorado, Florida, Nebraska, and the territories of Dakota and New Mexico conducted a special interim census, partially funded by the federal government, in 1885. These special state and territorial censuses are available online for subscribers of Ancestry. com. The 1885 Colorado and Florida censuses are also available online for free at FamilySearch.org.

Slave Schedules (1850–1860)

Slaves were enumerated separately during the 1850 and 1860 censuses. These slave schedules generally don't list slaves by name, however, instead distinguishing them only by age, sex, color, and the name of the slave owner. A free index and images to the 1850 U.S. census slave schedules is available online at FamilySearch.org. Ancestry.com includes images and indexes for the 1850 and 1860 slave schedules.

Mortality Schedules (1850–1885)

Mortality schedules were prepared in conjunction with the regular population census to record information about deaths that had occurred in the year prior to the census, including name, age, sex, color, marital status, birthplace, occupation, month of death, and cause of death. These mortality schedules survive for the years 1850 through 1880, as well as for the special federal census of 1885 for Colorado, Florida, Nebraska, New Mexico, and North and South Dakota. Mortality schedules are available by subscription on Ancestry.com. FamilySearch.org offers free access to the 1850 Mortality Schedule.

Agricultural Schedules (1850–1880)

Farmers that produced in excess of $100 worth of products (up to $500 worth on farms larger than 3 acres by 1870) were asked to provide information on their farm, crops, and livestock. If your ancestor was listed as a farmer on the 1850, 1860, 1870, or 1880 population census, you can find some of these schedules online at Ancestry.com (*http://search.ancestry .com/search/db.aspx?dbid=1276*). For the 1850–1880 agricultural schedules not online, check the online card catalog for state archives, libraries, and historical societies, as they are the most likely repositories of the original schedules. The National Archives also has many states, but not all, available for those years on microfilm.

ESSENTIAL

Many states conducted their own censuses, often during intervening years between the federal decennial census (generally, but not always, in years ending in "5"). Availability of state census records varies, depending on whether a particular state ever conducted a census, how often, and whether the records still exist. Genealogy blogger Joe Beine's list of links to online state census records (*www.researchguides .net/census/state.htm*) is a good place to start.

Agricultural schedules after 1880 were mostly destroyed, although the National Archives does hold copies for a select few states and territories for 1920 and 1930. In general, the only information readily available to researchers after 1880 are publications produced by the Bureau of the Census and the Department of Agriculture (USDA) with tabulated results and analysis by state and county, but no information on individual farms and farmers. These are available online on the USDA website under Historical Census Publications (*www.agcensus.usda.gov/Publications/Historical_ Publications/index.php*).

Manufacturing and Industry Schedules (1820, 1850–1880)

Manufacturing, mining, fishing, commercial, and trading businesses that produced more than $500 worth of goods or services were asked to report on the type and operation of their business, with questions covering everything from the kinds and quantities of raw materials used to the number of women and men employed in their operation. Many of these schedules are available online at Ancestry.com with the agricultural and other non-population schedules. You should especially follow up on these if your ancestor was listed in the population schedule with a manufacturing type of occupation such as flour miller or candle maker, but it is not uncommon to find farmers and others you might not expect operating a side business.

Veterans Schedules (1840 and 1890)

Living Revolutionary War pensioners were recorded on the back of the regular 1840 U.S. population schedules. In 1890, a special census was conducted for veterans of the Union Army and their widows. As with the rest of the 1890 census, only a portion of these special Civil War veterans schedules has survived. The 1840 Census of Pensioners (*www.us-roots.org/colonialamerica/census/1840/index.html*) is available online as part of a Colonial America site built and maintained by Kathy Leigh. The surviving 1890 veterans schedules are available online at Ancestry.com.

Defective, Dependent, and Delinquent (DDD) Schedules

The 1880 federal census included seven supplemental schedules that collected additional information on household members identified as belonging to one of the following (politically incorrect) classes: insane, idiots, deaf mutes, blind, paupers and indigent persons, homeless children, and prisoners. Ancestry.com has these 1880 DDD schedules online (*http://search.ancestry.com/search/db.aspx?dbid=1634*) for several, but not all, states. You can also access a Special Census on Deaf Family Marriages and Hearing Relatives 1888–1895 at Ancestry.com (*http://search.ancestry.com/search/db.aspx?dbid=1582*), which includes information drawn from questionnaires distributed to deaf couples, as well as their hearing relatives, as part of a research study conducted on the marriages of the deaf in America by the Volta Bureau in Washington, D.C.

Utilize Census Alternatives

City and county directories, as well as tax rolls, serve as an excellent resource in conjunction with, or as an alternative to, census records. Since they document at least some of the inhabitants of an area at a given point in time, both can be useful in cases where census records no longer exist or when you've "misplaced" an ancestor between the decennial censuses.

Tax Lists

Early tax lists generally include all white males over the age of twenty-one and indicate whether they owned land, slaves, or other taxable property. They usually do not include any other personal information. A Google search for *tax lists genealogy* brings up a wide variety of tax lists online, including 1790/1800 Virginia Tax List Censuses (*www.binnsgenealogy.com/VirginiaTaxListCensuses*), Eighteenth Century Tax Lists of Perquimans County,

North Carolina (*http://perqtax.homestead.com*), and Allegheny County, Pennsylvania Tax Records (*www.usgwarchives.net/pa/allegheny/taxlist.htm*)

City Directories

City directories are much like phone directories, a listing of an area's residents. They differ, however, in that they predate the invention of the telephone and often provide additional information about the listed individuals, such as the street address, place of employment, occupation, or name of spouse. Some also offer a separate street directory, sometimes referred to as a crisscross or reverse directory. This makes it easier to find neighbors, as well as nearby churches, cemeteries, and schools. City directories are compiled through door-to-door surveys and published at irregular intervals. Because they are published based on sales value, they are generally available only for larger cities and communities.

ESSENTIAL

Public libraries often retain copies of city directories published for their area. Check the website for libraries in your area to see if they have any city directories available for online browsing. Most won't, but you may be able to e-mail the library to request a lookup.

City or county directories are especially useful for tracking families between census years, for locating an individual's place of business, and for learning the layout of the area in which your ancestors lived. Some even include lists of residents who "removed" from the area within the past year and where they went. You can often find individuals listed by the year that they died with a date of death next to their name or a female listed by name and as "widow of John."

Despite their value to genealogists, city directories aren't always easy to find. The Library of Congress (*www.loc.gov/rr/microform/uscity*) has an extensive collection of U.S. city directories available on microfilm. While they are not available for online perusal or through interlibrary loan, the list of available directories is informative. FamilySearch also includes many city directories in its microfilm collection. City Directories of the United States of America (*www.uscitydirectories.com*) presents an organized directory of links to city directories that have been microfilmed along with the repositories where the microfilm copies can be accessed. It also includes links to city directory transcriptions that have been made available online. Ancestry.com offers indexes and browsable images of more than 10,000 city directories from cities and states across the United States in its U.S. City Directories collection (*http://search.ancestry.com/search/ db.aspx?dbid=2469*), covering the years 1821 through 1989. Fold3.com also has early twentieth- and late nineteenth-century city directories for more than thirty large population centers in twenty states in its online collection (*www.fold3.com/s.php#query=City+Directories*). Online genealogy teacher, Miriam J. Robbins, maintains the Online Historical Directories Website (*http://sites.google.com/site/onlinedirectorysite*) with links to city directories across the web. Or try a search for your locality and *city directory* in your favorite search engine.

Put It Into Practice

William Rowling, great-great-grandfather of Harry Potter author J.K. Rowling, married in England in 1872 at the age of nineteen. His marriage certificate names his father as Edward Rowling. Because the marriage occurred just one year after the 1871 UK census, it makes sense to turn directly to census records in order to learn more about William's family. An exact name search for *edward rowling* in the 1871 UK census at Ancestry.com brings up William's father as the first result—Edward Rowling, born about 1830 in Bassingbourn, Cambridgeshire, England, living with sons William, Henry, and Stephen. Edward is listed as married, but the wife isn't enumerated with them. (More on that in a minute.)

Next, head back one decade to the 1861 UK census. Again, the family isn't too difficult to find—but it will take a little more than an exact name search this time. Here the family is enumerated as Rowland, a name they did use for a time. It's close to Rowling, but not similar enough to come up in a Soundex search. A wildcard search for *row** in the last name field does the trick, however, when combined with a few other fields to help narrow down the results (*edward row** born *1830 +/– 2* years in *cambridge**). [Note: If you don't see the boxes for entering the birth location and date, then select "Show Advanced Search Options."] This wildcard trick for first and last names is something to try any time that exact search and Soundex search fail to turn up the expected results—select the box for "exact matches only" for the best results when using wildcards. Use of the wildcard for the birth location is also helpful here, covering both Cambridge and Cambridgeshire in one search as you don't know how it was entered in the database.

From the 1861 census, you learn that the mother's name is Sarah, born about 1831 in Southampton, Hampshire, England. Since the oldest child, daughter Harriet, is listed in this census as age ten, try going back one more decade to the 1851 census—the year Harriet was supposedly born. Here the standard searches come up empty, or at least they did, until several helpful researchers submitted a correction to the name and birthplace—click on the pencil icon to see the corrections. If this weren't the case, the next step would be to eliminate the last name entirely, and search for *edward* born *1830 +/– 2* years in *cambridge*. When this turns up nothing, try eliminating the birth county as well. A search for first name *edward*, born *1830 +/–1* year and spouse name *sarah* eventually brings you to the family.

It's no wonder they couldn't be found through traditional search methods! Edward Rowling, born about 1830 in Bassingbourn, Cambridgeshire, was actually indexed in the 1851 UK census at Ancestry.com as Edward Bowlings, born in Roystone, Cambodia. Royston is actually a township located within the parish of Bassingbourn, so the indexer wasn't as far off as he appears, but he or she should have been able to recognize Cambr as an abbreviation for Cambridge, not Cambodia, when viewing the England census. The handwritten last name on the census page does, however, appear more like Bowling than Rowling, with the final "s" added by the indexer actually a checkmark that follows each name on the page.

The point here is that names are easily and often mis-indexed, so creative searching should be something you are always prepared to do when looking through an online index. If you can't find someone by name, try other combinations of known information items. Be persistent! You can also try searching for another family member when the one you're looking for doesn't turn up. A search for first name *sarah* (no last name) born *1831+/–1* year in *southampton* would have also turned up the family.

Now that you've traced William's parents back to their first census as a family, return to the 1871 census. Remember Edward listed as married, but with no wife Sarah? Was it a mistake that he wasn't listed as a widower? Or is Sarah enumerated somewhere else? Now that you have her name, a search for *sarah rowling* born in *southampton* turns up Sarah Marie Rowling as a patient in St. Bartholomew's Hospital, London. Something else to investigate for the family tree!

Now that you know Sarah is still living in 1871, do you think she and Edward could still be living by the time of the 1881 census? Edward is the one who did a disappearing act in 1881, but Sarah Rowling, age fifty, born Southampton, is listed as a mother-in-law in the household of Frank Bennett in Medlock, Lancashire, England. Again a user-submitted correction makes her a bit easier to find—she was originally indexed as Sarah Rowley, but a simple wildcard search for last name *Row** would have overcome that. You know this is likely the correct Sarah Rowling because Henry Rowling, listed as a brother-in-law, is the right age and was born in the right place to be the son Henry Rowling you found living with Edward Rowling in 1871 (also further confirmed when Edward Rowling is found living with the Bennetts in 1901—see the next paragraph). Since they are listed as in-laws, however, Frank's wife, Sarah, is probably a Rowling child as well. If so, where was she in the 1871 census? That is something else to follow up on in additional records.

Further searches find Edward and Sarah appearing together again in the 1891 UK census, living in Hulme, Lancashire, England. The 1901 UK census finds Edward back with the Bennett family, unfortunately listed as a widower. You've now managed to locate the family (at least most of the members) in every UK census from 1851 to 1901—something to be proud of. The family wasn't overly difficult to trace, but it does exemplify many of the stumbling blocks you're likely to encounter during your own research—families that move around, families that aren't always enumerated together, names and locations that are mis-indexed, and so on.

CHAPTER 7

Hunt Down Family Connections

Marriage records are something a genealogist always hopes to find because they help to "tie the knot" between two branches of the family tree. They can offer evidence that a couple was legally married and may also indicate the bride's maiden name. Sometimes you'll even learn the bride and groom's date of birth or the names of the parents or other family members. Marriages also tend to generate a variety of documents, which increases your chances of finding a record that has survived through the years.

Marriage and Divorce Records

The most common civil record of marriage is the marriage license, issued to the bride and groom by the appropriate civil authority upon application for their marriage. Following the wedding ceremony, the license was returned by the minister or officiant to the county courthouse or town hall to be recorded in the register, with the date and location of marriage. An official certificate of marriage may have been issued to the couple; this certificate may be found among your family's papers.

In some states, particularly the southern states, you may also encounter a precursor to the marriage license known as a marriage bond. This financial guarantee was made prior to the marriage by the prospective bridegroom (or a relative or friend of the groom or bride) to affirm that there was no moral or legal reason that the couple could not be married. In cases where the bride or groom was under the minimum legal age for marriage, you'll sometimes find a record known as the *consent affidavit*, a letter or form completed and signed by the parent or guardian giving permission for the underage individual to be married.

ESSENTIAL

"Where to Write for Vital Records" (*www.cdc.gov/nchs/w2w.htm*) from the National Center for Health Statistics is a good starting place to learn about the availability of marriage and divorce records (as well as birth and death records) for the state you're researching. Vitalrec.com (*www.vitalrec.com*) also includes contact information and information on record availability for U.S. counties and parishes.

Civil marriage records in the United States are primarily found in the office of the county or town clerk. In some cases, however, older marriage records may have been transferred to the state archive, historical society, or library, while recent marriage records may only be available from the state vital records office. Individual state laws determine which agency is responsible. To further complicate matters, the date from which each state began to keep marriage records varies. Many states and territories were documenting marriages by 1880, but some did not officially record marriages statewide until well after 1900. In most cases, marriages were recorded at the town or county level prior to state registration, so you'll want to check county records as well. There is no nationwide index to marriage or other vital records in the United States.

Online, marriage records are becoming easier to find. The best place to start is FamilySearch.org, which offers free access to indexes and/or images of marriage records from many states and counties across the United States, as well as from elsewhere around the world. Fee-based site Ancestry.com also offers many marriage indexes and image collections. Alternatively, check the site for your state and county of interest at USGenWeb.org for links to marriage records, or do a search online for *marriage index* in your state and county or state and town (as applicable) of interest.

In the absence of a marriage license or certificate, evidence of a marriage may be found in other documents. If your ancestor was married in a church or other house of worship, the marriage was likely recorded in the parish register or church book, along with preliminaries such as the posting of marriage bans. Newspapers can also be a good source for marriage information, including engagements, announcements, photos, and even descriptions of the ceremony and reception. Look for a special section of the newspaper dedicated to wedding announcements, or in the local news or society pages. A marriage date may also have been recorded in the family Bible, on the back of a wedding photo, on a printed wedding or anniversary announcement, or in a letter, journal, or diary.

As with marriage records, divorce decrees relate to the family as a unit, and can often provide several details of genealogical value. These might include the wife's maiden name, the date and place of marriage, the dates of birth (or ages) of both parties to the divorce, the names and ages of any children, and the grounds for divorce. Divorce records are far less numerous than marriage records, however, and the manner in which divorces have been granted throughout history makes the records more difficult to locate as well.

Until the middle of the nineteenth century, the civil court rarely granted divorce. Instead, an act of the state legislature was necessary in most states. You'll find many early divorce proceedings among the records of these legislative acts. By the mid-1800s, almost every state had enacted some type of divorce law, allowing for the "judicial" granting of a divorce. Most of these divorce decrees were issued in a court at the county level. The particular court varies by location and time period, so divorce decrees may be found among the records of the Superior Court, Circuit Court, Family Court, Chancery Court, District Court, or even the Office of the Prothonotary. Do a search online for *divorce records* in your state and county of interest to learn which court would have handled the process for the time period in which the divorce likely occurred. Most states also now require that a copy of the divorce certificate be filed with the state department that oversees vital records—a good alternative for divorces that have occurred since about the mid-twentieth century. References to a divorce may also be found in newspaper notices or among family papers.

LINK

Several websites make it their mission to link to as many online marriage indexes and databases as possible. GenWed (*www.genwed.com*) links to numerous free marriage records and indexes at both the state and county level. Online Birth and Marriage Records Indexes for the USA (*www.germanroots.com/vitalrecords.html*) and Cyndi's List—Marriages & Divorces (*www.cyndislist.com/marriages*) also link to larger online marriage record collections, organized by state.

Many marriage and divorce records online are available only in the form of indexes or abstracts, although increasingly websites are starting to add digital images as well. These indexes typically include the name of the bride, the name of the groom, and the date of the marriage or divorce. Unless the site also offers digital images of the actual marriage record, you should follow up by ordering or accessing the original record, as it will usually include additional details as well as offer additional verification of what you found online.

Birth and Baptismal Records

Because of privacy laws, birth records are generally the most difficult vital records to obtain and often cannot be found online for individuals born during or after the twentieth century. In fact, as with death records, official birth records were not even kept in many states until that time. For these more recent birth records it is usually best to start with your living family members. Because a birth certificate is often required as proof of identity, many people have a copy of their birth certificate among their papers.

Just because fewer birth records are available online than other vital records doesn't mean that you should give up finding them. FamilySearch.org has one of the largest collections of vital records online, including birth and baptismal records for dozens of U.S. states, as well as many other countries around the world. Some of these free collections at FamilySearch are indexes only, while others also include digital images. Select "Search" from the home page of FamilySearch.org and then scroll down to "Browse All Published Collections" or "Browse by Location" to bring up a full list of available historical records.

QUESTION

Can I record the date of baptism in lieu of a birth date?
A baptism may have taken place days or years after the actual birth. For this reason it is important to record the date as a baptismal date, not a birth date. Most genealogy software programs include a special field for entering baptism or christening dates. In the birth field, just record the birth date as occurring before the date of baptism since that is all you truly know for sure, as in "bef. 13 April 1769."

Many state governments offer birth indexes and even certificate images online as well. Missouri, for example, offers a database of pre-1910 births (*www.sos.mo.gov/archives/resources/birthdeath*). Arizona offers not only an index but also images of the actual birth certificates (*http://genealogy.az.gov*) for births that occurred at least seventy-five years ago (so are no longer subject to privacy restrictions). West Virginia (*www.wvculture.org/vrr*) also has online images of birth records for selected counties and years. Ancestry.com offers a variety of online birth indexes among its subscription databases, including the North Carolina Birth Index (1800–2000), Kentucky Birth Collection (1852–1999), Minnesota Birth Index (1935–2002), and others. Check the website for the state archives, library, and/or historical society in your state of interest to see if they have put any birth records online. USGenWeb state and county sites will often include links to online birth indexes as well. Or, try a search such as *birth records arizona* to see what else might be available in your areas of interest.

Older baptism and christening records are becoming increasingly easy to find online in countries such as England, Scotland, and France. In the United States, however, church records are much more scattered and few baptisms and christenings have been transcribed and placed online.

Unearth Wills and Estate Records

After you've learned the details of your ancestor's birth, marriage, and death, you'll want to check to see if he left behind any estate records when he died. While "estate" seems to imply a large amount of property, estates are actually the sum total of an individual's possessions, including both property and debts, left behind at the time of death. The amount of real, or personal, property required to necessitate a court proceeding is determined by state or local laws in effect at the time of death. Not everyone will have owned enough property to generate estate records, but your ancestor also didn't necessarily need to be well off to have had his estate processed through the court system. If he had outstanding debts, property that needed to be divided, or anything else that needed to be settled after his death, it's likely that some record of that still exists.

Estate records document the processing and disbursement of an estate, whether the individual died *testate* (with a will) or *intestate* (without a will). If your ancestor left a will, an heir would normally present it to the court, creditor, or other interested party after his death. The court would hold proceedings and hear testimony to verify the validity of the will in a process known as probate. The court also officially appointed an executor—generally an individual or individuals named in the will by the testator—to handle the affairs of the estate. Often, executors were relatives or friends, but the executor or executrix could be anyone the testator considered trustworthy enough to handle his estate. Once the court approved the probate, the will was then generally recorded (transcribed) into a will book by the court clerk. In most cases, the original will (or a copy of it) also remained with the court, along with any other papers generated during the process of settling the estate, in a file often referred to as a probate packet.

When an individual dies without a will (which happens more frequently than you might think), the court generally appoints an administrator to handle the estate, and the distribution of property is made according to local law. These intestate proceedings, often called administrations, generate similar paperwork to the probate packets discussed previously, although they are sometimes referred to as administration packets.

LINK

For hands-on experience with estate records, the "Analyze an 1804 Inventory" case study at History Matters (*http://historymatters.gmu .edu/mse/sia/inventory.htm*) presents a typical estate with discussion of how a simple list of an individual's possessions can reveal routines, social status, and values. Michael John Neill's excellent case study, "Fishing for Clues in John Lake's Estate" (*www.rootdig.com/adn/john_ lake.html*), explains—with accompanying document images—how estate records can provide numerous insights into a family's life.

What exactly can estate records tell you beyond the fact that your ancestor died? The documents found in an estate, administration, or probate packet might include a complete inventory of the property of the deceased, a list of debts and creditors, appraisals, receipts, newspaper notices calling for legal heirs to come forward, witness testimony, letters from attorneys representing heirs, a copy of the will (if one exists), and other miscellaneous papers related to the settlement of the estate. Each of these pieces of paper represents the potential for learning more about your ancestor—especially the names of relatives (including the married names of daughters) and where they were each living. The list of personal property can be especially interesting, filled with items such as crockery, feather beds, pigs, brooms, and the like, which provides insight into the life your ancestor lived.

Estate records can usually be found with the court records of the county where the deceased was last living, or in other areas where he owned property, especially when they were in another state. Early records may have been moved to other repositories, such as the state archives. Check with the county clerk or the local genealogical or historical society to learn where the estate records are maintained. Some wills, especially those prior to about

1850 or so, have been published online, either in image or transcription form. Try a search such as *massachusetts wills online* and you'll turn up sites such as Wills of Our Essex County Ancestors (*www.essexcountyma.net/Wills*). Other examples of online wills and estate records include Probates Records Database (*http://archives.delaware.gov/collections/probate.shtml*), an online searchable index to Delaware probate records from c. 1680 to c. 1925; the St. Louis Probate Court Digitization Project, 1802–1900 (*www.sos.mo.gov/archives/mojudicial/stl_history.asp*), a collaborative project of the Missouri State Archives and the St. Louis Probate Court; and the State Archives of North Carolina (*www.archives.ncdcr.gov*), which includes digital images of wills dated between 1663–1790 in its MARS database, as well as an index to estate records for some North Carolina counties.

ALERT

Laws in most Eastern and Midwestern states, derived from the common law of England, allowed the female widow a dower right, or share (usually one-third), of her husband's estate for her lifetime. When a mortgage or other debts existed, dower rights may have held up final settlement of the estate until after the widow's death. When no estate record is found, a search of land records may turn up the division of land necessary to give the widow her "dower third." Research dower rights in your state and time period of interest to learn more.

FamilySearch hosts the largest online collection of digitized historical probate and court records with over 105 U.S. collections in this category online. In most cases, these records are not indexed and only available as digitized copies. Look for digitized book indexes to each county's probate collection and make sure you become familiar with the indexing system that is being used.

Searchable databases on the no frills SAMPUBCO website (*www.sampubco.com*) include indexes to 300,000 plus wills and probate files from more than a dozen U.S. states. Index searches are free, and you can order a digital or paper copy of most wills for a reasonable fee. Other major genealogy sites, such as Ancestry.com, also include will and estate records for various locations. Also check the local USGenWeb website and spend some time thoroughly searching in your favorite search engine to learn what may be available online for your area of research.

Chase Down Court Records

Most of the records previously discussed in this chapter, as well as land records and naturalization records, can be found in the town hall or county courthouse where your ancestors lived. This is because the local courthouse is generally where official business was conducted—where your ancestor would have gone to apply for a marriage license, file settlement papers for an estate, record a land deed, pay his taxes, register to vote, or transact other business of day-to-day life.

Court records also document cases involving civil and criminal actions. Don't be afraid to search these records because of what you might find. It's not unusual to discover relatives sprinkled throughout court records for minor civil proceedings involving property line disputes, bastardy bonds, public swearing, and unpaid debts.

Your ancestor did not even have to be accused of anything to appear in court records. He may have served on a jury, provided witness testimony for a friend or neighbor, or posted bond money for a relative. Or he might be named in county businesses transactions—assigned as a local tax collector or to oversee repair of a county road. Most of you will find few surprises, but even one or two unexpected mentions of your ancestor may help you in your search. If nothing else, court records can sometimes offer amusing fodder for your family history.

In the United States, every state has a system of local courts that handles most of the local business and transactions likely to have involved your ancestors. Use the Internet (e.g., *edgecombe county nc courthouse* or *south dakota courts*) to search for information on the court system and courts in the town or county where your ancestor lived—many states and counties have published guides and finding aids to their court records. The USGenWeb website (*www.usgenweb.org*) is also a good starting point for learning about local courthouses and the location of their records. Consider also that your ancestor may have used the courthouse that was most convenient to him, not necessarily the one that served the area in which he lived. Some business, such as the recording of land deeds, has to take place in the county or town of residence, but other official business (e.g., obtaining a marriage license) can be handled at any county courthouse in some states. If you don't find court records in the most likely jurisdiction, expand your search to neighboring areas.

ALERT

Many widely used groups of courthouse records—such as wills, deeds, and marriages—typically come with indexes, although not necessarily alphabetical. To keep things interesting, states utilize a number of different indexing systems, with names like *Russell*, *Cott*, and *Campbell*. Check the inside cover of the record book for instructions, or ask the court clerk for assistance. The 58-page book *Courthouse Indexes Illustrated* by Christine Rose, CG, CGL, FASG, provides a detailed look at over thirty different index systems.

Genealogical treasures can be found among almost all proceedings of the court, including civil, criminal, and equity disputes:

- The **civil court**, sometimes called the Court of Common Pleas or Quarter Sessions, oversees civil cases where one or more private individuals bring suit against another. These might be suits brought for unpaid debts, divorce, or support for the maintenance of children born out of wedlock. Civil court records may also contain name changes, road orders, naturalizations, and even livestock brand registrations.
- **Criminal court** oversees cases in which a law is alleged to have been broken and the state or local government files charges against an individual. Criminal cases include felonies such as murder, rape, and burglary, and misdemeanors like public drunkenness, petty theft, and breaking the Sabbath. Coroner's reports are sometimes found among criminal court records.
- A **court of equity**, often referred to as a chancery court, handles principals of equity as opposed to law. This might include divorce proceedings, adoptions, estate divisions, and other cases involving property rights. Powers of attorney and guardianship cases may also be found among the records of the equity court. These cases are generally handled without a jury.

In addition to courts handling civil, criminal, and equity disputes, specialized courts also existed to oversee certain matters. A prime example of this is a **probate court**—also called a surrogate court, orphans court, or court of ordinary—which deals with the administration of estates and other matters of probate. In areas without a probate court, these cases were generally handled by the chancery court, or other court of equity.

The majority of court records will *not* be found online, but many court offices maintain some sort of virtual presence. The courthouse website may include information on the various offices within the courthouse and the records under their jurisdiction, the hours of operation, and, in some cases, details on how to request record lookups by mail or e-mail. Some courthouse offices, especially the Recorder of Deeds, may have indexes or other historical records online. In some cases you can even find civil and criminal proceedings indexes online. The local library, historical society, or the USGenWeb website may have published online guides or indexes to local court files. FamilySearch has a selection of digitized copies of court records online, from the county court level to the State Supreme Court, as well as research guides to court records in the FamilySearch Research Wiki. You can also check the Family History Library Catalog online to see if any court records have been microfilmed for your locality of interest and request these for perusal through your local Family History Center.

LINK

State and Local Government on the Net (*www.statelocalgov.net*) can be useful in locating official government websites, including those for the local court system. In addition, many states offer online directories of their county courts, such as the one found at Texas Courts Online (*www.courts.state.tx.us*). Most USGenWeb (*www.usgenweb.org*) county sites also provide contact information for the county courthouse.

Identify Adoptions and Orphans

Sometimes your own family history or the search for one of your ancestors is stalled because the circumstances of an ancestor's birth are shrouded in mystery. The first step in such a situation is the obvious one—to discover the names of the unknown birth parent or birth parents. If you believe the individual was formally adopted, the next step is to contact the agency or state that handled the adoption for a copy of the adoption order (in most states this information is sealed), or "non-identifying information," which, governed by state law and agency policy, may include important details that aren't considered revealing enough to identify the birth parents. This non-identifying information may include information on the adoptee (such as the date of birth and place of birth) and the birth parents (including a medical history, education level, religious affiliation, age at the birth, financial status, other siblings, and a physical description). Laws governing the release of identifying and non-identifying information about adoptions vary from state to state and country to country. Adoption.com offers a useful online guide to state adoption laws (*http://laws.adoption.com/statutes/state-adoption-laws.html*), including what information is available and where and how to access it.

The Internet is also especially helpful in adoption searches because of the access it provides to reunion registries that match up searching family members who have been separated by adoption, foster care, or other means. The International Soundex Reunion Registry (*www.isrr.org*) is the largest such mutual-consent registry. You can find links to others in the Registries section (*http://adoption.about.com/od/registries*) of the About .com Adoption site.

If you manage to locate the name of a birth parent, or at least enough family details to offer the chance of being able to identify them, a variety of genealogy resources can be helpful in your search. Census records, newspaper notices and obituaries, online telephone directories, public record databases, the Social Security Death Index, and other resources discussed throughout this book can be used.

Adoption is not the only thing that separates a child from his parents. It's not unusual to find a child sent to live with family members, or even neighbors, after a remarriage or the death of a parent. A child may also have been bound out as an apprentice to learn a trade. Children didn't even necessarily have to lose their parents to be considered orphans, placed for a time under the responsibility of the county or local government. There are many records of orphans, especially in large cities, with at least one living parent who for some reason wasn't able to support them. These children might be traced to a poorhouse or orphanage or may have been reared by foster parents (related or unrelated) or even sent west on an orphan train.

A good place to search for information on orphans is the county courthouse. In some states, including Pennsylvania, Maryland, Delaware, and New Jersey, an Orphans' Court handled both the sale and division of real estate arising from estates, as well as the guardianship of minor children. In areas without an Orphans' Court, guardianship matters were usually handled by whichever court heard probate or equity matters, possibly in a special session. This court, depending on area and time period, may have been a Court of Quarter Sessions (county court), circuit court, or chancery (equity) court. A guardian was generally appointed by the court to take charge of a minor's property, not necessarily custody of the child; thus, a child could have a guardian even if one or both parents were alive—in cases where the minor inherited property in his own right from the surviving parent or a grandparent. But many true orphans can be found in the records as well, as they needed to have a guardian appointed to manage their parents' estate for them until they became of age—generally age eighteen for females and age twenty-one for males, although this age varies by locality and time period. Orphans' Court proceedings may contain records of orphans being bound out as apprentices as well.

ESSENTIAL

Because of the difficulty of adoption research and the possible emotional issues involved, it can often be beneficial to join an adoption search support group. The Adoptees' Liberty Movement Association (ALMA) (*www.almasociety.org*) is an all-volunteer group offering assistance, advice, and moral support to individuals searching for adoptive roots. The Center for Adoption Support and Education (*www.adoptionsupport.org*) is a national resource for families and professionals involved with adoption. Or, search online for *adoption support* to find a group near you.

Sometimes you'll get lucky and an Internet search will turn up Guardianship and Orphans' Court records online, as in the case of the Wills, Orphans' Court, Guardianship, and Letters of Administration database (*www.atlanticlibrary.org/collections/digitized/wills/index.asp*) on the website of the Atlantic County, New Jersey, library. FamilySearch has some court records relating to orphans and guardianship matters in its online collection of Probate Records. If you can't find what you're looking for online, check the FamilySearch Library Catalog online to see what guardianship and Orphans' Court records have been microfilmed for your area of interest, and search for the county courthouse online to learn how these records might be accessed directly.

Orphan asylums were established by governments, churches, and private charities, and their records are understandably scattered. Check with the local library or historical society to see if they have information on orphanages that operated in the area, or do an Internet search such as *orphans western pennsylvania*. Cyndi's List (*www.cyndislist.com/orphans/*) is an excellent place to find links to online resources and records on orphans, orphanages, and orphan trains.

CHAPTER 8

Look Local

Pinpointing where your ancestors lived is crucial to locating the written records that detail their lives. It can help identify the likely courthouse to check for civil records, where your ancestors worshipped, and even where they might be buried. Maps can help identify the ancestral homestead, visualize the places where your ancestors lived and died, and suggest possible migration routes once followed by your ancestors. Geography is also a powerful tool for distinguishing between two individuals with the same name.

Maps and Geography

Are you familiar with the area where your grandparents were born? You may know that it is a small Pennsylvania town called Shanksville, but you may not know what county it's in, or even whether it's located closer to Pittsburgh or Philadelphia. That's why the first thing you should do when you begin research in a new area is pull out a map. Online map services, such as Yahoo! Maps (*http://maps.yahoo.com*), Google Maps (*http://maps.google.com*), or Bing Maps (*www.bing.com/maps*), offer a host of features including address lookup, driving directions, satellite views, and zoom and pan.

LINK

When your research uncovers an unfamiliar place name, turn to a place-names database such as the United States Board on Geographic Names (BGN) (*http://geonames.usgs.gov*), which details more than 2 million places and features (towns, streams, mountains, cemeteries, and other geographical features) in the United States, including the names of places that no longer exist. Outside of the United States, you'll find similar assistance from the GEOnet Names Server (*http://earth-info.nga.mil/gns/html/*).

Locate a Lost Town, Village, or Creek

What if you can't locate your ancestor's town on a modern map? Place names change. Geographical and political boundaries shift. Communities fall into disuse and disappear. Look for the answer in a gazetteer created during the time period of the document where you found the place name referenced. A gazetteer is a book that names and describes places in a given area during a given time period. With your mystery town's description and location from the gazetteer, you may be able to unearth a map from the period and identify the town's geographical location.

A variety of gazetteers can be searched and viewed online. One good modern gazetteer is Falling Rain's Global Gazetteer (*www.fallingrain.com/world*), a database of nearly 3 million populated places around the world, organized by country. Clicking on a location name takes you to a page with the latitude and longitude, several small maps, and a list of nearby cities and towns.

Historical gazetteers can be used to locate towns that do not exist in modern times. While most are tucked away in libraries and archival repositories, many historical gazetteers can also be accessed online. Sites such as A Vision of Britain Through Time (*www.visionofbritain.org.uk*) include historical descriptions drawn from gazetteers. Try a search for *gazetteer [your county, state, or region]* to identify online gazetteers that may be useful in your research.

ESSENTIAL

You must know who had jurisdiction over a location to find records, but political and geographic boundaries are constantly changing. To help ensure that you're looking in the right place, AniMap Software for Windows, by Gold Bug (*www.goldbug.com/AniMap.html*), can display more than 2,300 color maps to show the changing county boundaries for each of the forty-eight contiguous states for every year since colonial times.

Explore the Lay of the Land—Virtually

Maps provide the opportunity to visually explore the places where your ancestors lived, as they existed at the time. A variety of maps can be of use to genealogists, including:

- **Historical Maps**—Historical maps come in many varieties. One of the most useful for genealogists is a landowner's map, which shows property parcels along with the name of each landowner. Historical maps may also show churches, cemeteries, and other areas of interest. Thousands of historical maps are available online, some for free viewing and others for purchase. One of the largest free collections is the Perry-Castañeda Library Map Collection at the University of Texas at Austin (*www.lib.utexas.edu/maps*).
- **Topographic Maps**—Topo maps, short for topographic maps, are a favorite with many genealogists because of their high level of detail. These maps emphasize physical features on the surface of the earth, from mountains and streams to cemeteries and railroad lines.

Large-scale topo maps are sometimes so detailed you can see individual buildings, churches, and all navigable roads.

- **Fire Insurance Maps**—Fire insurance companies often requisition detailed maps of heavily populated areas to aid them in determining the risk factors in underwriting a particular property. These maps can be useful for genealogists because they depict building outlines, property boundaries, and street names for more than 12,000 American towns and cities. The Digital Sanborn Maps, 1867–1970 (*http://sanborn.umi.com*), offers online access to a collection of more than 660,000 such maps. This database is available through subscribing libraries and institutions, so check with your local or state library to see if they offer it. Several state and city archives and libraries have also made digitized Sanborn maps for their locality available to the public on their website, such as Sanborn Fire Insurance Maps of South Carolina (*http://library.sc.edu/ digital/collections/sanborn.html*), available online from the University of South Carolina.

Technology now makes it possible to easily overlay a historic map directly on top of a current road or topographic map. The top layer can be made semi-transparent, allowing you to see through the historic map in the top layer and compare roads, rivers, and even old buildings and property boundaries with the current map or satellite image underneath. A number of large map collections offer the ability to view their historic maps as overlays, such as the David Rumsey Map Collection for Google Maps. Links to this and a number of other large collections can be found in the article "Historic Map Overlays for Google Maps & Google Earth" (*http://genealogy.about.com/od/ mapping_tools/tp/historical-map-overlays.htm*). State libraries and archives are also a good source for historical maps—use search terms such as *[place name] historic map overlays* to find websites such as North Carolina Maps (*www.lib.unc.edu/dc/ncmaps/interactive/overlay.html*).

Land and Property Records

Now that you know how to locate your ancestor's town on the map, it's time to take a closer look at the property and community that he called home.

Land is traditionally considered to be a valuable asset and, as such, great care has been taken in the recording of property ownership and transfer. People, understandably, want to have legal proof that their land belongs to them. For this reason, property records are among the most numerous records in existence, going back further in time and applying to more people than almost any other genealogical record.

QUESTION

How can I identify my ancestor's property on a map?
With a protractor, ruler, and graph paper you can draw a plot of your ancestor's property based on the physical description in the deed or grant, a process known as land platting. Try it for yourself with the step-by-step instructions in "Land Platting Made Easy" (*http://genealogy.about.com/od/land_records/ss/land_platting.htm*), or use a computer program such as DeedMapper (*www.directlinesoftware.com*) by Direct Line Software to draw the plat map for you.

Although beginners to family history research often overlook them, land records are a favorite resource of most professionals because of the valuable genealogical evidence they provide. According to leading genealogist William Dollarhide in "Retracing the Trails of Your Ancestors Using Deed Records" (*Genealogy Bulletin*, Jan.–Feb. 1995), "nine out of ten adult white males in America owned land before 1850." He goes on to state that this claim still applies to more than 50 percent of white males today. With those odds, all genealogists with white American ancestors should be using land ownership records in their family history research. A land record can place an individual in a specific location and time that, in turn, can lead to further records or help distinguish between two individuals with the same name. Land records are also a good source for names and relationships of family members, such as when a group of heirs jointly sell a parcel of inherited land.

Land records include a variety of different document types, including patents, deeds, mortgages, bounty land warrants, and homestead grants. Depending on the type of record and the time period, these may be found at the national, state, county, or local level. To understand which records might tell you more about your family, you will need to become familiar with the types of land records created in your geographical area of interest during specific periods.

Who Owned the Land First?

The history of land acquisition and ownership in America could fill up an entire book. But it is also important to understand a little about how land was acquired, distributed, and transferred among governments and individuals in the area where your ancestor lived so you'll know what land records might be available and where they can be found. Search online for specific information on land history and ownership in your area, with a search query such as *history land pennsylvania.*

States where land was originally controlled and distributed by the colonial or state government are known collectively as the *state-land states.* These include the thirteen original colonies, plus Hawaii, Kentucky, Maine, Tennessee, Texas, Vermont, and West Virginia. As you might expect, these lands were surveyed and distributed in a variety of different ways. In some cases the government controlled the allocation of land, and in others this control was granted to a private citizen or citizens, such as the Lords Proprietors in North Carolina and the town proprietors of the New England states.

The majority of the state-land states, from Pennsylvania and New Jersey southward, continued the British survey system of metes and bounds to legally describe a piece of land. This system used local features such as trees, fences, stumps, and creeks to describe the property's boundaries. The distances along or between these features were usually described in poles, rods, or perches—all interchangeable with a distance of 16½ feet. In New England, this system was supplemented by the drawing up of town plats—most in a roughly rectangular shape. The government granted this town plat to a group of town proprietors who then oversaw the sale and distribution of lots within the town.

Land in the state-land states was generally first distributed by means of *patents* or *grants.* This patent/grant is the initial transfer of title from the government or proprietor to the patentee/grantee. It is the first title deed and the beginning of private ownership of the land.

ALERT

Old land surveys are often hard to fit on a modern map because of magnetic declination, the difference between the true north (the axis around which the earth rotates) used for maps and magnetic north (the place the needle on a compass will point) used by land surveyors. Because the direction of magnetic north has changed over time, you'll need to adjust your survey plots to correct for this declination error. The National Geophysical Data Center (*www.ngdc.noaa.gov/geomag-web/*) offers a handy historic declination calculator for just this purpose.

Following the Revolutionary War, the new federal government started surveying and distributing the land under its control, also known as the *public domain*. The land in thirty states, often referred to as the *federal-land states* or *public land states*, was initially controlled and surveyed by the U.S. government before its transfer into private hands. These public land states are Alabama, Alaska, Arizona, Arkansas, California, Colorado, Florida, Idaho, Illinois, Indiana, Iowa, Kansas, Louisiana, Michigan, Minnesota, Mississippi, Missouri, Montana, Nebraska, Nevada, New Mexico, North Dakota, Ohio, Oklahoma, Oregon, South Dakota, Utah, Washington, Wisconsin, and Wyoming.

To keep things orderly, the government developed a new system for surveying its land prior to its being made available for purchase or homesteading, called the *rectangular survey system* or *township-range system*. The land was initially laid out into orderly squares organized along a *meridian* (imaginary line running from the North to the South Pole) and *base line*, which runs east and west. Meridian regions are divided into tracts of about 24 square miles, and these tracts are then divided into sixteen townships of about 16 square miles each. Each township is further subdivided into thirty-six one-mile square sections, each consisting of 640 acres, and these sections are further subdivided into smaller pieces such as halves and quarters called *aliquot parts*. Each piece of property in a public land state is identified in this manner in relation to a particular base line and meridian line. More detailed explanation of the rectangular survey system can be found online by searching for *public land survey system*.

In some states you'll run across several different systems of original land survey. For an extensive overview of land divisions and surveys in the United States, read *Land & Property Research in the United States* by E. Wade

Hone. And for information on the various Congressional acts that governed the distribution of federal land, and may have prompted your ancestors to migrate or settle in the location where they did, see "Timeline of U.S. Public Land Acts" (*http://genealogy.about.com/od/land_records/a/Timeline-Of-US-Public-Land-Grants.htm*).

Land in the public land states was first distributed into private hands in a number of ways. The most common of these include homestead grants, military bounty warrants, and cash purchases of land.

Dig for Deeds

Land deeds are the method by which land is transferred between individual owners, recording all land transfers following the original grant, warrant, or sale of the land by the government to the first individual land owner. These might include deeds of sale and gift, mortgages, estate settlements, and other land transfers. In addition to providing the location and description of your ancestor's land, a deed may also identify the names of neighbors or relatives; a relationship between the grantee and the grantor, if one exists; or a clue to the former location of the buyer (grantee) or next location of the seller (grantor).

When deeds are recorded, they are copied into deed books maintained by the county or other local jurisdiction. These can usually be found under the jurisdiction of the Registrar of Deeds at the county courthouse. In the New England states of Connecticut, Rhode Island, and Vermont, land deeds are kept by the town clerks. In Alaska, deeds are registered at the district level, and in Louisiana deed records are found at the parish level. Separate indexes to deed books were typically created by local officials. In most cases you'll find two separate indexes: one organized by grantor (seller), sometimes called a *direct index*, and one indexed by grantee (buyer), sometimes called an *indirect* or *inverted index*. The two indexes may also be combined in a single volume, with grantor and grantee entries both appearing interwoven in alphabetical order, or separated on facing pages.

Relying solely on an index to locate deeds has a few drawbacks, however. Deeds with more than one buyer or seller may be indexed only by the name of the first party. Some indexes also include only the deeds, and not other recorded instruments contained in the deed books such as slave bills of sale or livestock brands. When using a new index, it is good practice to conduct a small sampling of the deed records to confirm what may or may not be included. In cases where a thorough search is essential, then examine the deeds page by page.

ESSENTIAL

The Family History Library has microfilmed the deed indexes and deeds for many U.S. counties. You can request these microfilms for use at your local Family History Center. Do a Place Search for the county name in the online Family History Library Catalog (*http://familysearch .org/catalog-search*) to see what deeds they have microfilmed for your areas of interest.

Since you'll generally be working with deed records in the courthouse or at your Family History Center, it pays to be thorough to cut down on the necessity of repeat visits. Check both the grantor and grantee indexes for your ancestors, as you can learn a lot from both the purchases and the sales. Index entries that list multiple names are a special treat, as they may signify family members or a group of heirs. The designation "et al."—Latin for "and others"—following the name of a grantor or grantee often indicates such a deed. Before you leave, take time to make a copy of the deed index for your surnames of interest in the appropriate time period. This way you can easily order additional deeds by mail if you find others you need as your research progresses.

Locate Land Records Online

If you think your ancestor may have obtained land from the federal government, begin with the website of the General Land Office, U.S. Bureau of Land Management (*www.glorecords.blm.gov*). The database provides searchable access to more than 5 million federal-land title records (patents) for the thirty public land states, issued between 1820 and 1908. These include images of both homestead and cash patents, primarily from the eastern public land states encompassing the present-day states of Alabama, Arkansas, Florida, Illinois, Indiana, Iowa, Louisiana, Michigan, Minnesota, Mississippi, Missouri, Ohio, and Wisconsin. You can also access images of *serial patents* (land title records issued between 1908 and the 1960s) and *survey plats* and *field notes* (dating back to 1810). The General Land Office does not, however, contain every land record issued by the U.S. government.

Patents are the final proof of land ownership, but there is also a wealth of information to be found in the paperwork generated by the land application process. This includes not only those who actually obtained patents, but the many who never completed the requirements or who had their application rejected. Some of these land files—especially the homestead applications—can contain significant genealogical information, including the age or date of birth of the applicant, his marital status, name of the spouse, and size of the family. These application documents have been compiled into Land Entry Case Files, in the custody of the National Archives (*www.archives.gov/research/land*). The case files are also recorded in tract books, which serve basically as an index to both the patented and cancelled land entry files arranged by state and legal description of the land (numbered section, township, and range). Tract books for all federal-land states, except Alaska and Missouri, have been digitized and made available online by FamilySearch (*http://familysearch.org/search/collection/2074276*). Land Entry Files can be ordered online from the National Archives (*www.archives.gov/research/order/*).

ALERT

Look at an original land patent and you may notice a familiar signature at the bottom—that of the U.S. president in office at the time the patent was issued. Before you get excited, check the date as well. Patents dated after March 2, 1833, were actually signed by designated officials on the president's behalf. If you're lucky enough to have a pre-1833 original land patent handed down in your family, however, you may truly have a presidential treasure.

Since the colonial or state government distributed land in the state-land states, there is no nationwide database for these records. Instead, original land grant records can usually be found in the state archive or equivalent repository. They may also be found recorded in the county deed registers. Because of their historical value, many of these early land patents and grants are being digitized and placed online. Try a search such as *historical "land records,"* or *"land grants"* plus the name of the state or county in question to learn what is available online for your area of interest.

LINK

From 1775 to 1855, the U.S. federal government awarded grants of free land, called bounty land, to military veterans; initially to encourage volunteer enlistments, and later to reward military service. Many records generated through this process, including applications and bounty land warrants, can be searched and/or viewed online.

Deeds transferring land titles between private citizens are maintained at the county or local level rather than the state level. Therefore, you won't find quite as many deed records online. Many counties do offer online access to recent deeds and other property information. Digitizing historical deeds, however, takes time and money that many counties just can't afford. Exceptions, such as the New Hampshire County Registries of Deeds (*www .nhdeeds.com*) and Land Records in Maryland (*www.mdlandrec.net*), are becoming more and more common, however. Some early deeds may also be found in online collections hosted by state-level archives or historical societies. Do a search for *[county] [state] deeds* or check out the website of the Registrar of Deeds or Clerk of Court for the appropriate county and/or state to see what they may have online.

ESSENTIAL

For every record you find on the Internet, there are dozens that can only be accessed offline in archives, libraries, and similar repositories. Books such as *Courthouse Research for Family Historians* by Christine Rose and articles such as "10 Questions to Ask a Research Facility Before You Visit" (*http://genealogy.about.com/od/libraries/a/questions.htm*) will help you prepare for your trip before heading out the door.

County land ownership atlases are another source for information on landowners in the United States. What sets these maps apart from other maps is that they include the names of individual landowners at a given point in time, as well as county and township boundaries and other important historical information. Check with the local Register of Deeds, library, or historical society to see if such landownership maps exist for the area and time period in which you're interested. Some can also be found online in major map collections, such as the Indexed County Land Ownership Maps, 1860–1918, (*http://search.ancestry.com/iexec/?htx=List&dbid=1127*) at Ancestry.com.

Historical Newspapers

Your family didn't necessarily have to be famous or wealthy to make the news—at least not after the introduction of the penny newspaper in 1833 made newspapers easily available to the masses. Important life events such as births, marriages, deaths, and funerals often appeared in the local newspaper, as did land transactions, court proceedings, school achievements, and other information on the everyday life of the area's inhabitants. Beyond the names and dates, newspapers frequently contain firsthand accounts of important events and issues, and reflect popular thinking and cultural attitudes of the time. Even the advertisements are enlightening, offering insight into local fashion, trends, and the cost of living.

Prior to the Internet, only the most tenacious researchers used historical newspapers to research family history. They just weren't easily available, often existing only on microfilm at the local or state library. Newspapers also don't typically come with an index, so newspaper research generally involves a lot of research and guesswork just to select the newspaper and issue(s) most likely to contain information of interest. Once the search has been narrowed to a particular newspaper and time period, newspaper research can still involve hours spent in front of a microfilm reader scrolling through page-by-page, skimming line after line.

ALERT

Don't limit yourself to births, marriages, and obituaries when researching your family in old newspapers. Some of the best finds may come from the society and neighborhood columns, where you can get little snippets about visiting relatives, children joining the military or leaving for college, people suffering or recovering from a serious illness, and trips to visit friends and family in other towns.

Online access to historical newspapers has changed the scope of newspaper research, making it much more easily available to anyone interested in his or her family history. Many publishers and organizations have undertaken the digitization of historical newspapers in order to preserve and provide increased access to their rich history and commentary. The entire archive of the *New York Times*—dating back to its first issue in 1851—is just one such example of the many historical newspapers that have been made available for viewing via the Internet. These treasures of digital history present a great source for gaining knowledge about your family and the time and place in which they lived.

In addition to increased access, the digitization of historical newspapers allows for easier research with tools such as zoom, pan, and full-text search. The full-text search does come with a caveat, however. Most digitization projects use optical character recognition (OCR) technology to automatically recognize text within the digitized newspaper images. This process is much quicker and more cost-effective than manual indexing (can you imagine the effort the latter would take?), but does lend itself to inaccuracies. This is especially true for older newspapers where the typeface was a bit more flowery and may be harder for a computer to accurately decipher. Search results may include extraneous "matches" on words that the OCR technology believes are optically similar enough that they could be your target word. As a result, searching in historical newspaper databases can require quite a bit of creativity and patience, but the rewards are often immeasurable.

To locate historical newspapers online, first learn what paper(s) covered the location and time period in which you're interested. Then do a search for the paper by name and location plus terms such as *archive* or *historical*. There are also websites that link to online papers and collections organized by state, such as "Historic Newspapers Online" (*http://genealogy.about.com/od/newspapers/tp/newspapers_online.htm*). Many historical newspapers are also found in the following large collections that include content from newspapers across the United States as well as other countries such as Canada, Australia, and even Jamaica.

ProQuest Historical Newspapers

This collection of full-text and full-image articles from prestigious U.S. newspapers was first created in 2001 with the digitization of the *New York Times*. Other major newspapers now included in the fully searchable database include the *Chicago Tribune*, *Washington Post*, *Los Angeles Times*,

Atlanta Constitution, Boston Globe, Hartford Courant, New York Tribune, New York Amsterdam News, Pittsburgh Courier, Wall Street Journal, and *Christian Science Monitor.* Every issue of each title includes the complete newspaper in downloadable PDF format and full-text search with a variety of advanced search options. This collection is only available through subscribing libraries and institutions, and is not available for individual subscriptions. Check with your local, college, or state library to see if they subscribe to any or all of the newspapers in this collection. Many offer free in-library and remote access to their patrons.

NewspaperARCHIVE.com

This subscription-based service is one of the largest historical newspaper collections available online, but also one of the priciest. The Newspaper Archive database (*www.newspaperarchive.com*) contains more than 120 million full-page images from historical newspapers from around the world, ranging from 1607 to the present. Coverage varies by newspaper, so use the "Browse Papers" feature to see which publications and dates are available before subscribing. Online cancellation is available, but refunds are not offered for unused time. Most papers from the Newspaper Archive collection are available as part of a MyHeritage (*www.myheritage.com*) subscription, or may be accessible at Family History Centers, or through third-party subscription offerings such as Godfrey Scholar+ (*www.godfrey.org*).

Ancestry.com Historical Newspapers

Historical newspapers are available as part of the Ancestry.com subscription website. The Historical Newspaper Collection (*www.ancestry.com/search/rectype/periodicals/news*) offers access to more than 16 million pages from selected years of thousands of newspapers across the United States, United Kingdom, Canada, and Australia, dating back to the 1700s. Individual subscriptions to just the newspaper portion are not available; you have to subscribe to the entire Ancestry.com U.S. or World Record Collection.

Newspapers.com

In November 2012, Ancestry.com launched this stand-alone historical newspapers site, which features a nifty interface for viewing and saving newspapers and articles of interest. While there is some overlap between this site and Ancestry.com's Historical Newspaper Collection, each collection features slightly different subsets of papers. Newspapers.com features a growing collection of over 50 million newspaper pages from more than 1,800 newspapers across the United States. A clippings feature allows you to save, tag, and share your "finds," either publicly or privately. A discount subscription is available to Ancestry.com subscribers.

GenealogyBank

A product of the information provider NewsBank, GenealogyBank (*www.genealogybank.com*) offers more than 1 billion articles, obituaries, marriage notices, and birth announcements published in more than 6,500 U.S. newspapers, from 1690–2010. You can search the site for free and see brief excerpts that contain your search results, but you'll need to subscribe to view the entire article. A similar service, operating under the name America's GenealogyBank, is offered as a subscription service to libraries, so check to see if you have free access through your local or state library before subscribing.

Chronicling America: Historical American Newspapers

A joint project of the National Endowment for the Humanities (NEH) and the Library of Congress (LC), the National Digital Newspaper Program is a twenty-year plan to create a national digital resource of historically significant newspapers from all states and U.S. territories. The project's website, Chronicling America (*www.chroniclingamerica.loc.gov*), allows you to find information about American newspapers published between 1690 and the present, including the libraries that carry each title. The free database also allows you to search and read the currently digitized newspaper pages, which at this time includes newspapers published between 1836 to 1922 in thirty-five states, Puerto Rico, and the District of Columbia. As long as funding allows, the project will continue to expand its coverage.

For every newspaper you can access online, there are hundreds more only available in libraries and other repositories around the world. The U.S. Newspaper Directory, 1690–Present (*http://chroniclingamerica .loc.gov/search/titles/*) is a good starting point for discovering which newspapers were published, and when, for any place in the United States, as well as which repositories hold original or microfilm copies.

SmallTownPapers

Newspaper archive company SmallTownPapers (*www.smalltownpapers .com*) provides free access to more than 300 small-market newspapers from across the United States dating back as far as 1865. Coverage varies widely by newspaper.

In addition to these large collections, historical newspaper archives can also be found online digitized by public and university libraries, individuals, or even the newspaper itself. Visit the website of local, state, and university libraries that cover your area(s) of interest to find online digitized newspapers such as the Quincy (Illinois) Historical Newspaper Archive (*www.quincylibrary.org/library_resources/newspaperArchive.asp*). Turn to your favorite search engine to locate additional titles, using keywords like *[state name] historical newspapers* to uncover treasures such as New York State Historical Newspapers (*http://fultonhistory.com/Fulton.html*), a one-man show featuring over 22 million digitized pages from newspapers across New York State. Newspapers were also published for occupational, ethnic, and religious groups, so also search for those terms, such as *farming newspapers historic,* which brings up a number of neat collections such as the University of Illinois at Urbana-Champaign's Farm, Field and Fireside collection (*www.library.illinois.edu/dnc/fff*) of historically significant U.S. farm weeklies.

Libraries and Societies

A stop at the public library in the community where your ancestor lived is a must for any family historian. Libraries are a gateway to rich primary source materials on the history and culture of the region they serve, as well as the people who lived in the area. The library is usually the local repository for archived newspapers, city directories, school yearbooks, and other resources specific to the community. Many larger libraries also maintain a local history section, with family histories, community and local history books, photographs, and records such as census enumerations, cemetery transcriptions, and marriage indexes.

LINK

Use the Internet as a tool to find libraries that serve the locations where your ancestors lived, or that host records or special collections that match your research interests. PublicLibraries.com (*www.publiclibraries .com*) maintains listings and links to U.S. state libraries and college and university libraries, organized by state. LibWeb (*www.lib-web.org*) includes links to more than 8,000 web pages from libraries in more than 146 countries, including public, academic, and religious libraries.

Online, a library visit means an excursion to the library's website. Many libraries offer unique online content in the form of digitized original records, or transcribed indexes or databases. The University of Pittsburgh library (*http://digital.library.pitt.edu*), for example, provides access to historical maps and photos, transcribed census records, and the full text of more than 500 published works that relate to local Pittsburgh and Pennsylvania history. Another unique resource can be found on the website of the New York Public Library (*www.nypl.org*), where more than 600 Yizkor books (Holocaust memorial books) from the library's collection are available online in digitized format. Even smaller libraries may offer cemetery transcriptions or an index to obituaries that have appeared in their local paper. For example, the Cleveland Public Library (*www.cpl.org*) hosts an online Necrology File of cemetery records and newspaper death notices.

Collaborative databases, in which several libraries or societies pool their records and resources, are also becoming common online. In Indiana, the Vital INformation Exchange (VINE) (*http://web.isl.lib.in.us/vine/*) is a statewide database of vital records, obituaries, newspapers, yearbooks, and other local history resources from Indiana libraries, historical societies, genealogical societies, and related organizations. A group of libraries in central and northeastern Ohio have banded together to create the regional MOLO Obituary Index (*www.ohiofamilysearch.org*).

Even libraries that don't have online records can be helpful in your research. Most library websites make at least a portion of their catalog available for searching online. Look for a link from the site's home page. You may also find information on submitting lookup or research requests. Many librarians are willing to do brief lookups in indexed books, databases, and clipping files, or provide a copy of an obituary if you can provide a name and date. In some cases this service may cost you a few dollars to cover expenses and postage, but it is well worth it. More and more librarians are also offering online "Ask a Librarian" assistance, either through e-mail or chat.

Genealogists sometimes overlook university and college libraries, but they often hold unique historical resources. They can have many unpublished genealogies and histories in their manuscript division, as well as the records of churches and businesses. University libraries are often open to the public, although you may need to obtain a researcher card or pay a usage fee. You may also not be eligible to check out materials, or access specific online databases. Contact the library directly to inquire about their access policies.

ALERT

The interlibrary loan (ILL) service at your local library can be a goldmine for genealogists interested in materials held by libraries far from their home. While few libraries will lend non-circulating genealogical materials, you can often use an ILL request to borrow copies of microfilmed records, or to ask that they make copies of the index for your ancestors' surnames or a few relevant pages from a book or newspaper.

One tool used by many genealogists to locate library resources is WorldCat, a catalog of materials held in more than 10,000 libraries worldwide, including public, academic, and state libraries; archives; and historical societies. This includes special collections devoted to local history, which means you may find citations for historical newspapers, oral histories, family histories, cemetery records, historical photographs, family Bibles, town or county histories, and a wide variety of other materials. WorldCat can be searched directly online (*www.worldcat.org*), or accessed through "find in a library" links for book results in sites such as Google Books and Amazon.

Churches and Schools

In just about every town, you can find a church and a school. Throughout much of history these buildings have served as the center of the community, a focus of daily life for area residents. For this reason, church and school records often provide intriguing insights into the lives and personalities of earlier generations. They may also supply concrete information, such as dates of birth or baptism, marriage, and death, or proof of family relationships.

Religious Records

Church and synagogue records are a very valuable source for pre-1900 baptisms, marriages, and burials, but be prepared to face a few challenges if you are using them to help with your research. The existence of more than 100 different religious denominations can make it difficult to determine the church with which your ancestor had an affiliation. Churches themselves have appeared, disappeared, and merged over time. Record keeping varies widely. Some records are in the custody of individual churches, others in diocesan collections, and still others in national archives or other repositories. Generally, there are few catalogs or indexes to these church records, and the vast majority cannot be accessed online. In most cases you'll find it necessary to visit the church or archives in person, or to hire a researcher.

To locate church records, you must first identify the denomination of your ancestor, and the actual church that she attended. Don't just assume that your ancestors practiced the same religion that you do today. It's very common to find individuals or families who have changed denominations. In rural areas, the choice of churches was generally limited, and residents may have attended the church or parish most convenient for them. Once you determine the religion, a directory or a map from that time period may be able to help you pin down the closest church to where your ancestor lived.

When you have located the church, you next need to find out where the records are kept. Begin with an online phone directory or Internet search to see if the church still exists, and then contact it to learn about the availability of records for your time period of interest. If the church is no longer in existence, an e-mail or call to the local historical society or library, or to the regional headquarters for that denomination, may provide you with information. A thorough Internet search can be very helpful as well. Use terms such as *pittsburgh catholic genealogy*, which brings up the "Information for Genealogists" page from the Office for Archives and Record Center of the Catholic Diocese of Pittsburgh.

Many older church records have been published in book form or in local genealogical and historical periodicals. Look under your locality of interest in online library catalogs and in PERSI. The National Union Catalog of Manuscript Collections (NUCMC) (*www.loc.gov/coll/nucmc*) can be useful in locating church records held by libraries and historical societies.

ESSENTIAL

The Yearbook of American and Canadian Churches, published annually by the National Council of Churches in the United States and available for purchase from their website (*www.ncccusa.org/yearbook/*), lists all major denominations with contact information and a capsule history. ChurchTag.com (*www.churchtag.com*) is one of several church directory sites on the Internet.

One of the largest sources of transcribed and/or indexed church records online is the International Genealogical Index (IGI) at FamilySearch (*http://familysearch.org/search/collection/igi/*), which includes millions of extracted church records, primarily baptisms and marriages, from the 1500s to 1885. While you can search the IGI on its own, FamilySearch has incorporated the transcribed IGI records into its Historical Records collection, supplementing many of them with additional records and digital images. The USGenWeb Archives Church Records Project (*www.rootsweb.ancestry.com/~usgenweb/churches/*) hosts transcribed membership lists, church bulletins, church minutes, and records of baptisms, marriages, and burials submitted by volunteers. Most of the transcribed records are from the 1700s and early 1800s. Subscription genealogy sites such as Genealogy Today (*www.genealogytoday.com*) and Ancestry.com include databases such as church member lists, registers, and histories. An online search such as *church records oakdale pennsylvania* may turn up online databases, church histories, or other resources for church records in your locality of interest.

Even in the many cases where the actual church records are not online, you can do a lot of the background research on the Internet. The Family History Library has microfilmed records for many denominations, which you can learn about by doing a place search in the online Family History Library Catalog. The websites for regional and national headquarters for many denominations offer information on the availability of records for family history research, as well as online directories of churches, parishes, or synagogues. A search such as *researching methodist ancestors* can point to several helpful research guides.

School Records

From the seventeenth century to the present day, schools and other educational institutions have created records that may have information about your ancestors, including registration records, class lists, alumni lists, transcripts, report cards, school censuses, and class photos. If your ancestor went to college, you may be especially lucky, as colleges and universities tend to create, maintain, and preserve more comprehensive records than most primary and secondary schools. School fraternities and sororities also provide a potential source for records on such ancestors.

The one-room rural schoolhouse was a vital part of early American life, but these records, even if they have survived, may be hard to find. As the schools were closed, records may have been deposited with county or state repositories. Sometimes the local library or historical society may have these records or know where they are kept. Twentieth-century school records are usually much more comprehensive and can sometimes be found by contacting the school or school district directly. Try your favorite search engine to find schools in a particular location, using a search such as *schools lexington county south carolina*. The Board of Education in the state in which your ancestor attended school may also be of assistance in locating records. You'll often find, however, that many schools restrict access to personal information on people who may still be living. You may be able to get around these privacy issues by proving that you're a relative of the individual of interest and that she is deceased.

As with church records, most school records cannot be accessed online. The previously mentioned subscription site, Genealogy Today (*www.genealogytoday.com*), includes a number of transcribed school records and yearbooks. FamilySearch hosts digitized copies of school records from several states including the "Mississippi Enumeration of Educable Children, 1850–1892, 1908–1957." Some USGenWeb county sites have transcribed school records included among their online offerings. Search the online library catalog for universities and colleges to see what records may be available in the school archives. Collections of school records hidden away in libraries and archives may occasionally be found by searching the National Union Catalog of Manuscript Collections.

Yearbooks, school newspapers, and alumni registers and directories provide alternative avenues for research when the school records themselves are unavailable. If the school still exists—especially in the case of colleges, universities, or private schools—these resources may be available through the school library or alumni association. Online, Ancestry.com includes a huge yearbook collection (*www.ancestry.com/yearbook*) of more than 35,000 school yearbooks spanning the years 1875 to 1988 among its subscription databases. You can also find yearbooks and alumni lists on subscription site MyHeritage (*www.myheritage.com/research/category-10030/schools-universities*).

Local History

So much of what your ancestors did during their lives—their choice of occupation, who they married, and how they lived—has to do with the place they called home. A young man in a small, rural farming community, for example, was probably a bit limited when it came to his choice of brides. A large family living in the "big" city was more likely to rent than own their home. Researching the local history of the town, village, or city where your ancestors lived is a big step toward understanding what their life was like—the people, places, and events that impacted the course of their own personal history. This is what will help you place the raw facts of your genealogy—names, dates, and places—into historical context, and really bring your family tree to life.

LINK

The more you delve into your family's history, the more you're going to want to know about the history of your country and the events in which your ancestors participated. Digital History (*www.digitalhistory.uh.edu*) helps users reconstruct the past through a variety of primary sources, as does American Memory (*http://memory.loc.gov*) from the Library of Congress. The History sites at About.com (*www.about.com/education*) offer a wealth of historical information from medieval times to the twentieth century.

Much of your research into local history can and should be done in conjunction with the rest of your genealogy research. As you search an old newspaper for an obituary notice, for example, take time to look at the news headlines, the gossip columns, and even the advertisements to get a glimpse of what people were interested in during that time. When you're visiting the website of the local historical society or county government for information on available records, take a few extra minutes to click through on the History or About Us links, if available, to learn more about the area. As you enter information from census enumerations or marriage records into your research notes, be sure to add not just names and dates, but also details such as residence (with the street name when given) and occupation. It can be very interesting to track these over time.

One of the tools many genealogists use to visualize their ancestors' place in history is the timeline. Many genealogy software programs can help you create a basic timeline, or you can use special timeline software (search the web for *timeline software* or *timeline creator*). Augment important dates from your ancestors' lives with historic events such as wars, natural disasters, epidemics, and so on, looking for local events of importance, as well as national and world events. Knowing that your ancestors lived in the mid-1800s and actually "seeing" the events they lived through are two different things.

CHAPTER 9

Mine the Web
for Military Records

More than 42 million Americans, representing almost every generation, have participated in some type of wartime service. Men as young as fourteen and as old as sixty may have joined local militia units, making it likely that you'll discover at least one ancestor or relative with a military past. Military records can also document people who never actually served, such as the millions of young men who registered for the WWI and WWII drafts but were never called up for duty.

Find Clues to Military Service

Begin your search for military records by talking with living relatives and reviewing the documents and other information you have already collected. The goal is to identify ancestors who may have participated in the military and, ultimately, to determine when and where the soldier served. Clues to an ancestor's military service may be found in the following:

- **Family stories**—If a relative says that your ancestor served in the military, it is most likely true. Just keep in mind that memories get fuzzy with time, and the details may have been exaggerated or embellished a bit.
- **Photographs**—Search your family photograph collection for pictures of people in uniform. The type of photo and style of uniform can help determine the branch of the military and the war or time period in which your ancestor served. Patches, pins, insignia, and even belt buckles may help determine rank or unit.
- **Census records**—Occupational references may indicate military service. The conspicuous absence of a male relative during wartime may also offer a clue. Surviving Revolutionary War pensioners or their widows were identified in the 1840 U.S. federal census, and Civil War veterans or widows in the special 1890 Union Veterans Census (surviving only for the states of Kentucky [partial] through Wyoming, alphabetically, including Washington, D.C.). The 1910 federal census indicates whether the person was a "survivor of the Union or Confederate Army or Navy." The 1930 census designates military service in major wars through World War I.
- **Newspaper clippings**—People were proud of their hometown heroes, and brief mentions of local soldiers often made the community papers.
- **Journals and correspondence**—Writing letters or keeping a diary offered a distraction from the boredom of military camp life and the terror of battle. Such letters or journals may be found among your family's belongings or in a manuscript collection at a library or archive.
- **Death records and obituaries**—A soldier's obituary or death record may mention military service and provide details such as branch or regiment.

- **Local histories**—Published town or county histories often include stories and photos of local military units.
- **Grave markers**—A flag, emblem, engraving, or marker on your ancestor's gravestone may indicate military service. Many countries also honor their veterans with special headstones.

ESSENTIAL

Tombstone inscriptions and symbols are a good source for clues to military service. Acronyms and abbreviations may indicate the branch of military service, such as U.S. Air Force (USAF) or U.S. Navy (USN). Others may be less obvious, such as SS for Silver Star, GAR for Grand Army of the Republic, or UDC for United Daughters of the Confederacy. Search online for *military acronyms* or *military tombstone symbols* for identification assistance.

Once you have determined that an ancestor served in the military, there are a wide variety of records that may help to document his service. These include military service records, draft registrations, medals and ribbons, pension papers, discharge papers, pay vouchers, casualty lists, unit rosters, and bounty land warrants. From these records you can learn such details as date and place of birth, age at enlistment, occupation, and names of immediate family members. The path you take in your search will depend upon when and where your ancestor served, whether he was regular army or with a volunteer unit, and whether he was an officer or enlisted personnel.

Compiled Military Service Records

For military ancestors who served prior to World War I, compiled military service records, often referred to as CMSRs, are a good place to start. These are basically just what they sound like—an abstract of the available military information on an individual compiled from a variety of service-related records. Compiled military service records were originally begun in 1894 in an effort to reconstruct records of the American army and navy destroyed by fires in 1800 and 1814. The project eventually grew to also cover soldiers serving in *volunteer* units in wars between 1775 and 1902, including not only individuals from the American Revolution and War of 1812, but also those who served in various Indian conflicts, the Mexican Revolution, the American Civil War, the Spanish-American War, the Philippine Insurrection, and the Boxer Rebellion.

A compiled military service record consists of a series of cards with the soldier's name, rank, and unit, along with abstracted information taken from muster rolls, hospital records, pay vouchers, record books, orders, correspondence, and other military records. The cards for each soldier are kept together in an envelope, or jacket, along with any applicable original documents. There are also times when the records of two soldiers with similar names may be mixed within the same envelope, or the record of a single soldier split between two different envelopes (e.g., one envelope for S. Cooper and a second for Silas Cooper). The compiled military service record will generally provide you with your ancestor's rank, unit, the state from which he served, the date enlisted, and the length of service. You may also find the age, residence, a physical description, and date of discharge or death, or indications of other military-related activities such as hospital stays or a court martial.

The National Archives in Washington, D.C., is the official repository for federal military service records of personnel who served in the U.S. Army, Air Force, Navy, Marine Corps, or Coast Guard between the Revolutionary War and about 1912. This includes compiled military service records for Confederate army soldiers. Military service records, including compiled service records, can be ordered online (*www.archives.gov/veterans/ military-service-records/pre-ww-1-records.html*) or by mail using NATF Form 86 (which you can download online). Indexes and/or digitized images of these compiled service records can also be found online:

- Fold3 (*www.fold3.com*), in cooperation with the National Archives, offers subscription-based online access to the compiled military service records of soldiers who served in the American army during the Revolutionary War, as well as for Confederate Civil War soldiers (most of the Confederate records and some records of Union soldiers).
- Ancestry.com (*www.ancestry.com*) features an index to the compiled military service records for the volunteer soldiers who served dur-

ing the War of 1812; index and images for compiled military service records for Revolutionary War soldiers; and indexes and some digitized images of Civil War service records, including those of the U.S. Colored Troops (USCT). Use the Ancestry Card Catalog (*http://search .ancestry.com/search/CardCatalog.aspx*) to locate and search each specific database. Fold3.com is now owned by Ancestry.com, so some indexes on Ancestry.com link to digitized images on Fold3.com. A discount subscription to Fold3 is offered for Ancestry.com subscribers.

- The Civil War Soldiers and Sailors System (CWSS) (*www.nps.gov/ civilwar/soldiers-and-sailors-database.htm*) offers a free index of more than 6 million Civil War Confederate and Union soldiers compiled from the General Index Cards of the compiled military service records at the National Archives. Click on Soldiers or Sailors on the right-hand side to search for a name.

QUESTION

What if I don't know whether I have an ancestor who was in the military?
If you have an ancestor of the right age and at the right time to have served in a military conflict, it doesn't hurt to spend time searching military records—especially given the easy search capabilities of online databases. Just be careful not to assume the individual you've found is your ancestor, especially if you discovered his name in an index, without following up in additional records.

The War Department did not compile military service records for those who served in the regular army. The place to start researching pre-World War I enlisted Army personnel online is a set of helpful records titled U.S. Army, Register of Enlistments, 1798–1914 at Ancestry.com (*http://search.ancestry .com/search/db.aspx?dbid=1198*), digitized from National Archives microfilm publication M233. U.S. Marine Corps Muster Rolls, 1798–1958 (*http://search .ancestry.com/iexec/?htx=List&dbid=1089*) is a collection of regular lists of Marine Corps personnel which also includes some early enlistment details. FamilySearch.org is putting the U.S. Army Register of Enlistments

1798–1914 online, and also has a database of U.S. Navy enlistment records—Naval Enlistment Rendezvous, 1855–1891 (*www.familysearch.org/search/collection/1825347*). Additional information on pre-World War I records available for researching enlisted army personnel, as well as those who served in the navy and Marine Corps, can be found in the article "An Overview of Records at the National Archives Relating to Military Service" (*www.archives.gov/publications/prologue/2002/fall/military-records-overview.html*).

Pensions and Bounty Land Warrants

The men and women who served in the U.S. military during wartime have often been compensated in some extra way for their service. In the case of the Revolutionary War, War of 1812, early Indian Wars, the Mexican War, and the Civil War, the records of these veterans' benefits—pensions and bounty land warrant applications—are perhaps the most valuable resources available for genealogical researchers.

The federal government or state government granted military pensions to disabled and needy veterans, to the widows or dependent orphans of veterans, or to veterans who served for a certain length of time and lived long enough to receive the pension benefits. Pension files are often rich in genealogical information, containing such details as birth date and place, marriages, residence at time of application, property holdings, and names of minor children. Supporting documents, such as discharge papers, testimony from neighbors and fellow soldiers, marriage certificates, physician's reports, and family Bible pages, can sometimes be found included with pension files, especially in cases where the veteran had difficulty proving pension eligibility. These are the thick, juicy files that all genealogists drool over!

ESSENTIAL

If your direct ancestor wasn't involved in the military, or you can't find any records for him, look for the records of brothers, uncles, cousins, and neighbors. These may contain information and testimony that refer to your direct lineage. This is a research technique known as cluster genealogy.

The federal government, and some states, granted free land known as *bounty land* to veterans as an incentive or reward for service in the military. Bounty land warrants were issued from the colonial period until 1858 (for service through 1855), when the program was discontinued, to veterans of the Revolutionary War, War of 1812, and Mexican War. Bounty land was *not* available for Civil War soldiers, although Union veterans were later eligible for special homestead rights. Veterans or their heirs could claim this free bounty land by filing an application, known as a bounty land warrant application. If the application was approved, the individual was given a warrant that he could later exchange for land on which he could settle.

The government set aside certain land districts in the frontier areas where veterans could redeem their warrant for bounty land. Many historians believe that this was designed to lure the battle-trained soldiers and their families into areas where they could serve as a buffer against Indian attacks. Most veterans were too smart to fall for that ploy and instead chose to sell their land warrants to speculators. Therefore, your veteran ancestor may have applied for a bounty land warrant, but never received title to or settled on bounty land.

Many of the early Revolutionary War bounty land application files from 1789 to 1800 were destroyed in a War Department fire. Most of the surviving applications relating to Revolutionary War and War of 1812 service have been combined with the pension files because they contain similar types of information.

An excellent online resource for these records is the Revolutionary War Pensions database at Fold3.com (*http://go.fold3.com/revolutionary-war-pensions*), with both a name index and digitized images reproduced from National Archives microfilm publication M804. This database can also be accessed for free on FamilySearch (*www.familysearch.org/search/collection/1417475*). If your local library subscribes to HeritageQuest Online, its Revolutionary War Pension and Bounty Land Warrant Application Files database includes an index as well as digitized copies of the original handwritten records. This information was taken from the National Archives and Records Administration's (NARA) microfilm M805, which reproduces *selected* portions of the pension and bounty land applications filed by Revolutionary War veterans, or their heirs, between 1800 and 1906. Generally, there are about ten pages or fewer per file of the most genealogically significant documents. If you find an ancestor in the HeritageQuest database, you really should consider accessing the complete file at FamilySearch or Fold3 as well.

FamilySearch.org (*Civil War and Later Pension Files Index*—free) and Fold3.com (*Civil War and Later Veterans Pension Index*—subscription) each host a searchable name index and images of the pension index cards of Union Civil War veterans reproduced from NARA microfilm T-289, *Organization Index to Pension Files of Veterans Who Served Between 1861–1917*, with more than 3 million index entries documenting the pension applications of soldiers, sailors, and their widows. A similar Civil War Pension Index is available on Ancestry.com (*http://search.ancestry.com/search/db.aspx?dbid=4654*), reproduced from NARA microfilm T-288, *General Index to Pension Files, 1861–1934*. It's worth checking both the T-288- and T-289-based indexes, as they each may contain slightly different information.

ESSENTIAL

The descriptive pamphlets for National Archives microfilm publication T-289 and T-288 are available as free PDF download files from NARA and include a list of abbreviations, plus additional information about the records they index. Learn how to locate these and other NARA descriptive pamphlets (DPs) online in the article "Descriptive Pamphlets of the National Archives" (*http://genealogy.about.com/od/basics/a/nara-descriptive-pamphlets.htm*).

The War of 1812 Pension Digitization Project (*www.preservethepensions.org*), a collaboration of the Federation of Genealogical Societies and the National Archives, is digitizing the 180,000 pension files of soldiers who served in the War of 1812, containing a total of 7.2 million pages. The files digitized to date are available online for free at Fold3 (*http://go.fold3.com/1812pensions/*). A search engine query such as *genealogy pension* will turn up additional online sources of military pension records, such as the USGenWeb Archives Pension Project (*www.usgwarchives.org/pensions*).

Copies of military pension claim files for military service from the American Revolution up to just before World War I (1775 to 1912) and bounty land warrant applications for federal military service prior to 1856 can be ordered online from the National Archives (*www.archives.gov/veterans/ military-service-records/pre-ww-1-records.html*), or by mail using the National Archives Trust Fund's NATF Form 85. They will only copy up to 100 pages, however, and it's not at all uncommon for Civil War pension files in particular to run in excess of that, so you may get better results by hiring a professional genealogist to obtain the file in person from the National Archives. It's important to note that the National Archives pensions and bounty land warrants are based on federal (not state or Confederate) service.

Discover Revolutionary and Civil War Ancestors

There's something a bit special and awe-inspiring about having an ancestor who served in the American Revolution or Civil War—knowing that someone you are related to participated in the struggle to win the freedoms you enjoy today. Whether you agree with their reasons for fighting or the side for which they fought, it can be a real source of pride to have ancestors who were willing to fight and die for a cause they so strongly believed in. Learning about these ancestors and their convictions can also help connect you to a very important part of this nation's history in a way that almost nothing else can.

The American Revolution

Whether you're interested in joining a lineage society such as the Daughters of the American Revolution or Sons of the American Revolution, or just want to learn more about possible Revolutionary ancestors, a good place to start your online search is the Genealogical Research System (GRS) of the Daughters of the American Revolution (*www.dar.org*), which can be found in the "Online Research" section under Genealogy (*www.dar.org/ library/online_research.cfm*). The GRS includes a database of Revolutionary Patriots, men and women who have been accepted by the DAR genealogical staff as having contributed to the cause of American independence between 1774 and 1783, as well as other useful databases. If you find your ancestor listed as a Revolutionary Patriot, you can also use the website to order a copy of the most recent DAR application or file for your patriot ancestor.

Next, check out Fold3 (*www.fold3.com/revolutionary-war/*), which provides subscription-based access to a variety of digitized Revolutionary-era records from the National Archives. These include the previously mentioned compiled service records and pension records, as well as Revolutionary War muster rolls and payrolls, final pension payment vouchers, and the papers of the Continental Congress.

A few other excellent online databases for Revolutionary-era research include:

- **American Genealogical-Biographical Index** (*www.ancestry.com*)— This large index, sometimes referred to as the Rider Index for its original creator, Fremont Rider, includes indexes for many Revolutionary War-related publications. It is available as a subscription-based database on Ancestry.com.
- **A Century of Lawmaking for a New Nation** (*http://memory.loc.gov/ ammem/amlaw*)—This special collection in the free online American Memory exhibit of the Library of Congress includes some very interesting Revolutionary War pension claims and petitions for relief, as well as other sources for information on Revolutionary-era individuals. Follow the links to American State Papers and the U.S. Serial Set.

Many Revolutionary War soldiers fought in the state militia, and their records will usually be found among the appropriate state's records, not in the National Archives. Various state archives, historical societies, and other organizations have posted some of their state Revolutionary War records online. Examples include Pennsylvania State Archives' Revolutionary War Military Abstract Card File (*www.digitalarchives.state.pa.us*), Kentucky

Secretary of State Revolutionary War Warrants index (*http://apps.sos .ky.gov/land/military/revwar*), and Revolutionary War Rejected Claims and other databases from the Library of Virginia (*http://lva1.hosted.exlibrisgroup .com/F?RN=765708466*). Do a search in your favorite search engine for *"revolutionary war" [your state]* to find available records and documents. Fold3 and FamilySearch also have some state-level Revolutionary War records online.

A discussion of American Revolution research wouldn't be complete without a reminder that there was another side to the war. You may have ancestors who were Loyalists, or Tories—colonists who remained loyal subjects of the British crown and actively worked to promote the interest of Great Britain during the American Revolution. After the war ended, local officials or neighbors drove many of these Loyalists from their homes, and a majority moved on to resettle in Canada, England, Jamaica, and other British-held regions. The On-line Institute for Advanced Loyalist Studies (*www.royalprovincial.com*) provides an excellent starting point for further research into Loyalist ancestors.

The Civil War

The Civil War marked the most tragic chapter of American history. As with the Revolutionary War, the conflict tore apart families, friendships, and even towns. These divided loyalties mean that you may find you have ancestors that fought on both sides.

If your ancestor was born between about 1805 and 1847, chances are good that he may have fought in the Civil War. Even men in their sixties and boys in their early teens participated. But where did he serve, and for which side? The three most valuable pieces of information necessary for researching a Civil War ancestor are the soldier's name, whether he served for the Confederate or Union army, and the state from which the soldier served. With this information you can determine what types of records are available that might tell you about your ancestor and where he is located. Remember, there were two national governments in effect during those years—the federal government of the United States and the Confederate States of America. Combined with the massive destruction of property, especially in the South, this means that many of the existing records have been left fragmented and scattered among the National Archives, state archives, lineage societies, and other repositories. Plenty of excellent Civil War records do exist; they are just not all in one place. Therefore, the biggest hurdle in Civil War research is often in knowing where to look.

The first step in documenting your ancestor's Civil War service is to search service records and rosters for his name. The previously mentioned Civil War Soldiers and Sailors System (*www.itd.nps.gov/cwss*) is the best place to start. Here you can learn your ancestor's regiment, allegiance, and rank. With this information you can dig further into the database and bring up details on his unit. The subscription-based American Civil War Research Database (*www.civilwardata.com*) is another excellent resource for researching Civil War soldiers.

If you find your ancestor in either the Civil War Soldiers and Sailors database or the American Civil War Research Database, you can often learn more by accessing his complete compiled military service record (CMSR). As discussed earlier, these can be ordered online through the National Archives. Alternatively, Fold3 has digitized many, though not all, of these files and placed them online, where you can access them a bit cheaper, and a lot quicker!

QUESTION

Why aren't Confederate ancestors found in the National Archives? Actually, the National Archives does hold the compiled military service records of Confederate officers and enlisted men, containing information taken from documents captured by Union forces and from Union prison and parole records. Because the Confederate States of America operated as a separate government, however, Confederate pensions and other remunerations were authorized by the individual Confederate or border states, and the records are generally found in the respective state archives.

Once you've confirmed your ancestor's Civil War service, you can often learn further details about him in pension records. If he lived long enough, the chances are good that your Union Civil War ancestor applied for a pension. If not, his widow or dependents likely applied. These federal pension records are available from the National Archives and can be ordered online. As discussed previously, both Ancestry.com and Fold3.com offer subscription-based access to general indexes of these Union pension files. Fold3 also has online a small, growing subset of the complete Civil War Widows' Pension files.

The federal government did not offer pensions to Confederate soldiers until 1959, by which time the majority of Confederate veterans and their widows were deceased. Most Confederate states administered their own pension program, however. The veteran was eligible to apply for a pension to the state in which he lived, regardless of the unit in which he served. Generally, only indigent or disabled Confederate veterans, or their dependents, were eligible for pensions. The majority of these pension records can be found in the appropriate state archives, library, or historical society. Links to available online Confederate Pension Records can be found on About.com *(http://genealogy.about.com/od/civil_war/tp/confederate-pension-records.htm)*.

For ancestors who lived during the Civil War, either soldier or civilian, the following online resources may provide a source of insight into the war's impact on both individuals and the community:

- **The War of the Rebellion: A Compilation of the Official Records of the Union and Confederate Armies**—Commonly referred to as "OR" or "Official Records," this 128-volume set represents the most comprehensive and authoritative reference on Civil War activities, including military engagements, correspondence, orders, and reports. It can be accessed online through multiple sources, including Ohio State University's eHistory reference *(http://ehistory.osu.edu/osu/sources/records/)*.

- **Records of the Southern Claim Commission**—This commission reviewed the claims of Southerners who had furnished stores and supplies, whether voluntarily or involuntarily, for the use of the U.S. Army or Navy during the Civil War. Applicants were required to provide proof of lost property, along with satisfactory evidence of their loyalty to the federal government throughout the war. In support of these requirements, applications often include the testimony of neighbors, and mention family relationships and allegiances. Even if your ancestor never submitted his own claim, he may be mentioned in other claims as a witness or bystander. These records are available online in digitized format on Fold3 (*www.fold3.com/category_27/*).

- **U.S. Civilian Draft Registration Records**—Ancestry.com hosts an online collection (*http://search.ancestry.com/search/db.aspx?dbid=1666*) of over 3.175 million records of men (Union) who registered for the draft under required federal conscription laws in one of four drafts that took place between 1863 and 1865.
- **Confederate Citizens File**—One of the many hundreds of collections contained in National Archives Record Group 109, War Department Collection of Confederate Records, the Confederate Citizens File consists of about 650,000 vouchers that document goods furnished or services rendered by private citizens or firms to the Confederate government. The collection is reproduced online in its entirety as a database and digital images on Fold3 (*www.fold3.com/title_60/ confederate_citizens_file/*).

As with other genealogy records, a good search engine query such as *[your state] "civil war" genealogy* or *[your state] "civil war" records* will turn up a variety of useful databases and resources such as the Roster of Wisconsin Volunteers, War of the Rebellion, 1861–1865 (*www.wisconsinhistory.org/ roster*), and the Texas State Library and Archives Commission index to Confederate Civil War Pension Applications (*www.tsl.state.tx.us/arc/ pensions/index.php*). In addition to service-related records, be sure to search for maps, photos, and published histories, plus prisoner of war, hospital, and other records that may pertain to your ancestor or his unit.

Research Twentieth-Century Conflicts

If you're new to tracing your family tree, you may not yet have gone back far enough to explore the rich records generated by the Civil War and American Revolution. That doesn't mean you can't benefit from military records, however. World Wars I and II, the Korean War, and the Vietnam War all generated records that are useful for genealogical research.

Was He Drafted?

Almost every male U.S. resident between the ages of eighteen and forty-five completed a World War I Draft Registration Card in one of three separate draft registrations conducted in 1917 and 1918. These records include vital information on more than 24 million men—whether native-born, naturalized, or alien—born between about 1873 and 1900. More than 80 percent of the men who registered for the draft never actually ended up serving in the military, so they can be a valuable resource for learning about your nonmilitary ancestors as well.

Each of the registrations used a different form with a slight variation in the questions asked. All three include the individual's full name, home address, date of birth, age in years, occupation, the name and address of his employer, his citizenship status, a physical description, the city/county and state of the local draft board, the date of registration, and the signature of the applicant. The three registrations also included the following additional information:

1. June 5, 1917 (all men between the ages of twenty-one and thirty-one): Additional information included exact place of birth (usually including town), number of dependents, marital status, previous military service, and grounds for exemption.
2. June 5, 1918 (men who reached the age of twenty-one between June 5, 1917, and August 24, 1918): Additional information included exact place of birth, nearest relative's name and address, and father's birthplace.
3. September 12, 1918 (all men aged eighteen to forty-five who hadn't previously registered): No birthplace this time, but did ask for the name and address of the nearest relative.

The original WWI draft registration records are housed at the National Archives–Southeast Region near Atlanta, Georgia. The records have also been microfilmed and can be accessed through the Family History Library. Fully indexed, digitized copies of the original World War I draft registration cards can be accessed online as part of the subscription-based offerings at Ancestry.com, as well as in a free database on FamilySearch. Alternatively, you can request scanned reproductions of the World War I draft registration cards online through the National Archives Order Online service (*www.archives.gov/research/order/*).

World War II draft records also exist, but registration cards from the fourth registration of the seven conducted were the first to be fully available to the public due to privacy restrictions. This fourth registration, often referred to as the "old man's registration," was conducted on April 27, 1942, and registered men who were born on or between April 28, 1877, and February 16, 1897 (ages forty-five to sixty-four), and not already in the military. The original draft cards are held by each state's National Archives regional branch and are also available on microfilm from NARA and/or the Family History Library.

Ancestry.com and Fold3 offer an online, searchable database with digitized images of the currently open WWII draft registration cards, including both the fourth registration for all available states, plus a collection from multiple registrations for men in North Carolina. FamilySearch also hosts the fourth registration of World War II draft card images for free. Unfortunately, the records for the fourth registration in many of the southeastern states were destroyed before they were copied and will never be available. These include Alabama, Florida, Georgia, Kentucky, Mississippi, North Carolina, South Carolina, and Tennessee.

ESSENTIAL

Soldiers, sailors, and marines aren't the only ones with wartime memories. Your family history should also consider the ancestors who lived through the wars as well, not just those who fought. Talk to your living relatives, read firsthand accounts and memoirs, and research the area where your ancestors lived for a firsthand perspective of life during wartime.

As useful as they are for locating information about ancestors who may have served in the military, World War I and World War II draft registration cards do not include any details of actual military service. For those men who did enlist in the military following their registration in either draft, you should turn to military service records for further information.

Request Your Ancestor's Military Service Record

Service records consist of the information that the government collects and keeps on any military personnel. This might include the soldier's enlistment/appointment, duty stations and assignments, training, performance, awards and medals, disciplinary actions, separation, discharge, and retirement. Military service records are available for enlisted men who served in the regular army throughout America's history, as well as discharged and deceased veterans of all services during the twentieth century.

Military records from just before World War I to the present are held in the National Personnel Records Center, Military Personnel Records (NPRC-MPR) in St. Louis, Missouri. Access to many of these records is limited by privacy laws and, as such, they are not available online. Military veterans, and the next of kin of deceased military veterans, can order copies of these records through eVetRecs (*www.archives.gov/veterans/military-service-records/*), an online military personnel records request system.

ALERT

Don't overlook the most obvious source for twentieth-century military information—the memories of your living relatives. Collect those one-of-a-kind war stories and memories from the people who lived them before it's too late. If your military ancestor is already deceased, talk to his sibling, spouse, or children.

Unfortunately, a disastrous fire at the NPRC on July 12, 1973, destroyed an estimated 16 to 18 million of these military personnel files. This includes approximately 80 percent of the U.S. Army personnel records for persons discharged between November 1, 1912, and January 1, 1960, and 75 percent of U.S. Air Force personnel records for persons discharged between September 25, 1947, and January 1, 1964, alphabetically through Hubbard, James E. These records were never duplicated or microfilmed prior to the fire, so there are no surviving copies. The NPRC will attempt to reconstruct a destroyed service record upon the request of a veteran or surviving family member.

Search Conflict-Specific Databases

A number of databases are available online for researching veterans of World War I, World War II, Korea, Vietnam, and other twentieth-century conflicts. One of the largest is the World War II Army Enlistment Records file in NARA's Access to Archival Databases (*http://aad.archives.gov/aad*). This freely searchable database contains information on about 9.2 million men and women who enlisted in the U.S. Army, Enlisted Reserve Corps, and Women's Army Auxiliary Corps during World War II. These records contain a great deal of useful information about the enlistee, including year and place of birth, civilian occupation, marital status, education, and enlistment details. For those who died during World War I, World War II, or the Korean War, the American Battle Monuments Commission (*www.abmc.gov*) maintains a variety of databases of Americans interred overseas, missing in action, or lost at sea.

Bone Up on Military History

Don't end your search with your ancestor's military records. The web really shines as a tool for historical background research, offering easy access to unit histories, battle details, firsthand accounts, photos, timelines, and memoirs. You can picture what military life was like for your ancestor by learning about the battles he participated in and the activities of his unit. Most people aren't lucky enough to have letters or a diary left behind by an ancestor, but the letters and journals of your ancestor's fellow soldiers may offer similar, although less personal, insight. If your ancestor was awarded a medal, buried in a military cemetery, or imprisoned in a POW camp, you can learn about that, too. The Internet can also help you locate interactive maps, historical timelines, and photos of soldiers, ships, planes, and battlegrounds for enhancing your family history.

LINK

A great place to start your search online for conflict- or geographic-specific military resources is genealogy blogger Joe Beine's list of searchable military databases (*www.militaryindexes.com*). The military section of Cyndi's List also links to online military records (*www.cyndislist.com/us/military*) as well as websites devoted to individual regiments or battles.

Regimental and Battle Histories

Reading a history of the regiment or unit in which your ancestor served allows you to more fully appreciate what he experienced—from campaigns and battles to daily life in the trenches. Many regimental histories can be found online, especially for the U.S. Civil War. The Civil War Archive (*www.civilwararchive.com*), for example, includes thousands of regimental histories organized by state, as well as some soldier diaries and other personal history sources for Civil War soldiers. Search the Library of Congress (*www.loc.gov*) to locate published unit histories, or do a search online for the specific unit name, state, and war in which your ancestor was a participant.

Casualty Lists and Military Cemeteries

Casualty and remembrance lists, especially for twentieth-century and later conflicts, are fairly easy to find online with a quick web search, including sites such as the National World War II Memorial Registry (*www.wwiimemorial.com*), State-Level Lists of Fatal Casualties of the Korea War and Vietnam War on the site of the National Archives (*www.archives.gov/research/military/korean-war/casualty-lists/*), and a 34,000-plus name Virginia Military Dead database (*www.lva.virginia.gov/public/guides/vmd*) from the Library of Virginia. Major genealogy database sites, such as Ancestry.com and Fold3, also include such lists.

Military Heritage Societies

Many people think of joining a military heritage society such as Daughters of the American Revolution (*www.dar.org*), Sons of Confederate Veterans (*www.scv.org*), and General Society of the War of 1812 (*www*

.societyofthewarof1812.org) only after they have documented their military ancestor, but these organizations also serve as an excellent repository of knowledge to help you during the search process as well. Use Cyndi's List of Lineage Societies and Groups (*www.cyndislist.com/societies/lineage*) to find one which may fit with your military ancestor, and check out their website to see if they have a library, online databases, some type of research service, or even a forum or mailing list where you can ask questions of society members.

Military Medals, Ribbons, and Insignia

Online award databases and historical newspaper accounts are the best places to start your search for information on your ancestor's military awards. Home of Heroes (*www.homeofheroes.com*) is a good online starting point for identifying an unknown military ribbon or medal worn by your ancestor. Full-text Medal of Honor citations are available online courtesy of the U.S. Army Center of Military History (*www.history.army.mil/moh.html*). The Pennsylvania State Archives (*www.digitalarchives.state.pa.us/archive.asp*) features a database of World War I medal applications. Search online historical newspapers from the time period your ancestor served for award mentions as well.

CHAPTER 10

A Nation of Immigrants

Virtually all Americans are descended from immigrants. Some arrived via the Bering Strait during prehistoric times. Europeans, mostly English, came during the seventeenth and eighteenth centuries to colonize and settle the rich new land. Still others fled famine and political unrest in northern and western Europe. More than 500,000 were brought unwillingly as slaves between 1619 and 1808. Millions more arrived by foot, car, bus, train, ship, and plane from all over the globe. All told, more than 50 million immigrants have been welcomed to the United States, so at some point your family tree will branch out beyond America's shores.

Find the Birthplace of Your Immigrant Ancestor

One of the biggest challenges in tracing your family history is locating information about immigrant ancestors. Because most foreign records are kept at the town or village level, discovering the name of your immigrant's town, county, or parish of origin is an important goal. Without this information, it will be very difficult to expand your research to your ancestor's native country.

Begin by learning as much as you can about that person. Talk to living family members and search through family possessions or histories for evidence of the family's origins. Are there any marriage records, death certificates, naturalization certificates, photographs, funeral cards, newspaper clippings, military records, or letters from relatives back in the old country? Was the family surname changed at some point in the past? What religion did the family practice and/or what church did they attend? Were there friends or neighbors known to be from the same area? Are there any other clues that family members can think of that may point to the family's origins?

If that doesn't provide the information you're looking for, turn your search to public records, including vital, tax, census, land, military, and probate records. Begin with your immigrant ancestor's death. Death certificates, probate records, obituaries, and tombstones may indicate a birthplace or, at least, a country of origin. If your ancestor died after about 1962, try a search in the Social Security Death Index. With the information from the index, you can order a copy of the application he filled out when he applied for a social security card. These forms almost always give place of birth and names of parents.

After that, a good place to search for information on immigrant ancestors is in the federal census schedules. Begin with the most recent census in which your ancestor appeared and work your way back to 1850, or as far as you can. The 1900, 1910, 1920, and 1930 censuses each indicate the person's year of immigration to the United States and naturalization status ("Al" for alien, "Pa" for "first papers," and "Na" for naturalized). These may help lead to passenger manifests or naturalization records for your immigrant ancestor. The 1850 to 1940 censuses indicate the person's state or country of birth, which can help narrow down your search. The 1880 to 1930 censuses also indicate the parents' birthplaces; the 1940 census asked this question of only about 5 percent of the population. Sometimes you get lucky and find a census taker who writes in the town or county as well!

With the information you glean from census records you can often begin a search for your immigrant ancestor in passenger lists and naturalization records. Early naturalization and passenger records generally only provide the country of birth, but more recent naturalization records and passenger records (after about 1906) will usually indicate the town of birth as well.

ALERT

Expect inconsistencies in place of origin. Constantly shifting political and geographical boundaries in Eastern Europe, for example, may have led to various countries being recorded as the birthplace of your ancestor. It's also not uncommon for immigrants from small villages to say they hailed from a better-known town or city in the vicinity. Investigate multiple sources that list birthplace for verification, if possible, including records for collateral relatives who also immigrated to America.

Plunge Into Passenger Lists

Few achievements in family history research are as fulfilling as discovering your ancestor's name on a passenger list—often the first tangible evidence of his or her existence in America. If you've done your research on your immigrant ancestor, locating the actual manifest may tell you nothing new. But just seeing her name listed alongside those of her fellow passengers, and identifying the name of the ship she came over on, is a satisfying experience. And sometimes, especially with twentieth-century immigrants, the passenger list may provide that one clue you need to untangle your immigrant ancestor's story.

Most immigrants to the United States enter through a port city or border-crossing checkpoint. If they entered legally and under normal circumstances, some type of paperwork was generally completed to document their entry. The content and thoroughness of this information varies by time period, and the immigration records that were generated can be classified into several broad categories.

Passenger Arrivals Prior to 1820

From early colonial times through 1819, documentation of passenger arrivals was under the jurisdiction of the colonies (and later, states). The primary concern of these entities was the taxation of goods, not the transport of passengers. Ships' captains were not always required to maintain passenger lists. Documentation of passengers from this time period may come from a variety of sources, including: (1) a listing on the ship's cargo manifest, (2) notation of passengers in the ship's log, (3) publication of passenger arrivals in the local newspaper, and (4) lists created upon departure from the country of origin. In addition, names of ship passengers may be noted in private journals, in the archives of immigrant-sponsoring societies or organizations, or even attached to medical reports for ships quarantined due to onboard disease.

Pennsylvania offers one notable exception to the lack of required passenger documentation prior to 1820. Beginning in 1727, Pennsylvania required that all non-British immigrants be identified and take an oath of allegiance. Generally only adult male passengers over the age of sixteen were recorded, although some of the later lists also include women and children. These early Pennsylvania lists, totaling about 65,000 passengers of primarily German and Swiss decent, were originally compiled in 1962 by Ralph B. Strassburger and William J. Hinke. The three-volume series of books titled Pennsylvania German Pioneers has since been reprinted. Some of the passenger lists from this series have been transcribed and made available online at Pennsylvania German Pioneers Passenger Lists (*http://freepages.genealogy.rootsweb.com/~pagermanpioneers*). Ancestry .com offers a searchable database of the entire series as part of its U.S. subscription package.

There is no central repository for pre-1820 passenger records, and many of them have been lost or destroyed. Those that remain are scattered in libraries, historical societies, archives, museums, and private hands. The majority of the known pre-1820 records have been published in books and journals. Two excellent bibliographic reference works detail many of these pre-1820 passenger records: Harold Lancour's *A bibliography of ship passenger lists, 1538–1825*, third edition, and P. William Filby's *Passenger and Immigration Lists Bibliography, 1538–1900*, second edition.

William Filby has also indexed many of these published pre-1820 passenger lists in his *Passenger and Immigration Lists Index*. This work, originally published in three volumes and supplemented annually, names about 2.25 million pre-1820 immigrants. It can be consulted in many major libraries and is also available online as part of the Immigration Collection at the subscription site Ancestry.com. Additional sources for online research of pre-1820 passenger lists can be found in genealogist and blogger Joe Beine's bibliography of books, CD-ROMs, and online databases for lists of U.S. passenger arrivals before 1820 (*www.germanroots.com/1820.html*).

Another online resource for early passenger lists is GenealogyBank.com. This subscription-based site also offers a free list of passengers who arrived in the United States from October 1, 1819, to September 30, 1820 (*www .genealogybank.com/free*), covering arrivals at thirty-four ports in fourteen states and the District of Columbia.

QUESTION

Could my ancestor's name have been changed at Ellis Island?
Many immigrants arriving in America did ultimately change their names, to avoid prejudice or to better assimilate into society. This name change most likely did not occur upon their arrival in the United States, however. It wasn't the job of Ellis Island and other port officials to write down names. Instead, they checked the immigrant's paperwork against the passenger list created by the shipping company at the port of departure, not the port of arrival.

Customs Passenger Lists, 1820–1891

The federal government did not begin keeping a record of passenger arrivals until 1820, after Congress passed the Steerage Act of 1819. This act regulated the transport of passengers from foreign ports to the United States and required ships' captains to submit a list of their ship's passengers to the customs collector at the port of entry. From January 1, 1820, to approximately 1891, these passenger lists were kept by the U.S. Customs Service and are thus often referred to as customs lists or customs passenger manifests. They generally provide a minimum amount of information on the immigrant, including:

- Name of the ship and its master
- Port of embarkation
- Date and port of arrival
- Passenger's name
- Passenger's age
- Passenger's gender
- Passenger's occupation
- Passenger's nationality

The U.S. Immigration Service Assumes Control in 1891

The number of immigrants entering the United States grew so quickly that Congress passed the first federal law regulating immigration in 1882. Nine years later, the Immigration Act of 1891 moved jurisdiction of the immigration process to the federal government, under the new Superintendent of Immigration (which became the Bureau of Immigration and Naturalization in 1906). This office was responsible for processing, admitting, and rejecting all immigrants seeking admission to the United States and for implementing national immigration policy.

As part of this implementation, "immigrant inspectors" were stationed at major American ports of entry for the purpose of collecting and reviewing the arrival manifests, referred to as immigration manifests or immigration passenger lists. These lists begin about 1891 and continue until 1957, the exception being the port of Philadelphia, whose immigration passenger lists began in 1882. Although "Customs Passenger Lists" became "Immigration Passenger Lists," the information included on the two lists is virtually identical until 1893. Beginning that year, the federal government issued new standard forms with sixteen additional columns of information. Later revisions added even more information. These post-1892 passenger lists include the same information found on the earlier lists, along with the following additional details:

- Marital status
- Last town of residence
- Final destination in the United States, often including name of relative or friend

- Whether the passenger could read and write
- Amount of money the passenger was carrying
- Passenger's state of health
- Race (from 1903)
- Place of birth (from 1906)
- Personal description (from 1906)
- Name and address of nearest friend or relative in the old country (from 1907)

As with almost any rule, there are a few exceptions. One French immigrant's arrival in the United States is recorded on a 1946 passenger list, but the list itself provides none of the information you might expect for an immigrant at that time—listing only her name, age, and an application number. This is because she is listed along with more than 800 other women and their children on that ship as "applying for admission to the United States under the Act of December 28, 1945." The War Brides Act, which helped facilitate admission into the United States for foreign-born spouses of U.S. soldiers who married overseas during World War II, is just one of many such exceptions that may impact the information you'll find recorded on a passenger list. For a better understanding of the different types of laws that affected immigration into the United States, and the records these created, see "Timeline of Major U.S. Immigration & Citizenship Laws" on About.com (*http://genealogy.about.com/od/immigration/a/Timeline-Of-US-Immigration-Naturalization-Acts.htm*).

Keep in mind as you research that passenger records are not always available for all ports during all time periods. The port of Galveston, Texas, for example, lost the majority of its immigration records from the years 1871 to 1894 in the great Galveston hurricane of 1900. The National Archives holds a few extant passenger lists for San Francisco, but the official lists for that port were destroyed by fire in 1851 and 1940. Don't let this keep you from searching, however! Sometimes you'll find your ancestor immigrating through a port other than the one you expect, or you may find an alternate resource (such as an outbound passenger list from the departure city) that lists your ancestor. Online immigration indexes make searching much easier than it used to be, often allowing you to search across records of multiple ports in one step.

Locate Passenger Records Online

The National Archives is the primary repository for immigration records for passengers arriving from foreign ports between approximately 1820 and 1982. Microfilm copies of passenger lists up to about 1960 are available at the National Archives building in Washington, D.C. Some are also available at NARA's regional branch facilities, and most of the microfilms can be borrowed through your local Family History Center. Until the Internet became prevalent, this was the only feasible method for doing research in passenger lists. Now, however, the majority of U.S. passenger records prior to about 1960 are also available for online research through a variety of sources.

ALERT

Be sure when looking at online ship passenger manifests to click through to the next page in case the passenger information extends over more than one page (which it does for most post-1892 manifests). Check the last few pages of the manifest as well—you may find a list of individuals who died during the voyage, or who were detained for health or other reasons, such as "likely to become a public charge" (fairly common for young children or women traveling solo with no visible means of support).

One of the first large collections of passenger records to go online was the Ellis Island database (*www.ellisislandrecords.org*), which includes transcripts and digital images for arrivals at Ellis Island and the port of New York between 1892 and 1924. The immigration passenger lists prior to 1897 for the port of New York were actually destroyed in an 1897 fire at Ellis Island, but the customs passenger lists that were also kept for those years do survive and are included in the Ellis Island database. This free, searchable database includes approximately 22 million total records, along with ship photos and stories of the immigrant experience.

The "other" major New York port, Castle Garden, served as America's first official immigrant receiving station from 1855 through 1890, before being succeeded by Ellis Island in 1892. The Castle Garden website (*www.castlegarden.org*) offers a free searchable database of 11 million of the passengers who arrived at Castle Garden. These are transcriptions only, but Ancestry.com subscribers can access digital copies of the Castle Garden manifests.

The subscription-based U.S. Immigration Collection at Ancestry.com (*www.ancestry.com/immigration*) is the largest online source for passenger lists, including digital copies of virtually all readily available U.S. passenger lists from 1820 to 1960, as well as an index to the more than 75 million passenger names and 26 million crew names found on these lists. Nearly 80 percent of these records come from the receiving stations at the port of New York—primarily Ellis Island (including arrivals during years not included in the free Ellis Island database). The major ports of Boston, San Francisco, New Orleans, Philadelphia, and Baltimore are also represented in this collection, along with more than 100 other U.S. ports of arrival. The records are available only to subscribers, or through a free trial offer.

ESSENTIAL

Passenger lists often include a variety of handwritten annotations—numbers, symbols, crossed-out names, and so on—that were added by immigration officials at the time of the ship's arrival, or later as part of a verification check. Sometimes these annotations may provide a clue to additional records, such as a naturalization certificate or warrant of arrest. Find explanations of these annotations online in "A Guide to Interpreting Passenger List Annotations" hosted at Jewish-Gen (*www.jewishgen.org/infofiles/manifests*).

Some of the other immigration databases and passenger lists that can be found online include:

- **FamilySearch** (*www.familysearch.org*)—This growing collection of free immigration and naturalization records includes passenger lists from a number of U.S. ports. While some are indexed, many of the digital images are browse-only.
- **Immigrant Ship Transcribers Guild** (*www.immigrantships.net*)—This site offers free access to more than 14,000 individual passenger manifests

transcribed by volunteers. Click on the volume numbers and special lists links to view and search the available records.

- **National Archives** (*http://aad.archives.gov/aad*)—The Access to Archival Databases (AAD) includes in its Passenger Lists a searchable database titled "Passengers Who Arrived at the Port of New York During the Irish Famine," documenting primarily Irish immigrant arrivals during the period January 12, 1846, to December 31, 1851. About 70 percent of the passenger records list Ireland as the native country.

- **Galveston Immigration Database** (*www.galvestonhistory.org/Galveston_Immigration_Database.asp*)—More than 130,000 passengers who disembarked at the port of Galveston between 1846 and 1948 are included in this free, searchable database. Not included are arrivals between the years 1871 and 1894, along with a few during 1900 because of the destruction of records in the 1900 hurricane.

- **Olive Tree Genealogy** (*www.olivetreegenealogy.com/ships*)—Lorine McGinnis Schulze has transcribed a number of early customs and passenger lists and also organizes links to immigration records on other free and subscription sites.

- **Immigrant Servants Database** (*www.pricegen.com/about immigrantservants*)—A free online database of information on indentured servants, redemptioners (immigrants that gained passage to America through indentured servitude), and transported convicts who settled south of New England between 1607 and 1820.

Many individuals who were ultimately bound for the United States first immigrated into Canada. There are many immigration lists and databases available online for entry into Canadian ports, including those at Library and Archives Canada (*www.collectionscanada.gc.ca/databases/*) and subscription site Ancestry.com (*http://search.ancestry.ca/search/db.aspx?dbid=1263*).

Emigration (Outbound) Lists

Your ancestor most likely also left records behind in the old country when he came to the United States. These emigrant records created in the country of departure might include outbound passenger lists, visa or passport applications, or police emigrant records.

Britain: Outbound Passenger Lists 1890–1960

(www.findmypast.co.uk)

The National Archives (UK) in association with Findmypast.co.uk has created a searchable database featuring passenger lists for long-distance ships departing the British Isles between 1890 and 1960. Images of the passenger lists are available to download, view, save, and print. Searching is free; transcriptions and images of the passengers lists are available on a pay-per-view basis.

Hamburg Passenger Lists 1850–1934

(www.ancestry.com)

Between 1850 and 1939, Hamburg, Germany, served as the "Gateway to the World" for about 5 million European emigrants. An index to the existing Hamburg lists from 1890 to 1912 was initially created and placed online by the Hamburg State Archives, but was later moved to the subscription-based site Ancestry.com. Ancestry's immigration collection also includes digitized copies of the passenger lists for ships that departed from Hamburg from 1850 to 1934 (with a gap from 1915 to 1919 due to World War I).

Bremen Passenger Lists 1920–1939

(www.bremen-passengerlists.de)

The majority of the passenger lists from the port of Bremen, Germany, were lost during World War II. This database offers access to the 3,017 passenger records that survived.

Danish Emigration Archives

(www.emiarch.dk)

Emigration lists compiled by the Copenhagen Police from 1869 to 1908 have been transcribed and included in this free, searchable database. Information includes the name, last residence, age, year of emigration, and first destination of the emigrant from Denmark.

Norwegian Emigration Lists

(http://digitalarkivet.uib.no)

Click on English and then select "Emigrants" in the Shortcuts list to find data on emigrants that National Archives of Norway extracted from ships' lists, police emigration records, and other sources, including digital images. Norway Heritage (*www.norwayheritage.com*) is another excellent source for information on emigrants from Norway.

Border-Crossing Records—Canada and Mexico

Keeping records on alien arrivals at U.S. land borders was not required by early immigration acts. It wasn't until 1895 for Canada and about 1906 for Mexico that immigration authorities began to collect information on immigrants arriving in this manner. Separate card manifests were created for each individual that contain virtually the same information as that collected on a traditional ship passenger arrival manifest. These border-crossing records have been microfilmed and can be requested through any Family History Center. Online, Ancestry.com has an index and images of the records of aliens and citizens crossing into the United States from Canada via various ports of entry along the U.S.-Canadian border between 1895 and 1956.

The National Archives and Records Administration has processed microfilmed immigration records for individuals who crossed the U.S.-Mexican border between about 1895 and 1964 at land border ports in Arizona, California, New Mexico, and Texas. These are available for research through National Archives locations. Digital images of these records, along with a searchable index, are available online to subscribers at Ancestry.com.

LINK

No discussion of immigration research on the web is complete without mentioning Steve Morse and his One-Step search tools. These search forms (*www.stevemorse.org*) provide powerful interfaces for searching popular existing genealogical databases, including major immigration and naturalization databases such as Ellis Island, Castle Garden, and the immigration databases at Ancestry.com.

Naturalization Records

Naturalization is the legal procedure by which an alien becomes a citizen of a country. Every nation has different rules that govern these requirements for citizenship. The records generated by the naturalization process can help you learn key information about your immigrant ancestor, including the date and place of birth, ship, and port of arrival. How much you can learn, however, will depend upon when and where the naturalization took place.

Congress passed the first law regulating naturalization in 1790. As a general rule, naturalization was a three-step process that took several years and generated a number of different documents:

1. First, the prospective citizen filed a declaration of intent, also referred to as first papers, to become a U.S. citizen, in which she renounced allegiance to foreign sovereignties. The immigrant signs this document.
2. Following a prescribed waiting period—generally two to five years—the immigrant could petition a federal court for formal citizenship. This did not have to occur in the same court in which she filed her declaration of intent. The application completed by the individual in this step is called the petition for naturalization.
3. After the petition was granted and the immigrant made the oath of allegiance, a formal certificate of citizenship was issued to the petitioner.

Typically, the declaration provides more genealogically useful information than the petition. Prior to September 26, 1906, the declaration generally includes the name, country (but not town) of birth or allegiance, the date of the application, and the signature (if the individual being naturalized could write). Many included additional information, but the content varied dramatically from county to county, state to state, and year to year. Naturalizations after September 26, 1906, were handled on standardized forms and include more detailed information, such as the town of birth and the port and date of arrival.

As you can see, September 26, 1906, is a key date for naturalization research. Copies of all naturalizations after that date were forwarded to the newly formed U.S. Bureau of Naturalization for examination and are presently in the custody of U.S. Citizenship and Immigration Services (USCIS) (*www.uscis.gov*), which makes them easy to locate when you don't know where your ancestor was naturalized. Those more than fifty years old can be ordered online through the USCIS Genealogy Service (select "History & Genealogy" from the Services section of the left-hand navigation menu). These naturalization certificate files, known as C-files, generally contain a copy of the declaration of intent (to 1952), the petition for naturalization, and the certificate of naturalization. Occasionally, C-files also contain additional documents or correspondence.

ALERT

For detailed assistance in navigating the maze of available passenger records and locations, turn to the book *They Came in Ships: Finding Your Immigrant Ancestor's Arrival Record*, third edition, by genealogist John P. Colletta, PhD. *They Became Americans: Finding Naturalization Records and Ethnic Origins* by Loretto D. Szucs suggests a variety of ways to find naturalization records, as well as alternative sources for finding immigrant origins, and includes scores of document examples.

Prior to September 26, 1906, an alien could be naturalized in any court of record—including courts at the local, county, state, or federal level—and the naturalization documents are usually found maintained among the court's records. Often it was a matter of the alien choosing to travel to the most conveniently located court with the authority to naturalize, so you may want to begin your search by identifying the courts closest to the place your ancestor lived at the approximate time she was naturalized. Remember, the approximate year of naturalization can be found on the 1920 census if your ancestor was living at that time.

Some naturalization indexes and records can be found online. Fold3 is an excellent source, with digitized indexes and naturalization records for Southern California, Louisiana, Maryland, Massachusetts, New York, and Pennsylvania. FamilySearch has digitized images of naturalization records and some indexes for over a dozen U.S. states including California, Delaware, Illinois, Louisiana, Maine, Maryland, Minnesota, Missouri, New Jersey, New York, Ohio, Pennsylvania, South Dakota, and Texas, plus selected naturalizations for the New England states. Limit your search to the "Migration and Naturalization" collection and "United States" to see and search all available collections. Ancestry.com has many digitized naturalization records as well. For naturalization records found on various archives and personal sites, Joe Beine comes to the rescue with his list of Online Searchable Naturalization Indexes and Records (*www.germanroots.com/naturalization.html*).

Were They Eligible, or an Exception?

During certain points in American history, a variety of men, women, and children either were eligible to skip a few steps in the naturalization process or were granted automatic citizenship based on eligibility. Minor children, for example, were automatically granted citizenship upon the naturalization of their father. For a time (1855–1922), a woman could also achieve automatic citizenship either by marrying a citizen or upon the naturalization of her husband. Conversely, between 1907 and 1922, a female American citizen could lose her citizenship by marrying a man who was a foreign national, even if she never left the United States. From 1824 to 1906, minors who had lived in the United States at least five years before their twenty-third birthday (including those whose parents were not naturalized) were able to skip the declaration step, as were individuals who served in the U.S. armies (Union forces) during the Civil War.

Racial requirements also affected eligibility for naturalization as a U.S. citizen. The naturalization process was first opened to people of African descent on July 14, 1870. Native Americans born outside the United States were barred from citizenship on racial grounds until 1940. The Chinese were the first Asians to gain the right to naturalization, in 1943; most had to wait until 1952, when the racial requirement was stricken from U.S. immigration law.

Not All Aliens Were Naturalized

Aliens living in the United States were not required to become citizens, and during the nineteenth century, it really gained them little other than the right to vote. Alien residents could legally buy and sell property, hold a job, and get married without citizenship status. For this reason, many nineteenth- and early-twentieth-century immigrants—at least 25 percent according to answers recorded in the 1890 through 1930 censuses—lived most of their lives in the United States as aliens and either never began or never completed the process of naturalization.

If census or other records lead you to believe that your ancestor never pursued naturalization, don't despair. Alien registration and visa records are often similarly rich in genealogical details. Information was collected on noncitizen residents of the United States at various points during American history, including special wartime registrations of alien citizens of "enemy" countries and a nationwide registration effort in the 1940s. Beginning in 1924, aliens arriving in the United States were required to apply for immigrant visas, which offer yet another source for information on foreign-born residents.

The Immigration Act of 1924 prompted a major change in U.S. immigration. Beginning July 1 of that year, everyone arriving at a U.S. port of entry was required to present some type of entry document. This might include a birth record or naturalization certificate for U.S. citizens, a re-entry permit for alien residents of the United States, or an immigrant visa or other paperwork for noncitizens. Prospective immigrants wishing to settle in the United States were required to apply for an immigrant visa at a U.S. embassy abroad. Those traveling to the United States for a temporary purpose, such as a visit or to attend school, applied for a nonimmigrant visa.

ESSENTIAL

U.S. Citizenship and Immigration Services (USCIS) (*www.uscis.gov*) holds most of the twentieth-century records discussed in this chapter, including naturalization files (after 1906), immigrant visa files, alien registration forms, and alien files. Copies of these records can be requested for your deceased relatives through their fee-based Genealogy Program, although most records after 1956 are not eligible.

Fears of unknown enemies living within the United States prompted registration of resident aliens during wartime. These enemy alien registration records covered aliens who were living in the United States and were citizens of a country against which the United States had declared war.

The first such large-scale effort was driven by World War I, when from November 1917 to April 1918 all resident, non-naturalized "enemy" aliens, including their American-born wives, if applicable, were required to register with the U.S. Marshal in their county of residence as a national security measure. These alien registration forms documented citizens of the German empire living in the United States, including the date and ship of arrival, children's names and birth dates, parents' names and address, whether the alien was sympathetic to the enemy, names of relatives serving in the enemy forces, occupation and employer, a physical description, and a photograph and full set of fingerprints.

The majority of the World War I enemy alien records were destroyed in the 1920s by authority of Congress, but state and/or local copies of records for Kansas, Minnesota, Missouri, and the Phoenix, Arizona, area, as well as a few scattered other registrations, still survive. Selected records can be found online, such as this index to Enemy Alien Registration Affidavits, 1917–1921, of Kansas (*http://skyways.lib.ks.us/genweb/kcgs/alienbyco.htm*).

The Alien Registration Act of 1940 required all alien residents age fourteen and older to register with the U.S. government and be fingerprinted. Aliens entering the country registered as they applied for admission. This alien registration requirement applied to all aliens over the age of fourteen, regardless of their nationality and immigration status. Millions of the aliens who registered had already lived in the United States for many years.

Alien registrations completed between July 1940 and April 1944 were microfilmed and placed in the custody of U.S. Citizenship and Immigration Services. These records are searchable by name, date of birth, and place of birth, and copies may be obtained through the USCIS Genealogy Program.

Ethnic Research

Ethnic heritage is more than just a source of pride. It also offers alternative research strategies and resources for tracing your family tree. Different ethnic groups, both in the United States and abroad, preserve and maintain a variety of records of interest to genealogists. If you take time to become familiar with and explore these resources, you may learn something new about your own family heritage.

ALERT

Don't get too caught up in thinking of certain records or record groups as only ethnicity-specific. Your ancestors did not live in isolation and are likely to appear in record groups based on their locality or associations, no matter their race, ethnicity, or religious preference. Non-Chinese individuals are found throughout Chinese Exclusion Act case files, for example, providing testimony in the cases of their Chinese neighbors.

A variety of societies and organizations have been formed to collect, disseminate, and preserve the records and heritage of specific ethnic groups. These groups can often point you to specific records of interest for researching your ethnic ancestors. To locate such societies, look through the comprehensive directory of the Federation of Genealogical Societies Society Hall (*www.fgs.org/cstm_societyHall.php*).

Whether you're researching African American, Chinese, French-Canadian, Japanese, Jewish, Irish, Hispanic, or Native American ancestry, a variety of specialized databases relating to most ethnic or religious groups can be found online. Examples of excellent starting points include AfriGeneas (*www.afrigeneas.org*) for African American research and JewishGen (*www.jewishgen.org*) for individuals tracing their Jewish heritage. The National Archives maintains an excellent list of links to major websites for ethnic genealogy research (*www.archives.gov/research/topics/ethnic-heritage.html*), as does Cyndi's List (*www.cyndislist.com/categories/*). Specialized research guides and databases can also be found through your favorite search engine with search phrases such as *african american genealogy databases* or *chinese immigration history us.*

Put It Into Practice

Let's say we want to learn something about an old relative named William Park. William Park, a Philadelphia resident, was born in Ireland according to U.S. census and other records. The next step is to learn when he arrived in the United States, and the town or county of origin in Ireland. The best place is to begin by examining the U.S. census records, specifically the 1920 census since it asks for both the year of immigration and the year of naturalization. In William's case, the 1920 census gives his year of immigration as 1888 and the year of naturalization as 1895. The 1900 census also lists 1888 as the year he immigrated, although in 1910 he states it was in 1891. Still, that's only three years off, so it's a reasonable time frame in which you can search.

A search for *William Park* with an arrival year of *1888* and *Ireland* as the place of origin turns up a New York passenger manifest entry for a William Park of the right age, arriving on the *Ethiopia* in New York harbor on 24 April 1888. There is little detail on this passenger list to prove it is the correct William Park, although it is a good possibility.

Family papers uncovered a passport for William Park, so the next step is to search the U.S. Passport Application records online at Ancestry

.com. A search for *william park* born *1868 +/– 2* years with a residence of *philadelphia* quickly turns up his application for a U.S. passport in 1920. The document provides an exact date of birth (although the year varies from that given in other records by as much as five years) and that he was born in Donegal, Ireland. It also states his wife's name (Jane) and her date of birth (26 Oct 1870), his father's name (Robert Park), and that William arrived in the United States on a ship sailing from Londonderry on 12 April 1888 (yes, this is the *Ethiopia*, providing confirmation that the right passenger arrival record was found). The application also gives the address where he was residing in 1920, his occupation (watchman), a physical description, and a photo of William and his wife Jane. What a great bunch of clues!

Because a passport application generally indicates overseas travel, another search for passenger records is in order. A search for William Park in Ancestry.com's passenger arrival records for 1920 turns up a match on the S.S. *Haverford* that sailed from Liverpool, England, on 13 August 1920, arriving at the port of Philadelphia on August 26. William and Jane Park are listed as passengers on page eighteen, with helpful information on their naturalization status; William Park was naturalized in the Court of Common Pleas, Philadelphia, in 1895, and his wife Jane Park is listed as naturalized "by marriage." Because they are U.S. citizens, little other information is provided outside of their ages and permanent residence.

Since the ship departed from Londonderry, England, it is likely that FindMyPast (*www.findmypast.co.uk/passengerListPersonSearchStart.action*) will have a copy of the corresponding outbound passenger list for the *Haverford*, created as the ship departed England. Sure enough, they do—and it includes a very helpful piece of information, listing their address in Ireland as "C/O William Henry, Montober, Cookstown, Co. Tyrone, Ireland." Since William's wife is Jane Henry, this is likely the name and address of a relative they were visiting.

Additional searches of both Ancestry.com and FindMyPast.com for William Park (just to be sure nothing was missed) turned up another visit to Ireland in 1935, with a return on the *Caledonia* on 25 July 1935. The outbound list is especially helpful, giving the last address in the United Kingdom as "Devlinmore, Carrigart, Co. Donegal." Since it is known from previous research that William Park came from County Donegal, this provides a clue for further research.

The 1920 census says that William Park was naturalized in 1895 and he was a lifelong Philadelphia resident, so a stop at Fold3 is a next good step as the site has digitized naturalization records for Pennsylvania. Unfortunately, no online naturalization record was found for William Park, most likely because he was naturalized in the Philadelphia Court of Common Pleas and Fold3's PA naturalization records are from the U.S. Circuit Court. He does, however, appear as a witness on several other naturalization applications, including one for a Dell Park. Dill Park (the record was misindexed as "Dell") turns out to be living at the same address as William Park, and William Park is listed as a watchman—which matches the occupation he gave in census records. Looks like this might be a brother, or possibly a cousin, based on the birth year. More clues for you to pursue!

CHAPTER 11

Reach Out to Others

Discovering your roots can be a very personal journey, but it isn't something you'll easily accomplish alone. This is where the Internet truly offers an advantage for family history research, allowing you to easily connect and collaborate with other researchers. You can learn from and exchange data with others looking for similar information, discover previously unknown relatives, benefit from the experience and knowledge of others, or get help from individuals with access to records in far-off places. It's also really nice just to interact with other genealogists who share the same passion for family history that you do!

Make the Most of Boards and Lists

One of the easiest ways to connect with other researchers who may have information on your family is through genealogy-specific message boards and mailing lists. They serve as a prominent means of communication among family historians on the Internet and allow for a tremendous amount of research sharing. Best of all, they're free and convenient. Most even allow you to search through archived postings, and some offer e-mail notification when a new query is posted that matches your surname or region of interest.

Join a Genealogy Mailing List

You can learn a lot by joining a mailing list focused on the surname, topic, or region on which your research is focused. Subscribing is as simple as sending an e-mail to the list administrator. Once you've joined, you'll receive copies of all e-mails sent to the list by other subscribing members and can send your own messages that will be received by everyone on the list.

ESSENTIAL

A free Gmail e-mail account (*www.gmail.com*) is a good option for subscribing to mailing lists because Gmail elegantly combines all replies to a specific e-mail or topic into a single thread, or "conversation." The original e-mail and all replies are combined on one page, allowing lengthy mailing list conversations to take up only one line in your inbox. And when a conversation thread just keeps on going, Gmail even offers a mute button.

Most genealogy mailing lists offer two subscription modes:

- **List mode**—You'll receive each message posted to the mailing list individually as it is sent (or after it is approved by the list moderator).
- **Digest mode**—You'll receive periodic e-mails (usually daily) with several mailing list messages appended together. This can be a great method for reducing clutter in your inbox, but this mode can make it harder to follow a specific conversation.

After you subscribe, you'll usually receive a welcome e-mail within a few hours. Be sure to save this e-mail, as it will generally include important information on list rules and how to unsubscribe.

No matter what your genealogy research interest, there is probably a mailing list that applies—from individual surnames (such as CRISP) to research in specific counties or areas (such as the very active Bristol_and_Somerset-L mailing list at RootsWeb) or topics that you might want to stay on top of (such as genealogy DNA). The vast majority of genealogy-related mailing lists (more than 30,000) are hosted through RootsWeb (*http://lists.rootsweb.com*) on topics such as surnames and places, immigration, religion, prisons, and heraldry. Check out GEN-NEWBIE for beginner-level help on anything from research to software. If you're a more advanced researcher, there are plenty of options for you as well, including the ADVANCED-RESEARCH list and TRANSITIONAL-GENEALOGISTS-FORUM list. Alternatively, you can use your favorite search engine to search for a mailing list on a particular topic, such as *genealogy "mailing list" "pitt county" nc*.

ALERT

Genealogy mailing lists are similar to a community or neighborhood in that they reflect the personalities of their subscribers. Some lists are friendly with a number of off-topic "chatty" posts, while others are more strictly moderated with no off-topic discussion allowed. When you first join a mailing list it is a good idea to "lurk" for a few days to get a feel for the list and its members before posting your first message.

Delve Into Genealogy Message Boards

Genealogy message boards and forums are different from mailing lists. Messages are posted online rather than sent to your e-mail address. Some message boards are open for anyone to browse and post to, while others require you to join for full access. As with mailing lists, they are free. The downside is that you have to remember to visit the message board periodically to find new messages, but most boards will at least send you an e-mail notification when someone responds to one of your postings. Some will even let you know whenever a new message is posted that matches your surname or area of interest.

The upside is that message board postings will not clutter up your inbox like mailing lists do, so if you're short on time, message boards may be a good option for you. Because message board posts are archived online, most show up in Internet search engines. This increases the chances that your query for information on your great-grandfather Charlie just might be found by someone with some answers.

ESSENTIAL

Newsgroups, such as Yahoo! Groups (*http://groups.yahoo.com*) and Google Groups (*http://groups.google.com*), are similar to message boards, but they also incorporate the e-mail feature of mailing lists. In short, you get to choose whether you want new messages sent to you via e-mail or if you prefer to only read the new messages online. Many genealogical societies and genealogy research lists can be found on these sites.

Genealogy message boards and forums can be found in many locations online. The largest, most frequented boards are those at GenForum (*www .genforum.com*) and Ancestry.com (*http://boards.ancestry.com*). Although not a true message board, CousinConnect (*www.cousinconnect.com*) is another popular place for connecting with other researchers. It is dedicated solely to genealogical queries, and responses are sent directly to your e-mail. RootsChat (*www.rootschat.com*) is a popular genealogy messaging forum focused on Ireland and the British Isles.

Search the Archives

Message boards allow you to search or browse through past posts, providing an excellent tool for connecting with other researchers. The RootsWeb mailing lists are archived online as well (*http://archiver.rootsweb .com*), going all the way back to the beginning of the first genealogy mailing list, ROOTS-L, in 1987. Visit message boards and archived mailing lists for your primary surnames of interest and try searching for given names or locations from your family tree. Don't forget to search beyond the immediate family for spouses, cousins, siblings, and even neighbors. It's possible that people searching for those individuals may have information about your direct ancestors as well.

If you find a message you're interested in, even if it is an old one, take the time to reply with a brief message about the individual(s) you are researching and how you think they connect. This not only leaves a trail for the individual who originally posted the message, but it may also catch the attention of others researching the same family. For tips on posting your own genealogy queries on message boards and mailing lists, see the "Ask the Right Way" section later in this chapter.

Ferret Out Family Trees

You probably wouldn't believe the number of people who think that genealogy is nothing more than a hunt for an already completed family tree. Since you're reading this book, you probably already realize that it doesn't work that way. But with millions of people becoming involved in researching their family history, large numbers of family trees are available on the Internet, and your chances of locating at least a portion of your family tree online are better than you might think.

Find Family Trees at FamilySearch

The FamilySearch website offers two different ways to locate family trees, drawing from more than 4 billion names culled from pedigree charts and family trees submitted to the Family History Department of The Church of Jesus Christ of Latter-day Saints.

User Submitted Genealogies

This searchable database consists of lineage-linked conclusion trees provided to FamilySearch by users—previously contained in databases such as Ancestral File and Pedigree Resource File. These are family trees in basic pedigree format, without attached digitized documents or photos and with little, if any, source documentation:

- **Ancestral File** is a lineage-linked database that includes family trees submitted by family historians worldwide, created primarily from submissions gathered since 1979. Duplicate individuals from various contributors have been merged (not always correctly) and the only source information generally available for these trees, if any, is the name of the submitter.
- **Pedigree Resource File** was created to overcome some of the deficiencies of Ancestral File, and includes notes and sources when provided by the contributor. These family trees are generally more recent, submitted by users to the FamilySearch Internet service. Trees remain isolated from one another and duplicate individuals have not been merged.

User Submitted Genealogies can be accessed by selecting Search from the FamilySearch home page and then choosing the Genealogies tab.

FamilySearch Family Tree

FamilySearch Family Tree, which debuted to the general public in 2013, also features user-submitted family trees via a user-friendly pedigree interface. It includes family trees from Ancestral File and Pedigree Resource File, as well as trees directly submitted within the past several years by FamilySearch users. It is more much more robust than Ancestral File or Pedigree Resource File, allowing users to correct bad data, add source conclusions, and collaborate with other users researching the same individual. The goal of FamilySearch Family Tree is to create a single, lineage-linked family tree in an attempt to reduce research duplication and increase accuracy.

FamilySearch Family Tree is accessed through the Family Tree link on the FamilySearch home page. You will be required to create a free account and sign in to FamilySearch to use this feature. When you first log in you will be presented with a tree in standard pedigree format with yourself as the primary individual. Nothing other than your name will be included here unless you choose to add it, and it is not a requirement to search family trees submitted by other researchers. To use FamilySearch Family Tree to search family trees created by other individuals, select the Find link with the magnifying glass at the top of the page to access the search box. This Find feature only allows you to search for information on deceased individuals, to protect the privacy of living individuals also included in FamilySearch Family Tree. For more information on Family Tree, including video tutorials and user guides, see the FamilySearch Family Tree Training website (*http://familysearch.org/tree-training*).

QUESTION

How reliable is the information found in online family trees? Many of the family trees submitted online are works in progress and most probably contain at least an error or two. For this reason, you should never just download a family file you find online and add it directly to your own research without first taking some time to assess the accuracy of the information. They are sometimes, however, a good source for information you may not find elsewhere.

Member Trees at Ancestry.com

From the Ancestry home page (*www.ancestry.com*), select Search and then Public Member Trees from the dropdown box to search for your ancestors in family trees submitted by members. Search results will turn up family trees in a number of different collections, although Member Trees (both Public and Private) is their most current offering, with more than 4 billion names contained in over 46 million user-submitted family trees. Ancestry.com offers free online searching of their online Member Trees, and even nonpaying members who have been invited to view a tree are allowed to also view the attached records, assuming that the tree owner is a paying subscriber.

Public Member Trees can be viewed by all Ancestry subscribers, while Private Member Trees present only limited information online. Instead, you'll be offered the chance to connect with the person who submitted the family tree for further details through the Ancestry Connection Service. A free Ancestry.com guest account is required to access and use Member Trees. In addition to the trees at Ancestry.com, you can also submit to and search family trees through the free WorldConnect website (*http://worldconnect.rootsweb.com*) at RootsWeb.

Matches at MyHeritage

This rapidly growing popular database of lineage-linked family trees includes contributions by users to MyHeritage (*www.myheritage.com*), as well as companies they have absorbed such as GenCircles.com, FamilyLink.com, and Geni.com. Everyone can search the trees for free, but a subscription is required to view the most useful details. If you submit your own GEDCOM file to MyHeritage, or use their free Family Tree Builder program, you can also take advantage of "Record Detective" technology to match the people in your family tree file with other family trees in the database, as well as historical records. The site supports a total of more than 40 languages, which helps to deliver submitted family trees to a global audience.

Take Your Search Global at GeneaNet.org

This pedigree database boasts more international family trees than most and can be accessed in many languages as well. Because it was founded in France, GeneaNet (*www.geneanet.org*) is especially useful for searching family trees from France and other countries of continental Europe. There is a cost to upgrade to a Privilege Club membership, which offers enhanced search options and other features, but the family trees can all be searched and accessed free of charge. A handy e-mail alert can even notify you when new trees are added that match your criteria.

Search the Social Networks

Social networking sites offer yet another opportunity for connecting with others who may also be researching your ancestors. Facebook is one of the biggest these days, with a variety of genealogy applications such as FamilyBuilder's Family Tree (*http://apps.facebook.com/familytree*), available to help you connect your family tree to your Facebook profile. Facebook also has hundreds of genealogists talking back and forth to each other every day, plus pages for hundreds of genealogy groups and family history societies. If you are interested in communicating or collaborating with genealogists in a particular locality, check out the FamilySearch Research Wiki for its list of over 100 Genealogy Research Communities on Facebook (*www.familysearch.org/learn/wiki/en/Research_Communities_on_Facebook*). The Wiki has links to Facebook groups and surname pages as well. Sharing family history interests, surnames, and old family photos in your public Facebook profile can also help attract the interest of distant cousins, who may just have old photos or family stories that weren't passed down in your branch of the family.

Both genealogists and family members just waiting to be discovered can also be found on other social media sites such as Google+ (*http://plus.google.com*), Twitter (*www.twitter.com*), LinkedIn (*www.linkedin.com*), and the image-based sharing site Pinterest (*www.pinterest.com*). Use keywords such as *genealogy, family history,* or locality (*pennsylvania history*), surnames (*owen family genealogy*), or topics (*tombstone photos*), to find pages or groups that interest you.

ESSENTIAL

In order to read and follow many of the family trees you'll find published online, it will help to have a basic understanding of the conventional numbering systems used by genealogists. Three of the most common include the Ahnentafel, a numbering system for ascending genealogies, and the Register System and NGS Quarterly System, used for descending genealogies. Examples and explanations of each system can be found online through a Google search.

In addition to the sites discussed here, there are dozens of other lineage-linked family tree databases to be found online, as well as thousands of individually created family trees published on personal websites across the Internet. Many can be found by entering a search such as *bumgardner family tree* in your favorite search engine.

Ask the Right Way

As you search the web, you'll eventually come across other individuals researching the same ancestors. They may have information on your family that has been passed down to them, including treasured photographs, family stories, or even official documents and records. They may even have researched a family line that you haven't yet had the time or resources to pursue. The first instinct—and generally a good one—is to contact them via e-mail. Keep in mind, however, that while your shared interest in the same ancestors means they are likely to be related to you in some distant way, in reality these people are basically strangers to you, as you are to them. To better ensure that your e-mail is opened and answered, or your message board post isn't overlooked, consider the following:

- **Include a meaningful subject line.** E-mail from an unknown sender with a subject line of "Help!" is likely to be deleted without being read. Include the surname or full name of the individual you are writing about, as well as something like "genealogy" or "family history." Subject lines such as "Powell Genealogy" or "Family Tree of Archibald Powell" are more likely to catch someone's attention than "Hi."
- **Keep it simple.** Explain briefly who you are and how you received the individual's name and e-mail address, as well as how you are related to the family you are contacting them about. Consider this first e-mail as an introduction to test the waters. It's not the best time to share your entire life story.
- **Be precise.** Many people throughout time have shared the same name, so you'll need to include additional details to help people identify the individual you're interested in. Where did he live? About when was he born? Can you provide names of other members of his family? Briefly explain what you already know or where you've already searched for this individual.
- **Don't ask for the moon.** A genealogist who has been patiently researching his or her family for years isn't really going to appreciate an e-mail asking for "everything you have on my family." Most genealogists are exceedingly generous in sharing the information they have uncovered, but be reasonable in what you ask for. Asking for a few specific details, such as a marriage date or parents' names, is a good rule of thumb. They may offer to share more, of course, but they'll appreciate that you don't expect it of them.
- **Protect the privacy of the living.** While it's okay to share the names of your living relatives with other people, don't give people their birth dates, social security numbers, or other private information.
- **Offer to share information in return.** If you're asking for something specific, it generally pays to offer something in return. Perhaps you

have some old family photos, documents, or dates that this individual may be interested in.

- **Say thank you.** Take a few minutes to respond with a quick note of thanks for any information or response you receive, whether it is truly helpful to you or not.

These guidelines also apply to posting queries about your family online, whether on a genealogy forum or through a mailing list. Keep your query short and sweet, but include a relevant subject line, identifying details about your ancestor, and an overview of the places you've already searched.

ALERT

A genealogist should always give credit where credit is due. Don't add someone else's family history research to your genealogy database and represent it as your own work, or share the information without acknowledging the source. The many careful, painstaking hours that went into putting the research together deserve to be acknowledged.

Volunteer help can also be of tremendous assistance when researching your family tree. The genealogical community tends to be a very generous, giving group of individuals. All you have to do is ask a question and you'll usually get an answer. Help can be found almost anywhere you look, but the following groups are especially notable for the volunteer assistance they provide:

- **Books We Own** (*www.rootsweb.com/~bwo*): This free service has been around for more than a decade, connecting volunteers who own or have access to genealogy-related books and other published resources with people who need a quick lookup for their ancestor or a specific surname.
- **Find A Grave** (*www.findagrave.com*): A large network of volunteers has created this fabulous resource of gravestone photos and memorials from cemeteries around the world. The site includes over 102 million grave records and allows visitors to submit a tombstone photo request to volunteers closest to the cemetery's location.

Share Your Research

You can drastically improve your chances of connecting with other people researching your family line by making it easier for them to find you. Many people have connected with other branches of their family tree through an online website or community forum. Even the information posted through online obituary services and remembrance books has been known to bring families together.

One of the easiest ways to share your family history online is to upload a GEDCOM of your family history file to one or more of the lineage-linked databases previously discussed in this chapter. Your family tree doesn't need to be "finished" or even close to it, as long as what you do contribute has been well researched and you're comfortable with its accuracy, or you have noted places where your research is incomplete. If your family tree is still very much a work in progress and you are unsure of some of your information, look for a service that allows you to easily add information or make corrections as your research progresses.

When creating your GEDCOM file for online publication, consider how much information you want to share online and what you hope to achieve.

- To protect your relative's privacy it's best to remove personal information about living individuals before publishing your family tree online.
- Many people choose to include their sources, as this makes it easier for others to follow your research. Some family historians worry, however, that if they provide too much information, people will just take and add it to their own family tree without contacting the researcher, which works against the point of putting the family tree online in the first place. To avoid this, some researchers choose to eliminate their sources from online family trees, and instead include a note asking anyone who is interested in further information to contact the researcher.
- If you like to use the Notes field of your genealogy software for everything from contact information to personal thoughts, stories, and questions concerning your relatives, it is best to leave that on your computer and not make it part of your online family tree. That generally falls under the category of "too much information."

If you don't feel comfortable sharing your entire family tree online, there are other good options for reaching online researchers. One good way to connect with others who may be researching your family is to add your surnames to the RootsWeb Surname List (*www.rootsweb.ancestry.com*) free service that exists for the sole purpose of bringing researchers together. More than 1.2 million surnames are listed here, along with associated dates and locations where they are being researched. Each posting also includes the e-mail address of the person who submitted the surname so you can contact him or her directly. You can (and should) also post the surnames, dates, and locations that you're researching to the appropriate genealogy mailing lists and message boards discussed earlier in this chapter.

If you're creative and want to go beyond what most family tree databases offer, you may want to consider publishing your own family history website or blog.

Take a Class

Most people who take up a new hobby begin by buying a good beginner book or two or signing up for a class. You've already begun by reading this book, but if you're the type who likes more hands-on feedback, you might want to sign up for an online genealogy course. Prices vary from free to several hundred dollars, and the topics and lessons range from beginning research to advanced paleography or methodology. Most of the online genealogy courses are self-paced, and many offer quizzes, tests, and/or instructor feedback.

LINK

The National Genealogical Society offers an excellent set of guidelines and standards for individuals wishing to improve their skills and performance in genealogy. Their "Standards for Sharing Information with Others" (*www.ngsgenealogy.org/cs/standards_for_sharing_information*) discusses the responsibility of family historians when exchanging data, while "Guidelines for Genealogical Self-Improvement and Growth" (*www .ngsgenealogy.org/cs/guidelines_for_genealogical_self-improvement*) provides recommendations concerning ongoing education in family history.

Get Started for Free

Several free beginner genealogy classes with enough information to get you through the basics of family tree research are available online through various websites. About.com Genealogy offers an Introduction to Genealogy class (*http://genealogy.about.com/library/lessons/blintro.htm*) with self-paced lessons and self-grading quizzes. Genealogy.com offers a series of tutorials (*www.genealogy.com/university.html*) created by several genealogists, covering topics ranging from beginner genealogy to immigrant origins. Additional online learning opportunities are available from the National Genealogical Society, which offers a free Family History Skills course (*www.ngsgenealogy.org/cs/educational_courses/online_courses/family_history_skills*) for members, and Brigham Young University (*http://is.byu.edu/site/courses/free.cfm*), which includes ten genealogy topics among its free online courses. The largest collection of free online genealogy courses, however, can be found in the FamilySearch Learning Center (*http://familysearch.org/learningcenter/*), which includes several hundred family history courses, ranging from in-depth lectures with accompanying handouts, to short 5-minute video tutorials.

Learn from the National Genealogical Society (NGS)

In addition to its acclaimed home-study course, American Genealogy: A Basic Course, NGS offers several online and self-study PDF courses (*www.ngsgenealogy.org/cs/educational_courses*) including two U.S. census courses, and more in-depth courses such as Transcribing, Extracting, and Abstracting Genealogical Records; Genetic Genealogy; Civil War Records; and Working with Deeds. The online courses are self-paced, although they do have a six-month time limit, and offer a final self-grading exam upon completion. NGS members receive a member discount.

Enjoy an Online School Setting with Family Tree University

Experienced instructors at Family Tree University (*www.familytreeuniversity.com*) offer a variety of self-paced genealogy classes on topics such as finding ancestors in the U.S. census to Google Earth for genealogists. Each class is self-paced and includes a detailed course curriculum and instructor feedback.

Individual classes run about $100 each. They also offer an occasional online conference, with the opportunity to enjoy a full weekend of topics and speakers.

Earn College Credit or Enroll in a Certificate Program

A number of universities offer a variety of fee-based family history courses online. The National Institute for Genealogical Studies (*www .genealogicalstudies.com*), in association with the University of Toronto, offers a certificate of genealogical studies in American, Canadian, Scottish, Irish, and German records, as well as more general areas such as genealogy, methodology, and librarianship. You can also elect to take classes purely for personal enrichment.

In addition to its free classes, Brigham Young University offers several credit-based online genealogy courses through its independent study department (*http://is.byu.edu/site/*). Boston University has a four-week online Genealogical Essentials course, as well as a thirty-five-hour intensive, somewhat expensive program that leads to a "Certificate in Genealogical Research" (*http://professional.bu.edu/cpe/Genealogy.asp*). The instructors are top-notch, and the certificate program is offered in both a classroom setting at Boston University and online.

To find even more genealogy classes, both fee-based and free, enter a phrase such as *online genealogy class* in an Internet search engine, browse the listings at Cyndi's List (*www.cyndislist.com/education*), or follow Angela Packer McGhie's blog *Adventures in Genealogy Education* (*http:// genealogyeducation.blogspot.com*).

Attend Webinars

A number of genealogical societies, associations, and companies regularly offer free webinars online, featuring a variety of nationally known educators. Webinars are a great resource for genealogical education, especially for individuals who find it difficult to attend genealogy conferences and other live events. A wide variety of family history-focused webinars are available to choose from each month, many of them free and open to the public. Look for webinars from organizations such as Legacy Family Tree, the Southern California Genealogical Society, the Illinois State Genealogical Society, the Association of Professional Genealogists, and even the

National Archives. A fairly comprehensive calendar of upcoming genealogy webinars and online meetings is available online at GeneaWebinars (*www.geneawebinars.com*).

Connect with the Pros

As much fun as it can be to research your own family history, there can be times when it pays to turn to a professional for help. Maybe you just don't have the time to really dig into the records, or need some experienced assistance with putting all the pieces together. Or you might want to hire someone to do record lookups in a faraway city, or to take all of the bits and pieces of your research and turn them into a beautifully written family history. Sometimes you just need inside knowledge of local records, an experienced ear to bounce ideas off of, or a little extra help with a very stubborn problem

QUESTION

Aren't genealogy conferences only for professionals?
Contrary to popular belief, genealogy conferences and institutes offer all genealogists—from the beginning hobbyist to the advanced professional—the opportunity to learn something new. They also offer the opportunity to learn from some of the world's best genealogists, keep up with new techniques and methodologies, and sample the latest software and gadgets. You can even take a genealogy cruise!

Join a Society

Some organizations, such as lineage societies, genealogical societies, and patriotic organizations, focus primarily on preserving the genealogy and family history of their members and/or region and making it available to the world. By joining such a society, you not only enjoy extra access to their records, but can also benefit from the experience of the members. Most societies publish newsletters and quarterlies with record transcriptions, genealogy queries, articles on available records and resources, and news of interest to researchers. Many also offer some type of free or reduced-cost research benefits to their members, as well as the opportunity to include personal queries in their publications. Societies also generally arrange a variety of workshops, seminars, and research trips for their members. And, of course, there is the wonderful opportunity to network with other society members.

But what if the bulk of your research is not in your hometown? Do you join your local society? Or the society covering the area where your ancestors lived? Both situations have their benefits. Many genealogists choose to belong to their local genealogical society, despite having no ancestors from the area, for the chance to actively participate in the local genealogical community, in addition to joining societies in the areas where their ancestors lived. While you may not be able to attend the meetings or actively participate in the business of societies outside your area, membership still affords you the ability to keep up with the latest research news and resources through newsletters and quarterly publications. Many societies also operate mailing lists, so you can participate to an extent without leaving home.

Even if you choose not to join a genealogical society, most offer benefits to nonmembers as well. This often includes access to their library collection and a system for requesting research, lookups, and/or copies. Historical and genealogical societies are also good places to turn for inside information on records and repositories that will aid you in your research and for answers to your local research questions. They may have a website with searchable records, a forum for posting queries, or a mailing list that offers the opportunity to ask questions, request a lookup, or share the details of your family.

ESSENTIAL

Most genealogical and historical societies are nonprofit entities managed and run almost exclusively by volunteers. Despite the buzz over Internet genealogy, these groups are invaluable for their work in preserving our heritage for future generations. Yet the additional research opportunities offered by the Internet have left many societies facing declining membership, while operating costs continue to rise. By joining such a group, you help to keep them viable.

To find a genealogical or historical society near you, or that meets your research interests, visit Society Hall (*www.fgs.org/cstm_societyHall.php*) operated by the Federation of Genealogical Societies. This site offers contact information on more than 500 societies throughout the United States. Cyndi's List (*www.cyndislist.com/societies*) has several thousand links to societies and groups, organized alphabetically by the name of the society rather than geographically. You can also easily find many societies by entering a search such as *pennsylvania genealogical society* or *mennonite genealogy society* in your favorite search engine. Check out your favorite genealogical societies on Facebook as well! Search Facebook for your favorite societies, or use search terms such as *genealogical society* or *alabama genealogy* to see what's available.

Network with Other Genealogists

As mentioned previously, genealogists are connecting on a regular basis on Facebook, as well as through Google+, Twitter, mailing lists, study groups, and other networking opportunities. This gives you the option to ask questions of other genealogists at all stages of research, as well as the many genealogists in the process of transitioning to professional careers in genealogy. Here are just a few examples of the many ways genealogists are using the Internet to learn from one another and make new friends:

- **Facebook** (*www.facebook.com*)—If you have a Facebook account, or choose to create one, you can instantly find a few hundred genealogy "friends" to hang out with online. Become friends with a few genealogists you know well and Facebook will suggest others you might also know. It's great when you attend your first genealogy conference and already feel like you know everyone from Facebook!
- **Google+** (*www.plus.google.com*)—A huge, active genealogical community can also be found online at Google+, where you can add people whose posts or other content you would like to follow to your circles without them having to follow you back. It's a great way to make new friends, as well as learn from genealogy experts you might be too shy to friend request on Facebook.

- **Twitter** (*www.twitter.com*)—Yes, genealogists are using Twitter as a means to meet and learn from others who share their interest. It's a great place to find out about upcoming genealogy events or sales, get opinions on genealogy websites or products, ask questions, or just learn from (or laugh at) what other genealogists are talking about.
- **ProGen Study Groups** (*www.progenstudy.org*)—These groups are organized for aspiring professional genealogists that employ collaborative learning, focused on developing genealogical skills and best business practices.

Hire a Professional

To locate a reputable genealogist for your project, it is best to turn to a professional association. These groups work to ensure quality and ethics among professional genealogists, which can offer you a certain element of confidence in the person you are hiring. Two organizations within the United States provide credentials or certification to genealogists from around the world who have passed rigorous tests of their research skills. The Board for Certification of Genealogists (BCG) (*www.bcgcertification .org*) offers research credentials as a Certified Genealogist (CG), as well as in a supplemental teaching category, Certified Genealogical Lecturer (CGL). A second credentialing organization, the International Commission for the Accreditation of Professional Genealogists (ICAPGen) (*www.icapgen.org*), also offers testing of genealogists worldwide through comprehensive written and oral examinations. It offers the designation of Accredited Genealogist (AG). The Council for the Advancement of Forensic Genealogy (*www.forensicgenealogists.com*) is a professional membership organization for individuals working in the specialized field of forensic genealogy—"research, analysis, and reporting in cases with legal implications." The Association of Professional Genealogists (*www.apgen.org*) is another good place to turn when looking to hire a professional. This umbrella organization is not a credentialing body, but instead supports high standards in the field of genealogy and requires all of its members to adhere to a code of ethics.

ESSENTIAL

Week-long genealogical institutes such as the Institute of Genealogy & Historical Research (*www.samford.edu/schools/ighr/*), the Salt Lake Institute of Genealogy (*www.infouga.org*), the National Institute on Genealogical Research (*www.rootsweb.ancestry.com/~natgenin/*), and the Genealogical Research Institute of Pittsburgh (*www.gripitt.org*) offer an in-depth, intensive learning experience from some of the best instructors in the field. A huge bonus is the opportunity to meet and network with so many genealogists.

All four groups offer an online member list or database to assist you in locating a researcher by geographical location or specialty. Should you be dissatisfied with the work done by a member, each group also offers arbitration or other options to help in rectifying the situation.

CHAPTER 12

Dig Deeper

Genealogy can become addicting. As soon as you discover your ancestors' birth, death, and marriage dates, you may become enthralled with discovering more about them as people. But how do you dig deeper and get a more complete picture of who they were as people and what their lives may have been like? This chapter takes you through searching occupational records, finding family photos and postcards, delving into membership organizations, and even learning about your own DNA. There is always more to discover.

Books, Magazines, and Blogs

Earlier, you were introduced to the thousands of family histories to be found in books, journals, and other printed publications. But these publications can be essential for their guidance as well. From them you can learn about new or unusual record sources, less-used repositories, and current genealogical standards.

Books

One such fundamental guide book for genealogists is *The Source: A Guidebook of American Genealogy,* third edition (Ancestry Publishing, 2006) by Loretto Dennis Szucs and Sandra Hargreaves Luebking, which covers genealogical record types in great detail. This is a book that genealogists turn to again and again as they encounter new records or research situations. This third edition of *The Source* is also available for free online in the Ancestry.com Wiki (*www.ancestry.com/wiki/index.php?title=The_Source:_A_Guidebook_to_American_Genealogy*). Other very useful books in the same general category include Val Greenwood's *The Researcher's Guide to American Genealogy,* third edition (Genealogical Publishing Company, 2000), Holly Hansen's *The Handybook for Genealogists,* eleventh edition (Everton Publishing, 2006), and Ancestry's *Red Book: American State, County, and Town Sources,* third revised edition, edited by Alice Eichholz, PhD (Ancestry Publishing, 2004). The latter is also searchable as an online database (*www.ancestry.com/search/db.aspx?dbid=3249*) at Ancestry.com. These books are such standards in the field that you'll generally find them at any library with a genealogy section.

LINK

Wondering what books you should purchase for your personal genealogy bookshelf? There are numerous articles and lists of suggestions available online, including "Top 11 Essential Reference Books for Genealogists" (*http://genealogy.about.com/od/education/tp/books_reference.htm*) and "What Reference Books Should I Own?" (*http://blogs.ancestry.com/circle/?p=2089*). Or check out the books owned by other genealogists on LibraryThing (*www.librarything.com*) for many great ideas.

Just about every professional genealogist subscribes to, or reads on a regular basis, one or more genealogical journals. These scholarly publications typically contain case studies, compiled genealogies, articles on new research methodologies, critical reviews of current books and software, and previously unpublished source materials. Some of the most widely read genealogical journals are the *National Genealogical Society Quarterly* (*www.ngsgenealogy.org*), the *New England Historical and Genealogical Register* (*www.americanancestors.org/the-register/*), and *The American Genealogist* (*www.americangenealogist.com*).

There are dozens of other excellent journals published by state, ethnic, and local societies. Subscriptions to these journals may be either part of or independent of a membership in the society. As an alternative to the traditional published journals, the *Annals of Genealogical Research* (*www.genlit.org*) offers an online forum for genealogists to publish compiled genealogies, case studies, and other scholarly genealogical articles with the same high standards as found in the published journals. Only a few articles are published here each year, but it's free.

Magazines

Popular genealogy magazines publish articles of more general interest, discussing record types, websites, new online databases, software, and upcoming genealogical events. For Internet genealogy, the aptly named *Internet Genealogy* magazine (*www.internet-genealogy.com*) focuses entirely on researching your family tree online. Other popular print genealogy magazines include *Family Tree Magazine* (*www.familytreemagazine.com*) and *Family Chronicle* (*www.familychronicle.com*). The very popular *Ancestry* magazine ceased publication in 2010, but sixteen years of back issues can be viewed for free in Google Books (*http://books.google.com/books/serial/FTgEAAAAMBAJ*). An interesting digital option is the weekly Casefile Clues (*www.casefileclues.com*) by Michael John Neill, available by e-mail subscription.

Blogs

There are so many great genealogy blogs to choose from, it's hard to select just a few to bring to your attention. A large number of genealogists have Dick Eastman's blog, *Eastman's Online Genealogy Newsletter* (*http://blog.eogn.com*), on their blogroll (a list of other blogs that a blogger might recommend). He's the one that genealogists expect to keep them up-to-date with the latest and greatest in genealogy tools, software, and online resources of interest to family historians. *DearMYRTLE* (*http://blog.dearmyrtle.com*), also known as Pat Richley-Erickson, has a popular genealogy blog that continually informs and keeps genealogy fun.

The anonymous *Ancestry Insider* (*http://ancestryinsider.blogspot.com*) has worked for both FamilySearch and Ancestry.com, and provides readers with an inside scoop on both. *Genea-Musings* (*http://randysmusings.blogspot.com*), by Randy Seaver, is a pleasure to read because he updates almost daily, with a strong focus on search techniques and software, and lets his passion for genealogy really shine through in his writing. For an intelligent but lighthearted look at legal and DNA topics, don't miss Judy Russell's *The Legal Genealogist* blog (*www.legalgenealogist.com*). You can find links to over 1,700 excellent genealogy blogs through Chris Dunham's *Genealogy Blog Finder* (*http://blogfinder.genealogue.com*), and almost 3,000 in the Genealogy Blog Roll at Thomas MacEntee's *GeneaBloggers* (*http://geneabloggers.com/genealogy-blogs*). There is definitely a lot of informative family history–inspired writing going on out there in genealogy cyberspace, so go explore.

Occupational Records

Census records, marriage documents, obituary notices, and other sources of information on your ancestors will often make note of their occupation. This may seem like a trivial little detail, unnoticed in your quest for your ancestor's birth date or parents' names. Yet what your ancestors did for a living can tell you a great deal about them and what they found important in life. An individual's occupation may provide insight into his social status or place of origin. An occupation can also be used to distinguish between two individuals of the same name. Certain skilled occupations or trades, or even more unusual occupations, may have been passed down from father to son, providing indirect evidence of a family relationship. In short, an ancestor's choice of occupation can serve as a valuable guide marker in your path through their life.

Begin your search for occupational clues in your own home. Look closely at your old family photographs. Do you have any photos of your ancestor wearing a uniform, or standing in front of a family grocery store? Do the family papers contain any old business correspondence, pay stubs, farm or business ledgers, or retirement records? These may provide interesting information on your ancestor's work.

Other records previously covered in this book can also be excellent sources of occupational information. Census records from 1850 forward record occupations for each individual. By 1920, this occupational information had expanded to include not only the occupation or trade, but also the type of business for which the individual worked and his occupational status (self-employed, salaried employee, or wage worker). City directories can also be an excellent source for occupations as they tend to list the name of the business, rather than just the type of work the ancestor did. They are also available for many more years than the federal census.

QUESTION

My ancestor's occupation is not one that I recognize. What does it mean?
The world of work has changed greatly through the decades and centuries. For every new occupation—such as astronaut or web designer—that is born, another occupation name or term—such as ripper (seller of fish) or pettifogger (a shyster lawyer)—has fallen into disuse. Type *old occupations* into your favorite search engine to find a number of helpful lists and glossaries.

Death records are another place where you'll often find occupational information. Death certificates and obituaries often list the individual's occupation or former occupation. If you can find your ancestor in the Social Security Death Index (SSDI), send for a copy of his or her SS-5 application record; it will include, among other things, his or her employer's name and address. Marriage records often include occupational information as well.

Once you identify your ancestor's occupation, the Internet is an excellent resource for learning more about the industry or profession in which he worked. If your great-great-grandfather was a cordwainer (shoemaker), the website of The Honourable Cordwainers' Company (*www.thehcc.org*) offers a fascinating glimpse into the history of the profession, as well as a catalog of resources in the guild's library and links to additional online resources on the occupation of shoemaking. If you hear of an ancestor who purportedly invented something, search the U.S. Patent and Trademark Office database (*www.uspto.gov/patft*) to see if he ever patented his invention. A variety of links to such occupation-oriented sites can be found on Cyndi's List under Occupations (*www.cyndislist.com/occupations/*).

ESSENTIAL

Is your last name Barker, Cooper, Fuller, or Cohen? These and many other surnames originally derived from an individual's choice of occupation. A "barker" was a leather tanner. A "cooper" made barrels. The surname Cohen often derives from the Hebrew word for "priest." And a "fuller" is someone who "fulled," or softened cloth by stretching, pounding, or walking on it.

An Internet search for a specific occupation can turn up interesting details. Unless the occupation was very specialized, you'll want to include other identifying details in your search as well, such as place, time period, or even ethnicity. For instance, a search on Google for *history farming north carolina* results in over 100 million hits. However, narrowing the search further to *tobacco history pitt county north carolina* helps locate the interesting Pitt County Digital Tobacco History Exhibit (*http://digital.lib.ecu.edu/exhibits/tobacco/*) with census records, business directories, warehouse maps, newspaper articles, and photos documenting the importance of the tobacco industry in the area around the turn of the twentieth century. Try a variety of different searches for your ancestor's occupation, and you may be surprised at all of the interesting information that turns up!

State archives, local historical societies, and university libraries are also good places to look for information on various occupations as well as the records of businesses, institutions, and union and trade organizations. If the occupation was a common one in that particular area, such as with coal mining in Pennsylvania, you may find online exhibits with photos, documents, memoirs, and other valuable information. Most business and trade records will not be found online, but a search of online catalogs and manuscript collection finding aids can give you an idea of what is available offline, including membership lists, financial records, and occupational injury reports.

If the business, trade union, or other organization still exists, search the Internet for their website so you can contact them directly. They may be able to tell you what older records still exist and where they are stored. The U.S. Railroad Retirement Board (RRB) (*www.rrb.gov/mep/genealogy.asp*), for example, maintains records for individuals who worked in the rail industry after 1936, and their website includes information on how to request a search of those records for a fee. For railroad-working ancestors whose records aren't found with the RRB, the next step is to search for the records of the railroad companies themselves, most of which have been deposited with railroad museums and various historical societies. Again, the United States Railroad Retirement Board (RRB) comes to the rescue, with a list of depositories known to have railroad records, or try a Google search such as *pennsylvania railroad records*.

Membership Organizations

Many societies, associations, and organizations are in some way committed to preserving the shared history of their members. This might include the history and heritage of a business or occupation, a geographical region or time period, or even a military unit or engagement. Personal information found in the records of these organizations might include full name, dates of admission and membership, and the name of a sponsor. Because many fraternal societies offered some type of death benefit, you may also find the date of death, an obituary or funeral notice, and a notice of funerary benefits to family members.

ALERT

An unusual symbol on your ancestor's tombstone may indicate membership in a fraternal organization. A shield, helmet, or the letters "KP" or "K of P" may indicate membership in the Order of Knights of Pythias. The compass and square is a Masonic symbol commonly found on tombstones. A grave marker in the shape of a tree or tree stump often indicates a member of Woodmen of the World.

The number of societies that your ancestors may have joined is vast and includes ethnic, religious, charitable, political, fraternal, and social organizations. Most were formed for mutual benefit and protection purposes: to organize group medical care and life insurance, locate and obtain jobs for members, preserve the values of the members' homeland, or assist with assimilation into the New World. All offered a place for camaraderie and brotherhood. For these reasons, membership societies were especially important among immigrants, offering a sense of community identity while assisting with their transition into the larger American society.

Fraternal and benevolent organizations in America reached their zenith of popularity during the late nineteenth century, with an estimated one in five males belonging to at least one fraternal order. The Freemasons and the Independent Order of Odd Fellows were two of the largest societies, with nearly 1 million members each. The Order of Patrons of Husbandry, more commonly known as the Grange, also attracted a large following.

Lineage and hereditary societies, such as the Daughters of the American Revolution, have also been popular since the late nineteenth century. These societies each commemorate a different group of individuals, such as those who fought in the Civil War or the first colonists to settle a particular area, and generally restrict their membership to individuals who can prove lineal descent from a qualifying ancestor.

ESSENTIAL

Family organizations—groups of people who are descended from a single individual or are gathering information about all individuals with a particular surname—can be a good source for family history information, but not all of them are online. Try *Directory of Family Associations*, fourth edition, by Elizabeth P. Bentley and Deborah Ann Carl to help you locate active associations without an online presence.

Many lineage societies maintain active libraries and publish a periodical or newspaper for their members. Because membership in a lineage society generally requires documented evidence of descent from a specific qualifying individual, you can often glean significant genealogical information from its files. This might include membership application papers, pedigrees, and supporting evidence, such as pages from the family Bible, birth and death certificates, or military documents.

Clues that your ancestor belonged to a membership society can be found in many sources, including obituaries, tombstones, local histories, biographies, and family memorabilia. If you know or suspect that your ancestor belonged to a particular organization, the next step is to learn where those records might be located. Most fraternal organizations, lineage societies, and other associations do not have their records computerized or provide them online. You'll often have to contact them via e-mail, fax, or snail mail to obtain the information you seek. Contact information for such organizations can often be found online through a Google search.

Websites for many of the currently active fraternal benefit societies are linked to the American Fraternal Alliance (*www.fraternalalliance.org*). The Societies and Groups section (*www.cyndislist.com/societies/*) at Cyndi's List also offers thousands of links to ethnic and fraternal organizations, lineage societies, family associations, and other online societies and groups. Some organization websites, such as the Independent Order of Odd Fellows (*www .ioof.org/genealogy.html*) and the Grand Army of the Republic Museum and Library (*www.garmuslib.org*), offer information on how to conduct family history research in their records. A small number of transcribed rosters, bylaws, histories, proceedings, and other records from a variety of fraternal organizations are included as part of the online database at Genealogy Today (*http://data.genealogytoday.com/contents/Fraternal_Organizations.html*). Searching is free, but a subscription is required for full access.

Photos and Postcards

After spending hours and hours reading and learning about ancestors in old records, you can't help but wonder how they must have looked. Do the visual images you have formed in your mind really have anything to do with how your ancestors looked in real life? Which one of them passed down the red hair that has shown up in your children or the hooked nose that appears at least once in every generation? How did they dress? What did their homes look like? Were they happy? Photographs of your ancestors can truly bring them to life.

A quest for family photographs should always begin with your family. Contact every relative you know to see what photos they have and are willing to share. Don't stop with your immediate relatives, either. When searching for family photos and memorabilia, it is essential to search out and contact all descendants of an ancestor. You never know which of the descendants of your great-grandfather's eighteen children might have possession of the family photo that used to hang over his mantle.

LINK

Postcards are another visual source of clues to your past, offering a glimpse into the towns, clothing styles, occupations, and day-to-day life of your ancestors. Auction sites such as eBay (*www.ebay.com*) are a great place to find vintage postcards. Images from more than 10,000 towns and cities can be found in the online Curt Teich Postcard Archives (*www.lcfpd.org/teich_archives*). Ancestry.com has a database of over 115,000 historic U.S. postcards (subscription required), searchable by location.

If you encounter a relative who is reluctant to let go of original photographs, offer to make copies of the pictures or pay to have copies made. If he doesn't want the photo removed from his home, you can often make a pretty good copy with a digital camera, or arrange to bring a laptop computer and a portable scanner.

Locate Photographs Online

If you're unable to obtain photos from your family members, it's time to turn to the Internet. There are millions of photographs posted online and at least a few probably have some relevance to your family. Even if you can't locate a photograph of your ancestor, you may be able to find other photos of relevance, such as the town in which she lived, the place where she worked, or even her gravestone. Photo searches can also help turn up maps, scanned newspaper images, and other visual images of your family history.

Google Images search (*http://images.google.com*) is a great way to find ancestral photographs. Search for a specific surname, a town, or a cemetery to see what turns up. You may get really lucky and find a photograph of your ancestor, but Google Images search is also great for locating tombstone photos, scenic town views, and photos of historic events. Just be sure to investigate the copyright and permissions for a photo if you plan to use it in your family genealogy.

A large number of online photographs are hidden away from search engines in digital photo collections, such as the Prints and Photographs collection of American Memory (*http://memory.loc.gov*) and the Francis Frith collection (*www.francisfrith.com*) of more than 100,000 photos from across Britain. Ancestry.com also has hundreds of thousands of family photos, submitted to Ancestry family trees by users, available for searching and viewing in its Public Member Photos database (*www.ancestry.com/search/db.aspx?dbid=1093*). Because they are in a database, the individual photos in such collections won't generally turn up in a standard Internet search. Instead, you have to search each collection individually. You can find many such historic photo collections (*http://genealogy.about.com/od/historic_photos/tp/photo-collections.htm*) listed on About.com Genealogy. Flickr (*www.flickr.com*) is a definite must-visit for locating historic images from library, archive, and historical society collections. Broad Internet searches such as *england photos* or *historic railroad photographs* can also help locate relevant collections.

ALERT

County real estate or property websites are coming online every day to disseminate legal information on properties within the community. They are generally intended for tax and deed information, but many also include photos of the house or other property. This can be a neat way to find photos of older properties that used to be in your family. Look for links to Real Estate, Property Assessment, or Recorder of Deeds on the official county or city government site.

Another interesting source for family photographs online is what most genealogists call "orphan photos." These are photographs that have been found and rescued from flea markets, garage sales, and antique shops by thoughtful individuals, and placed online in the hope of reuniting them with a family member who will be glad to have them. Orphan photos can sometimes be found listed on genealogy message boards and mailing lists. There are also websites, such as Dead Fred (*www.deadfred.com*) and AncientFaces (*www.ancientfaces.com*), devoted entirely to archiving mystery, orphan, and other family photos online.

Who Are Those People?

Great-aunt Mildred left you the family album, but it's full of unidentified photographs of people you've never seen before. How can you learn to whom those faces belong and how they fit into your family tree? If you can safely remove the photos from the album, take them out carefully one by one to inspect the back for names, dates, notes, or a photographer's mark. Return each to the album immediately so you don't lose its position in the album or cause damage to the photo. If you plan to remove the photos from the album permanently, have your new storage solution handy so you can transfer the photos only once.

Next, contact living family members to go through the album and write down whatever they can remember about each photo. If your relatives live far away, have copies made of the photos and send them via postal mail; if your relative is online, then share them via e-mail or an online cloud service such as Dropbox, Google Drive, or SugarSync. Anything your relatives can remember may be helpful. If they don't know names, maybe they will at least know the branch of the family, recognize the backdrop, or be able to identify a single individual from a group photo. Have them look at items and props included in the photos as well.

LINK

Online digital photo sharing services, such as Flickr (*www.flickr.com*), Picasa (*http://picasa.google.com*), and DropShots (*www.dropshots .com*), offer a great opportunity for collecting and sharing ancestral photographs, especially if you have a large extended family. All three services offer options for sharing privately, and invited family members can add names, comments, and stories. Facebook.com and Ancestry Member Trees (*http://trees.ancestry.com*) offer additional options for getting family photos online.

Photos that remain unidentified can often be dated within a period of about a decade or so with a little detective work. By knowing the approximate date when the photograph was taken, you'll be more likely to identify possible names for the pictured individuals. Dozens of online tutorials can help you learn how to use clothing, jewelry, backdrops, photograph techniques, and other clues to identify the approximate date that a photo was taken. *Family Tree Magazine*, for example, hosts the *Photo Detective* blog (*http://blog .familytreemagazine.com/photodetectiveblog*) in which photo identification expert Maureen A. Taylor regularly discusses photo dating techniques using user-submitted photos as examples. *Family Chronicle* offers a brief online guide to Dating Early Photographs (*www.familychronicle.com/photoxtra .html*) with sample photographs organized by decade. They also offer two printed publications chock-full of reproductions of old photographs of known dates, offering numerous examples to compare with your own family photographs.

Save Your Family Photos Before It's Too Late!

Many family photographs, and the stories that go with them, are lost each year. Heat, humidity, and even bugs do considerable damage. Fire, flooding, and other disasters wipe out precious family memories. When there is a death in the family, relatives may divide up the photos, discarding the ones they don't want. Family photo albums and boxes of loose photos often end up sold with an estate or dumped in the trash. Almost every antique store has a section filled with old family photos, scrapbooks, and postcards—bits of family history that have been lost to anonymity.

If you have older relatives, consider letting them know that you would be happy to take care of their photos. If you want to make sure your photograph collection has a good home after you die, sit down and make sure all of the pictures are labeled (to the best of your ability), and make plans for a special family member to inherit the photos. If you have access to a digital scanner, or can afford to have a professional do the work for you, you may want to scan your ancestral photos into digital format and then save them to an external hard drive and/or online cloud service for long-term storage and backup.

DNA and Genetic Genealogy

Clues to your past cannot only be found in the records at the library and courthouse, they can also be found in your genes. DNA has been used for many years to identify people, but in the year 2000, DNA testing for genealogical applications hit the commercial market. DNA testing is best used to help confirm a link where no conventional source records exist or, in some cases, to determine if a person is part of a larger group, such as the Jewish Cohanim (or Kohanim) lineage.

Genetic genealogy tests look at the variations in the sequence of DNA from one person to the next. The more closely two people are related, the more similar their genetic material, or genomes. What's interesting is that all humans are about 99.9 percent the same. It's in that other 0.1 percent that you find the genetic differences that make you unique. Every once in a blue moon a small change or "stutter" occurs in this unique portion of our DNA. This "hiccup," or genetic mutation, is then passed down to a person's descendants. A similar mutation found in two people's DNA means that they share an ancestor somewhere in the past.

To help locate these genetic mutations, scientists have identified genetic *markers*, certain short segments of the DNA strand with known genetic characteristics. These markers, which can be found at specific locations, or loci, on the chromosome are essentially places where the same pattern repeats a number of times. Since the number of repeats within these sequences is inherited, people who match at a number of markers are almost certain to share a common ancestor.

QUESTION

Who should I have tested?
The answer depends on what you're testing for. In all cases, the oldest living generations (not necessarily age) are the most critical to test first since they are one generation closer to potential common ancestor matches. You also want to capture their DNA before it is lost forever. From there, select the relative(s)—grandparents, cousins, etc.—whose DNA is most likely to answer your specific question.

Genealogy DNA tests do not tell people precisely how they are related or who their common ancestor is. These tests need to be paired with accurate genealogy research to help determine the specific ancestral connection, and to track down relatives willing to be tested. For genetic genealogy purposes, three types of DNA provide the most useful information: Y chromosome, mtDNA (mitochondrial DNA), and autosomal DNA.

Y-DNA—Direct Paternal Line

In humans, each cell contains twenty-three pairs of chromosomes. Twenty-two of those pairs, called autosomes, are essentially the same in both males and females. The twenty-third pair, however, is the sex chromosome that determines gender. Males have one X and one Y chromosome in that pair, while females have two copies of the X chromosome. When a child is conceived, it receives one sex chromosome from each parent. The chromosome from the mother will always be X, but the chromosome from the father could be either X or Y. A child who receives an X chromosome from the father will be a girl; receiving a Y chromosome will make the child a boy.

Because the Y chromosome is the only human chromosome not affected by the constant reshuffling of parental genes, the DNA present in the Y chromosome is passed down virtually unchanged for many generations. This means that every male directly descended from the same distant male ancestor will have an extremely similar pattern of Y-DNA markers, making the Y chromosome extremely useful to genealogists. Since the Y chromosome is only present in males, the popular Y-DNA genealogy test can only be done on males, however. If you are a female interested in your paternal line, you will need to find a male relative (father, brother, cousin, and so on) who descends from the paternal line to be tested.

When you take a Y-line DNA test, your results will come back as a string of numbers. These numbers represent the repeats (stutters) found for each of the tested markers on the Y chromosome. These results have no real meaning taken on their own. Instead, you compare your results with other individuals to whom you think you are related to see how many of your markers match. Matching numbers at most or all of the tested markers can indicate a shared ancestor, generally referred to as the Most Recent Common Ancestor (MRCA). Depending upon the number of exact matches, and the number of markers tested, you can also determine approximately how recently this common ancestor was likely to have lived (within five generations, sixteen generations, and so on).

LINK

The International Society of Genetic Genealogy (*www.isogg.org*) exists to educate people about the use of genetics in genealogy through workshops, beginner tutorials, and an online forum. A number of blogs regularly address genetic genealogy in an easy-to-understand format, including DNAeXplained (*http://dna-explained.com*), Your Genetic Genealogist (*www.yourgeneticgenealogist.com*), and The Genetic Genealogist (*www.thegeneticgenealogist.com*). For more advanced questions, try the GENEALOGY-DNA-L mailing list (*http://lists.rootsweb.com/index/other/DNA/GENEALOGY-DNA.html*) at RootsWeb.com.

A special type of marker known as a Short Tandem Repeat (STR) is the one most often used in Y-DNA genealogy testing. In general, a DNA testing company will offer several different levels of tests—twelve markers, twenty-five markers, thirty-seven markers, sixty-seven markers, and so on. It is best to test a minimum of thirty-seven markers to achieve any sort of meaningful result. Basically, the more markers you test, the more conclusive your tests will be. The cost also goes up as the number of markers goes up, however, so most people choose to begin with a moderate number of markers (in the twenty-five to thirty-seven range). Almost all testing companies keep your DNA on file for a specified number of years so you can easily test additional markers at a future date if you so desire.

Mitochondrial DNA—Direct Maternal Line

If you're female, don't feel left out—you have your own special DNA test as well. Maternal DNA, referred to as mitochondrial DNA or mtDNA, is passed down from mothers to their sons and daughters. It is only carried through the female line, however, so while a son inherits his mother's mtDNA, he does not pass it down to his own children. It does mean, however, that both men and women can test their mtDNA.

The mtDNA mutates much more slowly than Y-DNA, so it is really only useful for determining distant ancestry. Your mtDNA results will be compared to a common reference sequence called the Cambridge Reference Sequence (CRS), to identify your specific haplotype, a set of closely linked alleles (variant forms of the same gene) that are inherited as a unit. People with the same haplotype share a common ancestor somewhere in the maternal line. This could be as recent as a few generations, or it could be dozens of generations back in the family tree. Your test results may also include your haplogroup, basically a group of related haplotypes, which offers a link to the ancient lineage to which you belong.

Autosomal DNA—All Ancestral Lines

Autosomal DNA is the DNA found in the twenty-two chromosome pairs, or autosomes, that contain randomly mixed DNA from both parents—basically all chromosomes *except* the sex chromosome. Autosomes contain almost the entire genome, or blueprint, for the human body, with one chromosome in each pair coming from the mother, and the other from the father. Because the DNA in each pair is inherited by both men *and* women, from both parents and all four grandparents, it can be used to test for relationships in all family lines—a potential goldmine for females and adoptees, as well as males. Autosomal DNA tests look at areas of the DNA known to vary from person to person, referred to as Single Nucleotide Polymorphisms (SNP, pronounced "snip") and compare the results to others who have been tested. A match is determined by how much DNA two people have in common, and how long the common segments are, measured in units called centiMorgans (cM). Due to random recombination of autosomal DNA as it is passed down through generations, autosomal testing is most useful for determining common ancestors within five generations, although factors such as cousin marriages and plain old luck of the recombination draw can potentially extend this period. On its own, autosomal testing cannot link a potential match to a particular surname or branch in your family tree. You can still connect matches back to a particular common ancestor, however, by having others in your family tested (e.g. mother, father, grandmother...) to help narrow your search to a particular branch of your family tree, and then compare genealogical research and localities with your potential matches to target in on the most likely common ancestor.

ESSENTIAL

DNA testing is easy and painless. Basically, you sign up with a DNA testing company and order the test(s) that you are interested in. They will send you a kit with a cheek swab (or in some cases a mouth wash or spit tube) with which to collect your sample. No blood is collected. You then send back the kit containing your DNA sample. Unless the lab is backed up, you will generally receive your results in about a month.

Test Your DNA

A variety of DNA testing labs specialize in genetic testing for genealogy applications. Each offers slightly different tests, pricing, and tools, and connects you to a different database of potential matches:

- **Family Tree DNA** (*www.familytreedna.com*)—FTDNA is the biggest genetic genealogy testing company, with a large online database of Y-DNA Surname Projects. They offer Y-line DNA (paternal surname), mtDNA (maternal surname), and autosomal DNA (Family Finder) tests and their website includes a variety of tools for analyzing your results and comparing your matches. Y-DNA tests are available from 12 markers up through 111 markers, and the Family Finder autosomal test includes about 710,000 SNPs. Individuals testing with FTDNA are all interested in genealogy at some level, increasing the likelihood of collaboration with DNA matches to identify the most recent common ancestor, and the company also provides a wide variety of tools for understanding and interpreting your DNA results.
- **23andme.com** (*www.23andme.com*)—As far as genealogy testing goes, 23andMe offers only a single product, which tests almost 1 million SNPs and incorporates both Ancestry and Health testing. The health-related portion of the test screens for over 100 potential traits and diseases (see Create a Medical Family Tree at the end of this section). The Ancestry test is autosomal so it tests for matches across all of your lines and also provides information on distant ancestral origins (Ancestry Painting). 23andMe has the largest database for autosomal matching, but since many of the people who use this service

test for health reasons rather than genealogy, it can sometimes be challenging to elicit responses from potential matches.

- **AncestryDNA** (*http://dna.ancestry.com*)—This autosomal DNA test compares over 700,000 SNPs and displays matches in common with other members of Ancestry.com, including a list of surnames you have in common, and a link to their family tree on Ancestry.com (if the individual has created one). You're also provided with a summary of your genetic ethnicity—the places that your ancestors lived hundreds, if not thousands, of years ago. Testing here provides access to another set of potential cousin matches and the ability to download your raw data, but the analysis tools are currently not as robust as the other autosomal testing services.

- **National Geographic's Genographic Project Geno 2.0** (*http://genographic.nationalgeographic.com*)—Geared specifically for learning about deep ethnic ancestry rather than genealogical matching, Geno 2.0 tests more SNPs on both the Y-chromosome and in the mitochondrial DNA than other companies and also tests markers in the autosomal DNA. The test covers 137,000 total SNP locations associated with differences among populations and provides information on deep ethnic origins on all lines. The one exception is that females will only receive their mtDNA and autosomal DNA results, but if they have a paternal male relative tested, they can link to him to display paternal Y-DNA in their results.

Get more bang for your buck! The chance of finding genetic cousins increases with every database that contains your DNA results. Some genetic testing companies will let you upload your results from other testing companies into their database for a lot less than the cost of testing with multiple companies. Third-party solutions, such as GEDMatch (*www.gedmatch.com*) for autosomal DNA and ysearch (*www.ysearch.org*) for Y-DNA, offer options for uploading your test results for free, along with tools for analyzing your results and connecting to individuals who have also uploaded their results to the service.

Join a Surname Project

Genetic testing for ancestral connections provides the most information when you have others with whom to compare the results. One of the best ways to do this is to join a DNA surname study in which men with the same surname compare their lineages and DNA test results to see if they are related. Women can play too, of course, but they'll have to find a direct-line ancestor with the surname to take the actual DNA test, as surname studies are based on Y-line ancestry. As an added bonus, many testing facilities offer a substantial discount to participants in group projects.

Many surname projects have their own website, so an Internet search such as *crane dna* or *crane surname study* may turn up just what you need. Be sure to search for variations of your surname as well (e.g., Crain, Craine, Crayne). For smaller or newly created projects, check the project listings at the various DNA testing companies. Family Tree DNA (*www.familytreedna.com*), for example, offers links to surname projects from its home page. Lists of surname projects can also be found on Cyndi's List (*www.cyndislist.com/surnames/dna*).

Create a Medical Family Tree

Many health conditions, from cancer to high blood pressure, tend to run in families. Some of these diseases are purely genetic. Most, however, are a mixture of genetic makeup and environmental factors. In these cases, you are not born with the condition; you only inherit a susceptibility or predisposition to developing it during your lifetime. By tracing the health problems and diseases suffered by your parents, grandparents, and other blood relatives, you can learn about your possible inherited risks. This information can help you and your doctor take preventive steps to lessen your chances of acquiring the disease or condition.

The Internet offers a number of resources for anyone interested in tracing his or her medical family tree. Online tools and guidance are available, for example, on the website of the U.S. Surgeon General's Family Health History Initiative (*www.hhs.gov/familyhistory*).

CHAPTER 13

Locate Records Abroad

America is truly a nation of immigrants, with the vast majority arriving during the past 150 years. In fact, 95 percent of Americans today have descended from individuals who did not live on this continent in the eighteenth century. That's a brief flicker in terms of world history. For you, this means it probably won't be long before your research leads you past America's borders.

A Nation of Immigrants

If you're worried that you don't have the skill for foreign research, don't be. The research skills and techniques that you are already using will readily transfer to research in a new location. Yes, there will be a few stumbling blocks, such as language barriers. You'll also need to spend time familiarizing yourself with the country's history, including changing political and geographical boundaries. But once you find that first ancestor in the "old country," you'll be hooked!

Before you embark into the records of a new country, you will first need to learn as much as possible about your immigrant ancestor from records within the United States. It is most important to identify his place of birth beyond just the name of the country, or even the state or county. The majority of genealogically relevant records in most countries are found at the local level—the city, town, village, or parish. In some cases, the records may be maintained at the state, departmental, or provincial archives, but even in many of these cases the records themselves are arranged by town or other locality.

The name of your ancestor's town or village may be found in a variety of records; some of the most likely include death certificates, obituaries (don't overlook ethnic newspapers), naturalization records (including those of any children or family members who also immigrated), marriage records, church records (including those of children), and WWI draft registration records (some of the forms asked for place of birth).

Limited space prevents going into extensive detail on genealogy research in countries around the world. Instead, this chapter takes a look at some of the major online family history resources available for each country, with links to websites where you can access further research guidance and resources on the countries where your ancestors once lived.

Canada

A large amount of genealogical and historical data for Canada is already available online, with more being added regularly. Most records are maintained at the province level, so you will need to have an idea of what part of Canada your ancestors came from before embarking on your research.

QUESTION

Where can I find Canadian records of birth, marriage, and death?
Civil registration of vital statistics in Canada is a provincial responsibility; available records and access will vary by province. Some archives and vital statistic offices, such as the British Columbia Archives (*http://royalbcmuseum.bc.ca/bcarchives/*), offer online indexes to historical birth, marriage, and death registrations. Others only provide information on how to order a certificate via mail. Try a search such as *canada vital records* or *alberta vital records* or *ontario marriages* to learn what's available in your area of interest.

Billing itself as a "gateway to Canadian genealogy," the CanadaGenWeb Project (*www.rootsweb.com/~canwgw*) is available in English and French with queries, lookups, and a FAQ (Frequently Asked Questions). Besides links to province-specific resources, you'll discover a timeline of Canadian history, information about famous Canadians, a cemetery transcription project, and a special website just for kids.

The Canadian Genealogy Centre (*www.collectionscanada.ca/genealogy/index-e.html*) of Library and Archives Canada has posted numerous (and free) online databases that are useful for anyone researching Canadian roots. Select a topic or enter a surname to find the 1851, 1901, and 1911 censuses of Canada; a variety of immigration records and passenger lists; naturalization records; land grants; and early marriage bonds for Upper and Lower Canada. Information and links to other sites that hold Canadian records of genealogical interest are also included.

ALERT

A free twenty-four-page guide entitled "Tracing Your Ancestors in Canada" is available for download in PDF format (*www.collectionscanada.gc.ca/genealogy/022-607.001-e.html*) from Library and Archives Canada. This guide describes the primary sources of genealogical information available in Library and Archives Canada as well as an overview of information in other Canadian centers.

A growing collection of Canadian family history records is available for free online access at FamilySearch.org. Select "Search" from the main page at FamilySearch.org and then scroll down to narrow by location to Canada to view over 75 collections of available records such as the 1851, 1871, 1881, 1891, 1901, 1906, and 1916 censuses. FamilySearch also has a large collection of provincial records, including vital, parish, estate, and land records.

The largest collection of Canadian family history records available online can be found on the subscription site Ancestry.ca (*www.ancestry.ca*). Almost 2,000 searchable databases include indexes and images for the 1851 through 1916 censuses of Canada, along with Canadian immigrant records and vital records from most provinces. Other interesting Canadian collections include the Canada Militia and Defence Forces Lists, 1832, 1863–1939, plus the historic Drouin Collection, with more than 37 million baptism, marriage, and burial records. This is a companion site to the U.S.-based Ancestry.com and includes the same records, although a Canada Deluxe membership that only includes Canadian records is available exclusively on Ancestry.ca.

Find information on more than 116,000 Canadians and Newfoundlanders who fought and died while in service to Canada at the Canadian Virtual War Memorial (*www.veterans.gc.ca/eng/collections/virtualmem*). Information in this free database includes the individual's military service number, unit and division, date of birth, and burial information. It also often includes that individual's hometown and the names of spouse and parents.

Since many of Canada's records are created and maintained at the provincial level, you'll want to check the archives, libraries, and other repositories in the province where your ancestors lived. The site That's My Family (*www.thatsmyfamily.info*) helps make this easy, offering a free online search interface for multiple databases from various provinces. Library and Archives Canada hosts the Directory of Special Collections of Research Value in Canadian Libraries (*www.collectionscanada.gc.ca/collectionsp/index-e.html*), a database of archival collections throughout Canada, searchable by keyword, title, and subject. You can also find a wealth of Canadian research guides and database links at Cyndi's List—Canada (*www.cyndislist.com/canada*) and About.com Genealogy—Canada (*http://genealogy.about.com/od/canada*).

Mexico, Central America, and South America

Records from the countries of Central and South America have become increasingly available online over the past few years, most due to the digitizing efforts of FamilySearch. You can also use the Internet to learn how to conduct research in these countries and find contact information and instructions for ordering records.

Find Records at FamilySearch

Available for free searching via the FamilySearch website (*www .familysearch.org*) are over 150 collections from the Caribbean, Central and South America, plus more than 65 collections specific to Mexico. The Mexico vital records indexes include more than 43 million baptism, 6 million marriage, and almost 400,000 death records from Mexico, a partial listing of records covering the years 1560 to 1950. FamilySearch also offers access to a searchable index and images of the 1930 Mexico census, plus dozens of browse-only (non-indexed) collections of Mexican civil registration records and Catholic church records from states across Mexico. FamilySearch also has census, Catholic church, civil registration, and some military collections for many Central and South American countries, including Argentina, Barbados, Bolivia, Brazil, Chile, Colombia, Costa Rica, the Dominican Republic, Ecuador, El Salvador, Grenada, Guatemala, Haiti, Honduras, Jamaica, Nicaragua, Panama, Paraguay, Peru, Puerto Rico, Uruguay, Venezuela, and the Virgin Islands. From the FamilySearch home page, scroll down and select a country of interest to begin navigating your way to available records.

LINK

Before you dig into the online databases, it pays to become familiar with the ins and outs of genealogy research in your country of interest. Guides to research and records in many localities around the world can be found in the FamilySearch Research Wiki (*http://wiki.familysearch .org*). Search or browse for your country of interest.

Locate Country-Specific Resources at GenWeb

Visit the North America Genealogy Project (*www.worldgenweb.org/index.php/northamgenweb*) to locate online resources and records and to connect with fellow researchers for the countries of Central America, including Belize, Costa Rica, El Salvador, Guatemala, Honduras, Mexico, Nicaragua, and Panama. For genealogy research in South America—encompassing the countries of Argentina, Brazil, Colombia, Chile, Peru, Venezuela, and others—the South AmericanGenWeb Project (*www.southamericagenweb.org*) serves as an online repository for source records, family histories, genealogy queries, and links to online databases. Both sites are free and fully supported by volunteers.

British Isles

There is a vast wealth of data available for the regions that make up the British Isles—England, Scotland, Wales, Ireland, the Channel Islands, and the Isle of Man. There is, in fact, much more than can be adequately discussed in this book. But to get you started, here are some of the largest and most useful online resources for genealogy research in the British Isles.

Some of the best jumping-off points include GENUKI, the Ireland & United KingdomGenWeb Project, and the FamilySearch Research Wiki. GENUKI (*www.genuki.org.uk*), short for GENealogy of the United Kingdom and Ireland, serves as a virtual reference library of genealogical information with relevance to the United Kingdom and Ireland. It's a great place to look for links to vital websites and primary source documents organized by region, county, and topic. The Ireland & United KingdomGenWeb Project (*www.iukgenweb.org*) has genealogical data and queries, along with links to eight country projects (British Overseas Territories, Channel Islands, England, Ireland, Isle of Man, Northern Ireland, Scotland, and Wales). Research guides organized by country and county can be found in the FamilySearch Research Wiki (*http://familysearch.org/learn/wiki/en/Main_Page*).

ESSENTIAL

If you're confused about the differences between the terms British, Great Britain, the United Kingdom, and the British Isles, you're not alone. It's important to learn the distinctions, however, because it not only affects how records are organized and where you will find them, but it will also prevent you from offending someone or appearing ignorant during the course of your research. Learn more from "What is British?" (*http://genealogy.about.com/b/a/255920.htm*).

Once you've spent some time exploring the records available at these volunteer projects, it's time to jump into online records and databases.

Census Records

Like census records in the United States, censuses in most of the British Isles were conducted every ten years—but in the second year of the decade (the years ending in "1") instead of the first. Because they cover the entire population, they are among the most comprehensive records available online for research in this region.

The free records at FamilySearch (*www.familysearch.org*) are a good place to begin your census research with complete indexes to the 1841–1911 England and Wales census, plus digital images of the 1871 census (other years are linked to images on subscription site FindMyPast). FreeCEN (*www .freecen.org.uk*), with its database of UK census transcriptions contributed by volunteers worldwide, is another good free resource. The statistics page (*www.freecen.org.uk/statistics.html*) includes up-to-date information on the counties and years covered. FindMyPast (*www.findmypast.com*), which includes the complete run of United Kingdom census images and indexes from 1841 through 1911, offers a free census index search and your choice of pay-as-you-go or subscription-based access to transcriptions and images. Ancestry.com (*http://search.ancestry.com/search/group/ukicen*), subscription required, has census indexes and images for all available years in England, Wales, Scotland, the Channel Islands, and the Isle of Man as part of their World Records Collection subscription. The official genealogy website of the Scottish government, ScotlandsPeople (*www.scotlandspeople .gov.uk*), offers subscription-based access to indexes and images of the

Scottish census, for the years from 1841 to 1871 and 1891 to 1901, plus index and transcription (no images) of the 1881 census. TheGenealogist (*www.thegenealogist.co.uk*) offers inexpensive subscription access to transcripts, indexes, and images for the England and Wales census 1841 through 1911. A variety of census indexes and images are also available at subscription-based British Origins (*www.origins.net*). GENUKI, as well as Census Online, are good places to find links to free census indexes, transcriptions, and images organized by region and county.

ALERT

The volunteer indexing project at The Genealogist offers rewards in the form of vouchers and subscriptions in return for time spent assisting in their transcription efforts. As a volunteer, you would participate in error-checking previously indexed entries, using special online tools. If you have some free time to offer and would enjoy free database access in return, consider signing up as a volunteer at UKIndexer (*www.ukindexer.co.uk*).

Census records for Ireland are not quite as easy to come by. The 1861, 1871, 1881, and 1891 census enumerations were destroyed by government order during World War I. The 1901 and 1911 Ireland census records, however, have been digitized and made available for free online use by the National Archives of Ireland (*www.census.nationalarchives.ie*). In the absence of earlier Irish census records, Griffith's Valuation of Ireland 1847–1862 can be searched online for free at Ask about Ireland (*www.askaboutireland.ie/griffith-valuation/*), or via subscription to Origins.net (*www.origins.net*) or Ancestry.com. Named for its director, Richard Griffith, Griffith's Valuation was an evaluation of every property in Ireland, conducted between the years 1847 and 1862. It doesn't offer details on family members as census records do but does provide a listing of the owner and occupier of each piece of property.

Civil Registration Records—Births, Marriages, and Deaths

Online access to vital records in the British Isles is a breath of fresh air after the inconsistent availability of such records in the United States. In addition, all British Isles civil registration records are open to the public, including even the recent records. England and Wales share the same civil registration system, while Scotland, the Republic of Ireland, and Northern Ireland each have separate systems.

ESSENTIAL

Ancestral Trails: The Complete Guide to British Genealogy and Family History, second revised edition, by Mark Herber is the best in-depth reference book for genealogists with British ancestry. For online research links and information, *The Genealogist's Internet,* fifth edition, by Peter Christian is another outstanding reference.

Civil registration in England and Wales was instituted nationwide on July 1, 1837. Searching these records is much easier than the painstaking state-by-state process most American genealogists are used to, because the General Register Office (GRO) maintains a national index of these births, deaths, and marriages. The alphabetical index, arranged first by year and then by quarter (March, June, September, and December), includes the surname, first name, registration district, and volume and page of the GRO reference. The mother's maiden name was added to the birth index in 1911 and the spouse's name to the marriage index in 1912. Online access to the GRO or BMD (birth, marriage, death) index is available from the following sites:

- **FreeBMD** (*http://freebmd.rootsweb.com*)—This massive volunteer project aims at creating a full transcription of the GRO BMD indexes for England and Wales. As its name implies, the database offers free access. The primary focus of FreeBMD is the period from 1837 to 1983, although the project is ongoing and does not yet cover the entire period. A copy of the FreeBMD database is also available for free searching on Ancestry.com, the project's financial supporter. Both sites offer the same data. Although FreeBMD offers links to the original index images, response times can sometimes be faster on Ancestry.com.
- **BMD Index** (*www.bmdindex.co.uk*)—This pay-as-you-go subscription site features the complete BMD index in the form of digital images from

the original record books. It also offers full name searching and better bang for your buck than other subscription-based sites. Searches only point you to the pages in each quarter where your ancestor's name might appear. You'll still have to view the actual pages—at least one for each quarter per year—to locate them in the index.

- **FindMyPast** (*www.findmypast.com*)—Previously mentioned for its census records, FindMyPast offers pay-per-view access to digitized images of all original GRO index pages from 1837 to 2006. It offers a surname-only search to help narrow down the pages you need to view.

When searching for marriages in the BMD Index, there's a technique you can use to identify the spouse in the pre-1912 marriage indexes. In the FreeBMD index, all you have to do is click on the hyperlinked reference link to view the other names appearing on the same page. If you already know the spouse's name, finding his or her name on that page will help confirm that you have found the correct index reference. If you don't know the spouse's name, you can use this to help narrow down the potential candidates. When viewing actual index images, you'll need to search the pages for both surnames (look for the more uncommon one first) to see if they appear on the same reference page. This means you'll need to know at least the spouse's last name. Of course, by ordering a copy of the actual marriage certificate, you'll be able to confirm the names of both parties in the marriage.

LINK

RootsChat (*www.rootschat.com*) is a free, easy-to-use messaging forum for anyone researching his or her family history or local history. The focus is on Ireland and the British Isles, but there are also discussions for other countries such as Canada and Australia, plus more general topics such as photo restoration.

Once you've located the reference to your ancestor's birth, death, or marriage from the GRO Index, you can easily order a copy of the original certificate online through the GRO's certificate-ordering service (*www.gro .gov.uk/gro/content/certificates*). Online fees for this service are comparable to what you would pay in person at the Family Records Centre in London or through the local register office. You'll need a valid credit or debit card to use this service.

Civil registration in Scotland began on January 1, 1855, and returns are kept at the New Register House in Edinburgh. The previously discussed ScotlandsPeople website (*www.scotlandspeople.gov.uk*) offers an index and online images of the original registers of births more than 100 years old, marriage records more than 75 years old, and records of deaths more than 50 years old. The best part about this service is that you don't have to wait for the certificate to arrive—you can view digitized versions of the actual handwritten register images online. Certificates of more recent births, marriages, and deaths can be ordered directly from the National Records of Scotland (NRS) (*www.gro-scotland.gov.uk*) through links from the ScotlandsPeople website. If you are looking for free research in Scotland civil registration records, two databases at FamilySearch (Scotland Births and Baptisms, 1564–1950 and Scotland Marriages, 1561–1910) include over 11 million transcriptions extracted from civil registrations. If you do find your ancestor in this database, you may want to confirm the entry by ordering a copy of the actual certificate.

QUESTION

What is the best website for researching Scottish ancestors?
A first stop for anyone researching Scottish ancestry should be Scot-landsPeople (*www.scotlandspeople.gov.uk*), the official family history website of the government of Scotland. It offers a wealth of genealogical data on a pay-per-view system, including indexes and registers of civil births, marriages, and deaths from 1855; records of births, christenings, and marriages appearing in parish registers from 1553 to 1854; census records from 1841 to 1911; and wills and testaments from 1513 to 1925.

Official registration of births, marriages, and deaths in Ireland began in 1864, although state registration of marriages for non-Roman Catholics began earlier, in 1845. The civil registration index is arranged alphabetically by year until 1877, after which each year was divided into quarters as in

England and Wales. FamilySearch.org (*www.familysearch.org*) offers free online access to the civil registration indexes for Ireland from the beginning of registration to 1958; excluded are index records from Northern Ireland after its creation in 1922. Certificate copies can be ordered online through the General Register Office of Ireland (*www.groireland.ie*).

Emerald Ancestors (*www.emeraldancestors.com*) offers a variety of vital records databases containing extracts and records from civil registrations for Counties Antrim, Armagh, Down, Fermanagh, Londonderry, and Tyrone. Monthly and annual subscription-based access is available.

Births, Marriages, and Deaths in Parish Records

Before the recording of births, marriages, and deaths in the British Isles became a civil issue, such vital events were recorded by individual parishes in the form of baptisms, funerals, marriages, and banns (the public declaration of an intended marriage between two individuals, often formally announced on three successive Sundays). The earliest date you'll generally find such parish registers in England and Wales is 1538, although many churches did not begin keeping records until 1558 or later. The recording of parish registers in Scotland, Ireland, and the rest of the British Isles began around the same time. After 1598 in England and Wales, a copy of the prior year's register for each parish was also forwarded to the bishop of the diocese. Known as Bishops' transcripts, these copies provide a second record of the valuable parish registers, and may have survived when the parish register has not.

ALERT

The British Newspaper Archive (*www.britishnewspaperarchive.co.uk*) is digitizing up to 40 million newspaper pages from the British Library collection at a rate of up to 8,000 digital images per day. Pay-per-view and subscription-based packages are available, or the papers can also be accessed through a Britain Full or World subscription to FindMyPast .com (*www.findmypast.com*).

The FreeREG site (*http://freereg.rootsweb.com*), a companion to the previously discussed FreeCEN and FreeBMD, offers free Internet access to baptism, marriage, and burial records that have been transcribed by volunteers from parish and nonconformist registers of the United Kingdom. Because these are transcriptions, you may want to check the information you find against the original parish register (or a microfilm or digital copy of the original) to verify that it has been accurately and completely transcribed.

Another free alternative for parish records is the Historical Records Collection at FamilySearch, which includes data collected and transcribed from parish registers from the British Isles by The Church of Jesus Christ of Latter-day Saints, as well as digitized images of registers and Bishops' transcripts for parishes in several counties in England, Scotland, Wales, and Ireland. Subscription-based access to many UK parish registers is available through Ancestry.com and FindMyPast.com.

In addition to the previously mentioned census and civil registration records, ScotlandsPeople also offers access to births, baptisms, banns, and marriages from old parish registers of Scotland from 1553 to 1854. The Emerald Ancestors site, previously discussed for Irish vital records, offers entries from a selection of parish registers for the period 1796 to 1924.

The Rest of Europe

Online genealogy research in Europe has made rapid advancements in recent years, with millions of documents and databases being placed on the Internet by local governments and various organizations. Vital records from the Netherlands, passenger records from Germany, and civil and parish registers from France are all available online once you learn where to look.

Ferret Out Family History in France

The French approach family history with a passion—evident in the many available genealogy projects and online databases to be found for this country. The records are fairly well preserved, despite several wars and much social upheaval, and date back well into the sixteenth century. The biggest drawback to French genealogy on the Internet is that most of the databases, records, and websites are only available in French. Don't let this scare you away, however. With a good French genealogy word list and the help of online translation tools you'll quickly be able to navigate your way around French records.

LINK

Many archives départementales in France have digitized civil, parish, and census records and have made them available online for free viewing. The Archives of France website (*www.archivesdefrance.culture.gouv.fr/ressources/en-ligne*) maintains a comprehensive and up-to-date listing of available online records by *département*.

You'll also want to familiarize yourself with the geopolitical divisions in France. Instead of counties, you'll find France broken up into *régions* (similar to our states) and *départements* (similar to our counties). Within each *département*, you'll find cities, towns, and villages, called *les mairies*. Archives are generally found at the *département* level, while local records are maintained by each parish and *mairie*. *Départements* in France are each assigned a number, so you'll need to learn both the name and number of the *département* to access appropriate records.

A good place to begin your research into French ancestry is GeneaNet (*www.geneanet.org*), a genealogy community for publishing and sharing family trees, connecting with other researchers, and locating records. While the site operates as a worldwide genealogy database, the primary focus is still on French ancestry. Because the site is available in English and several other languages in addition to French, it offers an easy introduction to French genealogy research. Search by surname and/or village to help locate databases that may contain information on your family and to connect with other genealogists who are researching your surname.

Another good gateway site to French genealogy is the FranceGenWeb (*www.francegenweb.org*) portal. Much of the site is presented in French, although some portions can also be found in English. Use FranceGenWeb as a gateway to find online databases and records, connect with fellow researchers, and locate the *départemental* GenWebsites. The Historical Record Collections at FamilySearch.org also include a few digitized record collections for France, primarily parish records.

When it comes to records of interest to family historians, France boasts an excellent system of civil registration records dating back to September 1792. Prior to that time, Catholic parish registers (*registres paroissiaux*) recorded baptisms, marriages, and funerals in much of France. The earliest parish registers date back to 1334, although the majority of surviving records date from the mid-1600s. These civil and parish records are being made available online, primarily on the websites of the various *départemental* archives, at a rapid rate. The French census, conducted once every five years beginning in 1836, is another useful record for researching French ancestors. These census records generally are un-indexed, which makes it hard to locate your ancestors in larger cities, but with patience they can provide you with a great deal of information about your family. Check the website of the *départemental* archive to see if they offer digitized images of their census records (*recensements de population*).

To learn more about French research, including notarial, military, and criminal records, visit the FamilySearch Research Wiki (*http://familysearch .org/learn/wiki/en/France*) and Anne Morddel's *The French Genealogy Blog* (*http://french-genealogy.typepad.com*).

Seek Your Ancestry in Italy

There is no central repository for most Italian genealogical records, so the first step in researching Italian ancestors is to identify the township (*comune*) where they lived, and the town hall (*municipio*) that holds the records of that comune. Civil registration was instituted in Italy in 1804, although the Napoleonic-era records are very inconsistent. Once Italy became unified as a country in 1860, civil registration again became a priority of the Italian government. The majority of these records of birth (*atti di nascita*), marriage (*atti di matrimonio*), and death (*atti di morte*) begin in 1866 and continue to the present day. As in France, the predominant religion of Italy is Roman Catholic, so Catholic parish records provide another excellent resource for vital records—baptisms (*atti di battesimo*), marriages (*atti di matrimonio*), and burials (*atti di sepoltura*). The majority dates back to 1563, although some church records begin as early as the 1300s.

FamilySearch is the largest source of online records for Italian genealogical research, with over 115 million Italian civil registration records from 1802–1940 being digitized and indexed from state archives throughout

Italy through special arrangement with the Italian State Archives (*Direzione Generale per ali Archivi*, or DGA). Select "Search" from the home page at FamilySearch.org, and then select "Continental Europe" and "Italy" to access available indexes and images. FamilySearch also has some Catholic and Evangelical church records, and military conscription records.

As with other countries around the world, Italy GenWeb (*www.italywgw.org*) offers a good resource for Italian genealogy, with online archives and records, how-to guides, and contact information for fellow researchers. ItalianGenealogy.com (*www.italiangenealogy.com*) and Finding Our Italian Roots (*http://italiangenealogyroots.blogspot.com*) also offer research guidance.

Don't overlook Italian resources within the United States. GenealogyBank (*www.genealogybank.com*) is digitizing and putting online for their subscribers six Italian American newspapers from California, New York, and Pennsylvania. The website of the Italian Genealogical Group (*www.italiangen.org*) includes a database of the surnames/areas that members, both past and present, are researching, along with a great collection of online transcribed records from local and regional archives (mostly from New York City).

Search for Roots in Scandinavia

The Scandinavian countries of Norway, Sweden, Denmark, Finland, and Iceland offer a wider variety of online genealogical records than most people expect. As with most European countries, the key to Scandinavian genealogy is in knowing the name of your ancestor's hometown or parish. This region's GenWeb sites, accessed through CenEuroGenWeb (*www.rootsweb.com/~ceneurgw*), offer good introductory information on the available records of interest to genealogists, as well as forums for connecting with other researchers.

As with most international genealogical records, a good place to begin is the free FamilySearch historical records collection. Click on "Search" from the main FamilySearch page (*www.familysearch.org*), and then scroll down and select "Continental Europe" to access vital records from Sweden, Denmark, Finland, Norway, and Iceland. The collections from Sweden are especially strong, with digitized images of a wide variety of church records. Ancestry.com and MyHeritage also have collections of genealogical records from the Scandinavia countries.

The Norwegian Historical Data Centre at the University of Tromsø (*www .rhd.uit.no/indexeng.html*) is working to computerize many of the historical records of Norway. The site offers free access to the complete Norwegian census of 1865, 1875, 1900, and 1910. This source also offers access to selected parish registers and other genealogical sources from the eighteenth and nineteenth centuries. Digital Archives (*http://digitalarkivet.uib.no*) from the National Archives of Norway lets you search transcribed and digitized records for free, including parish and real estate registers, probate material, court records, and books.

In Sweden, Genline (*www.genline.com*) offers online access to over 20 million digitized images of original Swedish parish registers on a subscription basis. The site is available in English, and you can buy a twenty-four-hour demo subscription for a reasonable price.

Selected Swedish church records are also available online, again for a fee, from the Swedish National Archives (*www.svar.ra.se*). This site also offers the complete 1880, 1890, and 1900 censuses of Sweden, plus tax registers, death records, and other databases of interest. Look for a link at the top of the home page to an English version of the site. The subscription website ArkivDigital (*www.arkivdigital.net*) has images of Swedish church records, and probate, military, and tax records for selected counties. Various subscription options are available; they also generally offer two weekends per year with unlimited free access.

The online database of the DIS Computer Genealogy Society of Sweden (*www.dis.se*) contains more than 22.2 million records of Swedes born before 1905 submitted by members. Searches of this database are free, but only members can access the full details.

ESSENTIAL

The Family Tree Guide Book to Europe by Erin Nevius and the editors of *Family Tree Magazine* provides beginner-friendly guidance for any-one researching European ancestors, with fourteen chapters, each devoted to a specific country or region of Europe. The fourth edition of Angus Baxter's *In Search of Your European Roots* is another good resource, with ideas for using various research approaches and sources in the countries of Europe.

In Denmark, the Danish State Archives (*www.sa.dk*) features a number of online databases including a probate index, census, and parish records, and the Danish Demographic Database (*www.ddd.dda.dk/ddd_en.htm*). Look for an English link on the site home page. The site also includes a link to the Danish Emigration Archives (*www.emiarch.dk*), where you can search a database of emigration lists compiled by the Copenhagen Police from 1869 to 1940 (the database only includes the years up to 1908). These lists give the last name, last residence, age, year of emigration, and first destination of almost 400,000 emigrants from Denmark. Don't miss the linked collection of online church books (*www.sa.dk/ao/Kirkeboeger/default.aspx*).

As you might expect in such a remote country, almost every member of the 300,000 population of Iceland is related to one another. You can check this claim out for yourself at Íslendingabók (*www.islendingabok .is*). Meaning "Book of Icelanders," the database includes Icelandic family trees and genealogies going back for more than 400 years, covering the roughly 720,000 individuals who were born in Iceland at some point in time. Unfortunately, only Icelanders are allowed access to this database.

Dig Deep for Your German Roots

Many genealogists believe that it can be harder to trace your roots in Germany than in any other European country because of changing boundaries and the destruction of records during the two world wars. Germany as it is known today wasn't even established until 1870, and German descent is no guarantee that your roots reach back to Germany at all. Instead you may find them in Poland, Ukraine, the Czech Republic, Slovakia, Russia, Hungary, Yugoslavia, or Lithuania. Even small portions of Belgium, Denmark, and France were obtained from German territory in 1919.

ALERT

Germans to America, edited by Ira Glazier and P. William Filby, is a sixty-seven-volume set of books indexing German arrivals to America between 1850 and 1897. A second series covers the 1840s. This series can be found at many major libraries—a partial list of libraries that have them can be found on Genealogy.net (*www.genealogienetz.de/ misc/emig/gta-holdings.html*).

That being said, there are several good sources of German genealogical information available online. Genealogy.net (*www.genealogienetz.de*) sponsors a variety of mailing lists, lists German genealogical societies, and links to a number of helpful databases. Some portions of the site are only available in German. Bremen Passenger Lists (*www.schiffslisten.de*) offers a searchable database of passenger departure records from Bremen for the years 1920 to 1939. All surviving records from this time period—3,017 out of 4,420 lists—have been transcribed and made available online by the genealogical society Die Maus. Subscription-based Ancestry.com includes over 500 German city directories and other German records in its World Deluxe collection. FamilySearch.org has over 50 German collections including city records, censuses, and church books.

For further research links to German genealogy on the Internet, check out the German Roots website (*www.germanroots.com*) maintained by genealogist Joe Beine. It includes a comprehensive list of links to online genealogy records, books, and other resources, as well as a basic research guide for German genealogy.

Explore Your Eastern and Central European Heritage

For most of the remaining European countries, access to online records is a bit limited. The Internet still comes in handy for research in the countries of Eastern and Central Europe, however. Online you can find a wealth of information on the changing political and geographical boundaries of the region, as well as maps, historical documents, and opportunities for connecting with other people researching your surnames.

Begin your search at the site of the Federation of East European Family History Societies (FEEHS) (*www.feefhs.org*), which is geared toward assisting North Americans in tracing their ancestry back to a European homeland. The site offers links to participating member societies, maps, and helpful online databases for research in Eastern Europe. It also includes a useful collection of ethnic, religious, and national cross-indexes. Another excellent starting point is the EastEuropeGenWeb Project (*www.rootsweb.ancestry.com/~easeurgw*) where you can access queries, family histories, and source records, as well as connect to the country GenWeb sites, from Albania to Yugoslavia. For the countries of Central Europe, you'll find many of the same resources at CenEuroGenWeb (*www.rootsweb.ancestry.com/~ceneurgw*).

If you have the name of the town or village in Central or Eastern Europe where your ancestors originated, ShtetlSeeker (*www.jewishgen.org/ Communities/LocTown.asp*) can help you determine its present-day location.

Moving on to country-specific databases and resources, the Polish Records Transcription Project (*www.rootsweb.com/~polwgw/transcribe .html*) at PolandGenWeb offers access to birth, marriage, and death records for many towns in Poland. The PolandGenWeb archives also include links to transcriptions of a few Polish cemeteries and other helpful information. Additional records for Polish genealogy research, including maps, gazetteers, obituary indexes, and cemetery listings, can be accessed at PolishRoots (*www.polishroots.com*). While there, check out the popular SurnameSearch registry, where you can register the surname you are researching and access a variety of surname databases.

For individuals with roots in what was Czechoslovakia prior to 1993 and is now Slovakia or the Czech Republic, It's All Relative (*www.iarelative.com*) includes a great deal of information on surnames, places, and databases to help you search your Czech, Bohemian, Moravian, Slovak, Lemko, or Carpatho-Rusyn family history. Other helpful sites for this area of Eastern Europe include the Carpatho-Rusyn Genealogy website (*www.rusyn .com*), The Carpathian Connection (*www.tccweb.org*), and Cyndi's List (*www.cyndislist.com/czech*) which offers links to hundreds of additional resources for researching ancestors from the Czech Republic and Slovakia.

ALERT

A number of free genealogy word lists have been compiled and placed online to help researchers tackle reading genealogical documents in French, German, Spanish, and other popular languages. These lists help researchers quickly identify common genealogy-related words, dates, and phrases along with their English translations. You can find a number online in the FamilySearch Research Wiki (*http://wiki.family search.org*) by typing *word lists* into the search box, or at About.com Genealogy (*http://genealogy.about.com/od/foreign_word_lists*).

A collection of several hundred small databases and records, plus family trees, useful for researching ancestry in the Eastern and Central European countries of Austria, Hungary, Poland, Russia, Slovakia, and Ukraine is available for searching at subscription-based MyHeritage (*www.myheritage .com*). Ancestry.com also has many databases available for this region in their World Deluxe subscription. Hundreds of thousands of free genealogy records are available for Eastern and Central European countries online at FamilySearch, including vital and other records from the Czech Republic, Germany, Hungary, Russia, Austria, Slovakia, and Ukraine.

Swiss family history is best begun at Swiss Genealogy on the Internet (*http://kunden.eye.ch/swissgen/schweiz-en.html*) where you can find an introduction to researching Swiss ancestors, the Register of Swiss Surnames, and links to websites about Swiss families. Another useful site is Swiss Roots (*www.theswisscenter.org/swissroots/genealogy/*), which serves as a gateway for Americans of Swiss descent looking to discover their ancestors. Here you can access a small handful of useful databases, learn a little about Swiss history and culture, and read about some famous Americans of Swiss descent.

Australia and New Zealand

Like the United States, Australia and New Zealand are fairly young countries where the majority of the population is only a few generations removed from its immigrant roots. Government-created records are scattered and inconsistent and many have limited access because of very restrictive privacy laws.

Records of birth, marriage, and death in Australia and New Zealand are maintained at the state or territory level. A good listing of the BMD Registrars, along with links to the registrars that offer free or fee-based online access to Australian birth, death, and marriage indexes, can be found at Cora Num's excellent website for genealogists (*www.coraweb .com.au/bdmau.htm*). This gateway site also includes well-researched links to archives, cemeteries, census records, convict records, and passenger lists for Australia. Once again, FamilySearch has a nice collection of free records for Australia and New Zealand, including births, baptisms, marriages, deaths, and burials, plus immigration passenger lists and Masonic records. FindMyPast (*www.FindMyPast.com.au*) has a huge collection of Australian records, including civil registration, census, church, and military records. Subscription-based site Ancestry.com also includes Australian vital records, plus electoral rolls, lists of assisted and unassisted immigrants, cemetery records, and much more.

ESSENTIAL

Maori are the indigenous people of New Zealand. It is believed that the Maori originally emigrated from Polynesia in canoes about the ninth century to thirteenth century A.D. There are currently a little more than 400,000 Maori living in New Zealand, comprising about 13 to 14 percent of the country's total population.

In New Zealand, registration of European births and deaths was first required in 1848 and marriage records in 1854. Registration of Maori births and deaths did not become compulsory until 1913, under a separate system of registration that applied to individuals of half or more Maori blood. The older New Zealand historical records (*www.bdmonline.dia.govt.nz*), not protected by law, can be ordered online by anyone for a fee.

The National Library of Australia in Canberra has a special section devoted to Australian family history (*www.nla.gov.au/oz/genelist.html*), with links to state libraries and genealogical societies as well as several databases for online research. These include immigration, military, and convict records, plus a huge collection of over 300 million digitized newspapers, photos, books, and diaries through their free online search engine Trove (*http://trove.nla.gov.au*).

Many people with Australian ancestry hope to discover a convict in their family tree. To this end, Convicts to Australia (*www.convictcentral .com*) includes a research guide, timeline, lists of the convict transport ships, convict databases, and stories of convict ancestors.

Asia and Africa

The large and diverse continents of Africa and Asia present a challenge for anyone attempting to research African or Asian family history. Very few records are available online. The Internet can still provide a great research tool for learning about the history of the area where your ancestors once lived and for connecting to other genealogists with research interests in the area.

AfriGeneas (*www.afrigeneas.com*) is the largest jumping-off point for Americans looking to trace their roots back to Africa, with records, forums, and mailing lists devoted to helping you connect your African American ancestors to their place of origin in Africa. Once you have at least identified your ancestor's country of origin in Africa, the AfricaGenWeb Project (*www .africagenweb.org*) may provide some assistance with directing your research efforts in Africa. If your ancestors were from South Africa, spend some time exploring the National Archives of South Africa (*www.national .archives.gov.za*), where you can search an index to several helpful databases. It is important to note that these are only indexes to available records. The actual documents will need to be requested from the Archives.

The AsiaGenWeb Project (*www.worldgenweb.org/index.php/ asiagenweb*) includes links to a variety of country websites, covering a broad area from Turkmenistan in the west to East Timor in the east. Many of these sites are actually in need of hosts and thus provide little in the way of useful information. The best include ChinaGenWeb (*www.rootsweb .ancestry.com/~chnwgw*) and JapanGenWeb (*www.rootsweb.ancestry .com/~jpnwgw*). For people tracing European ancestry in India, the Families in British India Society (FIBIS) (*www.fibis.org*) provides a number of useful lists and databases. Links to additional resources for British India can be found on About.com (*http://genealogy.about.com/od/india/tp/Research-In-British-India.htm*). An interesting site for those with Korean ancestry is the Korean History Project (*www.koreanhistoryproject.org*). Yes, FamilySearch. org and Ancestry.com have some historical records online for this region as well, including vital records for India, Sri Lanka, and the Philippines; Japanese American internment camp records; Indonesian naturalization and citizenship records; and Chinese jia pu (family histories).

CHAPTER 14

Putting It All Together

Now that you have learned the basic research steps, processes, and sources used in tracing your family tree, it is time to put everything into practice—to evaluate what you have uncovered and assemble it into a well-researched family tree, to publish or otherwise share your family history with others, and to protect your family's heritage from possible loss or disaster.

Evaluate What You've Found

Just as with a puzzle, each piece of information that you uncover about your ancestors needs to be evaluated to determine its appropriate placement in the family tree. What is the record telling you? Is the information complete? How convincing is it? Does it conflict with other information that you've found?

What Does the Document Say?

Reading old records is something you'll have to do often as you trace your family tree back in time. Handwriting styles were definitely different, and the writers weren't always very particular about punctuation and penmanship. Words may have had different meanings, and even dates weren't always as self-explanatory as you might think. An important step in evaluating the information you've found is to make sure that you've interpreted it correctly.

Even modern handwriting can be difficult for genealogists to read because of poor penmanship. As you go back in time, the difficulties only increase as you encounter unusual scripts and other handwriting oddities along with archaic spellings and usage. You don't have to be an expert in paleography to accurately read old documents, but some practice and experience definitely helps. Online tutorials can be extremely useful in this regard. The FamilySearch Research Wiki (*http://familysearch.org/ learn/wiki/en/Category:Handwriting*) includes handwriting tutorials for a number of countries, and the Learning Center (*http://familysearch.org/ learningcenter/*) features over 30 courses on reading old script (search "handwriting" to see the list). On About.com Genealogy, the Photo Glossary of Old Handwriting and Script (*http://genealogy.about.com/od/paleography/ ig/old_handwriting*) includes alphabets and example text for some of the most common handwriting scripts used prior to the twentieth century. For help learning to read documents written in British English between 1500 and 1800, the UK National Archives offers an outstanding practical online tutorial in paleography (*www.nationalarchives.gov.uk/palaeography*).

Dates in genealogy documents can cause confusion as well. A date in a marriage index may be the date that the marriage license was issued or the marriage banns were announced, not the actual date of marriage. Along the same line, people often confuse the dates for births and baptisms, and deaths and burials. Be sure to pair up the date with the correct event.

Once you go back far enough in your family tree, you may encounter different calendar systems, including the Julian calendar, French Republican calendar, various religious calendars, and the unusual Quaker system of dating. You may also find archaic usage relating to dates that you may not recognize. The term *instant*, for example, refers to this month, as in "the eighth instant." The corresponding term *ultimo* refers to the prior month. Examples of other archaic date usage you may encounter include Tuesday *last*, referring to the most recent Tuesday, and Thursday *next*, meaning the next Thursday to occur. Dates were sometimes recorded based on their relationship to another event, as well. A common example of this practice is regnal years, where the year is recorded by the number of years since the accession of the reigning monarch (e.g., 2008 is the fifty-fifth year of Elizabeth II's reign).

ESSENTIAL

In 1582, Pope Gregory XIII ordered that ten days be dropped from the Julian calendar that was in effect at the time and that the beginning of the year change from March 25 to January 1. This new system was the Gregorian calendar still in use today. Because of this calendar change, you may encounter events recorded with a double date, such as 20 March 1718/1719.

Sometimes genealogy seems to have a language all its own. As you dig into older records you'll come across unfamiliar terms and puzzling abbreviations. It is important that you look up the correct interpretation of such terms as you encounter them so that you don't miss any important clues.

Latin terms are the most commonly encountered in genealogical documents, from the legal language of wills and deeds to the Latin records of the Roman Catholic church. The abbreviation *et ux.*, for example, is one that you'll commonly encounter, from the Latin words *et uxor*, meaning "and spouse." Most of these words can be easily looked up online; check out the extensive Latin genealogical word list at FamilySearch (*http://wiki.familysearch.org/en/Latin_Genealogical_Word_List*) or consult a Latin-English dictionary. Other archaic and obsolete terms, such as those commonly used to describe occupations and medical conditions, can also be researched online. Try a Google search for the unrecognized term, or browse through the variety of online specialized dictionaries created for this purpose (search for *old occupations* or *archaic medical terms* to find such dictionaries and glossaries).

Prove Your Case

Proof in genealogy is very rarely an absolute. The information that you uncover during the course of your research may be used as evidence to support your conclusions, but you can really only call it proof if you and others find it convincing. A census record that lists your great-grandma living on her own as a widow certainly provides evidence that her husband is deceased. It isn't proof, however. The census enumerator may have made a mistake in entering the information, or the woman may have stated that she was a widow for any number of personal reasons. The evidence is there, but it isn't convincing enough to be considered proof when evaluated on its own.

ALERT

The Board for Certification of Genealogists (BCG) offers quality examples of genealogies, proof arguments, and research reports prepared by board-certified genealogists on its Sample Work Products page (*www.bcgcertification.org/skillbuilders/worksamples.html*). Other good discussions and examples of proof arguments and proof summaries can be found in the *BCG Genealogical Standards Manual*, and Christine Rose's book *Genealogical Proof Standard, Building a Solid Case*, third edition.

So what constitutes proof? Genealogists define proof as a combination of the evidence and reasoning that convincingly supports a conclusion. Evidence alone doesn't constitute proof. A single document can, on occasion, offer enough evidence to present a reasonable conclusion. Yet, the "proof" exists not only in the evidence drawn from that document but also in the fact that other reasonable sources were searched and no conflicting evidence was found.

You'll often encounter situations in your research where several elements of direct evidence conflict with each other. On the other hand, there will also be circumstances where no individual piece of evidence explicitly provides the information you seek. In these cases, the "proof" comes from analyzing each piece of evidence and creating a logical argument as to why the information, when taken together, carries enough weight to support your conclusion. This is a *proof summary* or *proof argument*, a detailed discussion of the problem, the evidence for and/or against your conclusion, and the resolution of the problem. To assist genealogists in determining whether their evidence and reasoning is sufficient to support their conclusions, the Board for Certification of Genealogists has defined a series of five elements that need to be met before a conclusion can be considered satisfactorily credible or "proven." Known collectively as the Genealogical Proof Standard (GPS), the five criteria are:

1. Reasonably exhaustive search for a wide range of high-quality sources
2. Complete and accurate citation of sources
3. Analysis and correlation of the collected information
4. Resolution of any conflicting evidence
5. Soundly reasoned, coherently written conclusion

A genealogical conclusion that meets this standard of proof can be considered convincing or "proved." This still doesn't imply that your conclusion is true or absolute, just that it is the most logical given the presented evidence. For additional help in understanding and using the GPS, see the book *Mastering Genealogical Proof* by Thomas W. Jones (National Genealogical Society, 2013).

QUESTION

I'm just doing this for my family. Why all the fuss over sources and evidence?
What difference does it make whether Great-Grandma died in Georgia or Alabama? Or where the birth date for Grandpa came from? Like anything else, family history is really only worth doing if you're interested in doing it well. The best way to honor your ancestors is to represent them correctly and take pride in your work.

You Can't Find Them! Now What?

In the process of researching your family history, you'll likely encounter research problems that just don't seem to have a solution. Perhaps your ancestor has a common name, making it impossible to sort him out from all the other men by that name that appear in the records. Maybe your ancestors pulled a disappearing act between the 1880 and 1900 U.S. census. Or perhaps you have followed your ancestors back to the point at which they "crossed the pond," only to have their trail sink into the Atlantic. What's the next step?

- **Retrace your path.** Review the information you have already collected. You've probably learned many new things since you first started tracing your family tree, and the information may reveal new clues when you look at it with fresh eyes. There may be names that had no significance when you first encountered them, or you may be able to better read the old handwriting now that you've had some practice. New sources also come online every day, so take time to retrace some of your Internet searches and revisit your favorite database sites to see what's new.
- **Check your assumptions.** Are you looking for the right name? Are you looking in the right place? Are you looking for the right person? Many brick walls are built from incorrect assumptions. If you have used a lot of compiled databases or published sources to construct your family tree, go back and check them against original documents. If your ancestors lived near a county line, check the neighboring county for records. Investigate all potential name variations for your ancestor as well—not just various spellings of the surname, but given-name alternatives including initials, middle names, and nicknames.
- **Branch out sideways.** The cluster genealogy technique introduced earlier in this book really comes in handy when your research hits a dead end. This is especially true in cases where ancestors seem to have disappeared. Because family, neighbors, and friends often moved together, you may find a clue to their former home or their new location by tracing the movements of the people with whom your ancestors had a connection. When you can't find an ancestor in a particular census, for example, conduct a search for their neighbors

from the previous or succeeding census. This technique also works well for passenger lists.

- **Don't do all of your research online.** For every genealogical record and source available online, there are hundreds more tucked away in archives, libraries, courthouses, and other offline repositories. The Internet is very valuable as a research tool, especially for the survey phase, but you can't use it as your only resource in a thorough family history search. Use online catalogs and other resources discussed throughout this book to become familiar with other potential sources of information about your family located offline, and then visit or write to the repository or hire a researcher to do it for you.

ESSENTIAL

If you're serious about genealogy, *Professional Genealogy: A Manual for Researchers, Writers, Editors, Lecturers, and Librarians*, edited by Elizabeth Shown Mills, is a must-have for your genealogy bookshelf. Two dozen leading professional genealogists contributed their expertise to this book. The chapters titled "Research Procedures," "Evidence Analysis," and "Proof Arguments and Case Studies" are especially helpful for their discussion of research methods with real-life examples.

One of the best ways to learn successful genealogical research methods is by reading and studying published case studies. These real-life examples are written by genealogists to describe a particular research process and the method by which they arrived at their conclusions. Many explore particularly confusing research situations, so they can be full of creative searching ideas. Others are particularly adept at walking you through the wide variety of genealogical sources that can be used to build a case. Numerous genealogical case studies and articles online even specifically offer advice on getting past genealogical brick walls. Michael John Neill has written two articles that may help inspire your creativity, titled "Brick Walls from A to Z" (*www.rootdig.com/adn/brickwall_a_z.html*) and "More Brick Walls from A to Z" (*http://blogs.ancestry.com/circle/?p=1396*). In addition, his article listings at Rootdig.com (*www.rootdig.com/adn*) include quite a few case studies and other real-life examples of working through apparent research dead ends. At About.com Genealogy you'll find "Brick Wall Strategies for Tracing Dead-End Family Trees" (*http://genealogy.about.com/od/basics/a/brick_walls.htm*), as well as a wide variety of other case studies (*http://genealogy.about.com/od/case_studies/*).

Other excellent examples include "Researching the Family History of Potential Slave Owners" (*www.examiner.com/article/summary-of-the-jefferson-clark-online-case-study*), a multipart example by Michael Hait, CG (Certified Genealogist), and the dozens of skillful case studies published by Elizabeth Shown Mills, CG , CGL, FASG, on her own website, Historic Pathways (*http://historicpathways.com/articles.html*).

Genealogy magazines and society quarterlies and journals are also filled with case studies demonstrating a variety of research skills and strategies. The *National Genealogical Society Quarterly* (*www.ngsgenealogy.org/cs/ngsq*), in particular, focuses on methodologies that apply to genealogical research across localities and time periods. Back issues are available online in digitized format for NGS members, and most major genealogy libraries have copies in their collections.

Protect Your Family History from Disaster

If you had to evacuate your house and only had minutes to get out, what would you take? Would you take the boxes of photos in the back of your bedroom closet? The photo albums on the coffee table in your family room? The computer in your study? The genealogy files in your basement? In a disaster situation you often won't have time to grab much and generally won't have time to go looking. You may not even be home when disaster strikes, which leaves you no time at all. Important pieces of your family history, even those that had survived for centuries, could be gone in an instant.

Back Up Your Computer Files

In the Internet age, people have come to rely on their computers for everything from online banking to digital photo storage. The downside of this reliance on technology, however, is that catastrophes such as fire, theft, computer viruses, and hardware failure can cause you to lose years of hard work or irreplaceable memories in an instant. Don't make the mistake of believing that it won't happen to you. It happens more often than you might think. But the results don't have to be catastrophic if you back up your genealogy files and digital documents on a regular basis.

There are a wide variety of backup options available, and with technology changing constantly it's probably best to explore these online. CD-ROMs work for small files, and most people already have a CD burner in their computer. For video or large photo collections, you'll want to look at DVD burners, USB flash drives, and external hard drives.

ALERT

For small, occasional offline backups of important files, such as your family tree file, sign up for a free e-mail account through a service that offers online e-mail storage, and e-mail the file to yourself. At the time of writing, Gmail (offered through Google), Yahoo! Mail, AOL's AIM Mail, and Windows Live Hotmail all offer anywhere from 15GB to unlimited storage of online e-mail. That's enough space to store plenty of documents and photos.

Online backup services offer another easy method for backing up your precious computer files and digital photos. You can store your data offline, away from your home where a disaster might strike both your computer and your backups at once, and use automatic scheduling of backups so there is no more forgetting to back up your files. Cost is a factor in such services, however. ConsumerSearch recommends the best online backup services (*www.consumersearch.com/online-backup-services*) based on their appraisal and rating of a number of online reviews.

Duplicate and Distribute

Sharing your family history like this is one of the best ways to assure that nothing important is ever lost. Make copies of precious photos and documents and mail them off to family members. Send relatives a GEDCOM of your family tree file. Create a genealogy website for disseminating your research. Upload your photos to an online photo-sharing service. All of these steps take a little time, but will ultimately safeguard your family history from potential disaster. Your family members will appreciate the gifts as well!

Don't Overlook the Hidden Dangers

Light, temperature, moisture, pollutants, and the odd bug or two all threaten the survival of family heritage. The solution doesn't have to be complicated, however. Basically, it's a matter of making the time to transfer your photos, documents, wedding dress, family Bible, and other family heirlooms into archival-safe boxes, albums, and storage containers. Once they're appropriately packed, they just need a safe home. Find a spot in your house that maintains normal indoor temperature year-round and is generally dark and dust free, such as a closet shelf, a storage trunk, or even under the bed. If you're in a flood-prone area, keep things above known flood levels. You should almost always avoid the attic, basement, and garage because they tend to experience large variations in temperature and/or moisture.

Information and supplies for proper storage and preservation of family photographs and documents are easy to locate online. Experts at the National Archives answer questions on storing photographic prints, when to remove photos from an old album, and how to safely attach photos or memorabilia to album or scrapbook pages on their Caring for Your Family Archives web page (*www.archives.gov/preservation/family-archives*). Archivist Sally Jacobs offers ongoing practical tips for genealogists and others interested in preserving their family's heritage on her entertaining blog, the *Practical Archivist* (*www.practicalarchivist.com*).

Publish Your Family History

One of the joys of researching your family history is sharing the results. Family trees can be displayed and presented in a wide variety of ways. A beautiful framed chart can be hung on your wall or presented as a gift. The stories of your ancestors can come to life through a published family history book. Old family photos can take on new life as a scrapbook. Your family history can reach a wide audience through a genealogy website or blog.

Write It Down

A written family history can be as short and simple or as long and detailed as you want. To most family members, it will be priceless, regardless of the size or complexity. The first step is to decide what you want your family history to be. Will you begin with an ancestral couple and document all of their descendants or work your way back up your own direct line? How many generations will your family history cover? Will you include family photographs? Who will buy your book or whom do you plan to share it with?

Once you've decided on some of the basics, the Internet offers a wide range of resources to assist you with your project. GenWriters (*www.genwriters.com/write.html*) has pulled many of these together in one place, with links to a variety of how-to articles and tips, plus a bibliography of family history writing guides.

If you don't want to do the writing or layout yourself, you can hire an individual or company to prepare your family history for you. Search for *family history publishers* or *genealogy book printer* to find companies that can help you with your project. If you're looking for someone to actually write the book for you, the member directory of the Association of Professional Genealogists (*www.apgen.org*) includes listings for quite a few genealogists who specialize in this area.

Scrapbooking Your Family History

With scissors, glue, pens, and maybe a few die-cuts and stickers, you can quickly spice up your collection of old family photos, and share your family story at the same time. Scrapbooking doesn't have to be fancy. The wide variety of specialty charms, stickers, papers, and other scrapbooking supplies available can certainly jazz things up, but journaling is what makes your history really come alive. Tell the "who," "when," and "what" behind every photo, and you've done the most important part.

LINK

Heritage fonts can do a lot to jazz up your family history project, whether it's for printing journaling and page titles for your scrapbook or to add emphasis to a published family history. Free Heritage Fonts (*http://genealogy.about.com/od/fonts*) includes themes ranging from medieval and Old English to the groovy 1960s to the Wild West.

There are hundreds of helpful tutorials, templates, journaling suggestions, and theme ideas for family history scrapbooks to be found online. The scrapbooking site at About.com (*http://scrapbooking.about.com*) will get you started with the basics, including demonstration of a variety of scrapbooking techniques and enough layout and design ideas and links to scrapbooking suppliers to keep you busy for years.

If you prefer computers to paper, you can create scrapbooks digitally as well, with special scrapbooking software or a graphics software program. At About.com Graphics Software (*http://graphicssoft.about .com/od/digitalscrapbooking*) you can learn all about this newer form of scrapbooking, including how to choose and use software, enjoy dozens of free downloadable scrapbooking kits, and find links to free online tutorials, downloads, and patterns all over the web. The *Shades of the Departed* blog (*www.shadesofthedeparted.com*) by Jasia is an excellent place to turn to find unique and beautiful digital scrapbooking kits with a family history theme.

Share Your Family History Online

Probably the easiest way to share your family history online is to publish your pedigree to one of the popular online pedigree databases such as RootsWeb's WorldConnect Project (*http://worldconnect.rootsweb.com*), Ancestry Member Trees (*http://trees.ancestry.com*), FamilySearch Family Tree (*www.familysearch.org*), or WikiTree (*www.wikitree.com*). All you have to do to use these free services is to upload a GEDCOM file from your family tree program and they turn the information into a series of online searchable pedigrees. This solution allows your family tree to be found by people searching the Internet, yet requires very little work or technical knowledge.

Another easy option for sharing your family history online is to create a page on a site that offers a set of easy tools for putting your family tree online.

Sites such as WeRelate *(www.werelate.org)*, MyHeritage *(www.myheritage
.com/family-tree)*, and GeneaNet *(www.geneanet.org)* let you build an online
family tree, collaborate with your family members, connect with other
researchers, and share photos and recipes. Many offer secure, password-
protected sites if you want to keep your family history in the family.

If you want a little more custom control over the layout, content, and design
of your site, you may want to create a full-blown genealogy website. There
are free hosting options, such as the popular Freepages *(http://freepages
.rootsweb.com)* at RootsWeb and TribalPages *(www.tribalpages.com)*, or
you might want to explore inexpensive hosting options geared specifically
for family websites, such as Related Families *(www.relatedfamilies.com)*.
Alternatively, you can purchase space, and even your own domain name,
through any hosting service. Many family tree software programs include
nice online publishing features to make sure the process of getting your
actual pedigree online is done in a nice, browsable format. For step-by-step
guidance, check out the NGS guide *Planting Your Family Tree Online: How to
Create Your Own Family History Web Site* by Cyndi Howells.

ESSENTIAL

For more control over your online tree, check out programs designed to
help you publish your family tree on your own personal website. These
include the Next Generation of Genealogy Sitebuilding *(http://lythgoes
.net/genealogy/software.php)*, Second Site *(http://ss.johncardinal.com)*
for users of the Master Genealogist, and Adam: The GEDCOM Family
Tree Builder *(http://timforsythe.com/tools/adam)*. Some programs, such
as RootsMagic and Legacy Family Tree, also have good online publishing options built right into the software.

Additional software options exist to help you get your family tree
information from your desktop genealogy program and then publish it
online (usually via a GEDCOM file). Explore further alternatives online in
the "Share & Preserve Your Family Tree" section of About.com Genealogy
(http://genealogy.about.com/od/preservation/u/share.htm).

Blogs are extremely popular with genealogists as an easy medium for
sharing their family history online. A blog, short for web log, is basically

a type of online journal with text, photos, and other goodies. You don't need to know any HTML or programming to use blogging software, and you can use it through a free online hosting service such as WordPress (*www.wordpress.com*) or Blogger (*www.blogger.com*). You can also install the software on your own website if you choose. A blog varies from a traditional genealogy site by having each entry dated, like a journal, and therefore people expect them to be updated frequently. This makes them a perfect medium for sharing every little setback and success of your family history research as it happens! Think of a blog as your family history research log. If this sounds appealing to you, you can learn the basics of starting your own family history blog in "Blogging Your Family History Search" (*http://genealogy.about.com/od/publishing/a/blogging.htm*) and learn even more from Thomas MacEntee's "A Genealogy Blog Primer" (*www.geneabloggers.com/genealogy-blog-primer*).

Dos and Don'ts of Online Genealogy

The Internet has definitely revolutionized genealogy. Computerized indexes make it possible to find individuals with very little information, on occasion without even a name. Digitized records make it possible to view page after page of records well into the wee hours, long after the library is locked up for the night. The availability of so many records in one place eliminates hours spent traveling to numerous repositories.

All of those benefits come with a price, however. Ease of publishing often results in half-done or shoddy research. The rush to put genealogical records online sometimes results in inaccurate indexes. The sheer wealth of available information makes finding the little bitty fact that you seek a very daunting task. To help you get started feeling comfortable with genealogy online, here are a few basic dos and don'ts.

Do Look for Source Documentation

Just because you find information online doesn't mean that it's true. Before you accept any statement of fact, look for information on the original source of the information. Many online databases will include a source or "more about" link. Family trees will, hopefully, include contact information for the submitter. Be sure to document both this original record and the online source where you found the information, so you can accurately assess the quality of the information and so others can follow your research trail.

Don't Expect to Find Everything Online

Many people begin their genealogy search on the Internet expecting to find their entire family tree online, already completed back several centuries. The trouble is, it usually doesn't work that way. You can absolutely do a lot of research online, but don't miss out on the fun and adventure of a visit to the local courthouse or family cemetery.

Do Your Homework Before Forking Over Your Money

Most of the commercial genealogy enterprises online are absolutely legitimate, but every now and then a website pops up with questionable business practices. Search the Internet for user comments and reviews of any website, software, or other commercial purchase before pulling out the credit card.

Don't Expect to Do It All for Free

You have probably noticed that certain subscription-based genealogy sites such as Ancestry.com keep coming up throughout this book. That's because even with the hefty price tag, these commercial subscription sites offer much more genealogical information online in one place than you'll find anywhere else. If you have a large family tree or plan to do a lot of research, a subscription will eventually pay for itself in time saved. If money is an issue, however, don't forget that many libraries offer free access to many subscription genealogy websites, such as Ancestry Plus and/or HeritageQuest Online. You can also search out the many free databases and resources highlighted throughout this book.

Do Not Publish Information on Living People Online

Your relatives probably won't be thrilled to find their birth dates and other private information online. Even just publishing their names along with the information on their parents can be too much, since many security systems use the mother's maiden name as identification. Use your genealogy software or a utility program to privatize this information before uploading your data online.

Don't Merge Family Trees

It's best to never import someone else's GEDCOM file directly into your own family tree. By taking time to enter the data into your genealogy software by hand, you get to learn about the new family connections. Otherwise you're letting software make all the decisions about who your ancestors are! If you do choose to import a GEDCOM file, however, make a backup of your main file first and import into the backup. This way you can revert back to your original file if the import has unanticipated results.

Do Give Back to the Genealogy Community

When you're first starting out, people will likely help you. After you've gained some experience, say thank you by helping someone else. Answer questions on a mailing list or forum. Do a few record lookups. Take time out to transcribe or index some records.

Don't Assume That Information on the Internet Is Public Domain

The majority of the articles, databases, transcriptions, and other genealogy information that you find online are protected by the copyright of the author. If you wish to repost such information in a blog, for a class handout, or on a mailing list or website, you need to get the author's permission. Acknowledging the source of the copyrighted material does not substitute for obtaining permission. For mailing lists and blogs, the best course of action is to use a very small excerpt (considered "fair use") along with attribution to the author and a link to the original content.

Do Back Up Your Data on a Regular Basis

You do not want to lose hundreds of hours of genealogy research or irreplaceable family photos because you haven't backed up your digital files. Find a backup plan that works for you and stick to it.

Don't Give Up

While the Internet exponentially increases your opportunities for locating your ancestors, it can also be an extremely frustrating experience to find just the right search combination. Use the search techniques introduced throughout this book and practice, practice, practice. It won't be long before you'll feel like a pro!

See It in Action

Now it's time to see how all of the research techniques you've learned in this book can be pulled together to research a family tree online. Several case studies written specifically to help walk readers through many of the records and resources introduced in this book appear on About.com Genealogy:

- Laura Ingalls Wilder: Fiction to Fact (*genealogy.about.com/od/case_studies/a/laura-ingalls.htm*)
- George Herman Ruth: A Wealth of Records Online (*genealogy.about.com/od/case_studies/a/babe-ruth.htm*)
- Robert Lee Frost: Following Families Through the Census (*genealogy.about.com/od/case_studies/a/robert-frost.htm*)
- Neil Armstrong: Researching Twentieth Century Ancestors (*genealogy.about.com/od/case_studies/a/neil-armstrong.htm*)
- The Mystery Box: A Descendant Genealogy (*genealogy.about.com/ od/case_studies/a/mystery-box.htm*)

I wish you success in applying the methods you've learned here to your own family history search. Enjoy the journey!

APPENDIX A

Further Readings

There are many excellent genealogy reference books available, covering a wide range of topics and localities. The selections listed here are among the cream of the crop, while also containing content applicable to any genealogist, no matter what your geographic or ethnic area of interest.

The Source: A Guidebook of American Genealogy, **3rd ed., edited by Loretto Dennis Szucs and Sandra Hargreaves Luebking (Provo, UT: Ancestry Publishing, 2006).**

The Source is one of those books that exists on just about every professional genealogist's bookshelf. Each chapter, written by an expert, covers a different body of genealogy research, showing what sources are available, how to find them, and how to use them. This is the definitive book for anyone researching American genealogy. Articles from the book are also online in the Ancestry.com wiki.

The Researcher's Guide to American Genealogy, **3rd ed., by Val D. Greenwood (Baltimore, MD: Genealogical Publishing Co., 2013).**

Another essential reference for researchers who focus on American genealogy is *The Researcher's Guide*, which identifies various classes of records used in genealogical research and tells where they are located and how to use them in research. This is both a reference book about available American records and a guide to the genealogical research process.

Ancestry's *Red Book: American State, County, and Town Sources*, 3rd rev. ed., edited by Alice Eichholz, PhD (Provo, UT: Ancestry Publishing, 2004).

If you need to know when a particular county was formed, what records are available, or where records are kept, this reference book will generally have the answers, with resources and historical information organized by state and county. Available online in the Ancestry.com wiki.

***Evidence Explained: Citing History Sources from Artifacts to Cyberspace*, 2nd ed., by Elizabeth Shown Mills (Baltimore, MD: Genealogical Publishing Co., 2009).**

While there is no one proper method for citing your genealogy sources, many researchers like to have a reference guide. *Evidence Explained* offers citation examples and models for thousands of different source materials, from Internet databases and images to census records and court records. Elizabeth Mills also shares her expert guidance in how to analyze for yourself what the essential citation elements are for different types of records that you may encounter. A PDF version is available for sale on the author's website at *www.evidenceexplained.com*.

The BCG Genealogical Standards Manual **by the Board for Certification of Genealogists (Orem, UT: Ancestry Publishing, 2000).**

If you're interested in becoming a professional genealogist, or just want to produce a quality, well-researched family history, this official manual from the Board for Certification of Genealogists brings together a wide array of research standards, along with examples of how to put them into practice. An updated version is planned for publication by early 2014.

Professional Genealogy: A Manual for Researchers, Writers, Editors, Lecturers, and Librarians **edited by Elizabeth Shown Mills (Baltimore, MD: Genealogical Publishing Co., 2001).**

This comprehensive manual for professional genealogists is also a must-have for the serious hobbyist. Twenty-three chapters cover a variety of genealogical skills and standards, each presented by a professional genealogist with expertise in the subject. Topics include every aspect of professional genealogy, including proof standards and ethics and operating a genealogy business, plus family history research and publication.

Mastering Genealogical Proof **by Thomas W. Jones (Arlington, VA: National Genealogical Society, 2013).**

The unique textbook style of *Mastering Genealogical Proof* helps readers to master the difficult concepts of genealogical reasoning and proof. Each chapter includes real-life examples and problems for further exploring the chapter's concepts, and answers are included in the back of the book.

Genealogical Proof Standard: Building a Solid Case, **3rd rev. ed., by Christine Rose (San Jose, CA: CR Publications, 2009).**

This small book provides a clear explanation and numerous examples of the *Genealogical Proof Standard* in action, as well as discussing the analysis and evaluation of evidence by which we build a case.

The Family Tree Problem Solver: Proven Methods for Scaling the Inevitable Brick Wall **by Marsha Hoffman Rising (Cincinnati, OH: Family Tree Books, 2005).**

When you hit a brick wall in your genealogy research, this book often comes to the rescue. The well-respected author offers a number of "brick wall" research techniques, along with case studies to demonstrate the techniques in action. She then delves into the most common types of genealogical research dead ends—missing records, ancestors who lived prior to 1850, and men with the same name—and the best ways to deal with them.

Hidden Sources: Family History in Unlikely Places by Laura Szucs Pfeiffer (Orem, UT: Ancestry Publishing, 2000).

Another excellent book geared toward getting you past your brick walls by introducing you to the vast variety of records in which you might discover your ancestors.

Trace Your Roots with DNA: Using Genetic Tests to Explore Your Family Tree by Megan Smolenyak and Ann Turner (Emmaus, PA: Rodale Books, 2004).

Genetics and DNA are science, so you can expect to have to stretch your brain a little to really grasp how the tests work and how they can be used in conjunction with traditional genealogy research to learn more about your ancestors. While this book isn't exactly light reading given the subject matter, it is a very user-friendly introduction written by two experts in the field. Due to its publication date, autosomal DNA is not covered in great detail.

Unlocking Your Genetic History: A Step-by-Step Guide to Discovering Your Family's Medical and Genetic Heritage by Thomas H. Shawker (Nashville, TN: Rutledge Hill Press, 2004).

If you want to dig even further into the science behind the application of DNA testing for genealogy, Thomas Shawker also does an outstanding job of explaining this difficult subject in layman's terms. Especially important are the chapters on why it is important for you to know about your family's health history and how to compile and interpret your own medical pedigree.

Finding Family: My Search for Roots and the Secrets in My DNA by Richard Hill (Grand Rapids, MI: CreateSpace, 2012).

This true, intensely personal story details how the author used genealogy and DNA to locate his biological family. In addition to being a fascinating read, this self-published book also serves as a useful guide for adoptees and others interested in exploring their roots.

Courthouse Indexes Illustrated **by Christine Rose (San Jose, CA: CR Publications, 2006).**

Courthouses across the country use a wide variety of indexing systems, many much more complicated than A–Z. This small guidebook includes illustrations and step-by-step explanations of over 30 different indexing systems that researchers might encounter.

Courthouse Research for Family Historians: Your Guide to Genealogical Treasures **by Christine Rose (San Jose, CA: CR Publications, 2004).**

Christine Rose has worked in more different courthouses (over 500) than just about anyone, and she shares her tips and expertise with readers in this well-written book. Learn how to make the most of your courthouse visit, including how to evaluate the records and use them to solve genealogical problems.

Digitizing Your Family History: Easy Methods for Preserving Your Heirloom Documents, Photos, Home Movies, and More in Digital Format **by Rhonda R. McClure (Cincinnati, OH: Family Tree Books, 2004).**

If technology intimidates you a bit, this book will help you tackle the project of digitizing your family history, from choosing a scanner or digital camera to using software to fix up your old family photos or preserve your old family movies.

Uncovering Your Ancestry Through Family Photographs **by Maureen A. Taylor (Cincinnati, OH: Family Tree Books, 2005).**

It takes practice and experience to learn how to find the little clues hidden in your family photos that can help you identify the people, place, or time period. Author Maureen Taylor specializes in this area and shares that expertise in this book, along with beautiful photographs to illustrate her points.

They Came in Ships: Finding Your Immigrant Ancestor's Arrival Record, **3rd ed., by John Philip Colletta (Orem, UT: Ancestry Publishing, 2002).**

This book is slightly out of date because it refers to using microfilm, when the majority of the records discussed are now available online; however, the steps and tips included in this book are timeless. Don't miss the excellent bibliography!

Land and Property Research in the United States **by E. Wade Hone (Salt Lake City, UT: Ancestry Publishing, 1997).**

Land records are among the oldest and best-preserved records available to American genealogists, but the variety of available land records and property laws can make them confusing to beginning researchers. This book is one to turn to again and again for land and property research.

Reading Early American Handwriting **by Kip Sperry (Baltimore, MD: Genealogical Publishing Co., reprinted 2008).**

Kip Sperry explains techniques for reading early American documents, provides samples of common alphabets and letterforms, and defines many of the unusual terms and abbreviations that you'll encounter. Numerous examples make it easy to practice what you've learned.

Ancestral Trails: The Complete Guide to British Genealogy and Family History, **2nd rev. ed., by Mark D. Herber (Baltimore, MD: Genealogical Publishing Co., 2006).**

This is a comprehensive book on British genealogy and family history with information for the beginner and advanced researcher alike. This excellent book begins with the basics of starting your family tree, and then walks you through the maze of British records and repositories. There is some Internet coverage, but this is still primarily a guide to offline, published sources.

Producing a Quality Family History **by Patricia Law Hatcher (Salt Lake City, UT: Ancestry Publishing, 1996).**

This excellent guide walks you through every step of producing a published family history of your family, including organizing your information; writing the narrative; and finalizing all of the little details, from choosing a typeface to creating a bibliography.

You Can Write Your Family History **by Sharon DeBartolo Carmack (Cincinnati, OH: Genealogical Publishing Co., reprinted 2008).**

This book is guaranteed to inspire almost anyone, even those of you who may not like to write, to successfully chronicle the fascinating tales of your ancestors. Her advice is practical and down-to-earth, taking you step by step through the process from researching to writing.

FREE DOWNLOADS!

Thank you for purchasing *The Everything® Guide to Online Genealogy*. To show our appreciation, we'd like to give you some free gifts to get you started. To access them, please visit *http://familytreeuniversity.com/ everything-online-genealogy*.

Starter Kit of Genealogy Forms and Worksheets

Track your work on your family tree with these essential forms, including:

- Five-generation ancestor chart

- Family group sheet for recording information about a nuclear family

- Research calendar for noting what you've done and future to-dos

- Checklist of sources and records to consult

- Decorative family tree to fill out and share

Type your information directly into the forms, or print out blank copies to write on.

Free Digital Issue of *Family Tree Magazine*

Get more help discovering, preserving, and celebrating your family history with a free issue of America's #1 genealogy magazine! Download your digital copy for timesaving tips, expert research guidance, the best web resources, tech tutorials, archival advice, and more how-to help to explore your roots.

Examples of Family Trees

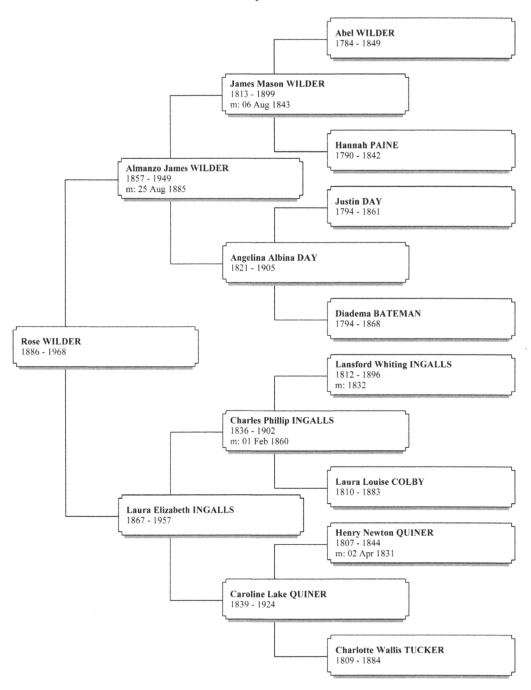

Abel WILDER
1784 - 1849

James Mason WILDER
1813 - 1899
m: 06 Aug 1843

Hannah PAINE
1790 - 1842

Almanzo James WILDER
1857 - 1949
m: 25 Aug 1885

Justin DAY
1794 - 1861

Angelina Albina DAY
1821 - 1905

Diadema BATEMAN
1794 - 1868

Rose WILDER
1886 - 1968

Lansford Whiting INGALLS
1812 - 1896
m: 1832

Charles Phillip INGALLS
1836 - 1902
m: 01 Feb 1860

Laura Louise COLBY
1810 - 1883

Laura Elizabeth INGALLS
1867 - 1957

Henry Newton QUINER
1807 - 1844
m: 02 Apr 1831

Caroline Lake QUINER
1839 - 1924

Charlotte Wallis TUCKER
1809 - 1884

More complete information on the family tree of Laura Ingalls and Almanzo Wilder, including additional details, updates, and sources, can be found on About.com Genealogy: *http://genealogy.about.com/od/famous_family_trees/p/ingalls.htm.*

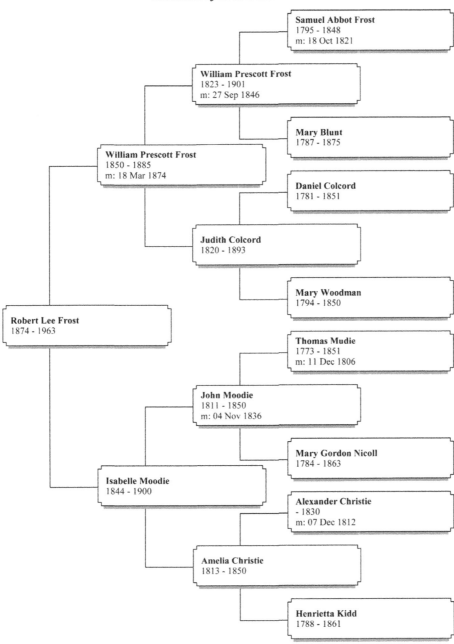

More complete information on the family tree of Robert Lee Frost, including additional details, updates, and sources, can be found on About.com Genealogy: *http://genealogy.about.com/od/ famous_family_trees/a/robert_frost.htm*.

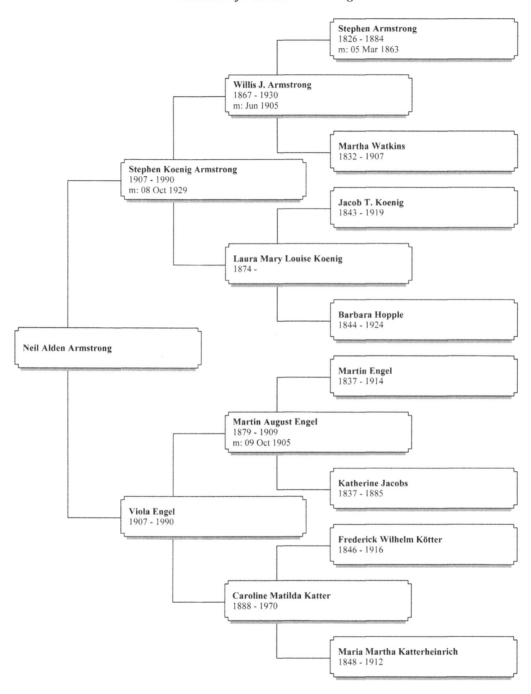

Stephen Armstrong
1826 - 1884
m: 05 Mar 1863

Willis J. Armstrong
1867 - 1930
m: Jun 1905

Martha Watkins
1832 - 1907

Stephen Koenig Armstrong
1907 - 1990
m: 08 Oct 1929

Jacob T. Koenig
1843 - 1919

Laura Mary Louise Koenig
1874 -

Barbara Hopple
1844 - 1924

Neil Alden Armstrong

Martin Engel
1837 - 1914

Martin August Engel
1879 - 1909
m: 09 Oct 1905

Katherine Jacobs
1837 - 1885

Viola Engel
1907 - 1990

Frederick Wilhelm Kötter
1846 - 1916

Caroline Matilda Katter
1888 - 1970

Maria Martha Katterheinrich
1848 - 1912

More complete information on the family tree of Neil Armstrong, including additional details, updates, and sources, can be found on About.com Genealogy: *http://genealogy.about.com/od/ famous_family_trees/a/neil_armstrong.htm.*

Genealogical Standards

Standards For Sound Genealogical Research

Recommended by the National Genealogical Society. Remembering always that they are engaged in a quest for truth, family history researchers consistently:

- record the source for each item of information they collect.
- test every hypothesis or theory against credible evidence, and reject those that are not supported by the evidence.
- seek original records, or reproduced images of them when there is reasonable assurance they have not been altered, as the basis for their research conclusions.
- use compilations, communications and published works, whether paper or electronic, primarily for their value as guides to locating the original records, or as contributions to the critical analysis of the evidence discussed in them.
- state something as a fact only when it is supported by convincing evidence, and identify the evidence when communicating the fact to others.
- limit with words like "probable" or "possible" any statement that is based on less than convincing evidence, and state the reasons for concluding that it is probable or possible.
- avoid misleading other researchers by either intentionally or carelessly distributing or publishing inaccurate information.
- state carefully and honestly the results of their own research, and acknowledge all use of other researchers' work.
- recognize the collegial nature of genealogical research by making their work available to others through publication, or by placing copies in appropriate libraries or repositories, and by welcoming critical comment.
- consider with open minds new evidence or the comments of others on their work and the conclusions they have reached.

Standards For Use Of Technology In Genealogical Research

Recommended by the National Genealogical Society. Mindful that computers are tools, genealogists take full responsibility for their work, and therefore:

- learn the capabilities and limits of their equipment and software, and use them only when they are the most appropriate tools for a purpose.
- do not accept uncritically the ability of software to format, number, import, modify, check, chart or report their data, and therefore carefully evaluate any resulting product.
- treat compiled information from on-line sources or digital databases in the same way as other published sources--useful primarily as a guide to locating original records, but not as evidence for a conclusion or assertion.
- accept digital images or enhancements of an original record as a satisfactory substitute for the original only when there is reasonable assurance that the image accurately reproduces the unaltered original.
- cite sources for data obtained on-line or from digital media with the same care that is appropriate for sources on paper and other traditional media, and enter data into a digital database only when its source can remain associated with it.
- always cite the sources for information or data posted on-line or sent to others, naming the author of a digital file as its immediate source, while crediting original sources cited within the file.
- preserve the integrity of their own databases by evaluating the reliability of downloaded data before incorporating it into their own files.
- provide, whenever they alter data received in digital form, a description of the change that will accompany the altered data whenever it is shared with others.
- actively oppose the proliferation of error, rumor and fraud by personally verifying or correcting information, or noting it as unverified, before passing it on to others.
- treat people on-line as courteously and civilly as they would treat them face-to-face, not separated by networks and anonymity.
- accept that technology has not changed the principles of genealogical research, only some of the procedures.

Guidelines For Using Records Repositories And Libraries

Recommended by the National Genealogical Society. Recognizing that how they use unique original records and fragile publications will affect other users, both current and future, family history researchers habitually:

- are courteous to research facility personnel and other researchers, and respect the staff's other daily tasks, not expecting the records custodian to listen to their family histories nor provide constant or immediate attention.
- dress appropriately, converse with others in a low voice, and supervise children appropriately.
- do their homework in advance, know what is available and what they need, and avoid ever asking for "everything" on their ancestors.
- use only designed work space areas and equipment, like readers and computers, intended for patron use, respect off-limits areas, and ask for assistance if needed.
- treat original records at all times with great respect and work with only a few records at a time, recognizing that they are irreplaceable and that each user must help preserve them for future use.
- treat books with care, never forcing their spines, and handle photographs properly, preferably wearing archival gloves.
- never mark, mutilate, rearrange, relocate, or remove from the repository any original, printed, microform, or electronic document or artifact.
- use only procedures prescribed by the repository for noting corrections to any errors or omissions found in published works, never marking the work itself.
- keep note-taking paper or other objects from covering records or books, and avoid placing any pressure upon them, particularly with a pencil or pen.
- use only the method specifically designated for identifying records for duplication, avoiding use of paper clips, adhesive notes, or other means not approved by the facility.

- return volumes and files only to locations designated for that purpose.
- before departure, thank the records custodians for their courtesy in making the materials available.
- follow the rules of the records repository without protest, even if they have changed since a previous visit or differ from those of another facility.

Guidelines For Publishing Web Pages On The Internet

Recommended by the National Genealogical Society. Appreciating that publishing information through Internet web sites and web pages shares many similarities with print publishing, considerate family historians:

- apply a title identifying both the entire web site and the particular group of related pages, similar to a book-and-chapter designation, placing it both at the top of each web browser window using the <TITLE> HTML tag, and in the body of the document, on the opening home or title page and on any index pages.
- explain the purposes and objectives of their web sites, placing the explanation near the top of the title page or including a link from that page to a special page about the reason for the site.
- display a footer at the bottom of each web page which contains the web site title, page title, author's name, author's contact information, date of last revision and a copyright statement.
- provide complete contact information, including at a minimum a name and e-mail address, and preferably some means for long-term contact, like a postal address.
- assist visitors by providing on each page navigational links that lead visitors to other important pages on the web site, or return them to the home page.

- adhere to the NGS "Standards for Sharing Information with Others" regarding copyright, attribution, privacy, and the sharing of sensitive information.
- include unambiguous source citations for the research data provided on the site, and if not complete descriptions, offering full citations upon request.
- label photographic and scanned images within the graphic itself, with fuller explanation if required in text adjacent to the graphic.
- identify transcribed, extracted or abstracted data as such, and provide appropriate source citations.
- include identifying dates and locations when providing information about specific surnames or individuals.
- respect the rights of others who do not wish information about themselves to be published, referenced or linked on a web site.
- provide web site access to all potential visitors by avoiding enhanced technical capabilities that may not be available to all users, remembering that not all computers are created equal.
- avoid using features that distract from the productive use of the web site, like ones that reduce legibility, strain the eyes, dazzle the vision, or otherwise detract from the visitor's ability to easily read, study, comprehend or print the online publication.
- maintain their online publications at frequent intervals, changing the content to keep the information current, the links valid, and the web site in good working order.
- preserve and archive for future researchers their online publications and communications that have lasting value, using both electronic and paper duplication.

Index

About.com Genealogy
  census records, 98, 108
  classes online, 208
  family histories, 46
  family trees, 266, 275
  GEDCOM files, 22
  genealogy searches, 58
  glossaries online, 15
  heritage fonts, 270–71
  overseas records, 238
  photo collections, 225
  resources online, 275
  state archives, 79
  word lists online, 254
  writing stories, 38
Abstracts, 26, 66
Access to Archival Databases
  (AAD), 77, 184
Adoptions, 127–30
African American Census
  Schedules, 102
African research, 256–57
Agricultural schedules, 110–11
American Ancestors, 76, 87
American Ancestors magazine, 76
American Genealogist, 217
American Memory collection, 78,
  153
American Revolution, 111, 156, 158,
  162–65, 168, 173, 222
*Ancestral Trails: The Complete
  Guide to British Genealogy and
  Family History*, 243
Ancestry.com
  birth records, 121
  church records, 150–51
  family trees, 201, 270
  genealogy searches, 46, 54, 61,
    71–74, 101–2
  historical records, 78, 89
  immigration records, 178–88
  marriage records, 119
  military records, 158–64, 167–73
  newspapers, 144–45
  obituaries, 85
  passenger lists, 183

  school records, 152
  wildcard searches, 54
  yearbooks, 152
Ancestry Insider, 218
Annals of Genealogical Research,
  217
Archival Research Catalog (ARC),
  77
Archives, searching, 45–47, 76–79,
  198–99
Archives.com, 85, 102
Armstrong, Neil, 275, 288
Asian research, 256–57
Atlanta Constitution, 144
Attics, searching, 38–40, 93
Australian research, 255–56
Authored narrative, 18–20

Backward searches, 35–48
Baptismal records, 120–22
Baxter, Angus, 251
Beine, Joe, 89, 111, 173, 179, 188, 253
Bennett, Frank, 116
*Bibliography of Ship Passenger
  Lists, 1538–1825*, 178
Birth records, 120–22, 242–47
Blogs, 217–18
Books, resource, 216–17, 277–83
Border-crossing records, 186,
  236–39
Boston Globe, 144
Boswell, Wendy, 50, 59
Bounty land warrants, 141, 157,
  160–63
"Brick Walls from A to Z," 265–66
"Brick Wall Strategies for Tracing
  Dead-End Family Trees," 266
British Isles research, 240–47
Brown, James, 82–83

Canadian research, 236–38
Carmack, Sharon DeBartolo, 27
Casefile Clues, 217
Castle Garden database, 182–83

Cemeteries, 90–92, 173
Census alternatives, 112–14
Census Finder, 102
Census Online, 102
Census records
  alternatives to, 112–14
  census images, 100–104
  census research tips, 98–99
  census years, 103
  checking, 97–116, 241–42
  children in, 107
  clues in, 106–9
  federal census, 98–100
  immigration records, 108
  information from, 98–99
  marriage records, 107–8
  military service and, 109–10, 156
  naturalization records, 108
  online indexes, 100–104
  research tips for, 104–6
  special census, 109–12
  state census, 109–12
"Census Tick Marks and Codes—
  Revisited Yet Again!," 100
Central American research, 239–40
Central European research, 254–55
The Chicago Manual of Style, 31
Chicago Tribune, 143
Christian, Peter, 243
Christian Science Monitor, 144
Chronicling America, 145–46
Churches, local, 149–51
Church of Jesus Christ of Latter-
  day Saints (LDS), 66, 69, 74
City directories, 46, 109, 113–14,
  147, 219
Civil registration records, 237, 239,
  242–49, 255
Civil War, 75, 78, 156–68, 173, 189,
  208, 222
Civil War Soldiers and Sailors
  System, 159, 166
Classmates.com, 59
Clooz.com, 25
"Cluster" research approach, 62–63
Collateral genealogy, 16

Colletta, John P., 188
Compiled military service records (CMSR), 157–60, 166
Computer files, backing up, 266–68
Computer files, duplicating, 267–68
Connecting with others
    contacting strangers, 203–5
    family trees, 199–203
    joining societies, 210–12
    mailing lists, 196–99
    networking, 202–3, 212–13, 226
    newsgroups, 198
    professionals, 210–14
    relatives, 58–59, 117–30
Correspondence/letters, 24, 38–46, 156–58, 167, 172, 176, 187
Courses on genealogy, 207–10
Courthouse Indexes Illustrated, 126
Courthouse Research for Family Historians, 141
Court records, 125–27
Customs Passenger Lists, 179–80, 182, 184
Cyndi's List
    genealogy classes, 209
    genealogy searches, 53
    military records, 173–74
    occupational records, 220, 223
    orphan records, 130
    overseas records, 238, 254
    societies, 212, 223
    surname projects, 234
    vital records, 120

Database searches
    free databases, 66–72
    strategies for, 53–56
    subscription sites, 73–76
Dates, recording, 29, 261
Daughters of the American Revolution (DAR), 163, 173, 222
Day, Angeline, 95
DearMYRTLE, 218
Death certificates, 88–90

Death Index (SSDI), 58, 61, 86–96, 219
Death records, 58, 81–96, 242–47
Deeds, 125–27, 135–41, 208, 225
Deeper searches, 56, 59–60, 215–34. *See also* Searches
DeepMapper, 135
Defective, dependent, and delinquent (DDD) schedules, 112
Derivative records, 18–20
Descendant tree, 16
"Descriptive Pamphlets of the National Archives," 162
Diaries, 19, 37–39, 45–46, 119, 156, 172–73
"Digging Details from Pre-1850 U.S. Census Records," 108
Digital archives, 45
Digital History, 153
Digital images, 18, 66, 75, 95, 101–2, 120–24, 226–27. *See also* Photographs
Direct lineage, 15–16
Divorce records, 118–20
DNA, 228–34
DNA project, 234
DNA testing, 232–33
Dollarhide, William, 135
Draft registrations, 73, 157, 168–70. *See also* Military records
Dunham, Chris, 218

Eastern European research, 254–55
Eastman, Dick, 218
Eastman's Online Genealogy Newsletter, 218
Eichholz, Alice, 216
Ellis Island database, 48, 50, 61, 179, 182–83
Emigration lists, 184–85. *See also* Passenger lists
Estate records, 122–25
Ethnic research, 191–92
European research, 247–54
Evidence, evaluating, 21, 259–66

Evidence Explained: Citing History Sources from Artifacts to Cyberspace, 32
Extracts, 26

Falling Rain's Global Gazetteer, 132
Family, finding, 58–59, 66–70
Family, interviewing, 40–43
Family Chronicle, 217
Family connections, 58–59, 66–70, 117–30
Family history
    previous genealogies, 44–46
    protecting, 266–68
    publishing, 268–72
    sharing, 44–46, 268–72
    storing, 268
Family History Library (FHL), 45, 66–69, 139
Family lineage, 16
Family Pursuit, 24
Family records
    adoption records, 127–30
    baptismal records, 120–22
    birth records, 120–22
    court records, 125–27
    divorce records, 118–20
    estate records, 122–25
    marriage records, 118–20
    orphan records, 127–30
    researching, 117–30
    wills, 122–25
FamilySearch
    census records, 101–2
    church records, 150
    family trees, 199–201, 270
    genealogy searches, 45, 54, 66–72
    historical records, 89
    immigration records, 183
    military records, 162
    overseas records, 239
    school records, 152
Family stories
    finding, 39

military stories, 156–57
publishing, 268–69
recording, 36–38, 42–45, 58
scrapbooking, 269–70
sharing online, 270–72
writing, 37–38
Family Tree Guide Book to Europe, 251
Family Tree Magazine, 217, 251
The Family Tree Problem Solver, 61
Family trees
basics of, 13–14
blogs for, 271–72
collateral genealogy, 16
creating, 37
descendant tree, 16
direct lineage, 15–16
examples of, 285–88
explanation of, 15–16
family lineage, 16
finding, 199–203
medical family tree, 234
pedigree, 15–16
previous genealogies, 44–46
researching, 16–18
software for, 14, 17, 22–24, 74, 270–72
Federal census, 98–100. *See also* Census records
Filby, P. William, 178–79, 252
Files, backing up, 266–68
Files, duplicating, 267–68
Findings, documenting, 31–33
Findings, evaluating, 21, 259–66
FindMyPast.com, 102, 185, 193, 241, 244–47, 255
"Find People Online: How to Search for Someone on the Web," 58
"Fishing for Clues in John Lake's Estate," 123
Fleming, Ann Carter, 27
Fold3.com
military records, 75–76, 78, 158–68, 170, 173
naturalization indexes, 188

obituaries, 85
Forums online, 196–99
"Free Military People Search," 59
French research, 247–49
Frost, Robert Lee, 275, 287
Funeral homes, 90, 92–93

Galveston Immigration Database, 184
GenCircles, 74, 202
GeneaBloggers, 218
Genealogical Data Communication (GEDCOM), 22–23, 202, 206, 267, 270–71, 274
Genealogical Proof Standard (GPS), 31, 263
Genealogical Proof Standard, Building a Solid Case, 262
Genealogical Research System (GRS), 163
Genealogical standards, 289–94
The Genealogist's Internet, 243
Genealogy. *See also* Family trees
classes on, 207–10
collateral genealogy, 16
direct lineage, 15–16
"dos and dont's," 272–75
genetic genealogy, 228–29
pedigree, 15–16
software for, 14, 17, 22–24
GenealogyBank, 74–75, 84, 87, 145, 179
Genealogy Blog Finder, 218
Genealogy Today, 76, 150, 152, 223
Genea-Musings, 218
GeneaNet.org, 24, 71, 202, 271
General Society of the War of 1812, 173–74
Generations
researching, 15–16, 47–48
skipping, 47–48
successive generations, 43–44, 47–48

Genetics
DNA surname study, 234
maternal line, 231–31
paternal line, 229–30
testing, 232–33
Geni.com, 74
GenSoftReviews, 24
GenWeb, 71, 240, 250, 253
GenWed, 120
Geographical locations, 30, 132–34
GEOnet Names Server, 132
German Genealogy Group, 90
German research, 252–53
Germans to America, 252
Glazier, Ira, 252
Glossaries online, 15
Graves, 90–92, 157, 176, 221. *See also* Cemeteries
Greenwood, Val, 216

Hait, Michael, 266
Handwriting styles, 260–61
The Handybook for Genealogists, 216
Hansen, Holly, 216
Hartford Courant, 144
Herber, Mark, 243
Hinke, William J., 178
Historical maps, 133
Historical Newspaper Collection, 144–45
Historical newspapers, 142–46
"Historic Map Overlays for Google Maps & Google Earth," 134
"Historic Newspapers Online," 143
Historic Pathways, 266
History. *See also* Family history
local history, 152–53, 157
military history, 172–74
researching, 76–78
timelines, 153
History Matters, 123
Hone, E. Wade, 137–38
Howells, Cindy, 53, 271

Images online, 18, 66, 75, 95, 101–2, 120–24
Immigrant Servants Database, 184
Immigrant Ship Transcribers Guild, 183–84
Immigration Collection, 183
Immigration Passenger Lists, 179–80, 182, 184
Immigration records
  birth records, 176–77
  border-crossing records, 186, 236–39
  census records and, 107–9
  customs lists, 179–80, 182, 184
  ethnic research, 191–92
  naturalization records, 186–91
  overseas records, 235–57
  passenger lists, 177–88
  researching, 175–94
  ship passenger lists, 177–88
Immigration Service, 180–81
In Search of Your European Roots, 251
Indexes online, 66, 88–90, 100–104
Industry schedules, 111
Information
  authored narratives, 18–19
  backing-up files, 266–68
  collecting, 18–20
  derivative records, 18–19
  duplicating, 267–68
  evaluating, 21, 259–66
  original records, 18–19
  primary sources, 18–20
  proof of, 262–63
  protecting, 266–68
  secondary sources, 18–20
Ingalls, Charles, 95
International Genealogical Index (IGI), 89, 150
Internet Genealogy, 217
"Interpreting the Tick Marks on Federal Censuses," 100
Interviews
  of family members, 40–43
  preparing for, 42–43

questions for, 42–43
  of self, 36–37
Isaacson, Karen, 53
Italian research, 249–50

Jacobs, Sally, 268
Jones, Thomas W., 31, 263
Journals, 24–26, 36–39

Keister, Douglas, 91
Korean War, 77, 168, 172–73

Lancour, Harold, 178
Land & Property Research in the United States, 137–38
Land deeds, 125–27, 135–41, 208, 225
Land patents, 135–40
"Land Platting Made Easy," 135
Land records
  historical maps, 133
  maps, 134–42
  property records, 134–42
  surveys, 137–39
  topographic maps, 133–34
Land surveys, 137–39
Lane, Rose Wilder, 95, 286
Latter-day Saints (LDS), 66, 69, 74
Legacy.com, 85
Legal Genealogist, 218
Letters/correspondence, 24, 38–46, 156–58, 167, 172, 176, 187
Leverich, Brian, 53
Libraries
  interlibrary loan, 148
  local libraries, 85, 146–49
  online libraries, 146–48
  searching, 78–79, 146–48
  websites for, 85
Library of Congress, 44–45, 78, 113, 145, 153, 173
LibWeb, 147
Lineage, 15–16

Lineage-linked databases, 71
Local history, 152–53, 157
Local searches
  churches, 149–51
  fire insurance maps, 134
  geographical locations, 30, 132–34
  land records, 134–42
  libraries, 85, 146–49
  maps, 132–34
  newspapers, 142–46
  property records, 134–42
  schools, 151–52
  societies, 146–49, 211, 217, 221–23
  strategies for, 131–53
Logs, maintaining, 24–25
Los Angeles Times, 143
Luebking, Sandra Hargreaves, 216

MacEntee, Thomas, 218
Magazines, 216–18
Maiden names, 28–29, 47–48, 62
Mailing lists, 196–99
Manufacturing schedules, 111
Manuscript collections, 46–47
Maps, 132–34
Marriage records, 107–8, 119–20, 242–47
Mastering Genealogical Proof, 31, 263
Measuring America: The Decennial Censuses from 1790 to 2000, 100
Medical family tree, 234
Membership organizations, 221–23
Member Trees, 23, 72, 201, 270
Memorial Registry, 173
Message boards, 196–99
Mexican research, 239–40
"Microfilm Publications and Original Records Digitized by Our Digitization Partners," 78
Microfilms, 68–69, 78, 100
Military cemeteries, 173

Military heritage societies, 163, 173–74, 222
Military history, 172–74
Military records
  bounty land warrants, 160–63
  casualty lists, 77, 157, 173
  cemeteries, 173
  census records, 109–10, 156
  compiled military service records, 157–60
  death records, 156
  draft records, 169–70
  draft registrations, 73, 157, 168–70
  family stories, 156–57
  finding, 76–77, 109–10, 156–62, 170–73
  letters/correspondence, 156–58, 167, 172
  military heritage societies, 163, 173–74, 222
  newspaper clippings, 156
  NPRC-MPR, 171
  obituaries, 156
  online records, 158–60
  pension records, 75, 160–63
  photographs, 156
  recent conflicts, 168–72
  remembrance lists, 173
  requesting, 171
  researching, 155–74
  Veterans Affairs records, 164
  wars, 163–73
Military service
  ancestors in, 156–71
  clues to, 156–59
  grave markers, 157
  local history, 157
  military cemeteries, 173
  military history, 172–74
  military records, 156–71
  photographs, 157
Military stories, 156–57, 171
Mills, Elizabeth Shown, 32, 62, 100, 265, 266
Mocavo, 50, 87

"More Brick Walls from A to Z," 265
Mormon Church, 74
Morse, Steve, 61, 87, 186
Mortality schedules, 110
MyHeritage, 24, 74, 101–2, 144, 152, 202, 271
Mystery Box: A Descendant Genealogy, 275
MyTrees.com, 71

Names. *See also* Surnames
  maiden names, 28–29, 47–48, 62
  naming patterns, 48
  order of, 28–29
  popular names, 61–62
  recording, 28–29
  similar names, 56–57, 61–62
  spellings of, 56–57
National Archives and Records Administration (NARA)
  ethnic research, 192
  immigration records, 182, 184
  military records, 76–77, 158, 161–62, 170–73
  passenger lists, 182
National Digital Newspaper Program, 145
National Genealogical Society, 31, 39, 207–8, 217, 263, 266, 279, 290–93
National Genealogical Society Quarterly, 217, 266
National Obituary Archive, 85
National Personnel Records Center, Military Personnel Records (NPRC-MPR), 171
National Union Catalog of Manuscript Collections (NUCMC), 47, 150
Naturalization records, 107–9, 186–91
Neill, Michael John, 123, 217, 265
Nevius, Erin, 251
New England Historical and Genealogical Register, 76, 217

Newsgroups, 198
Newspaper Archive, 85, 94, 144
Newspapers, 85, 94, 142–46
Newspapers.com, 145
New York Amsterdam News, 144
New York Times, 143
New York Tribune, 144
New Zealand research, 255–56
Notebooks, 24–26, 36–39
Note-taking, 25–26

ObitFinder, 85
ObitsArchive.com, 85
Obituaries, 82–86
Obituary Daily Times, 84–85
Occupational records, 218–21
OCLC WorldCat Catalog, 47
Olive Tree Genealogy, 184
OneGreatFamily, 71
One-Step website, 61, 87, 186
Online glossaries, 15
Online libraries, 146–48
Online message boards, 196–99
Online Public Access, 77
Online searches
  abstracts online, 66
  birth records, 120–22
  death records, 86–96
  forums online, 196–99
  images online, 18, 66, 75, 95, 101–2, 120–24
  immigration records, 177–88
  indexes online, 66, 88–90, 100–104
  maps online, 132
  marriage records, 119–20
  military records, 158–60
  online message boards, 196–99
  passenger records, 177–88
  sources online, 65–66
  strategies for, 65–79
  transcripts online, 66
Online subscription sites, 73–76
Organizations, 221–23
The Organized Family Historian, 27

Organizing Your Family History Search, 27
Original records, 18–20
Orphans, 127–30
Overseas records, 235–57
"Overview of Records at the National Archives Relating to Military Service," 159

Parish records, 246–49, 252
Passenger and Immigration Lists Bibliography, 1538–1900, 178–79
Passenger lists
    Castle Garden database, 182–83
    customs lists, 179–80, 182, 184
    Ellis Island database, 182
    emigration lists, 184–85
    Immigration Collection, 183
    immigration records, 177–88
    online passenger records, 177–88
Pedigree, 15–16
"Perfect Search Engine: How to Pick the Right Tool for the Job," 50
Periodical Source Index (PERSI), 46, 150
Personal stories
    finding, 39
    military stories, 156–57
    publishing, 268–69
    recording, 36–38, 42–45, 58
    scrapbooking, 269–70
    sharing online, 270–72
    writing, 37–38
Photographs, 223–27, 268. *See also* Digital images
Pittsburgh Courier, 144
Planting Your Family Tree Online: How to Create Your Own Family History Web Site, 271
Polish research, 254
Postcards, 223–24
"Post-em Note" feature, 74
Practical Archivist, 268

Prison records, 46, 112, 166–68, 172, 197
Professional genealogists, 210–14
Professional Genealogy: A Manual for Researchers, Writers, Editors, Lecturers, and Librarians, 265
ProGen Study Groups, 213
Progress, recording, 27–30
Project
    basics of, 13–14
    collecting information, 18–20
    documenting search, 31–33
    evaluating information, 21
    organizing, 22–26
    planning, 14–17
    recording progress, 27–30
"Proof argument," 262–63
Property records, 134–42
ProQuest newspapers, 144–45
PublicLibraries.com, 147
Publishing family history, 268–69

Quiner, Carolyn, 95

Red Book: American State, County, and Town Sources, 216
Relatives, connecting with, 58–59, 117–30. *See also* Family history
Religious records, 149–51
Research. *See also* Searches
    abstracts, 26
    authored narratives, 18–19
    backing-up files, 266–68
    basics of, 16–17
    of census records, 97–116
    "cluster" approach to, 62–63
    derivative records, 18–19
    extracts, 26
    genealogical standards for, 289–94
    logs for, 24–25
    note-taking for, 25–26
    organizing, 22–27
    original records, 18–19

primary sources, 18–20
    protecting, 266–68
    secondary sources, 18–20
    sharing, 206–7
    transcripts, 25–26
The Researcher's Guide to American Genealogy, 216
"Researching the Family History of Potential Slave Owners," 266
Research Wiki, 68–69, 127, 202, 239–40, 249, 254
"Retracing the Trails of Your Ancestors Using Deed Records," 135
Revolutionary War, 111, 156, 158, 162–65, 168, 173, 222
Richley-Erickson, Pat, 218
Rising, Marsha Hoffman, 61
RootsChat, 198, 244
RootsWeb, 70–74, 197–98, 201, 207, 230, 270–71
Rose, Christine, 126, 141, 262
Rowling, Edward, 114–16
Rowling, Henry, 114, 116
Rowling, J. K., 12, 114–16
Rowling, Sarah Marie, 116
Rowling, William, 114–16
Rumsey, David, 134
Russell, Judy, 218
Russian research, 254–55
Ruth, George Herman "Babe," 275

SAMPUBCO website, 124
Scandinavian research, 250–52
School records, 151–52
Schulze, Lorine McGinnis, 184
Scrapbooking, 38–39, 44, 227, 268–70
Search engine basics, 50–53
Searches. *See also* Research
    of attics, 38–39
    backward searches, 35–48
    basics of, 13–14
    census records, 97–116
    "cluster" approach to, 62–63

collecting information, 18–20
connecting with others, 195–214
database searches, 53–56
death records, 81–96
deeper searches, 56, 59–60, 215–34
documenting, 31–33
evaluating findings, 21, 259–66
family records, 117–30
genealogical standards for, 289–94
immigrant records, 175–94
local searches, 131–53
military records, 155–74
online forums, 196–99
online searches, 65–79
organizing, 22–27
overseas records, 235–57
previous searches, 44–46
recording progress of, 13–14
search engine basics, 50–53
strategies for, 49–63
tools for, 59–61
using wildcards in, 54–55
"Searching the Social Security Death Index in One Step," 87
Seaver, Randy, 218
Self-interview, 36–37
Shades of the Departed, 270
Ship passenger lists, 177–88
Slave schedules, 110
Slovakian research, 254–55
SmallTownPapers.com, 146
Social networking sites, 59, 202–3, 212–13, 226
Social Security Death Index (SSDI), 58, 61, 86–96, 219
Societies
    historical societies, 56, 78, 89, 118–23, 127–30, 150–51, 211–12, 220–21
    joining, 210–12
    lineage societies, 166, 174, 210, 222–23
    local societies, 146–49, 211, 217, 221–23

military heritage societies, 163, 173–74, 222
Software, 22–24
Sons of Confederate Veterans, 82, 173
Sons of the American Revolution, 163
Soundex, 57, 105, 114–15, 128
"Soundex Explained," 57
The Source: A Guidebook of American Genealogy, 216
South American research, 239–40
Special census, 109–12. *See also* Census records
"Specialized Dictionaries for Genealogists," 15
Spider's Apprentice, 60
Standards, 289–94
State archives, 79
State census, 109–12. *See also* Census records
Stories in Stone, 91
StoryCorps, 41
Strangers, contacting, 203–5
Strassburger, Ralph B., 178
Subscription sites, 73–76
Surnames. *See also* Names
    maiden names, 28–29, 47–48, 62
    popular names, 61–62
    projects, 234
    recording, 28–29
    similar names, 56–57, 61–62
    spellings of, 56–57
Surveys, 137–39
Swiss research, 255
Szucs, Loretto D., 188, 216

Tax records, 63, 112–13
"Ten Fabulous Sources for Family History Books Online," 45
"Ten Questions to Ask a Research Facility Before You Visit," 141
They Became Americans: Finding Naturalization Records and Ethnic Origins, 188

They Came in Ships: Finding Your Immigrant Ancestor's Arrival Record, 188
"Timeline of U.S. Public Land Acts," 138
Timelines, 153
Tombstones, 90–92, 157, 176, 221. *See also* Cemeteries
"Top 10 Places to Put Your Family History Online," 44
"Top 11 Essential Reference Books for Genealogists," 216
Topographic maps, 133–34
Transcripts, 25–26, 66

United Kingdom research, 240–47
U.S. Citizenship and Immigration Services (USCIS), 187, 190, 191
U.S. Federal Census, 98–100. *See also* Census records
USGenWeb
    birth records, 121–22
    cemetery records, 91–92
    census records, 103
    church records, 150
    court records, 127
    death records, 89–90
    estate records, 124–25
    genealogy research, 71
    marriage records, 119
    military records, 162
    pension records, 162
    school records, 152
    tombstones, 92
U.S. Newspaper Directory, 1690–Present, 146

Veterans Affairs (VA), 92, 164
Veterans schedules, 111–12
Vietnam War, 77, 168, 172–73
Virtual cemeteries, 90–92
VitalChek.com, 89
Vitalrec.com, 89

Vital records
    birth records, 120–22, 242–47
    death records, 58, 81–96, 242–47
    marriage records, 118–20,
        242–47

Wall Street Journal, 144
War of 1812, 158–62, 173
War stories, 156–57, 171. *See also*
    Military records
Washington, George, 98
Washington, Hansone, 82–83
Washington, William, 83
Washington Post, 143
Webinars, 209–10
WeRelate, 271
"What Reference Books Should I
    Own?," 216
"Where to Write for Vital Records,"
    118
Wilder, Almanzo, 94–96, 286
Wilder, James, 95
Wilder, Laura Ingalls, 12, 94–96, 275,
    286
Wilder, Rose, 95, 286
Wills, 122–25
WorldCat, 47, 148–49
World Record Collection, 144
WorldVitalRecords, 74
World War I, 77, 157, 162, 168–70,
    190, 242
World War II, 77, 168–73, 181, 185

Yearbooks, 147, 152

We Have EVERYTHING® on Anything!

The Everything® list spans a wide range of subjects, with more than 500 titles covering 25 different categories:

Business	History	Reference
Careers	Home Improvement	Religion
Children's Storybooks	Everything Kids	Self-Help
Computers	Languages	Sports & Fitness
Cooking	Music	Travel
Crafts and Hobbies	New Age	Wedding
Education/Schools	Parenting	Writing
Games and Puzzles	Personal Finance	
Health	Pets	

DON ASLETT'S

Mary Hart Berholz
—who Knows

CLUTTER
FREE!

_Finally &
Forever_

MARSH CREEK PRESS

Published by Marsh Creek Press, PO Box 700, Pocatello, Idaho 83204; 1-208-232-3535.

MARSH CREEK PRESS

Distributed by Betterway Books, an imprint of F&W Publications, Inc., 1507 Dana Avenue, Cincinnati, OH 45207. 1-800-289-0963.

ISBN 0-937750-12-3

Illustrator: David Lock
Designer: Craig LaGory
Editor: Carol Cartaino
Production Manager: Tobi Haynes

Library of Congress Cataloging-in-Publication Data

Aslett, Don, 1935-
    Don Aslett's clutter free! : finally & forever.
        p.   cm.
    ISBN 0-937750-12-3
    1. Orderliness.   2. Conduct of life.
3. House cleaning.
I. Title.
BJ1533.073A75   1995
648'.5--dc20
                                95-19944
                                CIP

ALSO BY DON ASLETT

More Help for Packrats:

> The Office Clutter Cure
> Not for Packrats Only
> Clutter's Last Stand

Business Books:

> How to be #1 With Your Boss
> Everything I Needed to Know About Business
> I Learned in the Barnyard
> Is There a Speech Inside You?

How to Clean / Professional Cleaning Books:

> Is There Life After Housework?
> Do I Dust or Vacuum First?
> Make Your House Do the Housework
> Don Aslett's Clean in a Minute
> Who Says It's a Woman's Job to Clean?
> 500 Terrific Ideas for Cleaning Everything
> Pet Clean-Up Made Easy
> How Do I Clean the Moosehead?
> Don Aslett's Stainbuster's Bible
> The Cleaning Encyclopedia
> Cleaning Up for a Living
> The Professional Cleaner's Personal Handbook
> How to Upgrade & Motivate Your Cleaning Crews
> Painting Without Fainting

ACKNOWLEDGMENT

When a book has a thousand-plus authors, they can't all be listed.

Packrats are clearly glad to exchange not only "stuff" but thoughts and solutions! I would like to publicly thank here the many people who sent me notes, letters, and articles and graciously gave permission to quote from them. Some of the material here, too, is from calls or comments made to me on radio or TV, or in conversation. I always carry a yellow pad to capture your wisdom and humor immediately, on the spot! Many of the quotes in these pages were pulled from long letters, and identities have been for the most part omitted or altered so that no families or feelings would be offended. Small changes have also been made as necessary to aid clarity.

There was a great deal of duplication and we've worked in the editing to assemble the best and most broadly useful of what you reported and recorded. (We also had some letters so pathetic or revengeful that we couldn't pass them on.)

Thanks again from all of us to all of you who took the time and invested the effort to write down your thoughts and ideas. Millions of lives will be influenced to the good because of it.

APOLOGY

The references to my other books in these pages might seem a bit overdone, but please bear in mind that 95% of the letters, calls, and comments recorded here were the direct result of someone's reading of those volumes. We did remove the majority of such references but some had to remain for clarity. And we added some references of our own, as to where you can find out more about specific subjects.

What are these books you'll be hearing more about soon?

The green book, the "convincer":
Clutter's Last Stand, 1984, Writer's Digest Books.

And the guide that takes you by the hand:
Not for Packrats Only, 1991, New American Library.

P. S. In the descriptions that follow of what you all did to dump your clutter, there may be some thrift stores and charitable service organizations you do not recognize. Such as Oxfam and Deseret Industries ("the D.I."), agencies headquartered in England and the mountain west, respectively.

TABLE OF CONTENTS

Introduction *1*

CHAPTER 1: *3*
  More Sightings of ULO's (Unidentified Lying Objects)

CHAPTER 2: *14*
  The Cost of Keeping it

CHAPTER 3: *33*
  More Incredible Excuses for Clutter

CHAPTER 4: *46*
  Help with "How To" (Dejunk!)

CHAPTER 5: *84*
  Moving Through It & Moving It Out:
  How to Identify Junk and What to Do with It Afterward

CHAPTER 6: *107*
  More Advice On... (All Those Things You Wanted to Hear More About)
  Books, magazines, and newspapers; paper (and computer) clutter; closets, clothes, drawers, junk bunkers; kiddie clutter, grown kid clutter; the junk room; jumbo junk; vehicle junk, garages; craft/hobby clutter; container clutter; sentimental clutter (including deceased people's); gifts; decluttering others; mental clutter.

CHAPTER 7: *183*
  Preventing Re-Junking

CHAPTER 8: *198*
  Success Report: "Yes, Fellow Rats, I did it!"

CHAPTER 9: *208*
  Write to Me

" Dear Mr. Aslett:
I finished reading Not for Packrats Only two weeks ago. Since then my wife has had a flurry of trips to Goodwill Industries and to the trash bin, as well as the agony of making decisions.

Your previous book Clutter's Last Stand caused us to move from our large ten-room home into a four-room condo. I thought we had taken all of the clutter out of our lives at that time. Not so.

Like you, we spend our winters in Hawaii and we used your previous book to clean up the stuff that had accumulated over eight years there. With that, I thought my life was complete and I could keep all the rest of my possessions.

Little did I know that you would write another book and the effect it would have on my life. My precious books are gone, and our shelf space has been cut in half. And various things I like to have for cooking are now in the possession of someone unknown to me.

I must admit, however, our condo looks better and our lives are more pleasant and it is all due to you. But please wait at least ten years before writing another book!"

" I confess, I'm addicted. Don't stop the presses. Please continue to author. This Aslett-addict will need a fix down the road."

It's Your Turn

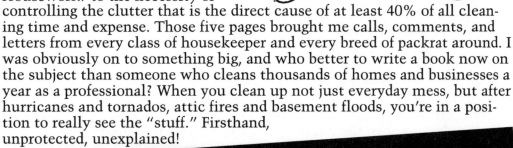

After all it **is** yours, that #1 cause of lack of self-esteem, space, and money. It's responsible for a lot of disorganization, arguments, and wasted time, too. I'm talking about JUNK AND CLUTTER. You have some, I know.

In 1980 I devoted a chapter of my first bestseller *Is There Life After Housework?* to the necessity of controlling the clutter that is the direct cause of at least 40% of all cleaning time and expense. Those five pages brought me calls, comments, and letters from every class of housekeeper and every breed of packrat around. I was obviously on to something big, and who better to write a book now on the subject than someone who cleans thousands of homes and businesses a year as a professional? When you clean up not just everyday mess, but after hurricanes and tornados, attic fires and basement floods, you're in a position to really see the "stuff." Firsthand, unprotected, unexplained!

Thus the first-ever book on dejunking was born, *Clutter's Last Stand*. It highlighted the sad, even silly situation that results from too much stashing and stacking, and made the case for decluttering in full detail. It attracted so much attention from the media—literally thousands of radio and TV interviews and newspaper and magazine articles—that the dejunking message was spread far and wide (I even dejunked with Oprah). All of this, plus a few choice junk contests around the country, brought forth more clutter confessions like you wouldn't believe. Letter after letter

let me in on not only the mental depression and everyday difficulties of living with clutter, but accidents, divorces, disasters, fights, arguments, real estate losses, and bankruptcies, all resulting from that junk nestled into our closets and cupboards, garages and sheds. There emerged a picture of clutter chaos that the most hardened packrat would never have imagined, on a doubleheader garage sale day.

It was clear now that plenty of people out there did want to rid themselves of junk, but they needed more help with how and what and when. Concentrating on the cures for clutter now, I did another book, *Not for Packrats Only*. It, too, hit junkaholics right in the old bin.

By now my cleaning company was in sixteen states, cleaning up over 40,000,000 square feet of human-occupied space per night. One of the most seriously junked spaces was obviously desks and offices, at home and at work. So now my first specialized dejunking book was published, *The Office Clutter Cure*, to help those office "stack" rats dig out.

Comments, calls and letters kept coming in, however, more requests for professional dejunking assistance, more media interest and features, everyone wanting ever more on dejunking. After three bestselling volumes already on the subject, I wasn't sure how much was left for me personally to say.

Then one day while I was sorting and rereading some of the letters and confessions sent in over the past year, Bingo, it hit me. YOU do. YOU HAVE SOMETHING (in fact a lot) TO SAY, you seasoned stashers, you hardcore hoarders. You were the perfect author for the next book. Having heard from thousands of you in both a serious and lighthearted vein, I knew how many great ideas and how much sound insight you had about "stuff." Now I realized you had an important message and heartstring-plucking stories of success and struggle that had to be heard. Thus this latest volume in "Don's decluttering library" came about, *Clutter Free! Finally & Forever*.

Here are the letters, comments, and confessions we've laughed and cried over, puzzled over and been inspired by. Now they're yours too. I think you'll find them eye-opening and enjoyable, and I promise that the peeks you'll get here into other packrats' problems and triumphs will help to free you. There are some super solutions here, so read carefully. Even if you only gain one good principle and use it every day for the rest of your life, think of the benefit!

I've carefully read and extracted, selected and organized what you shared and reported, revealed and confessed. And I made some remarks and observations of my own, whenever I was prompted to expand on the packrat point at hand. Whenever you see a big capital letter like the one on my name below, you'll know it's me talking. I've added a few charts and self-tests, too, which I hope you'll find fun and useful.

As before, I can't and won't try to tell you **what** to dispose of—the ultimate value of your possessions is your judgment and business, not mine or anyone else's. I'd rather teach the principles of freedom and control, and have you make your own choices.

If the comments and stories in these pages make you think of some of your own close encounters with clutter, feel free to call or write. Pass them on, share them—save a fellow sufferer today.

—**D**on Aslett
America's #1 Dejunker

More Sightings of ULO's
(Unidentified Lying Objects)

Junk and clutter are still accumulating out there—quietly, ominously, insidiously. Many a mini-landfill is in the making, at your friends', your neighbors', and yes, YOUR house. Junk is settling innocuously on any flat surface, moving into cupboards and closets, garages and kitchens, squatting blatantly in the open even as this is being written.

So, all you recovering or unreformed packrats out there, this is revival time. Time to wrestle the clutter problem to the ground again.

Lest you doubt the need for this, let's listen to what the letters I get every day have to say.

❝ The other night I got so sick of my junk I almost checked into a hotel to get away from it. Now that is 'junk desperation.'❞

❝ I can't throw a party or invite anyone over unless I keep people in the living room (but the bathroom is on the other side of the house!).❞

❝ *I enjoyed your book and am now considering throwing out some stuff. I have also bought a couple of extra cemetery plots in case I die before I get cleaned up.*❞

❝ *For the past eleven years I've lived in the same small apartment—constantly collecting but never willing to give anything up—something like the Dead Sea which has no outlet for its salty streams....*❞

❝ *When I first met my husband there was a VW engine in his kitchen.*❞

❝ **I'm so disorganized, I'm proud to have found the pen and paper to write with.**❞

❝ HELP!! My husband said he would only dejunk if you were to make a personal appearance at our house. (I'm **not** kidding.)

Here is a successful man who owns: 75 ties, 45 dress shirts, and 21 suits. His dresser drawers won't close without cramming stuff down in them, and he has two junk drawers, not one!"

66 I know someone who has an electrical power drill for every bit (to avoid the nuisance of changing bits)."

66 I can top that. I know someone with a tractor for every implement—so he didn't ever have to be bothered to unhook."

66 I have a frozen hummingbird in my freezer. When my husband complains about it, I point out that it doesn't take up much room."

66 *Your book* Clutter's Last Stand *was part of my divorce settlement. My husband wanted it back—I guess to remember me by."*

66 *My neighbor drained his swimming pool to create more space for his collection of lumber and spare parts."*

66 My wife is such a packrat, would you believe that at fifty-nine she still has the First Communion dress she wore when she was six? (I of course still have my electric train....)"

66 When my cousin has company she has to stay up all night to clear a path to one of the unused beds, and to find two empty hangers for the closet."

66 *I'd throw it away, if only I could find it."*

66 My husband has a real magazine problem. I kid you not, God be my witness, he gets lots of magazines, goes through them, and tears out three or four pages… then throws the pages away and keeps the magazines."

66 *I have always hated going into people's homes and seeing the mounds of junk holding residence under one rooftop. Junk glued to the refrigerator, stuff under the beds and couch, counters overflowing—every available surface covered.*

My mother-in-law's house looked like a museum. She had stuff on the ceilings (true!) due to no more wall space."

" I am from a family of junk addicts. When the local discount store burned, my uncle salvaged all of the eight-foot light bulbs and stored them in his barn. Who in their right mind was going to drive way out in the country and climb up to a loft to get a light bulb? He finally sold the barn and had to empty it. He donated the bulbs to the local school system. They sent a thank-you for 1,012 light bulbs.

He owns a large building that was empty but he is filling it up with all kinds of stuff. He has a collection of doors salvaged from buildings. (Gas station doors, restroom doors, lovely wood doors, extra-tall doors, etc.)

You've read about people whose houses were so full that there were magazines piled to the ceiling? My aunt had only two places to sit in her house… one was the toilet. Another aunt cluttered her bedroom so much that she slept in the spare room."

" I believe there is a little bit of a clutterbug in all of us. It is so easy to join this clutterbug club. I don't know when I first joined, but I am sure that I'm a lifer."

" Please help! My husband is the creative type that can improvise something from nothing or use throwaways for something marvelous in his workshop. I was a librarian and can't get rid of anything that looks like useful information. We would like to get out of our collecting trap."

" You know how some husbands take the garbage out? Well mine began bringing the garbage **in**.

For the past seven or eight years, he has been scavenging garbage dumps. (Yes, he has brought home a few real treasures, but he likes it ALL!)

He's brought home truckload after truckload of old, used clothing—baby stuff, children's, fat clothes, skinny clothes—you name it. Most of it is mildewed and covered with leaves and trash. He washes it and then piles it in the attic. One room upstairs has been as deep as three or four feet with this stuff. The attic spaces are full. He also brings home old rusty cans (paint?)—No labels, old papier mache duck decoys (no head), old mildewed mattresses, roofing tin, pieces of chairs, sofas, stoves, and toys. There have even been old fruit jars with blackened and questionable contents.

Two years ago he brought home a bunch of logs he'd found. We don't have a fireplace. They've laid beside the drive rotting ever since."

" Many people, I imagine, must send you their junk autobiographies. My parents, both intelligent, well educated professionals, have lived in junk-induced squalor, made up mostly of magazines and paperwork. When we were growing up my sister and I were not encouraged to invite friends over, and in all my childhood my parents gave only one party. They are finally dejunking the house, thanks to the earthquake last year, which cracked the foundation.

I'm no help—I just asked my mother to hang onto her maternity clothes until I can come up this summer to take a look at them (and I'm years away from having kids of my own). My sister wants to restore my father's 1953 Buick, now moldering, flat tired, in the back driveway. 'How can you sell it, Daddy? You proposed to Mother in that car!'"

" *Several years ago I purchased from a surplus store for 33 cents a rifle carrier that cost the Army about $8. I wasn't able to use it, but kept it for several years because I saved $7.63 by purchasing it. When we sold it at a garage sale for 50 cents, I maintained that we lost $7.88. My wife says we made 17 cents. Who is right?*"

" *I think we are in need of the books you mentioned. And I think we need them in a hurry because the junk from the garage is spreading. It's under the deck, it's under the addition, and it's even starting to build up in the basement. Before long it will take over the whole house! Help!*"

" I'm one of those savers—just a terrible one. I hate being one. I even pray that God will help me to be able to throw junk out. I will clean out my closet, throwing all of three things away, and then a half hour later, I may bring one back in from the garage."

" What have I been saving? Old magazines, a baby bathtub (baby is twenty-five years old), inch square pieces of fabric, yarn scraps not big enough to wrap around a finger, a blender motor that smokes, four sets of mixer beaters, at least a half dozen old broken eyeglass frames and loose lenses (outgrown fifteen years ago), a hamburger maker (last used when son #1 was on a mission twelve years ago).

I could go on for a week, but the D.I. truck will be here any minute."

❝ My husband is a real junker— he saves EVERYTHING. Recently he brought home an old broken toilet from his place of employment. I was disgusted with him and wanted him to take it back where it came from, but my neighbor, also a junker, came over and admired it and told him how neat it was. So now I am the only person on the block with a toilet flowerpot in their backyard."

❝ *It's called merchandise!!! I've been collecting it for forty years. We own a half-acre lot and the neighbors tease me that now I've got three quarters of an acre under cover. Every time I stack up an eight-foot pile of merchandise, I put a roof over it."*

❝ You must be writing your books just for me. I grew up saving everything I came in contact with. My grandmother let me know at an early age it was a 'sin' to throw anything away.

I still have the Valentine cards from my grade school days. The collection of things I have saved with no thought in mind about what I would ever use them for fills my entire basement. I paid to have these things shipped around the country and the world while my husband was in the Air Force."

❝ *Help! These piles and piles are pulling me down!"*

❝ I am sick over my cluttering. I truly am.

I cannot seem to throw anything away, and my life is **hell** this way. You can't imagine how I'm living— it's unimaginable and crazy.

I seem compelled to clutter and clutter and clutter. I want to change, but I feel powerless. I am completely stumped as to what to do. I can't afford to have someone come to my apartment to help me.

After I hear from you, I'll write again and take pictures so you can see for yourself."

That photo was ghastly, folks, too ghastly to print. (And I was afraid some of you might want to bid on some of those piles and stacks!)

❝ *Whole rooms of our home have been taken over by junk. As we 'do up' our Victorian house, the rubbish gets moved from room to room. What happens when we reach the end is anyone's guess."*

❝ The magnitude of my story makes writing this seem a chore.

I have lived literally buried under junk for approximately fifteen years. There have been times when the frustration and depression have been so overwhelming I've given up hope of ever being able to have a neat, attractive, orderly home. And times when in panic I've tried to make up for lost time.

Around 1971 or 72, my husband became interested in old bottles. He went to old house sites, dumps, etc., to dig for them. He brought everything he dug up home—no discernment or discrimination. He saved whole bottles, broken bottles, and shards. Then he began buying and trading. There are bottles on shelves (a whole room full of shelves, covered), bottles in boxes, bottles in old dishpans in several houses he owns.

This interest also led to interest in antiques and collectibles. I realize this is not so unusual, but wait!

He is also a golfer. A number of years ago he began going into the lake on the course to retrieve lost balls. Now this is a good way to economize, I know, but he wasn't satisfied only to meet his needs. There are grocery bags and boxes of golf balls stashed away.

He is also a hunter. He has saved the antler of every deer he has killed, plus many he has found in the woods. They number well into the hundreds. He also saves turkey feet and beards, and squirrel tails. These have attracted moths and other pests but no matter—he is undaunted.

I am not sure if he has ever discarded a worn out tire in the more than 24 years we've been married.

Shortly after his interest in bottle collecting began, he also began collecting every other collectible one could imagine: pottery, pot shards, old rusty car tags, dishes, magazines, newspapers, letters, store display items. He has a couple of four-foot stacks of old store ledgers in the basement—worm-eaten and rotting. And oh yes, old trunks (full ones). At yard and estate sales and auctions, he buys boxes full of (?) for one or two dollars and brings it all home. This interest led to periodicals (i.e. <u>Antique Monthly</u>, <u>Old Bottle</u> magazine, and several others). None could be thrown out. At one auction he bought a pickup load (stacked up even with the cab) of old chair pieces—I don't imagine there were more than five or six whole chairs in the lot. He intended to use them for parts or repair them and he did a few—the rest are stashed.

This led to an interest in woodworking. He began bringing home old lumber, doors and windows, etc. The old rusty nails he saved in jars.

All of this created a need for a larger home. We bought a huge old two-story house with a basement and a large amount of attic space. As we began the restoration, I imagined that at last we'd sort out, use, and/or discard this 'collection.' I was **wrong!** As we ripped out old lumber, cabinets, and miscellany, it had to be put under the house. 'We might need it for something.'

In the meantime, his father had acquired a warehouse, house, and garage. He has now filled up the warehouse and garage with his treasures….❞

Sorry folks, I can't let you read any more!

❝ My dad is one of those farmers you described with the back forty available for junking. He's brought us parts for our stove from his stash of old stoves out in the trees.

My dad throws old shoes in the chicken house because 'You never know when you might need some leather off one.'"

❝ I've been acquainted with the Green family for about two years now, and have had the unfortunate opportunity of helping them move twice.

Several years ago they lived in a spacious property in a rural community. They had a lot to begin with, but they're the type that eyes yard sales for anything that 'might be useful' somewhere down the road. Now their property already had a garage and barn to store this stuff, but they built additional sheds to contain and hide these treasures. For example, for years and years they saved tin cans because they could be useful sometime. Well... the cans never got used, and meanwhile the Greens decided to move to a smaller lot in a small town. It took them three years (no exaggeration) to move their stuff and figure out some place to put it.

Then they moved again, to Wyoming. Every vehicle and trailer (open trailers and trucks stacked eight feet above the usual level) was loaded—six such trucks and trailers, with two other passenger cars. Still they had more stuff than they knew what to do with. A double-car garage and a shed on the property they moved from was still packed with their things (and the new owners had the nerve to ask them to remove it!). Since I was in the area at the time, I had the honor of spending an entire day taking truckload after truckload to the dump or thrift store. There yet remains a 15' X 30' shed, packed floor to ceiling, sitting on that property.

Who knows how long it will take to move all their stuff this time?"

❝ When my grandmother died about three years ago, we as a family went in to take her house apart. We were really sorrowful and sad, but as we progressed with the project we at times found ourselves cracking up with amusement. She was quite the saver! We opened up an old oatmeal box and found it full of small metal disks. As we dug deeper, we found more and more and more of the disks in all kinds of boxes. They were even stored in the attic. We finally realized she had saved the ends off the cans of canned biscuits she fixed for breakfast almost every morning of the twenty-some years she and grandpa had lived in that house."

❝ My husband keeps everything. He says he might have a use for it later. He saves all of his empty oil and antifreeze jugs, etc. He has this big water barrel that we had chicken feed in and a bear got ahold of it and put holes in it so it's no good for feed or water or anything. But my husband keeps it to remember the bear—which he killed. He did finally find a use for the barrel—he puts his oil jugs in it, and it's full and overflowing!

My husband broke his leg this summer and had a cast on up to his thigh. When they took it off, he wanted to bring it home as a conversation piece. Thank goodness they talked him out of that one!"

❝ I'm married to a packrat. He has one room so full of papers no one can enter. He says he may need them some day. In seven years now, he's never looked at them. He still has every note he wrote in medical school. In his closet there are clothes he wore in college (he's thirty-eight years old). In the garage, closets, and drawers he has everything from old coffee jars with a little bit of paint in them, to parts, to things that have long since worn out and been discarded, to bunches of safety pins. Enough safety pins to pin every diaper in the world."

❝ *I helped a friend move away from home for the first time in her teens. We were going through numerous boxes, trying to pare down some of her belongings. I picked up an opaque plastic bag that rattled, looked in it, and decided to put it in the 'throw away' pile. My friend, who was usually very pragmatic, looked in the bag and said, 'I can't throw those out! My grandmother (her favorite, now deceased) gave those to me.' The bag was full of two-inch-high pink plastic figurines of all the presidents of the United States, up to 1974!"*

❝ ***Although I've only had a few avalanches so far, both my large studio apartment and my office are in the process of becoming total disaster areas. My dad refers to my***

apartment as 'The Ware-house,' and calls the highest pile in my main room 'the Matterhorn.'"

❝ *You asked what we were saving, Don? Here's a partial report: a kitchen sink which was replaced about ten years ago, avocado green carpet replaced at the same time after my husband tried melting a huge can of honey in the kitchen sink by turning on the hot water and then going out to work on the yard. I was out of town at the time and by the time he came in a few hours later, the flood made it necessary to replace the counter (which also is still in the garage), the linoleum, and the carpet.*

Next to the old sink in the garage is a toilet which we replaced about five years ago. We also have some tire rims we might use some day, and the boxes from my computer and other important things which we keep in case we might sell them someday. We also have photographic, model airplane, money management, and other magazines which are so old they are now collector's items. Also three Sylvania flash cube pillows which are worth money if we ever find the right person."

❝ At present, you'd have to levitate to get around my upstairs, and my children were trained from their earliest days to maneuver their way around piles and mounds like mountain goats."

❝ *I have nightmares of dying and having my obituary read: 'and she is survived by 137 worn-out toothbrushes.'"*

TEST YOURSELF

Judging by reader response, the "junker's self-tests"—the Junkee Entrance Exam in *Clutter's Last Stand* and Your Personal Clutter Checkup Exam in *Not for Packrats Only*—have been the most popular part of my earlier books. The following self-test was sent to me by a reader who was inspired to compose it after taking the quiz in *Packrat*. It was too good to pass up!

(This one, however, we might have to call the Are You Backsliding? Quiz or the Junkee Graduate School Entrance/Junker's Bar Exam.)

12

JUNKER'S QUESTIONNAIRE

by Ellen Esser

1. If junk burglars broke into my house today they'd
   a. Die laughing at my junk
   b. Call their friends to bring over the pickup
   c. Grab some pillowcases, stuff them, and run
   d. Leave; I don't have any junk

2. My junk could best be described as a:
   a. Pile
   b. Stack
   c. Heap
   d. Mound
   e. Mass
   f. Mountain

3. If I died tonight, I'd:
   a. Beg St. Peter to let me bring my stuff in with me
   b. Hope my executors read my will and bought the three acres to be excavated so that all of my junk could be buried with me
   c. Be somewhat embarrassed by the stuff I've left behind
   d. Not be concerned, because I'm not leaving any junk behind

4. If I won a $10,000,000 contest, I'd:
   a. Build a house four times as big as I have now, with a 1000 sq. ft. storage shed in the yard for even more junk
   b. Build a house twice as large and move in all my current junk, just have more room for it.
   c. Sort through my junk and only move half of it to my new house
   d. Start fresh with **no** junk

5. If I had to own my own business, I would most likely choose:
   a. a junkyard
   b. an antique-curio boutique
   c. a smaller personalized business with my own office suite and lots of equipment
   d. a dejunking/organizing business run from a 10' x 10' foot space in my well-organized home office

6. If I had one car and a two-car garage, I'd:
   a. Have to park on the street because that garage would be crammed with junk.
   b. Maybe have room to squeeze in the car **if** it was a compact.
   c. Have plenty of room for the car despite some clutter
   d. Have necessities (yard tools and trash and recycling cans) neatly along one side, and room for two large cars

7. To properly store all my junk, I'd need:
   a. At least two large self-storage rental units
   b. One large self-storage rental unit
   c. More Rubbermaid stuff organizers than I can afford
   d. Three or four of the smaller Rubbermaid stuff storers at the most

8. If I threw out ALL my junk for one trash pickup, I'd:
   a. Have to ask two or three neighbors to let me use their lawns as well as mine.
   b. Expect to hear some pretty nasty language from the trash truck personnel
   c. Be embarrassed, but…
   d. Have one extra 33-gallon bag at the most

9. If a neat, organized friend dropped in unexpectedly, I'd:
   a. Hide and pretend I wasn't home because I couldn't let her see the place
   b. Let her in and quietly die of embarrassment
   c. Let her in and pretend I was in the process of dejunking
   d. Let her in and smile—I'm dejunked

10. If someone gave me $2500 and I had to spend it by next week, I'd:
    a. Run to all the stores I could and buy, buy, buy whatever
    b. Think a day and then buy new "good stuff" and save all the old "in case"
    c. Buy what I need and only save half the old stuff
    d. Book a dream vacation away from all that stuff

11. When I travel:
    a. They get me for excess baggage every time
    b. I need two extra suitcases for souvenirs
    c. I bring a good-sized bag for souvenirs
    d. I come home refreshed and empty-handed

12. Dear old Hattie, bless her heart, passed on last week and I'm her only heir. Aunt Hattie was the "Queen Pack Rat" and I'm:
    a. Thrilled. I get all her stuff
    b. Pretty happy—I'll have to sort it but I'll keep at least half
    c. Discouraged, but not overcome—at least 1/4 of this is surely good and keepable
    d. Dismayed. Look at all this! I'll have to pay someone to haul it away

SCORE: Add up your score, giving yourself 5 points for each A; 4 points for each B; 2 points for each C; 1 point for each D.

12-15 You're dejunked and determined to stay there.

16-24 You're not immune to the junk virus, by any means—better start treatment now.

25-36 You have a serious case of junkitis, but you can be helped.

40+ It may not be as hopeless as it looks—recognizing the problem is the first step toward a cure.

ARE YOU A JUNKER?

• If your house caught fire, would you think twice about calling the Fire Department?

• Is the UPS person able to find a place anywhere on your porch or in your office to set a package down?

• Would your decorating style be best described as "wall-to-wall possession decor"?

• Do you dream of being reincarnated as a centipede or octopus so you'll have more arms for stuff?

Chapter 2

The Cost of Keeping it

Even if it's good stuff and even if you got it "free" (it was a gift, you found or inherited it, or it was a rock-bottom bargain at some closeout sale) clutter has a staggering price tag. The minute we get it home we start guarding it, constructing new closets and buildings for it, dedicating our guest rooms, car slots, sheds, and parents' homes to keeping it contained and protected (rent free, we think).

As we've talked about the tab these "treasures" ring up many of you say, "Boy, you're right Don, keeping sure costs!" But I detect a slight disbelief there still, after all it's just one man's opinion. And I know that until pack-rats are convinced their clutter is a negative, they'll defend it to the death.

So I decided you should get the raw report, the ugly testimony of toll direct from your fellow hoarders. Here are a few of the endless letters I receive revealing the true status of these "bargains" in the basement. Read 'em and weep—it's a big cost, and you're paying it every day.

See also Chapter 5 of <u>Clutter's Last Stand</u> and Chapter 3 of <u>Not for Packrats Only.</u>

COSTS OF CLUTTER: THE OVERALL COST

A great sociologist summed up the human quest these days quite simply:

How can I make more money?

How can I improve myself (live better)?

Interesting that more money (or what it will buy) is the very thing that holds us back from self improvement… as it leaves us tending stuff instead of tending our lives and the lives of those we love.

“ I was not only a packrat (trained by my 'Depression baby' parents), but a compulsive spender, 'antique' collector, disorganized, and a dirty mess. All this led to bankruptcy, the loss of a fifteen-year marriage, the loss of my career, and alcoholism. The 'free mule' you describe so unerringly in *Not for Pack-rats Only* was a monkey on my back."

❝ I began to consider seriously this relationship called **possession.** Previously I had regarded it as imposing a bond upon some item which attached that item to me: 'This is mine.' Only now did I realize that *I* am no less bound to *it*. I own these things only to the same extent that they own me!

Thus every possession carries two price tags. The original purchase price is the obvious and more easily measured cost. The other cost can be quite subtle and insidious.

Each and every possession exacts a continuing toll. Perhaps the price is paid in upkeep, in attention and time, or in concern over an item's safekeeping, or the memories it evokes. Sometimes a possession, no matter what its original price, is by its very presence in our house and the space it occupies, extremely costly.

As some of these things left, one by one or in the company of others—I felt a sense of relief. I was discovering that these things were not only cluttering up my home, possessing them was cluttering up my life!❞

First you have to shop all over for it, carry it home carefully, box it, and store it. Then you have to move it, move it.

Then you have to worry about it, protect it, dust, label, and list it. List it so you can remember what's in all those containers of precious, preserved junk.

COSTS OF CLUTTER: THE COST OF MOVING IT

❝ *It took fifteen weeks to help my mother-in-law move. The very last day my husband and I had to go in with three trucks and finish emptying the basement and garage because they couldn't get it all sorted and packed by the deadline date for the buyers. We drained every local grocery store of boxes and spent a fortune on garbage bags. My mother-in-law ended up having to rent two large storage units and the rest came to our house.*

When the emptying was done, we walked through the house. I had never liked how small the house was (or seemed), but when I saw it empty, I was shocked at the space!!! I never realized it just appeared small because of all the 'decora' insulation."

Imagine what everyone involved here paid in time and hard cash for this adventure! Not to mention all that lost living space over the years.

❝ I've moved eight times in fourteen years, and more than one of those moves has cost over $2,000. These are all moves within the same city, and from apartments! I had an eighteen-foot truck which I filled twice with only my possessions. It has always been easier to pack it all up than make any of those terrible decisions."

❝ I'd waited until three days before our scheduled move to start packing. And then it seemed as if I were in a 50's horror movie in which stuff just kept coming out of the walls. I opened yet another high cabinet (Eeeeeeeee!) to find it chock-full of forgotten belongings to be sorted, donated, discarded, or (shudder) moved—but to where?

Our new building, for all its modern conveniences, had practically no closet space and no storage area. I agonized over these nonessentials until the movers came and left with the furniture and the few boxes I had packed, leaving me to make trip after trip in my car to a rented storage locker and then to Goodwill. Finally, frantic to be done with this nightmarish move, and with the new tenants at my heels, I began heaving unlabeled, unexamined boxes from our garage straight into the dumpster.❞

—Regina W. Merwin
in the *Los Angeles Times*

The wife of a packrat sums up moving:

❝ My husband is going to take it all with him and sort it there.❞

❝ Several years ago we moved from a two-story, four-bedroom house into a duplex. It was a very disrupting experience. At the time, no one felt like dealing with twenty-five years' accumulation of stuff, so we simply (?) moved it and somehow stuffed it into a much smaller space. Had there not been a truly remarkable closet under the stairs in the duplex, we never could have done it. About six months after that, we bought a smaller house than we had come from, and again we moved everything. **I felt if I moved ever again, it would be too soon.**❞

COSTS OF CLUTTER: THE COST OF STORING IT

❝ In the last twenty-five years of marriage, we have moved three times and moved *everything*. Who says you can't take it with you? I didn't realize until now how much time I had spent **trying to figure out how and where to store everything** in each new home. I know how expensive shelves and cupboards are and it was getting depressing. You have saved us a lot of money. I was getting ready to buy a bunch of shelves for the basement so I could store the junk in a more organized manner. All the future junk I'm not going to buy and all the future storage units I'm not going to have to buy will save many dollars."

❝ *My husband, two children, and the family dog are all collectors of sentimental memorabilia. Our house, the average three-bedroom ranch style of the 50's, has undergone three major revisions to accommodate our junk. To finance these revisions (the last was 1500 square feet!) we've spent a lot of time increasing our earning power, so* **storage space has come at a high price both financially and in time spent earning money.** *Each revision is short-lived, and soon, we've once again outgrown the space we created for our 'special things.'"*

❝ *I have so much stuff I needed a big place, which I can't afford, and now I am threatened with eviction. But I can't afford to move because I've got too much stuff!"*

From a business magazine, on self-storage units:

❝ On a per square foot basis, storage centers rent for about the same as apartments."

A real estate agent on today's home hunters:

❝ *They don't want living space, they want more dead space for storage."*

I've cracked it! I've bought the house next door!

End the search for storage!

"**S**torage" is harder to find these days than real estate in downtown Tokyo. We've reached the pathetic point (once our house, garage, yard, sheds, office, and parents' house is full) of renting more room for it. And we still never have enough. Living was once the main purpose and focus of a home; we were excited to finally have a room for the kids, or a guest. Now STORAGE is the big question, space, and more space for… "stuff."

Intensive storage has now become a science, and all kinds of storage designing and organizing engineers and entrepreneurs have sprung up, all in pursuit—a seemingly losing battle—of a solution to the great storage shortage.

When solutions are found, they don't come cheap. Room additions, "Sears sheds" for the backyard, closet remodeling, high tech storage shelving, even file cabinets, bookcases, and trunks can easily run into the hundreds or thousands of dollars. Many storage devices and structures these days cost more than what they're storing.

94% of you reporting in say you need more storage space—I'd say **you have it already right at hand**—free. Just reclaim all those clutter-encroached areas and there it is, for the taking. Once all that junk is hauled out, your worthwhile stuff and you can live within your means: the space you already have.

Start today, thinking of dejunking as **space gaining**—it's a turn-on!!

COSTS OF CLUTTER: WASTED TIME

❝ I am always shuffling, moving, and sorting stuff, and I end up right where I was. I can't get ahead!"

❝ **All I ever wanted to do was write children's books and sew quilts. I love to cook and do a myriad of things, but I now realize I've spent the last ten years or so buying and storing stuff for 'someday.' (Needless to say, I've written and sewed very little.)**"

❝ *Junk and clutter **is** destructive and time consuming. I am sinking as I write this, wondering where the time has gone today. I should be getting ready for bed and an early workday tomorrow. I feel like the time between 7:30 a.m. and 9:00 p.m. (when I am writing this sentence) just disappeared, evaporated. I did not get to the laundry, the supermarket, etc. I pawed through my piles and bags*

and baskets of 'stuff' looking for things I needed."

❝ Time in a modern world is a precious commodity to be hoarded for things that are meaningful to us. My parents lived at a slower pace, isolated from other people. My life is ruled by the clock, in the office and at home, and **I have more important and enjoyable things to do than sort and organize and clean around a collection of junk**."

Sabotaged by junk!

My mother told me (without realizing it) a perfect story to demonstrate the time lost to clutter in other ways. She always saved all the old maps, even though fresh new ones were only $1.00. Taking along her aged collection of maps on a trip to Arizona once, she wanted to stop at an ancient Indian ruins there. So by the map she directed my father (clutching the wheel of a motor home) over 70 miles of rough and rocky mountain road, sheer cliffs and switchbacks, until they finally reached a dead end. They had to drive all the way back out in the dark to the main road (an interstate highway) and camped there for the night. The next morning they woke up and saw the ruins out the window, just three miles off the highway. Of course the Interstate (now 15 years old) wasn't on that antique map Mother had "saved" and insisted on bringing along. A new map would not only have eliminated some old clutter, but saved a half day of time, $50 in gas, and a lot of wear and tear on not just vehicle but driver and passenger.

Dejunking will save you time and help you become a better manager—by eliminating all those foulups, snafus, and miscarriages caused by clutter.

COSTS OF CLUTTER: IMPAIRED FUNCTION

❝ *Things have been tough for me in the last few months—my mother is ill (and impossible) and I am the designated caretaker. Trying to clean her house (alive with junk) is like trying to push a wheelbarrow of rocks up Pike's Peak in four-inch high heels.* **Murder!**❞

❝ *We got some big black Asian cockroaches from some firewood, and it was almost a year before I finally called the exterminator because I knew what a job it would be to move everything from the walls in the basement.*

We have a nice finished basement but we can't use it. It looks like people pay us to store things there.❞

"Walden, Updated"

What we have here is acquisition without assimilation. This tundra, the carpet of our home slowly deepens as pillows, books, curios, and memorabilia gather on every horizontal plane. We still have paths, we can move without hazard from one room to another, but once there the raw weight of too much seems to fall upon our hands, cuffing them. We have tried to clean through it all in one day, and it can't be done. It can't be done.
—Grace Longeneker

This next quote is a classic—one of my favorites. How could you sum up the everyday drawbacks of junk better?

❝ All major problems in our home seem to center around **the inability to find something.** I know that given a reasonable amount of time (two or three days), I could find anything. I know it is here somewhere because I never throw anything out. But when someone wants something RIGHT NOW!—I simply have no idea where it is. ❞

Rummaging begins at home

Rummaging is the unproductive art of hunting, digging, looking, searching for something with which you intend to be productive. It's not uncommon to spend five minutes sweeping the kitchen floor, and then ten minutes picking up the pile. Why ten minutes? You can't find the dustpan! You look under the sink, behind the garbage pail, in the closet, outside the door, and on the porch, but no dustpan. Finally you decide a piece of cardboard will do just as well and begin hunting for one. You consider using some box tops and coupons, but finally rip the corner off a shopping bag and start to scoop up the mess. Later you find the dustpan by the telephone. You have just used some of your life's time to rummage.

Rummaging is a waste of physical and emotional energy. Rummagers live on the edge, right up to the moment of their needs. They're always in the position of scrambling or frantically searching for the tool, the ticket, the assignment, the pattern, the phone number, the recipe, the warranty, the utensil, the attachment, or whatever. Rummagers spend 90% of their time rummaging and 10% doing. This can sure keep you from enjoying life.

Those who rummage physically will also rummage mentally. Their thoughts, ideas, plans, and expressions will be all jumbled and lumped together like their physical stuff.

And then there's the self-esteem angle on rummaging, the constant disgust and frustration with self. Not to mention how unappealing to others we are when rummaging—we really do resemble a confused, desperate rat darting about, building irritation into hysteria to "find it."

What is the root of rummaging? A bad habit of carelessness or "procrastination," to be sure. That tool, ticket, phone number, address, credit card, or whatever could have been put up or filed right after we were done with it, but it wasn't. Instead it was tossed in the rummage heap.

But then there's **all that surplus stuff all over, on top of and in the way!** Getting rid of it is the first step on the path to personal freedom.

" I have..."

...Or do you??

When you have something somewhere but you can't (with anything resembling convenience) call it up when a chance to use it comes around, you might as well not own it.

Things stashed away don't serve. "Saving" something is silly if not stupid, if a search is required to engage it. Then you don't have it, it has you. Not a good position to be in, in the storage compartment, or in life!

If something is buried long and deep enough, you don't have it. It's just a junk snipe hunt!

> **" Dear Mr. Aslett,**
> I thought you might enjoy
> this poem I wish I could live
> by:
>
> 'The right amount of junk
>   to save,
> I finally conceded,
> Is just enough so I can find
> What's needed when it's
> needed.'"
>
> —Sally Higley

How to become more efficient overnight!

For years I've been fascinated by what we humans are willing to do to gain speed and efficiency. When Howard Hughes' racing plane was finished, a beautiful sleek machine never even flown once, it was taken apart and re-riveted. Why? Because he had just discovered a rivet 1/32 of an inch flatter than the ones on it now.

A friend of mine in competitive swimming always shaved his head to make him more streamlined in the water—it made him ugly but it did make him faster. Even bicyclists wear tight silky trousers to cut the "drag" (wind resistance) as they pedal along.

Any time, anywhere, that excess is stripped off, we move faster and freer. Dejunking does exactly this, makes us faster and freer. Notice how all the people who seem to be running "behind" in life are loaded more heavily than the ones up in front.

A retired aeronautical engineer explained to me once that in air-craft design they always think of poundage in terms of its ability to cut or add flying distance. They have it down to a science, they know exactly how much every additional ounce of weight will end up costing over the life of a plane. In the case of missiles, for example, every pound of weight you could remove would add thirty miles to a missile's range.

The same is true in our lives— every extra pound takes up time and energy that amounts to thousands of miles of lost/missed distance over the course of a lifetime. So it's even smart arithmetic to unclutter.

COSTS OF CLUTTER: COST IN ACTUAL CASH

*" I am very neat and clean, but nonetheless I have a clutter dilemma. I am currently in the process of compiling 'stuff' to take to the flea market. I have two pickup truck loads… no room for a table to display my castoffs. I will be "picnic flea-selling"—that is where you put a piece of plastic or sheet(s) on the ground and let hungry onlookers go through it. I was very excited thinking what I could make from my sale— probably an easy $800 or $1000. But I became ill when I realized **my prices were 1/10th, 1/20th, and even 1/30th of what I paid for these things. Plus there was the time spent earning the money to buy them, the time spent shopping, lugging it all home, then storing it until moving day again.***

Gasp! This means if I make $1000 selling all such 'new but opened, stored, and moved' stuff, I spent at least $10,000 (or more) purchasing it!

A little less than a year's take-home salary. I am sick over this but I vowed I will never buy anything again unless it's absolutely necessary."

Now there is an economist (better late than never)!

COSTS OF CLUTTER: THE PHYSICAL HAZARDS

I think this one is eligible to be made into a movie....

❝ This past March I was making a move from my apartment in Ohio to one closer to work, in Pennsylvania. I had one last trip to make to collect my stuff out of storage. It was 33 miles, so I wanted to get it all in one shot, all my precious junk that is neatly boxed and never used. When I got to Ohio it took three hours to trek everything from the storage unit in the basement of

my ex-apartment, up steps, across a parking lot, and to my truck. By now snow is flying and I am cursing myself as to why did I **ever** save this stuff. Then, with the boxes all crammed in the truck, I set off down Ohio State Route 11. It was snowing and starting to get dark, so I was anxious to get home.

Cruising down Route 11 at about 50-55 mph, I noticed lids flapping on some of the boxes, but I thought I had those boxes wedged together so tight they would never pop off. I was wrong. About five minutes later, the lids did not fly off—entire boxes and their contents were airborne. I was in the left lane and frantically tried to pull over to get what flew out. Like possessed demons with minds of their own, my clutter was flying all over Route 11. The worst of it was that some blew directly onto a car window, causing the driver to swerve. After I came to a stop, I just sat in panic while I watched two more cars dodge boxes on the highway. I realized my clutter could have been fatal.

I looked in the back of my pickup and noticed several bare spots that had earlier been crammed full. I lost six, maybe eight boxes of useless clutter and almost caused an accident in the process. There was too much traffic to go along the highway and retrieve the stuff. I could see fragments all over, but to this day I have **no idea** what was in those boxes or on that highway, and have never missed anything valuable."

(**I** know some of you are headed for Route 11 right now to see if you can salvage any of that abandoned clutter. Forget it, a packrat in an old Packard got it all!)

I'm not sure you can get more graphic about the costs of clutter than these next accounts:

❝ A local property owner, long the subject of neighborhood complaints, has been charged more than $34,000 for a city cleanup of his property. The Gardena City Council voted unanimously to authorize the removal of hazards on the property, which includes a house, garage, and shed.

After a lengthy legal process which included numerous trips to municipal courts to get inspection and abatement warrants, the cleanup process began on June 16.

Trash and debris littered the yard to a point that it was declared a fire hazard. The interior of the home was in a state that violated numerous health and safety codes. To clean it up, the city had to hire two contractors: one to remove the junk and another to haul away 14 drums of hazardous household materials.

Because a warrant was in effect, police officers had to be hired to escort city crews and other workers while they were on the property. Legal and administrative fees eventually totalled more than $7,000.

The $34,000 cost has been added to the owner's tax bill, which will come due in its entirety in November."

—Joy Dockter
in the *Gardena Valley News*

❝ COLLECTIBLES KILLED COUPLE

Los Angeles—Their collectibles killed them.

Robert 'Sarge' Pauline, 72, and his wife of 18 years, Judy Ng, 42, haunted swap meets, auctions, and garage sales. They collected stereos, books, model trains, and trinkets that they crammed inside their small Van Nuys home.

The magnitude-6.6 Northridge earthquake crumbled the collectibles that were stacked high along all four walls of their bedroom. Rescuers found them in bed, facing one another, their hands covering their faces.

Emergency workers found the bodies under a 4-foot-deep pile of debris after digging for an hour.

'The stuff was piled to the ceiling, everywhere except at the door and above the head of the bed,' said Kent Ng, one of Judy Ng's brothers.

Family members said they never had been invited inside and had no idea about the overwhelming size of the collection the couple had amassed over the years.

Shrinking space inside the house apparently drove Pauline outside each morning to sip coffee and read the newspaper in his car, neighbors said."

—The Los Angeles
Daily News

It's confetti – you never know when it might come in useful...

COSTS OF CLUTTER: IMPACT ON OTHERS, ESPECIALLY OUR LOVED ONES

❝ I hate going to visit him because the kids have to be watched constantly. They might touch something 'valuable' or dangerous."

This is the saddest letter in this book—

❝After reading your books, I see that part of the clutter I have to get rid of is the desire for material things my mother taught us. I guess she was poor and when my father was successful she filled our house with velvet sofas and bedspreads (too heavy for me to lift from my own bed as a child), crys-

tal chandeliers, bisque and Dresden figurines. **All of these possessions took so much time to care for, time away from my sisters and me.** My mother worked and was seldom home, but I can remember her cleaning the chandelier better than I can remember her reading me a book when she had a day off. I almost got killed the day I used a Czechoslovakian cut crystal decanter to catch bugs and then broke it. These things had no value to a child."

What a message for we moderns this one has. Wow!

❝ We are all aware of the stream of young mothers who are leaving their children to strange caretakers so they can go to work. After closely observing the lives of a significant number of working mothers, I have noticed that most of the time it is not the MONEY they need that motivates them to work. It is an escape from their clutter. First the clutter produces depression. Then they develop a constant-buying mentality to give them a sense of worth in the midst of their clutter. Then their spending habit produces a 'need to work' state of mind.

I also have experienced far too often the negative effects on child training that clutter produces. **When my house is dirty and cluttered, my fuse is very short** and I often take it out on the children, yelling and commanding them and making unfair demands on them. Now that I have made a commitment not to buy anything unless absolutely necessary, and to have everything in its place at sunset, I am amazed at how my anger spurts have decreased."

How much time do **you** spend on a one-on-one basis with your spouse and children each day, vs the time you spend with your stuff?

Junk: The big fuse lighter

Another carryover from carrying all those extra pounds of stuff around is the friction it causes in our relationships with others. One woman, forever stacking and fighting her tipping piles of junk and then justifying them to other members of the family, talked about the ill feelings piled with those possessions. "Our doorstops are all broken off from slamming during arguments."

Think of the last five arguments around your house. How many of them were over junk and clutter? These things cause more fights, family squabbles, divorce, and dissention than anything except finances.

People fight over the space things take up, and then over the affection lost to them. We are really affectionate to mere objects. She will say "get rid of that old paint" and he will say "that's MY paint!"

COSTS OF CLUTTER: IMPACT ON US AND OUR VALUES

When some of us see a new home, we don't see a place for us, but a place for our stuff. The garage isn't for cars, it's for counter and closet overflow, that big back yard isn't for playing, but for parking the RV and other big toys. Ceiling height isn't a question of head room but of stacking and stashing potential.

Amazing, how if you're junked enough, clutter dominates your whole appraisal and value system. Places, purses, vehicles—even people—are all valued not for what they can give us as a person, but by what they can take of our hoard.

COSTS OF CLUTTER: MENTAL DISTRACTION

❝ I just graduated with a degree in Psychology, so maybe someday I will figure some of this out. I do know that the longer my life remains cluttered, the more emotionally cluttered I will be. Surroundings do that to you."

I wonder if it was a PhD degree? (Piled higher and Deeper!)

❝ Years ago, I saw a Japanese house that had been brought in its entirety to the Boston Children's Museum. That house made an indelible impression on me by its simplicity and functionality. I've held that house as an ideal ever since. **Clutter is visual noise**, and I can't hear myself think surrounded by the noise of useless possessions."

Out of sight, out of mind? No sir!

I've always maintained that clutter takes as much space in our minds as it does in our closets and cupboards, and a friend of mine, a noted food service expert, told me an interesting experience about his dejunking that seems to be one more little bit of evidence about this.

He decided to go through everything and get rid of all those things hidden away and never used. He went into every closet, drawer, and cubbyhole—all the areas where no one ever looked anyway—and removed only a few items from each hole, not really a big purge, and certainly nothing visible to the eye. For the whole next week, he said, all the friends that came over remarked "What's different here? Something is strange."

They could feel the junk gone! Do you believe that? I do!

COSTS OF CLUTTER: HOW IT TIES US TO THE PAST

Everyone I've ever met is on the alert for, if not actively searching for, an upgrade—more and better out of daily living. This is hard to achieve when you're eyebrow-deep in clutter. Clutter ties you into the same old routine because it anchors you to the past,

thus limiting your ability to take advantage of (or even be aware of) the future.

This thought could very nicely be put to music, and come to think of it, the perfect lyrics have already been written. Do you remember this little tune?

Please, release me let me go
Cause I don't love you any more.
Release me, and let me live
again.

❝ When I was finished with my decluttering project, I felt relieved, and actually looked forward to walking in the closet again rather than dreading it. I also felt that **giving up some of my past allowed me to deal with the present and future more easily.**❞

COSTS OF CLUTTER: HOW IT DICTATES AND LIMITS OUR LIFESTYLE

Wisdom from abroad—the U.K. (where the junker national motto is "God Save Our Things").

❝ My husband and I grew up in families where antiques and family furniture/ possessions were regarded as sacred

I'm sorry, I can't — I'm junk sitting!

relics to be owned and treasured in perpetuity. And when we were married, our parents in the kindness of their hearts cleared out their rooms, emptied their cupboards, and offloaded onto us all their surplus. As it was all so very 'good,' we did not feel justified in getting rid of it and buying something new and more appropriate; nor would it have occurred to us, as in the early 60's things were still quite hard. And in any case getting rid of anything would have caused great upset, great ruckus.

Subsequent moves, and the arrival of four children resulted in us buying a very large tumbledown Victorian manor in order to house the furniture, as well as the family. It wasn't long before **the continual effort and cost and all the repairs, cleaning, and maintenance of these things was causing a great deal of friction** as my husband was unwilling to give sufficient time, money, and labor to it, and who can blame him? His interests lay in other directions, and he had a very demanding job.

The situation was saved by my husband's redundancy at the age of forty-nine, and our having to move as a result. He undertook a complete career change. Having been in industry, he became a schoolmaster at a boarding school and we moved into a smaller, modern rented house at the school where the school undertakes to decorate and maintain the property free of charge. Bliss!

We had to get rid of half our household goods. My husband (and his mother backstage) fought disposal every inch of the way, but we really had no choice. Looking back, I realize how our inherited possessions dictated and limited our lifestyle. Indirectly they threatened our marriage—but we learned in the process. My husband's mother (a hoarder until the end) has moved to an old people's home, but has insisted on keeping quite a lot of family furniture for the grandchildren. Much of this is large and inappropriate, and is already having to be moved for the second time at great expense to another (fortunately free!) place of storage. We worked out that to move **each item** the second time around cost fifty pounds [$150.00 in U.S. currency]. As it happens two of my three older children are working abroad, and none of them look like they'll be getting a house in the near future.

I tell my children that even if we do not pass much family furniture on to them we shall be giving them something just as precious, **freedom to pursue a sensible and appropriate lifestyle, unencumbered by surplus possessions.**

Our families really believed that by giving us furniture they were saving us money, and it did to begin with. But times change, and the hundreds of pounds saved on furniture are nothing compared to the thousands spent keeping up a large old property—not to mention large fuel bills, etc. Also, after a while, the furniture itself became costly to maintain because much of it was passed on to us in bad repair—not a favor!"

> **" He who is attached to things will suffer much."**

" Discomfort, claustrophobia, confusion, and the need to have space available is what finally motivated me to dejunk."

COSTS OF CLUTTER: CARRYOVER INTO EVERY AREA OF OUR LIFE

" As I was reading *Clutter's Last Stand* I began to think of what was hidden behind my garage—seven years' worth of used motor oil in plastic jugs. The jugs had not weathered too well; some were cracked and leaking oil on the ground, what a mess! I finally decided to clean up this eyesore.

I found a place to recycle the stuff, but they only took five gallons at a time. That is quite a bit unless you have thirty-five gallons of the best refined in broken leaking jugs. As I rejugged this stuff I couldn't help but laugh and also cry over it. It speaks volumes about how I have let so many things go in my life. Rather than dispose of this stuff a few gallons at a time I put it off until I had a major oil spill on my hands. I realized I had also done that with my home, my wife and children, and even issues at the church I am pastor of."

Have you ever looked at the parallel between junk and drugs—their allure and effect is a lot the same:

1. Both are addictive
2. Both are expensive
3. Both make us feel good for a while but the long-term effects are another story
4. Both start small and innocent
5. Both grow quickly once started
6. Both distract and weaken us
7. Both fool us into thinking we're not hooked
8. Both require a cure before they will go away

Here's a drug that's already legalized!

TAX TIME IS ALL YEAR ROUND WITH CLUTTER

Every year April 15 looms as the day we have to account for our income and pay our taxes. I've often wondered what greater agony would result if every year on December 15th we had to report our current inventory of junk and clutter. An amusing thought, or maybe a terrifying one. While filling out my last 1040 (probably the tax form you use too), I altered one to fit those packrat profits. You might try filling this out for fun.

See page 30 for the Clutter Tax Return.

WHY DEJUNK? (ENDING THAT LOVE/HATE RELATIONSHIP WITH JUNK)

After forty years as a professional cleaner, working around and with all kinds of people and their possessions, I've come to the conclusion that we have a love/hate relationship with our clutter. We come up with endless excuses for keeping the relationship going (see Chapter Three), yet are constantly cursing that clutter for what it does to us.

In this chapter we've taken a look at what it does, why our clutter is killing us (even as we amass it and care dearly for it).

I could go on and say a lot more to counteract all those incredible excuses, but you being intelligent, progressive seekers of self-esteem, freedom, love, and wealth, only need a few reasons to rid. So let me now condense all the arguments for shedding that excess stuff into three lifesaving sentences. You'll hear these repeated and echoed over and over in this book. If you take few minutes to truly absorb them, I guarantee you'll be **cured**!

Why dejunk (now!)
1. People will treat you better
Being all piled and cluttered up reflects in your personality. It makes you seem slow, awkward, and disorganized—outdated, even. Clutter silently pulls you from dashing to dumpy.

Junk and clutter also signal insecurity and indecision, which are never comfortable to be around. This can undermine confidence in you or cause others to distrust you.

All those layers of junk also insulate you from others, and make access to you impossible. Before long it's obvious to other people that you'd rather tend junk than them, or more important things and issues. It's clear that your allegiance is to objects, you are going to serve "stuff" before staff, family, or friends.

Dejunking opens all kinds of avenues for being loved, wanted, and treated better. Nothing on this earth beats being treated well and loved!

2. You'll have more time and space to live
What are all of those "time management," "get organized," and "self-help" sources (books, seminars, sermons, psychologists, advisers, prescriptions) trying to give us today? More time and more space. So much of this is merely cosmetic or artificial stopgap tricks and gimmicks, so much of it either doesn't really work, or actually adds to our burden of clutter.

Getting is easy, disposing difficult. So keeping it all is our solu-

2040

Department of the Treasures—Eternal Refuse Service

U.S. Individual Clutter Tax Return

199_ (0)

Label

Use the preprinted label off one of your 10,000 catalogs

L A B E L   H E R E

Your first name and initial	Last name

If a joint return, spouse's first name and initial	Last name

Home address (number and street). (If a P.O. box, see page 7 of Instructions.)	Apt. no.

City, town or post office, state and ZIP code. (If a foreign address, see page 7.)

Your social security number

Spouse's social security number

For Privacy Act and Paperwork Reduction Act Notice, see Instructions.

Residential Anti-Clutter Campaign

▶ Would you donate $1 to stamp out clutter?   Yes ▨   No
Would you donate some of your spouse's stuff?   Yes ▨   No

Note: Checking "Yes" will not change your junk or reduce your refund.

Filing Status

☐ Single (there's only one of you, so you have more time and money to devote to things)
☐ Married filing joint accumulation
☐ Married filing separate stash (you couldn't even attempt to list it all together)
☐ Head of household (full of stuff)

Gross Clutter Accumulation

(purchased, gift, and purloined items all count the same)

	Number of Items	How Acquired	Cost New	Current Value
Clothes				
Paper				
Toys				
Sentimental stuff				
Collections				
Gadgets				
Hobby and sport clutter				
To be fixed stuff				
Attic/Basement/Garage junk				

Complete disposal within 10 days—5% tax credit

Basic Taxable Inventory
= _____ (A)
x _____

Anticipated clutter inheritance tax   ☐ I will take it   ☐ I will refuse it
If you check the first box here, add the amount inherited to the total at right.

Possible Exemptions

Under oath:
☐ I'm storing for friend or family   ☐ I'm an antique dealer   ☐ It was there when I moved in
☐ Child of the Depression   ☐ I'm Danish

Subtract 1% for each

Income	From all the garage sales in your lifetime	
Adjustments to Income	From line above subtract the following:	
Rent (house)	Subtract $50 per square foot for all the space in your home occupied by clutter, plus the total (direct and indirect) cost of any storage elsewhere	
Insurance	The percent of your homeowner's insurance coverage that is covering clutter.	
Containment Tax	(Cost of trunks, lockers, boxes, bags, Rubbermaid Keepers, shelves, extra closets and sheds. For depreciation allowance, see page 32.)	
Utilities	Energy (heat, lights, phone calls) consumed for a bunch of useless items	
Time and Energy	One hour of your time (at your current wage per hour) per cubic yard of clutter, per quarter	
Reputation Toll	Losses in community standing and personal relationships from clutter	

Adjusted Gross Clutter

Under penalty of being dejunked by a third party I certify that I have declared all my clutter past, present, and future.

Subtract line 30 from line 23. This is your **adjusted gross clutter**. If this line is more than -$30,000 and a child living with you became lost in the basement for the better part of a year, see "Earned Clutter Credit" (line 58) on page 20 of the Instructions. If you want the ERS to burn down your house and all clutter therein, see page 16 of the Instructions.

tion, but this quickly brings us to the point that "it" begins to keep us, through the cost of insurance, taxes, storage space, and our time to tend it all. Thus gradually we are diverted from the main road of our life going somewhere, to the side road of stuff. This is a dead-end road, and eventually we'll have to reverse out of it. When you lose sight of your real pursuit in life, when you find yourself fighting for time and space to live, you know it's time to dejunk.

Physical stuff, like junk and clutter, needs mental and emotional space, too—and it takes it—just look around (or in and under). You are surrendering your soul… for what?

Don't love what can't love you back.

Time and space—either you have it, or your stuff does. That should be an easy choice to make.

When the next big "self-improvement" seminar comes to town, let half of those signed up attend and the other half stay home and dejunk. I'll wager the dejunkers will benefit 5 to 1 over the seminar attendees in every department of learning to live better.

3. You'll save money

Excess has a price tag that doesn't get marked down, it just keeps mounting up. All that extra stuff you have costs extra money, and that usually means extra work at a job somewhere (= time away from your personal life and relationships). Soon we don't even have time to enjoy or pay attention to all that neat (if unnecessary) stuff—we're too busy working to pay for it.

Tending it all, too, doesn't just take a little of your storage space, a little time, and a little worry. Having anything costs money from one angle or another, and usually several. A $20 item (that you really don't need) on sale for $2, or even given to you, instantly becomes a liability in any accounting ledger. The minute you own it those expenses start mounting up—rent, depreciation, burglar-proofing, pest-proofing, your time to shuffle it around and try to figure out what to do with it—review the tally sometime to see the total cost. That $20 item you only paid $2 for can easily cost $145.50 in the end.

Even "free" isn't free. People can and do eat and drink themselves to death or ill health on free food. Carrying always has a cost, and many a fortune has been lost by burdening the boat with excess treasure. Junk and clutter have to be carried on the same inventory as the really needed things. Junkers are always "hunters," they have so much they always have to hunt around before they can find or do anything, at home, work, or play. This, too, costs.

Clutter makes constant, dependable deductions from our life's cash profits. If all of the money we've sunk in "stuff" were saved and invested better, the total, counting interest, would add up to thousands upon thousands of dollars of cold, hard cash. It's downright scary (and have you noticed how most good money managers aren't cluttered?).

The bottom line of all this is: It's not what you acquire that makes for happiness, it's what you become. Joy is loving and being loved. Eliminating junk and clutter from your life is the single biggest way to bring joy into it. We all know it, deep inside, and we all want to do it. Let's go to work on it!

Dejunking: why do it NOW?

❝ Before I read your book *Clutter's Last Stand* I did what I thought was a major dejunking. Then the basement flooded. I had to wash, dry, fold, and resort fifteen boxes of used clothes I was saving to give away to people.

Everything prior to the great flood (as it has come to be known) had been carefully sorted into seasons and sizes; I was proud of myself for being so organized. But it took me a month to get the clothes back into usable condition. I was so disgusted, and I felt selfish for keeping the clothes until they were nearly ruined.

I also had to get rid of boxes of curtains and sheets I didn't want anymore but kept anyway. Also destroyed were two bags of stuffed animals. I had to throw them away. If I hadn't been so selfish, perhaps they would still be being enjoyed."

For more on the cost of clutter, see Chapter 5 of <u>*Clutter's Last Stand*</u> *and Chapter 3 of* <u>*Not for Packrats Only*</u>.

❝ ON TOP OF MY CLUTTER

(to the tune of 'On Top of Old Smokey')

On top of my clutter
All buried in dust.
It just keeps on mounting
and driving me nuts.

Let's all take a minute
and pitch all that stuff.
And see how much laughter
Replaces our junk!"

—Paula Cooper Matthews

Chapter 3

More Incredible Excuses for Clutter

See? I told you it would all come in useful one day!

What or who creates a clutterbug? I've heard a lot of possible reasons over the years, from psychologists (professional and amateur), ministers, insurance adjusters, other pro cleaners, children, wives, and husbands of junkaholics, and probably above all from packrats themselves.

Let's hear it directly from that last group now, because junkers by and large are a sensitive and intelligent lot, with a keen eye and ear for "the inner workings."

ROOTS OF CLUTTER: THINGS SUBSTITUTED FOR FEELINGS

❝ I think your comment in one of your books about some objects coming to have an inordinate value, as if they had souls or lives of their own, is right on target. But it goes further, I think, especially in families with little love or warmth. **Objects that the parents handled or wore or prized come to be substitutes for the parents' love.** That would account for the vicious, angry fights over disposition of personal effects when someone dies, in such a case, among their children.

I grew up in such a home and for many years I did feel irrationally concerned with what my mother chose to give me. It took me a long time to get over it and even longer to understand that I saw her gifts as being equal to her love."

Someone in defense of their junk once said to me, "It's a lot more important to spend time with your kids than to go through everything and dejunk."

I agree with that. However you can do both, and you'll bless those kids to the same degree you get rid of the distractions.

ROOTS OF CLUTTER: SAVING FOR SECURITY/IDENTITY

❝ I know you approve—or at least don't disapprove—of keeping photos and MEANINGFUL mementos. But do you know WHY people keep things which actually have 'no value?' I didn't know but found out when I read *Culture Shock* years ago. As you probably noticed the more people have to move around, the more they are addicted to junk. (We are not talking about business travel. We are talking about people who live—either by choice or necessity—like gypsies, with no real home to call their own.) This junk gives them an illusion of being in the same place, i.e., having a permanent home. It serves as **an emotional anchor**.❞

❝ We are not talking about things but about identity. *I am my stuff.* This is who I am: A brown carton of my college notebooks, my great-grandfather's four-volume set of *The Cabinet of Irish Literature* published in 1893, my son's honor-roll certificates from the second grade forward, 317 World-War II-vintage computer boards. How awful. How weird. It gets worse. Every closet, drawer, shelf, and cubby-hole is a midden, *a time capsule of who I was, who I hoped to be, who I thought I should be.*❞
—Jane O'Reilly
in *Home and Garden*

What a profound summary of the clutter quagmire!

❝ *I talked with a social psychiatrist about the manic material acquisition addiction in American society. What he charged me $390 to find out is that we Americans use all our personal clutter of 'stuff' as an exhibition of who, what, and how we are. Our clutter is talismanic processing.*❞

Collector's Blues

Things won't let you down
Or run you around
Or leave you
Or deceive you.

Boxes and bric-a-brac
Never talk back
Or give you the sack.
They just stay in place
Taking up space
Till they're a cluttered disgrace.

You've no time to use them
Or sort them or choose them
Yet you can't bear to lose them.

—Janet Held

You wouldn't think we'd need to be told this, but we do indeed exist separate and apart from our stuff.

It's our character, actions, and feelings that really count, where our whole value in existence is. If we lose sight of this, we'll come completely unhinged if our house burns down or our storage bin is carried off by a tornado.

One great bit of advice I heard from a kindly elderly man once was "In life, don't let the tail wag the dog." I was little then and I didn't make the parallel to people letting their goals and pursuits in life be guided by the impulses of the moment rather than solid intelligent direction. Now that I know thousands of clutter collectors I see their decisions being guided by what they own, not what they want or need. Their clutter determines their spending, scheduling, travel, and conversation, and the tail is clearly wagging the dog. It's ok to have stuff, but as we see in so many of these packrat reports, silently and relentlessly, too often stuff has us.

These folks are getting much closer to the goal:

❝ **I don't need junk to tell me who I am** (and that I lack self-control if I'm overwhelmed by it)."

❝ I was a clutterbug in the highest, most cluttered, most catastrophic sense. **I kept everything out of fear.** And then I read your book, your warm humor, your love—and I was sold—on life—a new life of happy uncluttered clean homemaking."

ROOTS OF CLUTTER: INDECISION

❝ People who collect clutter also have trouble making decisions. When you can't decide what to do with something, you put it to the side and put off the decision process—and the clutter accumulates.❞

This is one of the reasons dejunking is emotionally tiring— we have to make ALL of those decisions NOW, one right after the other. It'll be a lot easier on you if you start today to train yourself to do it on a one-by-one basis—the minute a questionable item first crosses your threshold or comes into your hand.

ROOTS OF CLUTTER: HEREDITY

❝ *I was born with a bag-lady mentality.*❞

(Now there's an excuse I've never heard before!)

❝ *I am a a dyed-in-the-wool pack-rat. In defense, I must tell you that it was inherited. My father not only keeps all of his own junk, but often roots in other people's trash, and for years made trips to surrounding junkyards with a rake. He says as he got nearer, his hands would begin to perspire, and he'd begin to tremble in anticipa-tion. So you see, it's not all my fault. Add to that my Mormon heritage of 'waste not, want not,' 'store a year or two's needs,' etc., and is it any wonder?*❞

❝ *It HAS to be in the* **genes.** *It must be. In our family we call it 'the Clancy creeping out in us.'*

Here's why: I've already told you about Mom. Her eighty-year-old sister lives next door to where Mom did, where she has lived ever since she and her late husband built their home sixty years ago this year. She has a full basement and two storage sheds. In them she has every washer and dryer she has ever owned! One shed is so full she can only look in the door. She has never thrown away an item of clothing, and **her washroom is so full of junk that every time she gets ready to use the washer or dryer, it takes her fifteen minutes to move things around so she can use the appliances.** *I have warned her kids what they have to look forward to!*

Then there's an eighty-three-year-old brother. When I went south this

The first thing you'll need, son, is a *junk bench...*

winter, we went to take him a cake around Christmas and found him in his—get this!—three-room storage building. I doubt that he has ever thrown away a single thing in his entire life. He didn't let us in farther than just inside the door, but I've heard that he has some things that are collector's items such as old toys and other miscellanea that if sold would put him (and probably his heirs too) on easy street for life. He told us that he started collecting when he was six or seven years old. He is caretaker of the family cemetery and keeps such things as faded old flowers off the graves. I also saw old two-liter Coke bottles, old unusable mattresses, and everything else imaginable. He even went so far as to tell his son and daughter that when he died, the storage shed was to remain locked and never be opened.

Then there's my cousin, daughter of the above-mentioned aunt, who is definitely a clone of her mother. Last year, she finally gave her deceased husband's long-out-of-style suits to Goodwill—after the heating company looked in her basement and said, 'We can't install a new heating system in here until you clean it out. There's no room to work.' Her husband died in 1981 and she now is seeing someone who is a perfectionist housekeeper. They've been dating about three years but she has seldom let him beyond her living room. I shudder to think what will happen when they marry, though she tells him she's a terrible housekeeper and he just says 'That's ok. I'll clean the house.'"

That poor guy, when he loses her in the clutter on their wedding day he'll probably have a hint of what's coming.

This heredity excuse is one of the most popular, "I'm a Dane and the Danes are big-time packrats." There are lots of claims to a pure cluttering line in the global geneology—it somehow seems that a pure dejunked race or strain should appear once in a while to even things out!

Junking by Age Group and Generation

1 to 8 Parents and other people heap it on.

8 to 18 You do what everybody else does—collect what's "in."

18 to 30 You don't have much cash so you go to garage sales to top out your heaps.

30 to 40 You're more selective—"status" objects are the focus now.

40 to 50 Some kid stuff (strollers and some of that grade school artwork) finally goes.

50 to 60 Your teenage drill team and baseball outfits finally go.

60 to 70 You ditch your maternity wear, and begin to consider dumping some stuff on your kids.

70 to 80 You start collecting again for the next life.

80 to 90 Your stuff is about the only security you feel in a non-caring world—so you hang on to it for dear life!

90 to 100 You've hit the jackpot—What you have left is at last **truly antique.**

ROOTS OF CLUTTER: THE URGE TO OVERDO EVERYTHING

❝ *Your letter and book came just when I was doing some serious soul-searching. I had just prayed that very morning and asked the Lord to help me to be moderate in everything. My natural tendency is to go overboard, and I have to be so careful.*❞

❝ My mother is a bona-fide junkee, and a very **obsessive** person in everything she does. She overeats, overtalks, overbuys, overcooks, you name it, she overdoes it.❞

❝ I come from a dysfunctional family (two alcoholic parents) and cluttering is my current **obsessive-compulsive addiction**. I'm creative (into art, various crafts, writing, etc.) a perfectionist, a procrastinator, very shy, an under-achiever, and not good at setting priorities, problem-solving (except in my creative pursuits), decisionmaking, or letting go.❞

Suddenly for the first time I think I finally see the value of a "shrink." They may not be needed for the brain, but for the basement, the attic, our closets. Plenty of us need a shrink, and as soon as our stuff is shrunk, wellness is in sight.

ROOTS OF CLUTTER: REFLEXIVE/INGRAINED SAVING

❝ I keep these things because I was a 'Depression Babe.' Everything was precious in those days. I've still got an old set of my false teeth I replaced years ago, because Mother's only set broke in hard times and she went without teeth for three years. I used to dream about something pretty for my hair—I can't bring myself to throw away a bobby pin now.❞

Gads, for a minute I thought she was keeping the teeth for a hair clamp!

So much of cluttering amounts to accumulating **much more than we could ever use of something.** For many of us this goes beyond practicality and prudence into sheer reflex and mindless habit. Sensible saving is one thing, but salting away ten, twenty, or more times than you could ever use of something is a waste of time, space, and money (as well as a hogging of resources that someone somewhere else on this crowded planet really needs).

Before you save the next thing, think:

1) How many of these/how much of this do I already have?
2) Do I really have room to keep it?
3) How long will it last in storage?

4) **When** will I use it?

❝ *I was brought up in a family that really believed '**waste-not-want-not**'.*

When you grow up hardly throwing away anything but banana peelings and eggshells, what a punch in the gut it is when you finally do figure out you could actually have been trashing all that mess you've been walking over and around all those years."

❝ *Growing up, I was taught to say 'please' and 'thank you' and to save things 'just in case.' Forty years later I found myself living among 'just in case' piles and 'someday I'll need it' drawers."*

❝ *In its quiet way junk and clutter whispers a belief in immortality, because surely deep inside we know we'll never manage to use or wear it all in our lifetime."*

(**A**men!)

ROOTS OF CLUTTER: CUTESY COLLECTING

❝ We live in an old stone farmhouse built somewhere in the 1800's, that just seems to absorb **as if by osmosis,** antiques and collectibles... which I do so enjoy finding at yard sales and flea markets... or at least I did until I read *Clutter's Last Stand*."

❝ **We live in a 100-year-old log and stone house, very conducive to collectibles.** *Country Living*

Clutter Crossword

A member of the audience handed this to me after one of my decluttering seminars, and I thought you might like to pull out one of your 143 pencils and give it a try.

Across
2. A sophisticated name for junk
4. We collect these on our vacation
6. What we stuff our junk into
8. How our storage room looks
9. What we wish our junk would become
11. One half of wall junk

Down
1. When we clean we put our junk in
3. Rhymes with gutter; makes our house look messy
5. What we will be when we die and find out that we can't take our junk with us
7. We put our junk in the back yard on
10. The other half of wall junk

was my favorite magazine—I've since cancelled my subscription."

Pretty desperate, huh? Two letters in a row blaming their clutteritis on a poor old stone house!

❝ *The day I bought my fortieth 'dried apple face gnome,' I was trying to find a place to display it when I suddenly found myself wondering: do I really enjoy looking at these things all that much, or is seeking them out and shelving them just something to do?"*

ROOTS OF CLUTTER: BUYING TOO MUCH

How many of you are these folks' kissing cousins?

❝ *Every time I talk to her she is overwhelmed by her messy/cluttered house, which she 'can't get to' (she works full time). So she moans and groans 'Whatever am I going to do?' Next sentence, 'Oh, I just got a... [diamond watch, bed for the third bedroom, new electric frypan, etc.]' Now she has to find a place for the second-best frypan, and the sofa bed that was in the third bedroom is now jammed into the already over-full living room."*

❝ I have the bad habit of **stockpiling**—buying too much stuff for when I run out, i.e., four new bottles of shampoo for when the one I'm using now is gone. Uncounted boxes of stationery for when I run out. Numerous birthday cards in variety packs—I still buy them individually too. Notebook paper (three packs of it), index cards, even flour and sugar (three bags of each), canned veggies and soup."

ROOTS OF CLUTTER: INSULATING THE SELF WITH STUFF

❝ There is something I would like to share. I'm a homemaker, and having the house decluttered is a little scary for me. I think my junk was **my excuse not to live today** because I could worry, putter, complain, and so on about my junk. I have lots of free time now. My home keeps itself clean and now I have time for me, to do projects I want to do. Because of my junk it seemed selfish to do what I wanted before because there was **so much work to do** (my excuse). My husband and I have also discovered how important having fun is. We would never allow ourselves this because of stuff (excuses) and we needed to make fun a priority."

❝ Clutter *narcotizes our sense of purposelessness* as we surround ourselves with objects and projects, obligating ourselves beyond our capacity. Frantic busyness confers a weird sense of immortality. We always have tomorrow to look forward to, because there's so much to do! (So we can avoid facing more profound questions.)"

—Barbara Sullivan in *The Chicago Tribune*

What made me do it?
- [ ] eyes bigger than stomach
- [ ] need to feel rich (such as from a giant horde of clothes clutter, 70 or 80% of which is probably unwearable by you at this point in time)
- [ ] optimism and romanticism (failure to be realistic)
- [ ] nostalgia/sentiment
- [ ] empathy/pity
- [ ] compulsion to collect
- [ ] desire to preserve it for posterity (how's that for self-delusion?)
- [ ] thrift real or imagined
- [ ] investment ("it'll be worth money some day")
- [ ] simple greed/the urge to hoard

More of those Amazing Junker's Excuses

❝ *My husband says he can't get rid of his stuff for all the reasons commonly mentioned. But the best is because* **when he's President** *it will be necessary for history. They'll put his kindergarten papers in a museum.*❞

❝ *My husband has twenty-year-old love letters that he won't throw out because his old girl friend put so much work into them.*❞

❝ I guess coming from a family of eight, we saved everything and took care of it because '**we might need it someday**,' or '**we paid good money for that**.'❞

❝ Our small grandson wanted to keep his old bicycle tire tubes because 'they **might heal themselves**.' I guess that's why we all keep junk.❞

❝ ***I'm keeping it because I'd like to use it up.***❞

I've heard this, believe it or not, said about pantyhose with major runs in both legs, pocketknives with no blades left, and fifty-gallon drums of axle grease.

❝ *I'm saving it* **until I get a nicer home**.❞

❝ *I am enclosing my 'weird junk' for amusement. These are shoulder pads from T-shirts. I removed them because I look ghastly in shoulder pads, but didn't throw them away because they matched the shirts.*❞

❝ Please send me a copy of your Junkee Entrance Exam. Maybe with that, or your book I'll be able to bring myself to throw out all the old Christmas cards I have in boxes in the basement. I'm keeping them until I find time to cut off the backs to use for writing grocery lists.❞

❝ My husband is a real junker! One day we were cleaning out our storage locker and I came across a nice pair of men's boots. I asked my husband why he never wore them and he said because they were three sizes too big! This prompted me to ask why he had them in storage, why didn't he get rid of them? He said, with shock in his voice, 'Becky! These are **real deerskin** boots, and **Dad gave them to me**! They're worth a lot of money!' His dad, by the way, is still living. We pay $66 a month to rent a storage space for stuff like that."

❝ *A thought occurred to me as I read of the couple who entered your "worst junk" contest and won with a goat brassiere. They had carried that thing around for years (they didn't have a goat), thinking it might come in handy some day—AND IT DID! They won a vacuum with it."*

Besides, you never know when a well-endowed goat might wander into your yard. Don't count on the same lift from the rest of your clutter!

As you can see from this small sampling, it hasn't been hard to come up with excuses for collecting and clinging to clutter. We've all heard, and I've recorded, some of the most creative menageries of lame logic imaginable to justify ownership of unused stuff.

To give you an idea of the magnitude of the "Excuses to Cling," let me list those in the letters we just read, plus a few of the most

common others from letters and comments I receive.

Here are only forty or so—judging from the average junker's repertoire there are easily another thousand or so out there somewhere. Before you giggle at any of the following, consider some of the justifications that have issued forth from your own lips (if they're as good/better send them to me!)

For fun I've put a checkbox by each of these excuses—check any you've used yourself, or thought of using. (In case you need to be convinced that you need to read on.)

If you think I've missed a few, check out Chapter 3 of <u>Clutter's Last Stand</u> and Chapter 11 of <u>Not for Packrats Only</u>.

Mess? What mess?

44

- [ ] "It's in my blood."
- [ ] "I wouldn't have any identity without it."
- [ ] "I'm compulsive."
- [ ] "I can't let it go to waste."
- [ ] "It fits into my 'country' decor."
- [ ] "I collect these."
- [ ] "I'm a shopaholic."
- [ ] "In case I become famous."
- [ ] "Someone put a lot of work into it."
- [ ] "I might need it some day."
- [ ] "I paid good money for that."
- [ ] "It might heal itself."
- [ ] "I intend to use it up."
- [ ] "It's too nice to use/wear."
- [ ] "It matches."
- [ ] "I'm going to use it to _____"
- [ ] "It's made of real/solid _____"
- [ ] "It was a gift."
- [ ] "I might win a junk contest with it."
- [ ] "It only has ___ holes in it."
- [ ] "It's part of a set."
- [ ] "I'm going to fix it"
- [ ] "I'm keeping/saving it for parts."
- [ ] "We only used this once!"
- [ ] "It's brand new."
- [ ] "It's still perfectly good."
- [ ] "It's an antique."
- [ ] "It was here when I moved in."
- [ ] "I'll use it for a spare."
- [ ] "I'm saving it for the kids."
- [ ] "It's a conversation piece"
- [ ] "I'm going to finish it some day."
- [ ] "I'm going to take it up again someday."
- [ ] "I'm going to go through these someday."
- [ ] "I'm going to convert this into _____" (i.e. a planter or picture frame)
- [ ] "We might move to _____ and need this."
- [ ] "It may come back in style."
- [ ] "I'm going to wear it _____(to paint/work in the yard)"
- [ ] "It may be valuable some day."
- [ ] "It may come in handy in hard times."
- [ ] "They don't make things like this any more."
- [ ] "I want to show my grandchildren my roots."
- [ ] "I'll always be ready for…."
- [ ] "It still has the tag on it."
- [ ] "It was a bargain/great buy."
- [ ] "As soon as I throw it out, I'll need it."

Let's take a closer look at "But it's still perfectly good!", for example—one of the great classic excuses to rat-hole stuff.

A few years back when Clint Eastwood did the western *Pale Rider*, the movie company built the "town" in the Sawtooth Basin near Sun Valley, a short distance from where I lived.

They did a fine job, those were nice solid buildings even with carved banisters on the stairs. When they were finished shooting they dozed down all the buildings, burned them, picked up the few nails that were left, and all looked just as before.

Now that got to me, all that wasted firewood, and the loss of a possible park or tourist stop.

I stewed over it a month or two until someone familiar with the legal and safety considerations and costs involved in retooling or moving it all computed it up for me. It amounted to more time, energy, and risk than burning it, so they actually did a wise and unwasteful thing. The town had accomplished its mission, made a good movie, provided lots of jobs for the locals and now it was given back to nature. That's a good plan in anyone's book. Sure there might be a bit of wear or life left in something, but getting it out often calls for more than it's worth.

TEN WAYS TO TELL A PACKRAT

1. They can walk sideways smoothly, from all their experience threading through narrow canyons of junk.

2. They are agile and dextrous—they can climb over any obstacle and squeeze into any space to reach things in remote areas.

3. They always have large purses and bulging pockets.

4. Their whole countenance lights up at trigger words like "Sale," "Bargain," "Free," and "You can have it, if you want."

5. They drive a van or station wagon, even if they don't have children.

6. Their suitcases have sprung hinges, or are stamped "Excess Baggage."

7. Their vehicle lurches, no matter when or where you say "Garage sale!"

8. They brag excessively about it, if and when they do happen to toss out one single piece of garbage.

9. A stricken expression comes over their face when someone else throws something away and there is no way they can politely retrieve it.

10. No matter what hobby, pastime, or activity you mention, they already have everything you need for it.

Chapter 4

Help with "How-to" (Dejunk!)

This may seem immodest, but let me start off here by saying that so many people have commented—so forcefully—on what a help my other books have been, that I'd be doing you a disservice if I didn't mention it.

❝ *Your book gave me a 'jump start' into decluttering.*

I brought it home and decided to just look through it. Little did I realize that you don't just **look** *at this book. Two hours later I had read enough to know that my 'dejunk' time had arrived.*

I took the Junkee Entrance Exam and my score was NOT one to be proud of. The next morning, 6:00 a.m., it was downstairs to the junk room. By 8:00 a.m. there were six

boxes of 'treasures' ready for the garbage truck. Such things as 26-year-old high school books, broken containers (without lids), empty film containers, bent straws, flower pots (complete with soil), and many more valuable treasures.

I felt so good all day knowing my junk room was six boxes lighter. **For five days it was up at 6:00 a.m. to dejunk.**

On Friday I took the exam again. WOW! Not only did I feel better, but my exam score increased from 107 to 210.

I now know what you mean when you say 'Life truly begins when you discover how flexible and free you are without clutter.'
IT'S TERRIFIC!!!"

❝ My main secret to getting started, that kick-off (or should I say kick out?) oomph for dejunking (is that word in the dictionary yet?) is reading a Don Aslett book! Your books are like having a guardian angel on the shelf just waiting there to help me. **Even just flipping the book open and reading chapter headings gets me stirred up!**"

❝ *I read your books in between junking sessions (at piano lessons or soccer practice) and get more inspired all the time. I look forward to going at those piles of clutter and have to tear myself away to fix meals or make Halloween costumes.*"

❝ *After reading* Clutter's Last Stand, *it hit me like a bolt out of the blue. I'm Mrs. Clutter, married and have been for some thirty-three years, to the original Mr. Clutter. Looking back on our habits of 'saving' everything because it might come in handy someday, I began to realize that the only thing we ever throw away is garbage. (And Mr. Clutter goes through that sometimes.)*

I took the Junkee Entrance Exam and passed with flying colors. Now that it was clear I was a terminal junkee, should I give up or fight?

Well, my eyes had been opened for the first time to how bad things really were. I decided to **get off my duff and ATTACK!**"

❝ *I was quite motivated by your book. It was one book I didn't read just to say 'Well, I'll have to do that someday.' It was one that jolted me to action.*"

❝ My mother and I are sentimentalists who have never been able to throw anything away. Worse, she did all the cleaning around her collections and stacks and boxes while I was growing up, so **I didn't learn much about housework, but I did learn to stack things.** Last year my life reached new lows. My stacks were at an all-time high, and I needed new space and air in my life. I bought your book and had an eye-opening accident with it. I left it on the toilet with the rest of my junk and it fell in! It was just clean water so I pulled it out, and cleared off my oak desk so that nothing was on it but that wet book (on plastic). I turned one page a day that summer to dry it out while I hired my niece to help me **live** the book.

The book is still water-swollen, the cover is off, but it's my bible!"

❝ I was afraid there would be nothing left in my room!

Last Christmas my Mom got a book called *Clutter's Last Stand*. That wasn't

48

the worst part! The scary part started the day after Christmas. When I woke up Mom was already throwing things out. When I asked her why, she said she had got to Chapter Two in the book and just had to start getting rid of this old junk. I immediately closed my bedroom door. She could throw out all her clutter but she wasn't going to get near mine.

The second step was to warn Lora. She said 'Oh, that doesn't matter. I don't have any clutter anyway.' Then I explained that Mom was only on Chapter Two and that things would probably get worse as time went on.

The book had some good points. **It made Mom realize that used wallpaper and mashed bridesmaids' bouquets were not good!**

Every day she read a chapter or two and then threw out more junk. Mom threw out clothes that no one would ever fit into again. She made grease rags out of old diapers. I told Lora we should get that book away from Mom before it was too late. Every day she gave us a lecture. What a holiday! When company came the only thing Mom talked about was how everyone should get rid of their junk and how much good this book had done her. 'Dejunking' was one of her favorite words.

After Mom had thrown out junk for a few days she started going to other peoples' places and throwing out their junk. Then the dreaded thing happened. I got the urge to clean my room and throw things out. I'm sure glad I got over it. Lora quickly caught on to how much fun it was to throw things out. She re-read and threw out the letter collection she started in 1982.

By the time school began things were back to normal because Mom had lent the book out to people. It's a good thing she hasn't got it back yet or she might re-read it and start all over again."

Why were my previous books on this subject so successful? Because I spent twenty years observing and assimilating YOUR clutter problems and successes. "Clutter" and "Packrat" are filled not with theories, trends, or tips but frontline insights and firsthand lessons you learned when you left your junk behind. We don't need to take the room to repeat them here. These books are available in bookstores and libraries (or from a dejunked friend or neighbor who has a copy). If you can't find them I can send you a personally autographed set:

Since those books were published, you've come up with more good "How we did it in Des Moines" documentaries and data, and here it is now, for help with that always difficult business of "how to."

But first let me answer a big question about clutter I never focussed on much before:

WHEN ARE THE PERFECT TIMES TO LAUNCH INTO YOUR LITTER?

Notice I said "times," not "time," because dejunking is not:
1. One big mood
2. One big marathon
3. Completed after you've done it all once.

No matter how thorough your siege or surge of dejunking may be, junk never rests or remains static. So the more times and places you can find and use to thin it, the better. You probably have some of your own favorites; you may be able to find a few more in this list. Any time any of the following events are scheduled into your immediate future, piggyback them with dejunking—they fit right together.

Deep or "Spring" cleaning—Prior to any big cleaning project hold a massive garage sale and make two trips to the dump. Get rid of all that clutter before you start. Don't clean it or clean around it even one more time—evict it! Otherwise all that junk will slow you down, and thwart the deep

cleaning effort before it even gets off the ground.

Putting away/ Taking out seasonal stuff—  Since we don't see it all the time, we're especially likely to ignore the condition of seasonal stuff. Take a hard look at, after you pull it out or before you put it away. Maybe you should just pitch it.

Getting ready for a trip or vacation—We seem to get an instinctive urge to put our lives in order then anyway.

Painting/Papering/Paneling—When you get a look at those fresh crisp "new" rooms you have when you're done, you aren't going to want to clutter them back up. So don't!

Installing that new rug or no-wax floor, rug shampooing—"Clearing the floor" is 75% of the decluttering battle won. Now just dispose rather than re-impose!

Moving—Why pay to have utter clutter moved across the country, or even across town?

Redecorating—Don't just re-upholster, re-paint, re-finish, re-arrange, and re-evaluate—RE-

MOVE (some of that junk). This alone will give your home a whole new look.

Remodeling—By the time you move it all out of the contractor's way, and clean up all the plaster dust, sawdust, plain old dust, and bent nails he or she drops all over it, you'll want to be rid of a lot of that stuff anyway.

Building—Most of us, thank heaven, draw the line at moving junk into a totally new home.

Big-time party or company coming to stay—Pride and shame are strong emotions you should take advantage of!

The search for some important lost paper or object—Why not can any clutter you unearth along the way?

Divorce or breaking up with someone—Dejunking is a great outlet for disgust and cure for depression.

Weather bound—Rain, snow, and cold often postpone travel, visits, and events. This usually means some nice surprise surplus time and a good chance to surprise your stuff!

Community donation drive—PTA, church, etc. A chance to get rid of some excess to a good cause and they pick up sometimes, too—a double blessing.

Sundays—My favorite "de-treasuring" day. Indeed a day of rest and we never rest better than after we've been relieved of a burden. And the extra reflection of Sunday makes for wise selection.

DECLUTTERING CATALYSTS/JUMP STARTS

It's clear from all your cards and letters that in decluttering, as in cleaning, getting started is the hardest part. Here's a few ideas for getting over that first big hurdle— getting going. (It'll get a LOT easier after that.)

Meet the Junk Monster

❝ Thank you for sending the poster of you and the JUNK MONSTER. [Pictured on the back of *Not for Packrats Only*.] It's great! My daughter took one look at it and said it was horrible and then started to clean out her room. I wish that picture had been around a few years ago now that I see the results it is producing as far as my daughter is concerned. On the other hand, my husband had a very startled reaction to it. I can't repeat what he said, but some

The Junk Monster
At home in Don Aslett's Cleaning Museum, Pocatello Idaho.

cleaning out was done in the barn. All I did was leave the picture on the table for anyone to see and didn't say a word. **That picture is worth a thousand words!!!!"**

Yes folks, that is what a junker looks like inside.

Have people over

We all know about this one, and it's one of the best. Just don't let them stay more than two weeks, or they'll start adding to the problem instead of aiding it!

❝ I found out my mother-in-law and her new husband were coming to visit for a few days. Here was the push I needed to dejunk my house."

❝ What motivates me to declutter? Well, one thing that ALWAYS works is **having people over for dinner on a regular basis.** I'm an absolute fiend when company is coming! It's a sure sign to me when people never have anyone for dinner that they're hiding something... usually junk and clutter. Just this past year I found another way to clean up my act. I went on a Christmas **open house tour** of some homes in my area. I got some great decorating ideas, and was also motivated to throw out some tacky things which had somehow crept in unawares."

Anything that causes us to suddenly **look at our surroundings in a new way**—through the eyes of others—will usually work: not just having company, but taking a photograph (cameras have incredibly unsympathetic eyes), knowing that the fire inspector or real estate appraiser is coming, etc.

Take advantage of the "soiled and spoiled" release

❝ *My husband and I had read about half your book and been inspired to clean, dejunk, and live better lives when the **water heater** in the basement **sprang a leak**. This was a great blessing. Not only do we now have a new, much more efficient heater, but we've used the dampness as an excuse to pitch great mounds of stuff that we'd been hanging onto. Although nothing got very wet but some old carpet on the floor, we've been on a roll for the past two weeks. Most of our time and energy has been spent boxing up stuff for charity or the trash collectors, and we love it!"*

❝ Among the 'stuff stashes' I left behind at Mother's when I went off to take a new job out of state was the attic of the garage. It was a big garage and it had a second story just as big above it for storage. I had it packed to the rafters. There was everything up there from old waders to assorted tree trunk sections, crab traps to ancient jacks and hubcaps, antique photography equipment to homemade wine to my second-best mandolin. All was fine up there for years until some adventuresome mouse (tempted by my aged ears of Indian corn, or perhaps my 88 packets of leftover garden seeds) moved in.

By the time I had occasion to be sifting through this stuff next in search of some elusive item, I discovered that mice had multiplied big-time. They had worked over EVERYTHING and what they didn't chew, they soiled or stained. I could hardly believe that those little creatures (which I formerly thought of as cute) could do so many kinds of damage to so many kinds of things—books, magazines, posters, letters, clothes, blankets, linens, sleeping bags, shoes, stuffed animals, leather-covered decanters—you name it! I had to haul everything out of that hot crowded space, carry it through a trapdoor and down a ladder to the garage proper, and go through it. Amidst lots of cussing and tooth-gnashing, a lot of things **did** get relegated to the trash."

This one is very dependable too, and you don't even have to wait for a natural or man- or woman-made disaster. Just start going through some of those aged mounds and stacks, and you'll find lots of things that aren't quite as you imagined anymore.

Once something is defaced , we aren't quite so willing to grant it a place.

Saved isn't Saved!
—*Aslett 23:2*

You kept it, but when exhumed, reclaimed, called to active duty, its condition is always short of its "shoulds," thanks to:

Leakage, crushage, breakage, stainage, mouseage, mothage, rottage, fadeage, and just plain age.

That folks, is the reality of stor**AGE**!

Make a list of what you COULD part with

❝ Organization is my middle name. I like to read books on time and space management as a challenge (do they have any ideas better than mine?). I really do sort my first aid kit every few months and purge my clothes twice a year. So when I began reading *Not for Packrats Only*, it was purely for pleasure. As I read I thought 'If I had any junk, which I don't, this would be fun to follow. This is good advice, but of course it doesn't apply to me....' But as I kept reading, my mind began to wander around my house and into my cupboards. **Without even getting up from the couch, I made a page-long list of junk I had to admit I was harboring!** It included:

• a broken piece of Grandma's pie plate

• wedding gift crystal and candlesticks galore

• a part for my '66 Chrysler that I couldn't identify but my brother might be able to

• seven rabbit cages (and no rabbit)

• dozens of plastic forks

• magazines I intended to cut and file articles out of real soon

• guitar, had seventeen years and never played

• set of six crab dishes (I'm a vegetarian)

Thus began my dejunking project."

Get sick of it

❝ As for getting started on dejunking, well, it takes me about a month of seeing clutter everywhere and feeling all cluttered up inside to get **so sick of it** that I do something about it today. But it's a bit like getting back in shape—**it never takes as long the next time as it did that first time.**"

You never know when this will strike—it may be a matter of months, or it may not come to pass till you've been stumbling over clutter for thirty years or more. But when it hits—that moment of truth for all junkers—"SICK OF STUFF!"—there's no mistaking it, and there'll be no stopping you!

Launch into a home improvement

Just about any home improvement you undertake will nudge you toward the universal home improvement—dejunking. (Just don't save all that scrap afterward, and "the old one" of everything, or you'll be back where you started!)

❝ *My main motivation to declutter was our desire to have a new bathroom—it was either the books that I had already read (or would never read) or the new jacuzzi, so the books had to go.*"

66 *We thought we'd really dejunked and come clean. But our crisp new (and now 'clutter-free') house just didn't look like we'd anticipated. First revelation: When we decided on this new house, what we saw was the builder's model—furnished and decorated for display. Clean, neat—* **no** *knickknacks,* **no** *plants,* **no** *clutter. Return home, look around—ugh! Still there, though less than before. Ugh! again.*

Second revelation: carpet is awful! So:

Out with old carpet, in with new. This is equivalent to **moving.** *New carpet looks terrific. Rooms are empty—don't want to put anything in them but must!* **1/3** *went back in.* **NO** *plants, no morose little brass animals, etc. Life is sunny, cleaning equals vacuum, dust surfaces of tables, squirt glass. Easy."*

66 We had our house reroofed (looks so nice!), and they had to tear off the old roof, rotten sheeting, etc. So they got debris in the attic, which we've been filling with our version of debris for almost thirty years, and now we **had** to clean it out. We actually have two attics, and I was pretty embarrassed because the roofers could see right down into them and see what we have accumulated. When they peered down through the dust motes, it must have been akin to archaeologists peering into an unplundered pharaoh's tomb. The attics are all dry and snug again now, and safe from other prying eyes.

Well, a new roof makes everything else look horrible. Soon as we can accumulate some more $$$, we will proceed with fixing this dump up. We have thrown out a lot; **our daughters can't grasp it yet, that we have actually THROWN STUFF OUT!** Our garbage collector must have been shocked, too. From one garbage can a week, we put out the maximum, seven, for the past three weeks. And have burned a lot of burnables."

I wondered who those guys at the ball game were talking and chuckling about!

66 My husband's a trucker, and after a kitchen fire, we stored the contents of four rooms of our home in the trailer of his semi, while repairs were being made to the house. When we tried to get everything back into those rooms, however, it wouldn't fit. (This is one of the Laws of Accumulation—when things are removed from a container—no matter the size, be it box or house, they won't go back in.) We had to weed out some clutter as we returned our personal things and the furniture to the renovated house. **We were able to dispose of a lot of unneeded things because we didn't have time to agonize**—that trailer was needed to earn a living!"

Get an ultimatum from someone else

66 For years I've been a serious packrat with junkaholic tendencies. I have been fighting my way out from under fifteen years of accumulation and clutter. My husband of fifteen years was becoming a bear over the condition of our home. When he started yelling 'No more shelves' and 'Where am I supposed to sit?', I knew I had to act."

Now the big question, lady—did you act?

Whether or not this particular "push" will work is very uncertain, to say the least! Most rats have a highly developed territorial instinct, and an ultimatum or opposition from someone else is more likely to cause them to retrench, than to remove anything.

For help with the delicate matter of decluttering others, see Chapter 14 of Not for Packrats Only.

Move

I've heard a lot of you say, "The very best way to dejunk is to move!" and there's no doubt it amounts to shock therapy. When we stay in one place quietly accumulating things for years and years/forever, we become pretty oblivious to it all. But when suddenly faced with packing and loading it all up, and then paying to have it trucked somewhere, even the most hardened junker begins to think in terms of weeding down. Most "moving" testimonies are moving indeed!

❝ Dear Don:

I am a packrat of the highest order. And have packratted for many years. Our house was always orderly and tidy on the surface, but stuff was crammed into every available storage area. We had a big old farmhouse in the country with **a cavernous basement, a barn, and a chicken coop. All were filled with stuff.*** Then one day last spring my husband came home from work and said 'I'm being transferred. I leave next week.'

We were fortunate and sold the house in three weeks. During that time I weeded out and threw away—and felt proud of myself. Then the moving company representatives began arriving to give estimates. Each was worse than the last and each one said 'My, you do have a lot of stuff.' Even though my husband's company was paying for the move, I was outraged at the cost. I was told that in order to get into the price range I found acceptable, I'd have to unload about 4,000 pounds of stuff.

We also knew that we'd be moving to an apartment or a rental house while we looked for a new house. We would have to pay for the second move, and to save money, I'd have to do all the packing. I looked at all the junk and clutter and everything else and felt overwhelmed.

Panic can make the worst (or best) packrat into a ruthless unloader. As I went through cupboards, drawers, closets, basement, and barns, I asked myself, **'Is this worth my effort to pack it?'** For a lot of the stuff, the answer was no. I hate to pack. And if I'm going to pack, the stuff I pack had better be worth it.

Within a month's time, I did get rid of slightly more than 4,000 pounds of stuff. On moving day, our stuff on the truck weighed in at about 8,000 pounds. I felt triumphant.

It didn't last. Four months later we were ready to move into our new house. The reality of packing everything in the house again seemed overwhelming. **While I packed, I kept discard boxes right beside me. In no time at all I found it a lot easier to put things in the discard boxes than to wrap and pack them.** When the moving van arrived this time it was a small truck and we were moved out of the old and into the new house in four hours (including a half-hour lunch break).

We now have a house with ten closets, a full attic, a large basement, and two-car attached garage. Six of the closets are empty, the attic holds twelve small boxes of books, the basement is virtually empty, and the garage holds two cars and four garbage cans. And that's the way I intend to keep it. Your book is a constant reminder, and when I'm tempted to store something I ask myself: 'Is this thing worth packing?' I don't think I will ever forget the horror of moving twice in four months.❞

*Don't tell anyone, folks, but this describes my editor to a T.

Arrange a temporary separation from your stuff

❝ *With a move quickly approaching, I wanted to get started on the packing process. However, my place was still being shown by real estate brokers and I knew it would show better with the pictures on the walls, etc. So I started packing things that wouldn't be missed—extra knickknacks and things that adorned shelves, tables, and beds. When all the extra stuff was packed away, I looked around and was delighted with the CLEAN look of everything. My home looked so neat and clean and fresh and open and organized and light. Those knickknacks and extras may stay packed forever! One prospective buyer delayed the real estate broker until I came home because he wanted to meet the woman who kept such a neat and well-organized home!!!!"*

❝ *We thought we had sold our house, so we began moving many of our possessions out and into storage (at Mom and Dad's). The offer fell through and we ended up staying in our house. By this time, we had lived for three months without many of our much-needed (so we thought) things and never really missed them."*

Gadfrey, a new business opportunity—a fake listing service.

"I've never really missed it"— you'd be amazed how often I hear this particular testimony (you could almost call it a heresy) from former hard-core clutterers, after they have parted with some junk. You can give yourself a temporary divorce or trial separation from your hoard, a taste of clutter-free living, by moving to a motel or a cabin in the woods for a couple of months—bringing only the essentials along. You too will soon be amazed at how little of it you miss. You might even rediscover some real zest for living.

Would joining a monastery do it?

❝ **Dear Don,**
Your remark about joining a monastery as one solution to clutter put a smile on my face. I live in a monastery and believe me, there are monks who have little and monks who have everything. There are lots of ways to live the vow of poverty!"

Amen!

What about a pro dejunker?

Many of you have asked if you might need a professional dejunker to dig you out of your bondage. Dozens and dozens more have called and asked me:

1. To take on the job of dejunking them, as a professional.

2. To give them direction or authorization to become a pro dejunker themselves, a "shrink of stuff."

It's your call, for sure, to seek help or to be a helper, but remember dejunking isn't a matter of finding some elusive flaw in character or cupboard. There's a lot of plain old plug-along work that has to be done. We acquired all this ourselves, and only we know its real price and place. No professional can perform as well as you in this, or with surer or better long-range results. And if you can do it yourself you'll be saving the $30 or $40 an hour you'd have to pay someone to pry into your personal affairs.

Maybe we should declare a national decluttering day?

❝ When I was leafing through Carol Fields's *Celebrating Italy* (William Morrow & Co., 1990) recently, I came across a paragraph that reminded me of your clutter removal recommendations:

Italians make it clear that they hope the New Year will bring new things by tossing old, useless possessions out the window at midnight. It is an energetic, if symbolic way of getting rid of the bad that has accumulated during the past year. On New Year's Eve Day, Americans are used to seeing pages of old calendars drift out of office windows and flutter slowly to the streets below, leaving the financial districts of many big cities buried under a blizzard of white paper. But in Italy what comes out the windows is anything from a used bar of soap to shoes, old

glasses and terracotta dishes, even couches and refrigerators, and they come flying like missiles. With fear and trepidation do Italians walk about on that night, pressing flat as they can against walls of buildings, never knowing when something will come whizzing by. Cars are not exempt from assault. Sometimes so many objects land on an automobile that its owners have to wait for the street cleaners to unearth it. Newspapers carry long articles detailing the carnage: '500 injured and 3 dead' the headlines read one year, all casualties of what they call 'toasts with blows.' The crashing sounds of broken pottery are often accompanied by loud firecrackers or shots or the popping of champagne corks—noise expressing high spirits like those of the Romans centuries before, with the added intention of driving away evil spirits."

A national decluttering day (little less exuberant, perhaps) isn't a bad idea—although we probably need at least one a quarter, or maybe one a month, here in the U.S.

❝ Declutter Day. A good name for a national holiday, don't you agree? The world should stop producing and consuming for 24 hours while we all get rid of those unused canning jars, etc. February would be a good month for this holiday."

UN Clutter

Some of you have asked me (as a world traveler) what other countries' clutter is like. Let me put it in a verse if I may:

The question was, "Do they have as
   much, as we in the USA?"
Piles of junk, and clutter too—all that
   stuff that's in our way.
All I can tell, as I travel, well, only here
   do we have the room.
In Japan, each house has maybe one
   fan, and only a single broom.

In our dwellings here, we have room to
   spare, maybe even a second place.
While living quarters, south of our
   borders, may be smaller than our
   closet space.
Here in the States, we collect plates,
   and even display them (it's kind of
   rude).
In Russia they compete just for something to eat, the focus is all on the
   food.

While we rent storage for broken
   lamps and cushionless couches
In the Himalayan hills, they find
   thrills, in what can be carried
   in small back pouches.
We have so much, we can hardly
   touch, without some navigational planning.
Longer and better do the
   Polynesians live, with time to
   enjoy sun tanning.

So we live clutter heaped, with extra
   everything, and all kinds of fine
   enamel,
While Arabs move about, and well
   make out, with nothing but a tent
   and camel.
And in China and Korea, where they
   make junk, that is sold for plenty
   yen,
Why glory be, they are clutter free,
   because we buy it all from them.

Why did we get all this, too much!
   Were we just putting on the Ritz?
I've heard it said, 'twas descended and
   bred, It came directly from the
   "Brits."
That's not quite fair because "over
   there" some piles may be higher and
   quainter
But they've been collecting for centuries longer and the call of the mall is
   fainter.

We came to acquiring late, but applied
   ourselves so enthusiastically
The only question seems to be "who
   has more than me?"
The land of the free soon meant the
   land of MORE
We became a world leader in clutter,
   too—the proof is just inside our
   door.

Where to Start

WHEREVER YOUR IMPULSE LEADS YOU

❝ I started out thinking I would dejunk my bedroom. After looking things over, I realized there were things in the bedroom that belonged in the closet. The closet was too full to hold anything else, so the closet needed to be cleaned first. The closet had things in it that belonged in the sewing closet. The sewing closet was so full that the door wouldn't close. The process seemed endless. I decided that the sewing closet was the place to start."

A stitch in time...

We are sometimes forced to dejunk in a certain order (to make room for house guests, or clear out an area for the contractor who is doing our remodeling, for example). But in general it works best to follow your immediate impulses here, because then you have only the dejunking itself to do, not overcoming your resistance to it.

❝ *I just bought myself a Mother's Day present, your*

Not for Packrats Only. I bought it on Monday and started reading it at 10:00 p.m. I got up after a couple of pages and threw away the sample shampoo and conditioner samples I had just received in the mail.

I am starting in the little areas to gather up steam for the monster areas like my office."

A strategy that almost always works!

TRY A "WEEKEND RETREAT" FROM CLUTTER

Lots of people vote for and use a weekend jump start.

Here's a sample attack plan.

Monday—Thursday
Scowl at the stuff that's been polluting your premises.
Read *Clutter's Last Stand* to fortify your sense of purpose.
Make friends with someone with a pickup.
Make reservations Sunday evening at the finest restaurant in town, for the celebration!
Leave Friday evening and all day Saturday open.

Friday 5 p.m.
Unplug the phone and the TV. Put a quarantine sign on the front door.
Prepare a sign for yourself with the following lettered on it:

Does/will this enhance my life now or ever? Does this love me back?

Now you want to have the capacity and options for disposal all set up so you won't have to break the mood of dejunking to divest. So clear yourself some vacant space and have four dispersement boxes ready:

Junk: The obvious disposables.

Charity/family: Still-good stuff that isn't doing anything good for you—you don't like or need it.

Sort: Useful things that need to be put somewhere else if they're going to actually be used.

Emotional withdrawal: Stuff you know you should get rid of, but you can't quite face it yet. Seal it up in a box until you're ready (or have forgotten what it even is), then dump.

Use opaque bags or boxes for your discards so you can't see the contents and be tempted to reevaluate.

Pour or empty the target or starter cache (drawer, closet, container, even room)—all of it—OUT into the middle of the floor onto a big tarp or sheet. Don't pick at it where it is. If things are still tucked tightly and tidily in place you might just leave them; if you have to pick them up and re-place them, you'll think twice!

Allow no interruptions and be guided by the spirit of freedom and the thought of the regained dignity and respect to come.

When you can't take any more, quit and wait till next weekend to continue. Dejunking is exhausting.

If you are a team person, the right friend or relative can be invaluable here: to serve as a rooting section as well as actually help out. They can immediately remove the junk from view after you've made your judgments, and set more stuff before you, to help you get through it all as quickly, and with the least trauma possible. They can affirm that you're doing the right thing and urge you on. They should be a non-clutterer, and sincerely want to help you simplify your life.

They can also help you celebrate—not just enjoy looking back at all you've been through together, but discuss and plan further strategy.

EASY STARTER PROJECTS: RIDICULOUS/OBVIOUS STUFF

66 I started with the shoelaces from old tennis shoes. I'd saved them for years and years, before I threw them out a few months ago. When I looked at them, I realized they weren't even any good! The ends were gone and they were full of knots and splices in the middle where the middle had worn out."

Picture this:

66 And then there were the **totally black slides** you mentioned. I never thought them unusual—after all, they were 'part of the set' of good photos (many of which were ugly or useless and ought to be thrown out, too). When I read your comments I couldn't stop laughing. Even now! Why on **earth** would anyone save totally black slides? Maybe I thought a picture would finally appear on them, or I'd finally remember what they were supposed to depict."

66 Deciding where to start was no problem. I knew there were **six sneaker boxes full of old letters going back to grammar school**. (I'm twenty-three now.) I decided the memories were just as special and took up less room. So I

thinned them out and went back days later and thinned them out some more until I got down to one half a box full. (Some things I do want to keep.)

The next area was my desk and three drawers full of broken toys from childhood, extra replacements to everything and anything, old expired coupons, and free gift offers (I'm a sucker for 'free')."

EASY STARTER PROJECTS: EXCESS DECORATIONS

I was called in on a fire loss job years ago, and it turned out to be a modest house where a malfunctioning furnace had exploded. It burned part of the room it was in and thoroughly smoked the interior of the house.

The whole place was sooted and had a heavy fire odor, so **everything** had to be cleaned. My cleaning company had done many jobs like this over the years (so we thought!). When I arrived the insurance adjuster informed me that "the lady of the house"—they always get the blame—had "an unusual amount of contents." So I bid the job a little higher and went home to get crews and trucks. We cleaned off the clinging smoke film and had the walls ready to paint, and then started in on the contents—namely the knickknacks. There were little figurines and statues and decorations hanging and set around everywhere—over 200 (a record) in the first room alone. Every room after that yielded an equally amazing number. Even the bathroom had at least 30 such things. By evening we were way over my budget and bid, and we were told there were more in the basement—like tons more, boxes and boxes of them that she hadn't got around to displaying. If I remember the billing list I believe we ended up cleaning well over 7,000 whatnots—in one house.

I love the personality of tasteful porcelain and the warmth of well-chosen decorations, but an entire regiment of them is too much and it begins to take its toll on your time and life. You don't need 7,000 to have too many. Do some departing, send some on a mission, a gift adventure; it will definitely reduce stress and cleaning time and expense. (The bidder who does your cleaning might not be as naive as I.)

There were 147 blankets in that little house, too—a record for three beds! You don't want to hear the rest of the story.

EASY STARTER PROJECTS: JEWELRY BOX

“ *I decided to do something about my cluttered, unused jewelry box and its contents. I like jewelry and the kids have given me many presents of it over the years. Unfortunately their tastes and mine sometimes haven't agreed. Between my stirring of the contents and their stirring to find something they could wear, my jewelry box was a mess. Up until this time I couldn't bear to throw a broken piece away ('someday I'll fix it,' or 'the parts can be used for something else'). I'm also quite sentimental and items from my childhood and the like meant a lot to me. The box was now crammed full and I seldom touched it. My husband had given me a few basic good pieces (earrings, bracelet, and necklace) and* **I wore these pieces all of the time. It was easier and quicker than facing the tangled mess.**

I finally made up my mind to clean out my jewelry box. I spent six hours one Saturday doing it. I had to untangle all of my chains, etc. **I made four piles: broken jewelry, jewelry to give kids, jewelry I would wear, and sentimental jewelry.** *I had a garbage bag handy and I threw away anything that was broken. That hurt! Most of the unbroken items I didn't want any more I gave to my daughters, who loved them. This made me feel better and less guilty. Some things like typing pins from high school, church award pins, and items from my grandma, I couldn't part with. They held too many memories of hard work and love.*

The result was a pleasantly roomy jewelry box with everything arranged neatly. I'm wearing more of a variety of jewelry nowadays. I also feel better when I look at my jewelry box!”

A fine job, indeed, and hopefully your winnowings won't teach your daughters the art of junking a jewelry box!

EASY STARTER PROJECTS: SPICE RACK

❝ Dejunking my spice cupboard!
What I did: Took everything out of the cupboard. I haven't seen anything so bare as my lazy Susan with all the spice jars and cans removed. It looked like last year's Christmas tree with all the orna-ments and tinsel off. Then I thor-oughly cleaned and scoured the far reaches of every corner in that cupboard. The lazy Susan gleamed in silent admiration. It was difficult to junk that chocolate flavored Weight-Watcher extract that was so important to me just eight years back. My eyes teared as I heard the resounding crunch of that Swedish wasabread as it hit the bottom of my 33-gallon trash can. It was especially sad to notice that only two packages had been used. Surely that expiration date had to be wrong: January 1978. Likewise, it was hard to believe that those little silver candy pearls could have glued themselves to the sides of the bottle so tightly. They ricocheted like hailstones off the side of the old cocoa can lying at the bottom of the trash can, near the pile of half-burned candles from Grandma's 75th birthday party. (Grandma died in 1984; she was ninety years old.)
After completing the project, I felt like I had accomplished a herculean task, as I stood there admiring a bright, sparkling-clean lazy Susan filled with shining bottles and cans of up-to-date spices and extracts **just waiting to be used**.❞

All very admirable... but what happened to the bottle those silver candies were in?

EASY STARTER PROJECTS: UNDER THE SINK

A nice nonemotional easy start-ing place for most of us. **Dejunk your cleaning arsenal**—ancient unused cleaners, aerosol cans with missing snouts, spray bottles with one half inch of cleaner left in the bottom (no matter what angle you hold it at, you can't get any out), rusty cans, threadbare rags and shedding sponges, fourteen kinds of dried-up floor finish, etc. Most of this is so awful you won't even bat an eye as you trash it. (That funny smell under the sink will disappear too.)

EASY STARTER PROJECTS: CARRY-ALONG CLUTTER

Notice that most people will get right up to the ticket gate, park entrance, or checkout counter, and then and only then will they start hunting and pawing and rummaging through their purse, pocket, or wallet for what they need. And notice the frowns and scowls from the audience (the rest of the line).

I loved this woman's summary of the situation—(Webster's wife, I think).

> **❝purse** (`pars) n. *1.* a sum of money given as a prize. *2.* a portable junk drawer"

Note that word "portable." The dumbest clutter imaginable is clutter you have to pack around with you everywhere you go, every day of your life. Extra pounds (or even ounces) in the purse are almost as bad as extra pounds on the paunch—dejunk it today. "My chiropractor told me not to carry my purse anymore," an audience member in Richmond, Virginia told me. (The reason wasn't its collection potential, it was the weight of the purse pulling down her arm and shoulder.)

You can relieve yourself of your carry-along clutter almost anywhere there's a trash can handy—so now you know what to do during your next long line wait.

While we're on the subject of purses, this little dejunking ballad, written by Sid Herron and performed by him at one of my decluttering seminars, delighted the audience. There's some great wisdom here and I didn't want you to miss it.

Purse of the American Wife

Copyright 1992 by Sid Herron, used by permission.

It all started one afternoon, when I needed to wash the car.
I could have got my own car keys, but I didn't want to walk that far.
I said, "Baby, can I borrow your car keys?" She said, "Well sure I guess,
My purse is there in the bedroom, just try not to make a mess."

I grabbed her purse, and to my surprise, it weighed about thirty pounds!
I started looking frantically for somewhere to put it down.
Then I tripped on her high heel shoes, and I fell back on the bed;
The strap broke and the purse flipped over—landed upside down by my head!

Chorus
Now there's nowhere to run to, nowhere to hide;
The stuff's scattered all over the bed, and it won't fit back inside!
Look out! I think I saw something moving there! We've found three new forms of life!
Another lost civilization's been found in the purse of the American wife!

Verse 2
I said, "Baby, do you actually carry this thing? I wouldn't do that on a dare!"
Then I suddenly realized why she needed chiropractic care!

I said, "I see the need for the lipstick, and
the powder that you put on your nose,
But what on earth would you ever do with
a half a pair of pantyhose?"

You wouldn't believe all the things I
found! I could hardly believe my eyes.
She still had every old credit card back to
1965.
I found an old jar of baby food, though
our youngest child is ten.
Unless she knows something I don't
know, I don't think we'll ever use it
again.

Here's a subway pass for a town we
lived in in 1984,
And there's enough pieces of makeup
here for her to start her own beauty
store.
Well, I suppose that old Vegas postcard
just might someday be rare,
But you gotta wonder what she's gonna
do with all those Life Savers covered
with hair!

Verse 3
She's got three pounds of business
cards from people that she hates.
She's got so many pocket calendars,
how come she's always late?
When I finally found the key ring underneath the cosmetic case,
I dang near put my eyes out with her little
spray can of Mace!

She finally came to my rescue, it was just
in the nick of time,
'Cause I was fightin' off the rabbits' feet
with a bag full of nickels and dimes.
I sorta hid in a corner while I let her take
control,
Somehow she made the purse just suck
it back in, like it had its own little black
hole!

I never did wash the car that day, I was
lucky to escape with my life.
But I can tell you for certain now, I have
more respect for my wife!

That women have some kind of special
power is something I no longer doubt,
'Cause they can bend the laws of time
and space to make purses bigger
inside and out!

EASY STARTER PROJECTS: SHOES

I dare you—in fact I double dare
you—to toss out just one pair of
shoes. You ladies have at least five
pair that could and should go out
this minute… the platforms, the
wedgies, running shoes split in six
places, the sandals that always
pinch your toes, and the spike heels
with one heel missing—120%
unfixable. Toss one pair in the junk
box now. It will strengthen your
moral fiber and intimidate your
spouse (who could toss a few shoes
too).

When you're done with shoes
and on a roll, move on to leaky
boots and flattened slippers!

EASY STARTER PROJECTS: MEDICINE CHEST

Some "time experts" say we spend at least six years of our life in the bathroom. You might wonder what we're doing in there all that time, until you start examining the overstuffed shelves of our cosmetic crazed, over-perfumed and over-prescribed society. We're so hung up on health and beauty preparations that "the medicine cabinet"—a separate little closet just for them alone—is a standard, hallowed, unquestioned part of every American bathroom. Medicine cabinets get bigger with every home show, and this is by no means the only place in the house occupied by our self-dosing and self-improvement chemical collection.

Most medicine cabinet clutter rots or ages out before it ever runs out. At least half of it hasn't ever worked for you. But it's all still there behind that mirrored door, filed away in hopes of a second-, third-, or fourth-round cure. The very sight of all this is enough to make you sicker.

Then morning, noon, and night you have to rummage through all this to find the things you do use (and hold a box in front of you to catch what catapults out when you open the door). A simplified, stripped-down medicine cabinet could gain most of us up to twenty minutes a day—enough time to write a book in a year!

Part of my job as public health officer at the 1993 National Scout Jamboree (30,000 boys and 5,000 leaders attending) was to help set up the health center tents. As I saw all those cases, bottles, packages, and boxes of medication unloaded, I asked a brilliant young doctor there what in his opinion was **the most unnecessary part** of medicine cabinet clutter. He pointed at a big tray of "cold medicine" nearby, and said "There isn't a drug in there that really does anything." Mouth-wash, for another example, is a magnificent marketing ploy (and fly repellent).

He then revealed a couple of other good reasons to declutter that cabinet.

• Such as all that leftover medication we save for "future needs." When later (even years later) a similar problem arises, we take the leftovers. They may even make us feel better, so now we don't bother to go to the doctor. But just because the symptoms of something diminish or disappear, it doesn't mean the condition the medicine was prescribed for is gone. It can still be there, doing damage.

If and when we do finally go in for some medical attention, the drugs we've taken thoroughly confuse any observations the doctor might make or samples he might take to get our actual diagnosis. This is bad, bad medicine.

• Keeping all this old stuff also encourages casual pharmacizing—"prescribing" and distributing drugs to other family members and friends. (People even keep and use deceased people's prescription supplies—DON'T!!) You don't know what someone else's allergies may be, what else they're taking, or for that matter what's even wrong with them!

• Pills, powders, liquids, and creams all lose potency over time—some within as little as two weeks! Take a gander at the expiration dates on everything in there (OTC remedies, too) and I guarantee you'll start dumping.

• The less crowded your drug storage area, the less chance for mistake when reaching for a bottle.

• Aged medicine can be dangerous—the antibiotic Tetracycline, for example, actually becomes toxic with time.

To dispose of old medication safely, you can flush it down the toilet. Remove the pills or capsules from the bottle, have them all together in a bunch, and flush the toilet. Try to toss the pills into the commode just as the water swooshes down, so it will take the pills with it before they can settle at the bottom. If any are left in the bowl, flush again until you're sure all have been flushed. (Some of that stuff might be powerful enough to have some cleaning action, and we professional cleaners would probably be tempted to swab as we flushed!)

Now pitch the empty bottles into the trash.

If you don't feel comfortable doing this, or if you have something that can't be flushed, take it to your pharmacy. Most pharmacies are happy to safely dispose of old medications for you.

❝ We threw out about fifteen pounds from our medicine closet. We found prescriptions dating back to 1964. There were three boxes of borax powder (we never could find it when we needed it, so would buy more).❞

❝ My friend was inspired after I told her my dejunking story. She donated her unworn clothing and hauled out nine pounds of makeup from her makeup 'collection.' She laughed when she told me it included makeup she had bought in high school.❞

❝ For a basically healthy family, we had a staggering amount of outdated prescription drugs, over-the-counter drugs, and various ointments and vitamin supplements. It made me feel healthier to get rid of it all!❞

❝ When I came to page 87 in Clutter's Last Stand, the call to action hit. I attacked the medicine cabinets in both bathrooms. Anything that hadn't been used lately (as evidenced by a layer of dust) came out. Powder, makeup, medicines, and bottles with unknown contents. It all went in the garbage. It didn't take long and it was finished.

Then I reopened the cabinets. (I love basking in accomplishment.) They looked great—so neat and uncluttered. Even so little an area dejunked **gives me a lift mentally and physically.**❞

How long has it been there?

Very likely too long to do you much good.

Drugs of any kind are best stored in a cool, dry place—in our warm humid bathrooms, many prescription and over-the-counter medications deteriorate quickly. The shelf life of drugs and other remedies does vary, depending on the manufacturer, among other things. But the following is a good general idea of the lifespan of some common inhabitants of our medicine cabinets:

pain relievers
aspirin/bufferin—1 year
acetaminophen (such as Tylenol)—2 years
ibuprofen (Motrin, Advil)—2 years
Codeine with acetaminophen—1 year
Darvocet-N-100—1 year

anti-inflammatories
Such as Naprosyn and Lodine—2 years

antihistamines
Such as Dimetapp, Contac, Chlor-Trimeton, Benadryl, Bronkaid, etc.—2 years

nasal decongestants
Such as Sinex, Sinarest, Privine—18 mos.

cough syrups
Such as Robitussin, Contac Cold Formula, Terpin hydrate—no more than 1 year

antiseptics
iodine, merthiolate, Campho-Phenique, New-Skin—3 years
rubbing alcohol—2 years
hydrogen peroxide—1 year
witch hazel—3 years
Caladryl (poison ivy remedy)—3 years

antibiotics
Terramycin A, Minocin tabs or caps—2 years
Amoxicillin tabs and caps—2 years
Bacitracin, Erythromycin—2 years
Polymixin B sulfate powder—3 years

antifungals
Such as Monistat 7, Lomotrin, Nystatin—2 years

cortisone creams
Such as Cortizone and Cortaid—3 years

eye drops
Such as Murine, Cortisporin Opthalmic, Tetracycline Opthalmic, Mycitracin Opthalmic—2 years

antacids
Such as Alka-Seltzer, Tums, Pepto-Bismol, Gas-X—2 years

diarrhea remedies
Such as Kaopectate, Imodium—2 years

laxatives
Such as Metamucil, Dulcolax, FiberCon, Feen-a-Mint gum—3 years

prescription ulcer medicines
Tagamet and Transderm—2 years
Zantac—1 year

high blood pressure medications
Such as Lopressor and Lasix—2 years

female hormones
Such as Premarin and Provera—1 year

birth control
Birth control pills such as Ortho-Novum 7-7-7—1 year
Condoms—1 year

other prescription medications
Prednisone—3 years
Nitroglycerin (heart medication)—1 year (3 mos. once opened)
Synthroid (synthetic thyroid hormone)—1 year
Prosac (antidepressant)—2 years
Zorax (herpes medication)—3 years

vitamins, minerals
1 to 3 years

How I Managed to do it!/ This Works For Me

"**H**ow did you manage to do it (dejunk)?" is a question reformed packrats get asked a lot. Let's listen to some of their answers now.

❝ *How did I manage to do it? I just shut my eyes.*"

❝ I gave a thorough cleaning to the first floor by taking these steps: First, **made a list of everything that had to be done**. Second, **did it**. Third, **checked off** each item as it was done. As I saw progress on the list, I felt that things were getting done instead of feeling overwhelmed by what wasn't completed. Four, **had a takeout lunch** so as not to feel I was adding more cleanup into the job.

(What looked like a very long list was completed in three and a half hours!)"

❝ Having had my consciousness raised by your two books, I'm now trying to make a concerted effort to improve things. I'm finding **chipping away at one pile after another, a little at a time**, most productive so far. When I have an occasional breakthrough (literally and figuratively), I go for it and continue working on that one area until I run out of steam and/or time. I'm fifty-five years old and my three-year plan is to try to improve the clutter by the time I'm fifty-six, control it by the time I'm fifty-seven, and eliminate it by the time I'm fifty-eight."

❝ **It's true that it's hard at first to let go of clutter, but** *it gets easier and easier until it really is FUN!*"

❝ *A fellow clutter collector asked me the other day how I was able to do the major dejunking I've been doing recently. It was largely a matter of time, I told them—after years and years of clinging and saving, I finally reached the point (I'm almost fifty) where I was **able to see and willing to admit** all the things I would never use.*

I want the space all that stuff is taking up now, too—to live and move, and have uncrowded room for the things I really do cherish."

❝ I decluttered to a point and then was stuck at a certain 'level of tolerance.' I would get sucked into the items left as if they were looking into my eyes and saying, 'Don't throw me out. Don't you love me?'

So what I did was make a list of everything I owned, a pretty detailed list, but within reason. Then I went off site with the list, where I could have a better perspective. I wasn't as emotionally attached to the title of the object as to the object itself. I could see each item on the list more coldly and compare it to the real gems that I'm passionate about."

❝ *We cannot see junk when it is put away with good items.*

It is completely futile to attempt to pick out of a bin, for instance, the outdated, the worn out, and the never-used items. Because they become invisible, camouflaged among the good, usable, valuable ones.

*In order to clean out a drawer or a closet or a barn, **it is necessary to empty it completely.** One then puts back, in good order, the things one chooses to keep. What's left is clutter."*

❝ *I find that the time while I'm watching television is also a good time for small uncluttering projects. The other day I went through my sewing box and pared down to a few spools of thread of essential colors, one small pack of sewing needles, a few straight pins, a thimble, and a pair of scissors. I was now able to put it in a smaller box. My partner saw what I was doing and did the same with hers. We had enough excess to create a whole sewing kit in my old box, which we will be selling at our next garage sale."*

❝ *I find that dejunking is easier if I make a goal of one bag a day, of stuff either to junk or give away."*

✶ One thing I've found helpful is to **time myself** in how long this or that takes to do. It doesn't take 'all afternoon' to empty jars and wash them, just two hours. I estimate (or overestimate) how long something will take and then I time it. I try to see myself on the other side of that particular chore—in two hours, for example, it will be done."

✶ I've been **keeping a notebook** about each drawer or closet that I clean—what I got rid of, what I did with it, and how I felt afterwards. Since I have such a mountain of junk to move this exercise is helping me to see that I'm making progress."

✶ *Here is **the order** I went in:*
1. House, room by room
2. The Final Frontier—attic, utility room, under the house
3. Outlying areas—cars, yard, Mom's, locker, work
I ran into a funny problem at Mom's. Although I was ready to dejunk my childhood stuff from her basement, she wasn't ready for me to!
4. Paper—scrapbooks, letters, photos and negatives, writings
*This was the most time-consuming. I took months to fill scrapbooks, photo albums, and baby books. Also, there is proof here more than anywhere that **'organized' and 'neat' are not synonyms for 'junk-free.'** These items were all neatly organized in boxes, such as the one marked 'To Paste in Scrapbook'—it dated back seven years!"*

✶ *I took seriously your 'use it or lose it' rule. I put pet toys OUT to be used, I put special things from childhood ON DISPLAY to be enjoyed. After displaying for a while some kitchen utensils that I felt had sentimental value, I was able to let them go. And I felt like a genius when I connected these two items: a collection of cat mugs with no way to display, and a nifty but useless Coke crate. I put one mug per wooden slot, and it made a great display of both!"*

✶ Yesterday while I was **home alone (the best time to do this)** I cleaned the top shelf of one kitchen cupboard and bagged up never-used cups and saucers.
When I declutter I **seal the bags or boxes of discards** and warn my husband and daughter to keep out until it all goes to a thrift store. I even got rid of several decades of *National Geographic* this way."

✶ **By constantly working at it**, the process gets easier and easier. The last time I had to clean out the 'catch-all' closet in my guest bedroom (I was expecting company), the process was quick and painless. With all the practice I've had, I can quickly decide to throw it out if it has no immediate use, or if I forgot that I even had it.
I will be moving in about a month or so, and my new living quarters will be smaller. What a great opportunity to declutter even

more! My niece will be holding a garage sale and has generously offered to include my things. I can happily get rid of things that were too valuable to throw out even though I was not using them. (A Weber grill, some exercise equipment, a daisy-wheel printer, old end tables, motivational tapes, etc., etc.)"

❝ *I love the uncluttered look of my house and my closets now.*❞

HOW OTHERS CAN HELP

❝ Dear Don:

Why it is so much easier, even irresistible, to clean other people's junk? We have to forcibly stop ourselves from starting right in on it. Any way we could turn this around, to help us get a little more enthusiastic about tackling our own?"

Part of this is plain old packrat curiosity, of course—we want to see just what that other person has by way of stuff. Two good friends could take advantage of this by trading dejunking jobs. Or one could serve as the "dumpster's advocate" for the other. Here's a few more ideas on this:

❝ After decluttering, I had eleven giant silver garbage bags in my living room for a week and a half. I just couldn't call Goodwill. My daughter came over at eight a.m. and headed for the phone."

❝ *Over the years I've hired four different nieces to help me find the courage to dispose of my 'treasures.' One time, when I really dug to the bottom of everything, I ended up spending $250 in wages to one of my nieces before I was through.*

I am ready now to pay a niece to stand beside me and force me to discard things."

❝ I'm a great junk collector. About once a year, *my friend comes and throws my junk out and I do her sewing and mending for the year.* I've never missed anything she threw out. I do this on a day my husband is not home because he saves more junk than I do."

❝ Just thought I would share my favorite dejunking idea.

For the past ten years I have hosted a 'white elephant party' for twenty-four of our close friends. We all bring our **worst, most awful** junk in gayly wrapped packages. Then we all take turns choosing and unwrapping a 'gift.' It is a hilarious evening laughing at how bad junk can be. Anyone unable to attend gets everyone else's junk left on their front porch.

We all do a lot of dejunking as we hunt for our worst possible junk."

I've heard of others who get together on New Year's to share and compare what they got for Christmas that they hate.

❝ Forced to clean out an unfinished 'catch-all' room because of plans to finish it—this particular 'nightmare alley' had been catching clutter for nine years—I couldn't quite bring myself to attack it. So I turned to the buddy system for help.

I took four **Polaroid snapshots** of the room from various angles, pasted them all on a sheet of paper, and **wrote a 'caption' under each one:** Having a… Wonderful Time… Wish You… Were Here. I sent them to a daughter, knowing she'd get a laugh, and hoping she'd could come and help me go through it all and coax me into parting with things. She has always come through for me in emergencies. (And she did this time, too.)

We work well together, she understands my idiosyncrasies, and can encourage me when I need it most. I trust her judgment and practical decisions. Plus we can visit, reminisce, laugh, and ponder over why I have some of this stuff, anyway. Or where it came from to begin with. (We've concluded it's breeding and multiplying.)

Relative or trusted friend, it doesn't matter, as long as it's someone who can encourage you to reach your goal—in this case, of an empty room to remodel!"

❝ *My idea is to form a group of people in the same circumstances and work together to throw away—pack out—straighten up—till we feel free to hire help.*

One rule: no exchange of junk between members.

Goal: one 'humongus' garage sale. Anybody interested?

Get in touch with Marion Bartholomew 419-294-3245."

❝ *Perhaps all of my life I have fought clutter, and sad to say (before reading your book), clutter seemed to be winning. My analysis of its roots parallel some you discuss—so well!—in your book—upbringing, junky habits, presents, but most of all, no support system for 'allowing' and guiding an all-out personal war on clutter."*

It might help if we declutterers could report our small victories to each other, the way other kinds of recovering addicts do, in a sort of public testimony:

Mini-Milestones/ Small Beginnings

❝ I recently started throwing rubber bands away. Even the big wide ones that come on broccoli."
(**Gasp!**)

❝ I can now bring myself to dispose of old clothes without clipping all the buttons off first."

(**Clap, Clap...**)

❝ I cast out my first film canister last week (the minute I removed the film from it!)"

(**Atta girl, way to go...**)

❝ The installers asked me if I wanted the old rug and I said NO!"

(**That's the spirit!**)

❝ I finally admitted that four coolers (for a family of two) was probably enough."

(**More, more!**)

❝ I finally had the courage to get rid of the stuffed baby alligator a friend from Florida gave our children sixteen years ago!!!"

(**Awesome!**)

❝ I was able to trash an ancient stack of Sunday newspaper magazine sections without a sigh (even the 1982 Kentucky Derby memorial issue)."

(**Bravo!**)

❝ I managed to ditch my entire collection of empty margarine tubs, lids and all."

(**Encore, Encore!**)

❝ I declined a free sewing kit at the airport (it had a plastic thimble in it, too)."

(**Faint, faint!**)

❝ I saw one of those Xerox paper boxes (complete with top!) in an alleyway and just turned my head."

(**Beyond belief!... Where was that?**)

A little TIME & MOTION input on decluttering

CAN'T FIND THE TIME TO DEJUNK?

In so many of your letters and conversations "not being able to find the time" to dejunk keeps popping up.

Well, there is some good news and some bad news here. The bad news first: You don't find time, you don't save time, manage time, take time, or make time either—the only thing you can do with time is **use** it, poorly or well. Time goes on, it passes, with or without your input—it doesn't wear your or anyone else's harness. Time is oblivious to your junk and clutter, either the collecting or disposing of it. So if you are waiting for some time to get your stuff under control you might as well move over and accept junk and clutter as a constant companion.

Now comes the good news. It isn't time to do it that's holding you up—you have all the time in the world, the same amount as anyone else, all you ever will have. Schedules aren't based on time, they're based on decision. Once you DECIDE to dejunk you have "the time."

If you don't believe me, watch how it goes when you're invited to something. If it's something you don't care all that much about, something you can easily pass on—you're too busy, other priorities are too pressing, "you'd love to, but..." your schedule just doesn't permit.

If it's something you'd really love to do, on the other hand—visit your favorite fishing hole, or get together with Miss or Mr. Highly Desirable—watch out. Schedules are re-shuffled, priorities re-prioritized, resolutions thrown to the wind, hours swiped or reclaimed from something else. What we really WANT to do, there's always time for.

If something is rewarding enough, we get up/home early, or wait an hour or two later. Well no class, show, date, or lottery can reward you like being junk free—the time you invest here will give you back some breathing space.

"Too busy" is the limpest of all excuses, because your good time, and plenty of it, is used stacking, storing, cleaning, tending, moving, finding, and fighting over your stuff. Over a lifetime it probably adds up to at least a hundred times the amount of time needed to remove it. Dejunking is one of the few moves that really **can** give you time.

So now one more excuse not to dejunk is gone—"not enough time."

HOW DO YOU PICK THE RIGHT PROJECT FOR THE TIME?

" I had no trouble getting lots of dejunking ideas—my problem came in deciding on the one that could be accomplished in the amount of time available."

If you have only a small amount of time to work with, you may not want to start in something that will end up spread out all over in everyone's way if you have to quit in the middle. But in dejunking, practical considerations and logistics aren't nearly as important as **mood.** Pick the decluttering project that you just **feel most like doing** now—because when you're in the mood, you can move mountains of clutter in a surprisingly short time. And if you don't feel like it, the smallest area or assignment can take forever.

When the urge to purge something strikes, that's the thing to tackle now, whether it's the linen closet or the backyard. Morale holds us back far more often than the number of minutes available.

" I can only squeeze in about an hour of dejunking a day, so I go for one contained area—i.e., a linen closet (I have two), the buffet, one cupboard, etc."

> **66** **Can't get to sleep?** Get up, clean out some drawers, or dig into any other quiet small to medium decluttering project. Then climb back in bed and sleep the sleep of the righteous."

DEJUNKING BY DAYS OF THE WEEK

Some folks like to take this approach. A weekly dejunking detail doesn't have to regiment you, but it can help form some useful habits. This is my own "daily decluttering agenda"—you could make up something similar to suit your own schedule and inclinations.

Monday: has the most mail and newspapers (and we're usually feeling fresh and aggressive)—a great day to pare down/go after that paper clutter.

Tuesday: Clothes, closets.

Wednesday: Garbage/trash day. Kid clutter. Holiday leftovers.

Thursday: Kitchen clutter (never any shortage of that!).

Friday (relief day): Any kind of "It's been holding me down" stuff. Office finish off/catchup.

Saturday: Exterior clean up and clear out day—vehicle, shop, and storage shed junk.

Sunday: Reflection and purification day—photos, sentimental stuff, return borrowed and snitched stuff, pack up discards for charity.

HOW LONG WILL IT TAKE?

Your whole decluttering agenda, that is? Don't be surprised or get discouraged if you don't get instant results. Most of us have spent our entire lives accumulating, so we can't expect sorting and pruning to be an overnight process. Here are a few reports from the "worst case" end.

66 *How long did it take me to dejunk? About six weeks, with some preliminary work. I worked 33 hours a week at my regular job during this period and dejunked all day on free days and weekends."*

66 I started in August and finished almost a year later, but the majority took only about **three months of working a couple of hours a week** on it. After that the scrapbooks took several more months."

66 After reading your book we spent *142 hours* ruthlessly decluttering. I need another 142 hours this summer to do my basement and garage."

66 *I see that I've only just begun and I've been working one year on this!"*

66 My first step was to buy every one of your books, and read them. That was **a year and a half** ago and all of that time, I have been working toward the goal of total dejunking. It is taking me a long time because I don't have unlimited time to devote to this. I work 6-8 hours a day out of my home, and am also a mother and wife, which is a full-time job in itself. There are simply not enough hours in my day. But I am making progress."

78

And this is one more war that can be won by steady progress.

You may not have anything like the agenda these folks had. But any packrat deserving of the title usually does have a LOT to go through. Hence the importance of the following topic.

KEEP ON DECLUTTERING (HOW TO MANAGE TO KEEP GOING)

❝ Worst problem was **facing the project day after day.** The 7.1 Loma Prieta earthquake (Oct. 89) left me thinking, 'Why did you spare my stuff, Lord?'"

❝ How do I feel now? Organized. Isn't that what dejunking is? I'll open that closet door when I pass, just to see. Maybe I'll go attack the shelves of memorabilia next. But I think I'll take a nap first. I'm exhausted!"

❝ How did I manage to get all the way through? Obsessive will. I seem to thrive on really hard projects."

If we kept a "Dejunker's success scorecard" it might look something like this:

    STARTERS 57
    FINISHERS 17

Yes, there is some difficulty here in keeping going, sustaining your enthusiasm after the big committed start.

Tackling those stacks takes mental as well as physical energy, and one of the biggest obstacles to clearing out the clutter is running out of steam before you run out of stuff.

Getting started in anything (going to school, getting yourself in shape, or any ambitious project) is more fun and exciting and goes faster than all those middle miles before the home stretch. And in decluttering, especially, it's all too easy to "lose it" before we lose it (the junk).

There is no one simple foolproof formula for enduring to the end—especially when age (yours or its), sentiment, or sheer mass come into the picture. But some of you have shared some interesting ways to keep going:

- I **cover my bed** with stuff when I start, so I can't go to sleep till I'm finished!

- I **invite my Mother-in-Law over** when I feel my resolve weakening.

- I make a **master map** of all the areas that need to be dejunked before I start, and mark things off as they're finished. This way, no matter how discouraged I may feel at any given moment, I can see that I'm still making head-way toward the goal.

- I **give myself a quota**, say an hour or half hour a day (with one day a week off for good behavior). Then I don't worry about where I am in the whole dejunking agenda, just that I keep putting in my as-signed dejunking time each day. Sooner or later I get enough done that a sense of momentum and accomplishment carries me the rest of the way.

- I **keep track of how much I dispose of** in each decluttering session—how many garbage bags or cans full. This helps give me a sense of accomplishment (I get secret pleasure out of amazing the neighbors on garbage collec-tion day, too!).

- I keep a '**Gone Clutter List**' (list of things I got rid of, was able to finally part with) as I go along. I go back over it when I need the strength to go on.

- I remind myself of **all the room there'll be** for new/good stuff when I'm done. Having the room at last for the things you really care about is a thrill.

- I think of it as a **treasure hunt**. What will I find today that I've been looking for for months (or forever), or that hasn't surfaced for so long that I've forgotten I have it?

❝ I have always hated housework, including decluttering. **But the joy of finding that lost memento or forgotten picture is worth the momentary pain of cleaning."**

❝ There were some surprises, such as a book I found that I had never read."

❝ You neglected to mention the **monetary savings** that can occur through dejunking. I recently found a check for over $200 that I had shoved in a drawer one time because I was too busy to deal with it when it came in. I often find coins in bags of otherwise useless junk, per-fectly good light bulbs and other items. I recently discovered that I had ten brand new photo albums stashed away in a closet—enough to last me at least five years."

I cleaned up!

Now let me share two big helpers of my own, boiled down from hundreds of mights and maybes:

1. Make your path public! Tell family, friends, associates, even outsiders of your commitment and schedule to dejunk. By doing this you've pledged yourself publicly to the effort, and all those other folks will suddenly all become disciples of discipline, prompting, asking, questioning you when things seem to be simmering down. Having to report on and answer to all this is one strong incentive to keep going.

2. Leave a starting place when you stop: When it's easy to pick up where we left off, we're more inclined to launch further into it than be lazy. If there's a handle to grab when you re-engage in your dejunking duties, you'll find keeping going easier.

It's kind of like fueling and servicing the car the night before or right after you return from a trip, instead of waiting until you're ready to take off on the next one. A fresh, easy, ready start makes going inviting.

So whenever possible, don't leave things in the middle of a mess. I always finish and clean up my present project and then in anticipation set out the next pile of clothes, paper, etc., all ready to dive into at a minute's notice. This also sets the next dejunking step clearly in my mind, so I've already begun dejunking it mentally before I get to it. All of this works to create a positive "can't wait to get to" attitude, rather than one of "have to" dread!

Practice these two big "keep going" helpers and a lot of that old, tired, discouraged feeling will go away!

GETTING DOWN WHEN YOU'RE GETTING RID

> 66 Not all of this dejunking was pleasant. There was the parting, the disagreements, the labor, the reality. Some sadness, too."

Have you ever been in one of those training programs where they tell you what it's going to be like when you get in the thick of it all—be it combat, a job, an athletic event, or the big campout? As I'm getting the skills and tools to launch myself into something, I love to have the trainer tell me how I will feel, what I'll see, all the dangers and disappointments before I start. Then when those surprises, disasters, and discouragements come, I won't get depressed or lose my sense of direction.

Well, dejunking has its low points, too:

1. There is always more stuff to deal with than you have time and boxes for. The rooms and areas you're working on will seem to expand before your very eyes.

2. You almost always get emotionally exhausted before you get physically tired (probably from all that aged guilt and accelerated decision making).

3. You'll question your own sanity before you're through, for some of the stuff you saved.

4. You'll suffer waves of "this serves me right."

5. You'll get little support from those nearest and dearest to you

while you're in the midst of it, but plenty of opinion, criticism, and sarcastic remarks.

6. You always have to clean up after you've cleaned out.

Just remember that like those sneaky gas gauges, it takes a long time to move off "Full," but once you reach Half it goes down fast!

ONCE—OR EVEN TWICE— MAY NOT BE ENOUGH!

❝ I am still working on my house today. It seems I get to a certain level and it feels great. Then gradually I realize something is still bothering me and I can finally see that there is still some clutter I hadn't noticed before. I grew up with chaos so anything better feels good at first."

❝ Cleaning my basement gave me the incentive to clean out the rest of my house. I went from room to room tossing things. When I was done I really felt good. But a few months later I went through the rooms again as well as the base-ment. I found more things I had to admit to not wanting. I thought I got it all the second time.

Last week I bought your book, and I shocked myself again. I made a list, for you to perhaps enjoy reading, of the things I eliminated the third time around.

• A juicer I bought four years ago for a stomach ailment. I used it for **one week.**

• From my husband's closet, shirts, sweaters, and jackets from years ago with the tags still attached—I gave them away.

• On my bedroom wall, a shadowbox that had some fifty knick-knacks. I never had time to dust it, so it looked terrible. Gone! (All that time, I had a nice framed photograph shoved under my bed because there was no place to hang it. Now I can finally hang it up.)

• A backpack half filled with art supplies. In the meantime, my daughter's backpack was torn and difficult to carry to school every day. I gave her mine and threw hers out.

• In the laundry I had a broken tin hutch filled with a set of encyclopedias I never used once in seven years, and a lot of other unused books. I donated the books and threw away the hutch.

• Next to the hutch was a desk filled with pure junk. I decluttered it and gave the desk to my children. Now my laundry room is empty and I can install a countertop along the wall to fold clothes on. I've always had to fold them on the floor (then I trip over them).

Also in the laundry room is an exercise bike which is great for hanging freshly dried shirts on the handles of. I'm looking for a taker.

• In the bottom of the china closet, the boxes the china and crystal came in, in case I ever move. I threw them out.

I have china service for **sixteen**. How pathetic! I've never used more than eight of anything at a time and then only three times in eight years. I really enjoy displaying my crystal and china, but I only display half of it. I'm giving away the other half.

• In the basement I found patches of screen for repairs, empty (not half empty—EMPTY) paint cans! Flower pots, decomposed flower bulbs, empty baby food jars, two bed frames, and two dressers I was going to refinish (**when?**)."

DEJUNKER'S PARALYSIS CAN BE OVERCOME

❝ For years, I just kept saving things and didn't even notice the clutter. My main rooms such as living room, dining room, kitchen, and bedrooms looked neat on the surface, but my closets and drawers were filled to capacity with outdated, unworn clothes, dozens of shoes I never wore, and vast assortments of kitchen gadgets and souvenirs of all kinds. **Whenever I didn't know what to do with something, I'd simply shove it into a closet or drawer, or in the attic, cellar, or garage.** I felt comfortable in the house and no one ever looked in these places anyway, I would tell myself.

However, my husband had passed away, my property taxes were going up, and maintenance of the house was getting to be more than I could afford. So I decided to put the house up for sale. Now I was faced with the dilemma of what to do with all the clutter. Surely I couldn't show the house to anyone in such a state of disarray. I set about to try and dejunk the premises.

I armed myself with a couple of boxes and decided to tackle the attic first. I soon found out what a discouraging task it was going to be, as I found myself amidst boxes of sentimental items, remnants of my children's past, such as old carriages, playpens, and games, the first couch my husband and I ever bought, and assortments of old clothes still in wearable condition. It was so cluttered up there I could hardly walk around. I reminisced there for about two hours and decided to give up. How could I possibly part with this stuff?

I moved on to the garage and decided that most of the stuff there was either still usable or had never been used. There was an old sled there that my son could pass on to his future child and an old lawn mower that he might use if he ever gets a house of his own. **I was paralyzed with inertia.**

The cellar was filled with enough things to start a plumbing supply or hardware store. There were also old rusted tools and gadgets that seemed to blend into the walls, so you didn't even notice them!

I realized I was facing a serious situation and could not show the house until I found some way to clean up.

Then I came across your book. I read and reread it until I had enough inspiration to tackle the debris. I decided to take the day off from work and work on this problem, while I still had the motivation.

I followed the guidelines you set up in the book and tried to keep my emotions in check. Before I knew it, I had piles of trash in the street and it wasn't as hard as I had thought it would be. I had now developed a new philosophy about my junk. **I only save the things I actually use and have adequate storage for.** I have put aside boxes of sentimental things to work on. Other usable things I no longer want, I give to charity. It is wonderful to start seeing empty spaces and I find I don't have the compulsion to fill them up.

I worked on this about two months and admit I'm exhausted, but I have no regrets. I can now take prospective clients on a tour of my house and not worry if they ask to see the attic or the garage. Several have remarked how neat and orderly my house is! What a proud moment!

Just want you to know that I couldn't have done it without your book—and I'm grateful."

FREE, FREE AT LAST!

When you sum up this business of "dejunking," the need for it vs the struggle to do it, it really has little to do with the actual stuff involved. The willpower or motivation you need isn't necessarily going to come from a carefully charted course, a companion, or a "die if you don't" decree.

Think about it a minute. It all comes down to whether you really want—and how bad you want—the rewards of a junk and clutter free life. When and if you can finally focus on the grandeur of personal freedom, high self-esteem, the increased respect of others, and all that recovered space, time, and money—then any dejunking process is a piece of cake. We get so caught up in the mechanics of

staying the execution of all our expensive and exciting keepables that we miss the whole reason to master this, to get clutter under control. **The reward, the relief of not having all this so astonishingly beats the burdens of having it, that it's downright ridiculous to keep on imposing such a sentence on our very life.**

If you can tune in to the rewards of ridding yourself of it, the how, what, when, and where will come easily and naturally.

Chapter 5

Moving Through It & Moving It Out:
How to Identify Junk and What to Do with It Afterward

At least five thousand times in the last ten years—in calls, comments, cards and letters—I've been quoted the "junker's favorite scripture":

> ***"One man's junk is another man's treasure."***

In 98% of cases this verse turns out to have been mistranslated. It should read:

> ***"One man's junk is another man's junk."***

However much I may believe this, I also believe that every one of us should have complete freedom of that critical determination: Junk or treasure?

So I won't attempt to judge your junk, but in this chapter you will find some great helps from your fellow packrats to ease the evaluation process.

BACK TO THAT TRICKY BUSINESS OF JUDGING JUNK

What was the hardest thing about your decluttering campaign?

❝ Incredibly hard to decide what to do about valuable or really good (but excess) stuff."

❝ One of the things that really gets in the way of dejunking is the inability to make decisions. You look at a thing and you can't decide whether or not you want it, need it, or like it, or if you ever will. There are things you have that you know you want, and things you know you definitely don't want, but it's those **things you have no strong feelings about one way or the other** that cause trouble. It's easier to shove them in the back of a cupboard so you don't have to decide.

The problem with this is that the next time the thing surfaces, you have to decide all over again, and if you decide not to decide and shove it in the cupboard again, then you just have to deal with it again some day. Or if you die, then your heirs have to deal with it and that just isn't fair."

" I have been a reluctant junker for some years—keeping things not because I wanted to, but because I felt guilty about throwing them away."

Ah yes, the ambition killer, the big hangup. If it wasn't for this business of trying to decide what is junk and what is not, what to keep and what to banish, clutter wouldn't be much of a problem. THIS is what slows us down and holds us back, and in fact it's what created most of our piles and stacks in the first place. Anyone else's clutter, we can divide the wheat from the chaff in a second; our own is another story. To speed the process we all yearn for something like one of those mechanical coin sorters where you just pour a random mix of coins into the funnel at the top and somehow each type of coin falls swiftly into its respective slot.

This evaluation process is so intensely personal, so unquestionably subjective, that no matter how much good advice or input we get from anyone else, only WE can make that final judgment.

But there are some pretty dependable criteria others have used

and you can use to make it, and let me remind you of what they are:

Some Junk Judging Guidelines

(Courtesy of *Clutter's Last Stand.*)

Is it clutter or is it not? Is your dejunking fever being cooled down by cold feet? Are emotional ties and guilt diluting your ability to be ruthless and strong? If indecisiveness sets in, here are some guidelines that may help.

It Is Junk If:

☐ it's broken or obsolete (and fixing it is unrealistic)

☐ you've outgrown it, physically or emotionally

☐ you've always hated it

☐ it's the wrong size, wrong color, or wrong style

☐ using it is more bother than it's worth

☐ it wouldn't really affect you if you never saw it again

☐ it generates bad feelings

☐ you have to clean it, store it, and insure it (but you don't get much use or enjoyment out of it)

☐ it will shock, bore, or burden the coming generation

If you can check one or more of the above truthfully, then it's probably junk. Do yourself, your house, and posterity a favor—pitch it! It's robbing you of peace of mind and space.

It's Not Junk If It:

- ☐ generates love and good feelings
- ☐ helps you make a living
- ☐ will do something you need done
- ☐ has significant cash value
- ☐ gives you more than it takes
- ☐ will enrich or delight the coming generation

If you can check a few of the above comfortably, then it's probably not junk—enjoy it and feel good about its place in your life.

Here are a few more questions you can ask yourself to help make the big decision.

DO I REALLY NEED THIS?

We all ask ourselves this question, the problem is we seldom answer it. We put the item in question back so we can ask it again and again and again and again and again.

❝ I have a good helper in my three-year-old. She points to things and asks, 'What's this?' If my only answer is 'stuff,' out it goes!"

❝ Every time I'd unpack something that **made me feel heavy and cramped**, I'd let it go. It was inevitably an item that I never really used or cared about, but clung to because I thought I needed it. Out it went, Alleluia!!"

❝ I served in three different armies for a total of nine years. When you have to shlepp everything on your own back you get a pretty good idea of WHAT is essential."

DOES IT WORK?

One of my codes of life, that's proven its value over and over:

Don't own anything that doesn't work.

Owning anything that won't run or work is a downer and a disadvantage from every angle. So all that "To fix," "Might be fixable," and "Waiting for parts" stuff should be on top of your list to deal with.

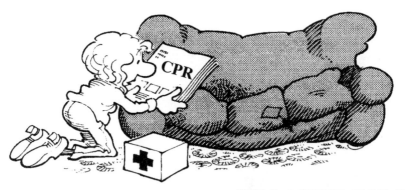

Fix it or deep-six it. Get it in working order, or out of your life.

One card I received had a short course for this:

❝ If it's dead, revive or bury it. If you can't identify it, it's dead."

Discard unmendables, unmentionables, unusables, unreadables, unwearables.

AM I USING IT?

(Make yourself a sign or place card that says this.)

❝ I was very impressed with the statement in *Clutter's Last Stand*: 'Think USE as you go through your closets, boxes, and piles.' This is more to the point than thinking 'Where shall I store this?'

So now I must go through my entire house with this new thought in mind, 'Think USE.'

On Saturday I started cleaning my basement. It was so different to think in terms of '**what will I use it for, and when**?' I was shocked to see how few things I really knew I would use again."

❝ Have nothing in your houses that you do not know to be useful or believe to be beautiful."
—William Morris

WILL I EVER USE IT/GO BACK TO IT?

❝ *...I had been saving a magazine article about how to raise hyacinths, tulips, and daffodils indoors for over twenty-five years. I finally realized I didn't have anywhere in the house or garage where bulbs could be placed at the proper temperature to raise indoor flowers. The magazine article got thrown out, and when I finish dejunking I'll celebrate by spending $1.39 for a bunch of daffodils."*

❝ **I have not thrown all my 'junk' away. But at least I've stepped past the stage of purposeless saving, without even having had illusions of possible future uses or purposes."**

❝ Dejunking is like dying in little pieces. It's hard to admit you can't (or won't) ever go back again. Looking at my French dictionary, ancient paint supplies, and yellowed music, I told myself, 'You haven't done these things for over fifteen years and you NEVER WILL AGAIN. It's okay to get rid of them,' but I felt that if the things I'd done through my life were over, then I wasn't sure who I was. I felt safer being a conglomerate of the twelve-year-old me artist and the fifteen year-old-me musician than just the current me.

I defined myself by my past activities, and admitting that things were obsolete was hard."

❝ My 'decluttering' rules include:
1. If you forgot you had it, THROW IT OUT.
2. If you won't use it for a year or more, THROW IT OUT.
3. If you didn't use it for the last year, THROW IT OUT.
4. If you have two (same size frypans, teakettles, whatever) and you only need one, THROW ONE OUT."

P.s. "OUT" can mean many things these days—not just trash it, but sell it, or give it to a friend (see p. 100).

The Packrat's Official WHAT ARE THE CHANCES? Calculator

At last, a way to shear through the doubt and uncertainty that often surrounds ostensibly valuable stuff that's been in limbo for quite a while now.

   WILL I EVER FIX IT?
      TAKE IT UP?
      TAKE IT UP AGAIN?
      FINISH IT?
      WEAR IT?
      WEAR IT AGAIN?
      READ IT?
      FIX IT?
      EAT IT?

1. First, get a piece of paper and pencil.

2. Now pick up the item in question and give it a good look. If it's gone to pot in storage (there's a good chance of this), you can end this exercise right here.

3. If it's still good, when did you put it in storage, or on the shelf? Put the number of years ago it was down on your paper, and then multiply it by five percent. (Feel free to round your numbers off to the nearest decade or century.)

4. How strong is its pull on you now? If the idea of getting around to it still is mighty appealing, stay with the figure you have. If your feelings about the object or activity are closer to "so-so," multiply the figure you have now by 2.

5. Subtract the percent you have now from 100%, and you will have the ACTUAL likelihood that you will ever interact with it again.

DO I REALLY CARE ABOUT IT?

❝ *Into the drawers everything went. Now I've gone through all that stuff. I asked myself* **'If there was a fire, would I save this?'** *A 'No' response helped me to gather all the nonessentials and finally get rid of them. I have gone through my whole room, little by little each day. I am 75% junk free."*

Wonder how many packrat firemen get burned fingers trying to save junk?

❝ **If you really value something and want to keep it, you will find a place to store it. You can often find a place to store it by getting rid of things you don't use."**

❝ If I'm stuck as to whether or not to keep something, I say 'Would I go out of my way to buy this if I didn't have it?' If the answer is no, it's gone. Sometimes I've kept things just because I owned them."

IS IT WORTH CARING ABOUT?

❝ The advice from *Clutter's Last Stand* that really sticks in my mind is **'Don't love anything that can't love you back.'** That alone was worth the price of the book. Is it available on a plastic, sequin-encrusted refrigerator magnet?"

WHERE AM I KEEPING IT?
Disgrace by PLACE— the real indicator of value

Ever notice how certain clutter rates certain places? **Where** something is stashed or located is a clear indicator of worth—we may have made these judgments unconsciously, but they're usually right on!

Just for fun, let's run through a little 1-10 value rating here ("Wow, that's a 10!").

GOOD STUFF 10

10 With me (in purse, car, briefcase) Most of this does have some real purpose—just get rid of the "antiques" mixed in.

9 On the dresser top This is usually live, active stuff—it just needs to be organized better.

8 In new closets or drawers We don't let anything but good stuff in here—let's keep it that way now!

7 In old closets/drawers Doubtful—needs a good going-through.

6 At the folks' By the time we reclaim it, much of this is beside the point.

5 Paid storage Mainly vanity, or failure to face facts.

4 Attic Forgotten (for good reason).

3 Garage Lying in wake, waiting for death certificate to be issued.

2 Basement/crawl space Long gone/we're going to let it rot before we throw it away.

1 Just outside Trash. Anything not valuable enough to be stored in a garage, shed, or barn probably isn't valuable enough to keep.

JUNK

Average Junk Quotient/ Content of:	
Bookshelves	33 1/3%
Furniture	25%
Clothes Closets	50%
(to get more precise here:	
clothes bars in closets	50%
shelves in closets	80%)
Toys	65%
Upper cupboards in kitchen	70%
Souvenirs	90%
Boxes in the attic	85%
Boxes in the cellar	95%
Things left on the porch	90%
Things stored in the garage	85%
Things stored in sheds	97%

DOES IT GENERATE GOOD FEELINGS?

It is my practice to respond to all mail, and I pulled this exchange out of an old file.

"Dear Mr. Aslett:
I am eleven years old and reading your books is a lot of fun! I REALLY like your book *Clutter's Last Stand*. Those 101 Feeble Excuses for hanging onto clutter are great.
If it's all right, I have a question for you. I have a scrap of cloth that is very pretty, but it is of no use to me. I used to have a box full of scraps, but I threw them out. (Thank goodness—they caused a lot of complaints.) Now I would like to know if I should get rid of that last scrap (P.S. I can't throw it away, but it's a newsence!)
Please wright,
Mary Catherine"

Dear Mary Catherine:

If that remaining scrap of material is pretty and you like it and it enhances your life, then it isn't junk, so I would make it into a nice picture mounting, or something you can display. We may not live in the past, but wow do we learn from and savor it. Anything that has a good feeling and good memories is well worth keeping and actually finding a place or use for. True beauty these days is a rare thing, because there is so much tinsel and artificial and "twinkee" stuff around. Compared to that, a healthy piece of fabric is wonderful! Let me know what you do with it, and keep up the dejunking of the old worthless stuff that has a tendency to bury the good stuff!

Thanks for reading my books, enclosed are two more, autographed just for you. The *Packrat* book is just as fun as my first one.

Your friend,

Don Aslett

"I have a lot of things I need and two small collections I love—many books (some I use as references, some I read three or four times and then give or throw away), and a Snoopy and Woodstock collection that makes me smile, laugh, feel good, remember people and places and really enjoy."

GOOD—anything that does that is wonderful, not junk.

" *Those old ballet slippers that symbolize a long-ago dream may be just as important to your good life as an extra pair of sheets (although the sheets are entitled to better storage space).*"
— Ann Guilfoyle
in Home Free

IS IT WORTH STORING OR FILING?

" Here is one little insight I gained from my dejunking process. I decided to use a fairly complicated index card system for my boxes of seasonal stuff and 'usable junk' in my basement. Every single thing in these boxes is written down on an index card. The cards are filed alphabetically and have a reference number so that I can go immediately to a box and find the item. The greatest part about this system is when I was going through the

stuff, **I'd be darned if I was going to make an index card for some dumb, useless thing.** It became a great weeding out of all those borderline items. So if it's not worth packing carefully in a box and making an individual card for it, then OUT IT GOES. And I never have to wonder if something is 'down there somewhere.' If it's in my card file, I have it. If it's not, I don't."

WHO AM I KEEPING IT FOR?

" In order to dejunk, I ask myself 'Who am I keeping this for?' If it's for someone else, I get rid of it. My sons have already told me they don't want any of my junk. So 'Why am I keeping this?' If it is because Aunt Molly will be hurt if I give it away, I get rid of it. Am I keeping it because I'm afraid I won't be able to afford one in the future if I find I need one? I get rid of it. I have always been given whatever I need, either free or at a price I can afford. **Hanging on to things shows a distrust and lack of faith in life.** If everyone hoards there is scarcity, when everyone shares there is plenty for everyone."

Let's take a break here and enjoy another of those unique dejunking ballads by Sid Herron.

Heave Ho

Copyright 1992 by Sid Herron, used by permission.

Heave ho, time to throw,
    All of the clutter and junk must go!
    Time to take a cold, hard look
    At all of my possessions.

Heave ho, time to throw,
    All of the clutter and junk must go!
    Life's not long enough to hoard
    Engine cranks from Model-T Fords
    And similar obsessions!

My mother as a little girl
    Lived through the Great Depression.
    To throw a thing away required
    A psychiatric session.

My father was a gambling man
    From Vegas up to Reno,
    And when he died, he left me towels
    From fifty-three casinos!

My brother was a victim
    Of their clutter, there's no doubt;
    Walked in a walk-in closet once,
    And never did come out!

Chorus

Heave ho, time to throw,
    All of the clutter and junk must go!
    Time to take a cold, hard look
    At all of my possessions.

Heave ho, time to throw,
    All of the clutter and junk must go!
    I don't have room in my garage
    For the running boards from my
    brother's old Dodge,
    Or old spark plug collections.

My cars sit in the driveway,
    There's no room in my garages.
    My freezer's got no room for food,
    It's full of old corsages.

My floor is stacked with magazines
    On subjects esoteric,
    From Szechuan food to remedies
    For diseases dysenteric.

I'm afraid to move my sofa
    For fear of what's behind it;
    I'd love to get my carpet cleaned,
    If I could only find it!

DO I STILL FEEL THE SAME ABOUT IT?

❝ It's funny how many of my prized possessions have suddenly begun to look like junk, and it surprises me how many of those things have been thrown away by me in the last three days.❞

❝ The 'good' china and glass-ware I intend to sell. They are no longer 'me' and I have two sets of casual china I enjoy looking at much more and which I can put in the dish-washer.❞

❝ One item I had trouble with was a knitted snowsuit—thirty-eight years old, full of holes, only one mitten. I had loved it for years, but now I looked at it objectively and realized **it was not what I cracked it up to be.** Since I had a picture of my brother in it, I decided it was time to give it away.❞

❝ Dejunking is a matter of constant redefining. Just because last time I sorted, I decided to keep something doesn't mean its number isn't up now.❞

❝ (Oh lovely, liberating fact!) **Your feelings about the stuff DO change!** Not always, but often, especially if it's been there for quite a while.

As you're going through it, you'll feel that wonderful freeing moment—of realizing you **can** get along without it, spare it now. Interesting, how with the exception of those few real heartstring-tuggers, the older the stuff is, the more likely this is to happen. It's almost as if we had to hold things in limbo for a certain amount of time before we've paid our dues and can be set free.❞

❝ Another thing I discovered about dejunking my life is that many things that once seemed so valuable I must save them, now seem senseless and stupid. It's funny how our **perceptions change** through life's many turns. But the things that are really important will always be important and they are things that have no monetary value and they take no space in drawer or closet. They are things you carry with you at all times, inside.❞

WHAT IS IT WORTH TO ME NOW?

❝ **Dear Mr. Aslett:**
I'm a little—no, a lot—concerned with the word 'de-junk.' It makes an assumption that I think is counterproductive: Excess=Junk. I don't think that's absolutely the case. I'd like to see more of a focus on growth, maturity, new points in life= opening up space (literally) and *letting go of possessions that are no longer appropriate to that new moment of life.* It's baggage (objective), not junk (judgmental).❞

I couldn't agree with you more. The key question about any object, how we can tell whether it's junk or not, is What is its value to us NOW?

A Face-the-Facts Junk Judging Appraisal Sheet

...for anything you're undecided about

Is continued ownership the answer?

An honest appraisal of its worth TODAY.

(You could think of this as a clutter excuse lie detector.)

I had a place/room to keep it
☐ I honestly still have plenty of room for it

I thought it might come in handy some day
☐ I have actually used it

I thought I needed it
☐ I do need it

It's an investment
☐ I could actually sell it for cash now

It was a homeless object and I felt sorry for it
☐ I still pity it enough to give it a place

I intended to take this (hobby/craft/sport/skill) up some day
☐ The chances are 60% or better that I will

I intended to fix it some day
☐ The chances are 75% or better that I will

I got it for parts
☐ I really have used it for parts

I wanted to impress people
☐ People are impressed with it now

I thought it was beautiful/interesting
☐ I still think it is

It was the last of its kind
☐ Its uniqueness is still worth it

I'd never had one
☐ I'm savoring it daily

Other people had one
☐ I still care about keeping up with the Joneses in this particular way

It was a gift
☐ It is still giving

It was so sharable
☐ I've shared/am sharing it

I intended to give it to_____
☐ _____ is still alive, and I have their current address and enough postage to send it

I wanted to show people I could afford it
☐ I still can afford it, in time and money

It was too good to let go
☐ It's still that good now

IF ALL ELSE FAILS, THERE'S STILL THE EMOTIONAL WITHDRAWAL BOX

My friend Gladys Allen originated this as a means of dealing with the really tough cases, the stuff you know you should get rid of, but can't quite bring yourself to. Seal it up in a box or bag and tuck it on a shelf or in a corner somewhere. Then in a month or two or six, whatever it takes, after its pull on you has lessened and your memory of it has dimmed, you can quietly lift it from the shelf and dispose of it. (If, on the other hand, you haven't forgotten for a moment what's in there, it should probably stay.)

Amazing, how this works.

> " What a wonderful invention the 'Emotional Withdrawal' box is! A marvelous device for testing whether things are going to be missed or not!"

" I've decluttered a lot but I'm not perfect. I still have my 'fat clothes' in bags in the closet—'in case' I regain those 72 pounds. To me they're good luck charms—if I throw 'em, the pounds return and I'll wish I had them. So every week I run my lambswool duster over the bags.... Stupid? You bet. Every week I say 'out' and then 'Well, they're my *emotional withdrawal* bag and I'm not ready yet.' And on they stay. Are such good luck charms legitimate?"

You bet! Remember the general guideline for "keepers"—keep it as long as it's doing something for you! Any shelf excess that kept the excess off me personally, I'd keep dusting forever.

On the other hand, if it isn't performing any positive function in your life, GET RID of it!

" I've never been extremely disorganized or untidy, but like everyone else, I'd unthinkingly hang onto clothes and household items that were either outdated, unused, or disliked. I was acting—or failing to act—out of habit, misplaced sentiment, or just plain ignorance of the fact that I did indeed have the power and the right to make conscious decisions about shaping and controlling my environment. You helped me see that I was allowing my possessions to accumulate and invade my space and my consciousness—in effect, **to govern me**."

" **Dear Mr. Aslett:**
I'm writing to tell you about the impact your books on clutter have had on me and my life. I had been collecting 'treasures' for almost thirty years, throwing away nothing—clothes, books, toys—heirlooms all. Other books only told me how to organize my junk. I was already a master at organizing, fitting, cramming,

and saving. I knew I had a problem—a big one—but I never considered throwing anything away. You *gave me permission* to just junk it!"

My books (including this one) do have a little different philosophy and thrust than many of the other writers on the subject. If I may quote another of your letters:

❝ Some of these other books have some good ideas but they are too slanted to **hiding** junk and clutter. I don't want to hide 'stuff'—I want to get **rid** of it. (It still takes space to hide stuff, no matter how attractive the containers.)❞

...NOW QUIT WORRYING ABOUT CASTOPHOBIA

Castophobia? That's fear of regretting what you just dejunked. You've all mentioned it to me over and over: "You wait, Don. **The minute I get rid of this I'm going to need it.**"

This may have actually happened somewhere sometime, but if you haven't needed something for the last five or ten or twenty years, you're unlikely to ever. Once in a while we pump up our "might" or "maybe" imagination up far enough to start whining about something we discarded. But in reality (if we were honest with ourselves) actual need for the average clutter castaway is rare. So quit worrying about the "resurrection" potential of things.

I've taught, spoken to, and worked with thousands of people, helping them in the process of downsizing their lives in the later, "now that the family is grown and gone" years. One of the most dreaded decisions they ever have to make is going from a big house with plenty of space to a smaller apartment or condo or whatever. People pre-grieve this process for years and protest it violently. Yet when they're back still actually taking care of it all they can't keep up with it. **100% of the people I know who finally took the step were elated,** exuberant over it afterward—"the best thing I ever did." Shedding, ridding themselves of what had evolved to "too much" was a progressive step that changed their lives for the better. **None** of them, not a single one, suffered any Castophobia.

So cast out those morbid fears and charge ahead.

> **❝ *I agree with you about rarely regretting the action to let something go: it has only happened to me twice in all my years of dejunking, and I'm not sure I really would use those two 'precious' things if I still had them.*❞**

A FEW LAST THOUGHTS FROM A FELLOW RAT THAT MAY HELP YOU TO RID:

"Even if there was a war, I wouldn't want this anyway."

"If it doesn't fit, get rid of it."

"I've/We've outgrown it."

"If I don't have a place for it, I don't want it."

"I'll/We'll never miss it."

"5 of one thing is enough. 10 is too many."

"The kids don't want it."

"You're not throwing your life away, you're saving it."

NOW WHAT DO WE DO with what we weeded out?

❝ You've convinced me there's a need to get rid of some junk— now I need some hand-holding to know what to do with it once I've decided I don't need it."

❝ There's a philosophical thing about keeping good material in circulation. Somehow it all has value and it does seem immoral simply to toss. If I'm not using it, someone else has a right to it, especially if they're struggling financially."

When it comes to dealing with the remains, undertakers have that down to a science, even a financial plan. In the case of clutter, tossing is by no means the only option— there are other and often better ones, such as **share, activate, donate, recycle, or trade.**

I devoted an entire chapter (Chapter 12) in <u>Not for Packrats Only</u> to this subject.

Here are some ideas from my readers now.

SELL IT?

❝ Recently, I sold some unlovely antique furniture and with the proceeds bought some lovely modern pine which is 'user friendly,' and actually works. So much antique furniture is decorative rather than functional—what a relief to be rid of it after all these years!"

❝ I lived in the same 2,850 sq. ft. house with a large two-car garage for twenty-four years. It was amazing how much my partner and I had collected over the years. So much wasted space just keeping dusty old neglected stuff.

We began by having garage sales, taking things to Goodwill and to the Shelter in our neighborhood. In just the last three months before we moved (which was only three weeks ago), we had three garage sales and made over $1,000. Most of the things were priced $.10 to $5, so you can imagine how much we got rid of! I was really on a roll. Then I sold a diamond ring I had for twenty-four years which I never wore and was costing me $15 a year to keep in a safe deposit box. I bought a couple of Treasury Bonds with the money, so now I earn $180 a year instead. I've sold exercise equipment that lost its novelty, filing cabinets which I emptied by uncluttering my paper trail, and bookcases by selling books I would no longer read.❞

❝ Being raised in rural America with parents who remember the 'Great Depression' and a work ethic that only farm mules have, we began to brainstorm ideas for the dissolution of the past twenty-two years. Money won out and Saturday, August 4, was the day of the great GARAGE SALE. To get ready for it we spent two weeks of hard labor. Many tears and cynical words were laced with uproarious laughter and in the end the results far outweighed the effort.

We're leaving in a few days for a family vacation to San Francisco where we will have no trouble at all spending the found money from our sale. But even better than the shopping is when we return with our precious bargains, there will be room to store them!❞

❝ *I had two yard sales and went to the flea market twice. (I bought a pickup to do this in, too, talk about clutter expense!)*❞

❝ I once had a garage sale with my sister and spent more money buying her stuff than I made selling mine.❞

❝ *I couldn't work in all the clutter, so I started to sell all my 'antiques.' I wound up buying more 'antiques' and spending more $ (on all the classified ads, show entrance fees, and big budget mail order lists).*

I'd rather sell it than give it away because it's the only income I've got now. But selling—even on a full-time basis—takes time and **labor** *(whew!), planning and effort. Garage sales, flea markets, antique shows, mail order lists—whew!*❞

❝ Thought about keeping all the better items (ha ha!) for a rummage sale, but a lot of time, effort, and hassle goes into one, and the Salvation Army is the luckier for it.❞

❝ The dismal failure of my yard sale has convinced me to never have another yard sale. I donate most everything to charity and it saves me a couple of days of life every year. **Fifty dollars for approximately three days work is a low-paying job!** Thank you!"

❝ I had been considering holding a garage sale, but after reading your view of them, I itemized over $900 worth of clothing and household items, donated them to charity, and **was able to deduct that amount from our income tax**."

Peddling it does beat piling it, but selling your excess isn't necessarily the perfect answer or a big bonanza. People can be so impractical when it comes to this. They'll spend $200 in order to make $20.

They pay for ads and signs and take days off from work to hold a garage sale. They may have paid $25 for something and they got taken. It is junk. They don't use it, but won't give it away. They feel they have to get at least 50 cents out of it. It is like the owner's validation of owning it.

The following might be more promising approaches:

❝ *Several people I know have garage sales and for a share of the cost of the newspaper ad ($2-$3) they will let me add some items to their sales.*"

❝ My sister had an interesting garage sale. Her boys took out the kitchen chairs and propped up Garage Sale signs on them—there wasn't any sale planned and I guess the boys do what they please. Anyhow, people started coming over, so my sister started carting out stuff and selling it. My daughter too contributed some items on the spur of the moment. In a couple of hours they made quite a bit of money and cleaned out some junk and they didn't have pre-sale jitters, either."

If you're still looking for your kitchen chairs, Ma'am, my wife got them for $1.25 each (but they don't match our other eight).

❝ *I know a bunch of women who have an '**auction sale**' and exchange their clutter. For a baby shower they have an 'auctioneer' that auctions off stuff they bring to the 'sale' and they buy each other's stuff by bidding for it. The proceeds then go toward the baby shower, and everyone is stuck with different junk. They have fun, the new mother has money instead of gifts, and the junk gets moved around (if not out).*"

Great—this wears it out, gets someone else's germs on it, and gets it out the door.

In case you're wondering what to do with stuff left over from garage sales, put it on the curb neatly and let curb shopping take over. I've seen Jaguar owners loading old bed springs, etc.

If necessary borrow a "Sold" sign and set it in front of the house. People think others are careless and desperate at moving time and that they throw good stuff away.

GIVE IT AWAY (TO SOMEONE WHO REALLY WANTS OR NEEDS IT)

One of the best solutions for "good stuff." It's just about always better to give than to retain.

❝ I read *Not for Packrats Only* twice in one week. Suddenly some mental fog cleared. It dawned on me that it was not necessary to sell things! After all, so much has been given to us!

After trying unsuccessfully to sell some of the furniture we no longer needed, for example, I discovered that one of our children wanted a bedroom set and another was casting a wistful eye at my grandmother's Victorian table and chairs. That took a little doing, as we had to ship things from Texas to Idaho and Michigan, but now I have a whole room for my 'office' and a small kitchen area in which to collapse with a cup of coffee, shell the beans, or check through the mail. This is a much more satisfying use of available space, and less furniture makes it easier to clean."

❝ I am glad to send nice things to my sister, it takes care of gift giving for a while. I used to buy her soaps and inexpensive stuff and now I send her something good that didn't cost me anything and I just send it as a surprise. Those are the best gifts, as one doesn't need a reason."

❝ Let's all help to overcome the impression that to be a REAL gift, such as a birthday or Christmas present, something has to be new. (To the extent that people will sink to recycling the most awful stuff—such as things *they* got from someone and didn't like—as gifts, because thank god those 'new' stickers and labels are still hanging on there, however precariously, so the thing is still new!)

If we can manage to legitimatize used or previously owned stuff as gifts for official gift-giving occasions, it would help the national economy (and our dejunking effort) a lot. After all, people go to garage sales and shove and claw their way past others for choice previously owned stuff."

❝ *Lots of stuff had to find a 'good home' before I could let it go, so I gave jewelry as gifts and dolls to a collector. My music books, which I hated to just send to Goodwill, I gave to a local youth symphony.*"

❝ I had quite a store of fabrics and sewing supplies, but then I developed allergies that prevented me from doing much sewing. And my children are all gone now. How to dispose of all those dollars worth of fabric with good conscience?

It took three years after converting to the dejunking principles to be able to do this. Then I did the following: First, I let my daughter, who sews, select any fabric she felt she would enjoy for her home or her children. I still had a great deal left, so I **started to listen and become aware of who sewed** in our church. I mentally assessed their financial standing and the size of the family. Then with happy heart I gave my remaining store of fabric to a struggling family with six children. The mother will always be my friend, and I have a warm feeling in my heart when I see one of her children in well-made clothing. I also have three big empty drawers in my linen closet. Everyone profited!"

❝ *Eventually we realized that we would undoubtedly move again some day, and about three years ago I began trying to dispose of things. First I went through the linens and gave the excess towels and sheets to the Salvation Army. Next were the canning jars. We had both current usable ones and antique ones. Ten boxes of quart jars went to the county agent, who found someone who needed them. (We have a vegetable garden, and I still can and freeze food, but now that there are two of us instead of five, pint jars fill the bill.) The antique jars that I wasn't using to store pasta and such in the pantry went to a local farmhouse museum, where they are now used in demonstrations for schoolkids. Four boxes of insulators collected during the '60's (it was a lot of fun then, but we're not interested now) went to the telephone company museum.*"

❝ I have been the lucky recipient of many giveaways. When my uncle and aunt moved they had a whole billiard table covered with stuff that **we were all invited to look at and take anything we wanted.** I'm all in favor of it.

The native Indians of British Columbia had a good thing with the potlatch. Wealth is not to be hoarded but given away. A native person's wealth was based on how much he could give away, not how much he had. It is significant that our government banned potlatches, as ours is definitely an insecure, hoarding society. (Potlatches were made legal again in 1952, but they weren't the same anymore.)"

❝ If you can't bring yourself to throw something away because it is a good, usable item, *send it to your favorite charity and deduct it off Schedule A on your income tax.*"

Yes, charitable decluttering can be profitable, too.

❝ *My tax records this year will include donations to: The Salvation Army, Goodwill, Hurricane Victims, The Women's Center, Fire Victims, and the homeless. A quilter's group got exactly .5 tons of fabric (I still have the other .5 ton). My family got some of their gifts* **back**. *(What was I going to do with* puppets?*) I donated sewing and craft supplies to a women's jail to make baby quilts—it cost me over $40 to mail the boxes. I set my brother up in an apartment (when he came out of the service this year) with kitchen and bath stuff. A girl I work with got an apartment and I gave her stuff to get started. I must say all this was such a time and money waster! NO MORE COLLECT-ING!!!"*

❝ *Here are some good places I've found to dispose of things:*
<u>*clothes*</u>—*Church and syna-gogue 'clothes closets.' Call church.*
<u>*pots, pans, towels, etc.*</u>— *Halfway homes for ill. Call your local state agency that cares for the mentally retarded, etc.*
<u>*books*</u>—*State hospitals. The American Association of Univer-sity Women often stages sales*

to sell our old books to others.
<u>*newspapers*</u>—*Often vets can use. I don't know why. Call vets. Bird rescue centers also use tons of them (for bird cage bottoms). Call centers.*
<u>*boxes food and household items came in*</u>—*Preschool and kindergarten teachers can use these to set up 'stores' and markets. Your empty Quaker Oats box is a big deal to some kid.*
<u>*all of the above*</u>—*Go to a large neighborhood and put up a FREE sign."*

When it comes to the question of giving things away, watch that "dog in the manger" impulse. Clutter clinging does feed that selfishness at the bottom of our soul.

❝ When we moved here there were spare gutters in the rafters. I found out the previous owners had promised them to the neighbors across the street who had no gutters. I wouldn't give them up! Eventually they bought new ones. It hit me later how selfish I was being. I'm so ashamed. And now I'm stuck with these gutters I will probably never use."

❝ *Clutter's Last Stand*, which I have read for the third time now, has been a great help to me, and I'm able to pass some of the sugges-tions along to my elderly public health clients, many of whom need help in decluttering.

Many elderly people are willing

to 'let go' and recycle items if they know these things can serve a worthwhile cause or help someone else. Here are some possibilities for places junk can go. All of these may not apply to every town everywhere, but I'll list them anyway.

1. **Local florist shops** may take plastic pots, glass and ceramic vases, baskets, or anything you have received flowers in. These items must not be cracked or chipped, and preferably washed. Often they will give several free carnations in return for things like this. Ninety percent of my clients have been in and out of hospitals several times and have cupboards half full of vases and baskets, so I really encourage this type of recycling. One woman has no less than one hundred assorted vases and the like in her basement. She's saving them for a rummage sale she'll never have.

2. **Excess dishes**. Many could be given or sold to antique shops—what they don't want can be given to a local thrift shop or the church's annual rummage sale.

3. **Pots and Pans**. Again, to the thrift shop or church rummage sales. Or ask your family members if they can use them now. You never know what people need.

4. **Clothing**. Luckily we have a local state-operated thrift shop, also a state hospital nearby that will take used clothing. One of the local

churches needs used clothing year round for mission quilts.

5. The **books** you keep for show don't impress anyone. They can readily assess your knowledge by talking to you. Give what you don't read to a library book sale (our town has one each spring and fall), to a thrift shop, or to the kids or grandkids.

6. **Bibles and church literature** in excess. Call a local church or two and ask whether or not they want them. Otherwise they can go to the thrift shop or possibly an older child or grandchild.

7. **Furniture**. Ad in paper, free ads in supermarkets or laundromats (or on the bulletin board of a senior apartment building). Or call up the next fundraiser auction that comes along and ask if they will pick it up."

❝ As a starving design student, I know of one more excellent place to reincarnate clutter. **Art schools (and probably elementary, junior high, and high school art departments)** are full of resourceful, but broke people who can actually use many kinds of household junk to make something useful.

For example, 100% silk or any 100% plant fiber can be made into handmade, acid-free paper (like this notepaper) if the school has a paper studio, which could probably also use hoses that are in good condition, five-gallon buckets with covers, the stuffing from older life jackets (which makes great paper—the other sources of the same fiber, abaca, charge a high price for it), embroidery floss, screening, working electrical fans (to dry the paper), etc. They can also use acid-free mat board (archival board), though probably not most kinds of paper that people just have lying around the house. They can use chicken wire for the underlying structure of sculptures, etc. Wood pieces, lumber, sheet metal, and plaster mix can be used in sculpture as well. They may also be able to use tile (for mosaic) and cloth (if there is a fashion department).

Art schools can also use good and SAFE wood shop tools and metal working stuff (welding equipment, safety glasses, gloves, tin snips, etc.) as well as Plexiglas.

Art students spend a lot of time drawing objects, too, so old vases, bottle collections, lamps, etc., might be accepted, though I would call first. Perhaps **an object with sentimental value could be traded for a drawing of it** which would take up less space. I guarantee an art student will take store mannequins, too, if you put up a sign on the school bulletin board.

I think an art school is the perfect… uh… dumping ground for stuff that you were going to use for art or crafts. **All the guilt of never getting around to doing the crafts can be alleviated by giving it to a talented person who will appreciate and use it.**

P.S. Uh oh! Did I just ruin everybody's excuses?"

Don't worry, Ma'am—*real* pack-rats have excuses you've never even imagined!

❝ If you're in one of the arty occupations such as writing or photography, you may be able to solve your clutter problem by donating all your files and drafts to some lucky university.❞

❝ There are plenty of good places besides Goodwill to dispose of things. Such as:

• State hospitals always have people leaving them to go back out on their own. And they need *everything*.

• Art teachers can make good use of the most surprising things. Call the art chairperson in any school district to discuss what you're looking to get rid of, that they might love to have.

• Your state or city art council has a list of local artists. The secretary of the council, or someone there, will know which of those artists are doing 'Found art.' Call and check with them, and those two huge boxes of engine parts or that collection of radish peelers may have a new home.

• Boy Scout and Girl Scout troops. They love to get stuff and can usually use it, no matter how junky it may seem. Old tubing of any kind, for instance, can be cut up and used to make all kinds of things."

❝ *My husband surprised me by not only offering to clean up and reduce **his** stuff, but by offering to drive all our excess items to a variety of recipients such as the local Baptist Church (five large boxes of art supplies for school), a nearby hospital (three large grocery bags of magazines), and my brother Jimmy (hardware, paint and painting equipment, spare parts, roll of wire fence, large tub of nails and lumber left over from* deck building, and some pieces of particle board). I was working and couldn't do it. Today I will assist with the main body (clothes, books, kitchen and dinnerware, glasses and coffee cups, fabrics, picture frames, old pictures, folding beach chairs, extra barbecue and ice chests, ten pairs of shoes, linens, etc., etc.). The majority of these items are in superb condition and will go to 'animal birth control assistance' in San Jose, or to Temple Bethel in Aptos. Both hold rummage sales to raise money for their objectives.

I was very tempted to call Goodwill pickup, but this labor-intensive stage was actually the best part, **as we saw again and again how thrilled the recipients were, with items geared to their specific needs.**"

❝ I recently gave away a station wagon full of clothes and misc to a poor friend (a housing activist with a PhD in Theology!). There was so much stuff that her little boy had to hold the (never used) ice cream maker in his lap. Her roommate told me later that she came home and danced with joy. My friend said that if I had been able to read her mind and heart I could not possibly have done more perfectly. She had to give speeches to civic groups but had very ragged clothing, and she really needed the things I gave her for her house like old extra drinking glasses and odd pots and pans, etc.

It did a lot for me, too. I had no idea how intensely relieved I would be. I felt so free, so incredibly light (what a strange word, but

accurate) when my friend drove off with her big old car packed to the ceiling."

❝ I do have one suggestion about **books**. Yes, I tossed a bag that were worn, torn, and outdated. But our library accepts books. Many (such as paperback novels) are put in circulation until worn out and others are sold in twice-a-year sales to raise funds for such things as good children's books and reference books. I sorted my books and took those that were still current enough and in good enough shape to my local area branch. The paperback selection is always getting use when I'm there and they do wear out. Even so, if just three or four more folks get to pass some pleasant relaxing reading time with a book you've enjoyed, it's worth it. (I really cleaned out—two shopping bags of hardcovers and three of paperbacks.)

If you donate books to the library instead of tossing them, the library can serve all reading tastes and interests at less taxpayer cost, and can sell a few to get a needed item or two as well."

❝ I culled our library (books are my weakness) and brought several bags of books to the used book store, where we get credit for books we want to purchase."

66 While my main outlet for books is an orphanage, your books I consider reference material. I shall 'SAVE-or' them for quite a while.

If you come across anyone with decent children's books or used Don Aslett books, the Tupelo Christian Academy, P.O. Box 167, Tupelo MS 38802 would be pleased to obtain them. Send them to the attention of the librarian, and books or tapes can be sent more cheaply at library rate. Of course new books are always a treat, too."

66 *I am (and have been) giving away National Geographics (believe it or not), Smithsonian, Audubon, etc. I have two bags of magazines and books that I know I will never read again ready to take to the local Veterans Administration medical center. The center said that they would love to have them."*

GIVE IT BACK TO WHERE IT CAME FROM

66 *I took four truckloads of 'stuff' and left them on my ex-husband's doorstep (mildewed eleven-year-old high chair, broken commode seat, broken vacuum cleaners, old baby stuff—our youngest is nine, wedding pictures, etc., etc.). I'll bet he was surprised when he got home. His girl friend told a friend of mine that I was ruining her life—she had to sort through all that and organize a garage sale."*

Now there is real revenge—sending it home to roost!

TRASH IT

66 High-rise buildings with trash chutes are wonderful for dejunking! You get the thrill of hearing that stuff going down the chute and landing in the compactor (and sometimes even shattering!). There's also the advantage of irretrievability; once that stuff gets out of your hand and on down the chute, it's **gone**!

You don't get this advantage living in a house—if stuff goes into a trash can you can still get it back right up till the minute it gets dumped into the truck next Tuesday. (And I've seen people chasing after the truck to get something back.)"

Some of us feel like we've spent our lives at the end of that chute!

(IF ALL ELSE FAILS) BURN IT

66 Having a woodstove has been a great boon to ridding myself of excess paper goods (and also stuff from long ago Creative Writing classes I didn't want anyone to read)."

66 *Where I am employed, they put out a warning to all employees that the next person getting caught filling the twenty-foot dumpsters would be fined **and** fired. GASP! That was me!!!*

So I have reached the point where I can no longer burden the world with my stuff—I have resorted to BURNING—no traces, no remains. We are allowed to burn Tuesdays and Saturdays, and on those two days my neighbors think I am having a ritual in my burn barrel. It is such a good feeling though."

Chapter 6

More Advice On...
(All Those Things You Wanted to Hear More About)

This chapter is devoted to the categories of clutter you wanted to hear more about.

The nature and size of the "entries" here is a direct reflection of your interest in the subject. If it's in here, it's because your letters talked and asked about it. You might call this a little encyclopedia of "Everything you wanted to know more about and weren't afraid to ask."

BOOKS

❝ Please, if you would, more about books and magazines."

❝ Today I boxed up five extra cookie sheets, a drawerful of extra-clever kitchen gizmos, my collection of twenty-three already-read Louis L'Amour books, and about thirty other paperback books. Then on the next shelf up, I saw those two sets of Art History Encyclopedias that a friendly clutter remover gave me ten years ago, covered with ten years worth of dust."

❝ I finally occurred to me that I didn't need my own library of classics. Not a single volume had ever been cracked, and I was just using them for shelf dressing, when you get right down to it."

❝ Just what was filling that giant cardboard barrel in the corner of the garage? Half-read romances, and a variety of coverless and broken-back paperbacks, many of which weren't worth reading the first time around."

It was instilled in us all in childhood, that special reverence for the printed and bound word. And it's nice to know it's still there, even in the days of audio and video. But a book, hardcover or paperback, just another form of packaging—it's still content that counts. Does it delight you, is it useful? If not, get rid of it.

(Intellectual or other pretensions aren't a good enough reason to keep it, either.)

As I've noted elsewhere, more than 50,000 new books are published each year. If you're worried about waste, you probably waste more money throwing away a plastic knife and fork than by getting rid of a worthless book.

66 I have always had a great aversion to tearing books. But there was **one 300-page book that I was saving for a single diagram on a single page.** Needless to say, my stock soon became 299 pages lighter."

66 *I went through four years of college texts, sorted out all the ones I'll never use again, sold them back to the bookstore, and received at least a hundred dollars. For a starving graduate student, this was a good thing!"*

66 **You don't have to choose between keeping a whole book and trashing the memorabilia in it.** I cut pages that I wanted to keep out of my high school yearbooks (are you shocked?), pasted them in my scrapbook, and tossed the rest (50 lbs.). Similarly, I cut the flyleaf page out of gift books I didn't care for and put the inscription in my scrapbook, and gave away the still-good books."

66 **Only keep those books that you may need to refer to, or that you want to read again. Give away the rest."**

66 *My greatest problem all along has been books and magazines. I have hundreds of them, not including all the old National Geographics and Reader's Digests from 1975.*

I no longer save magazines because of a single article. And I don't buy new books except as gifts. If I like a book, I will buy it and read it, but taking extreme care to keep the pages clean and the book in good condition. Then I give it to someone else at Christmas."

66 Yesterday I finished reading your book and began on my bookshelves. First the cookbooks—I weeded out a pancake cookbook (I can't stand pancakes), a dumpling cookbook (don't remember when, where, or why I bought it), and various others. Next were books on fixing computers (wishful thinking when I got those), teaching myself new languages, and books for computers other than the one I own. Next came history books I won't read or ones I have read that weren't very good. Then it was the 1/4 used puzzle books I've had forever. Those I put in a bag to donate to the local hospital. Next were all the German language books I'd purchased to read to keep up on my German! Hah! That was quite a stack. Then came the incomplete set of American history books from Time-Life. I'd had them over ten years. **Moved them four times, but never read them.** Out they went."

MAGAZINES

❝ *Help! The library was dejunking magazines from five years ago and my husband brought them home! Now what?*❞

For a few insights into the time-honored American custom of saving old magazines, let me transport you for a minute here to one of my "clutter consciousness-raising" seminars:

"Did you know, ladies and gentlemen junkers, that if all the *National Geographics* saved were moved to one area of the world, it would tilt the earth out of orbit?

Do you know the real reason doctor bills are so high? It's not the service or the insurance, it's the cost of hauling away all those *National Geographics* that hundreds of patients a week bring to the office!"

By now the entire audience is searching desperately for an excuse to hang onto those fine photos and precious printed masterpieces.

A woman clears her throat so she can speak loudly. "Some day my great-grandkids can look through them for the pictures."

(596 heads nod in relieved approval.)

"Ok gang, I've got a question for you. How many of you notice that as life goes on and you grow older, that you have more time than you've ever had?"

5, 10, 15 seconds of silence follows.

Not one hand goes up. **Not one!** We're all getting busier and busier, in fact after retirement some get so busy they hire help.

"Let's have the real truth, folks. If today, tomorrow, when that nice new *National Geographic* shows up, you have no time to read it, you just store it—**if you didn't have time to deal with it this week, then how much time will you have for it ten years from now? Face it. When you come across it then in a box in the basement, covered with mouse manure and mildew, are you going to be any more likely to open it?**"

Some woman gave me her address to put in this book, as a place to send unwanted *National Geographics*, kind of a one-woman humane shelter. I considered it, but the idea of facing charges of conspiracy to clutter was too much!

This next reader raises an interesting point.

❝ After reading *Clutter's Last Stand*, I parted with **lots** of magazines. Have you ever weighed a year's worth of magazines?

Country Living (12 issues) ---------- 15 lbs.

Colonial Homes (6 issues) ----------- 5 lbs.

Architectural Digest (12 issues) --- 22 lbs.

National Geographic (12 issues) -- 12-14 lbs.

Five Ethan Allen and Pennsylvania House catalogs -------------------- 12 lbs.

My major triumph thus far has been disposing of twenty-four years' worth of *National Geographic.* We had saved them for our son, who wanted them for his children, but when he divorced.... We found a good home for them in the library of a new school and our cabinets were some 300 pounds lighter."

It was reported in *National Geographic* itself once that one fellow has 412,000 of those weighty volumes!

66 *Read a magazine from cover to cover, tearing out things you wish to save as you go along, and then THROW OUT the magazine. (I used to have piles and piles of magazines that I was saving for a rainy day.)"*

Magazines are great for a quick pass—the articles and the advertising are designed that way. But don't forget they can make a quick pile, too, and they're worthless that way.

66 My first project was to get rid of six years (seventy-two issues) of *Changing Times* magazine. I quickly went through them and tore out the few articles I definitely wanted to read. It was really hard not to let myself read 'Latest News from Washington' which was now one to six years old. But I kept telling myself that I would gain nothing by it, and my time was too valuable to waste on outdated junk. We stopped subscribing a year ago because we never had time to read it. It is very helpful when we need it, but **the Public Library carries it too.**"

66 Using what you said in your book I was finally able to persuade my husband to throw out the ten years worth of back issues of *Byte* magazine that he was going to go through 'someday.' He even canceled the subscription when I pointed out he **hadn't taken one out of the wrapper in six months.**"

That's sad, silly, and solved!

66 *The thing I had dreaded most was going through my beloved collection of church magazines (I even saved all the church newsletters). Some of them went back to the 1860s. My husband constantly harassed me about them, and he didn't even know that I was gradually filling in those issues I didn't have.*

But guess what? I've weeded out hundreds of them, keeping mostly only the past few years, because we use them as resources for talks and lessons. I called the Church Historical department in Salt Lake, but they had them all, so I called the St. George library, and learned they have a no-check-outs history room and ***are delighted to be able to fill in some of their gaps. So others can enjoy them and I'll be able to 'visit' them whenever I want.*** *Isn't that great? Thank you for that suggestion.*

I have to admit that when it came right down to it, it was a very wrenching, emotional experience, and I had to compromise a bit by keeping one from each year."

66 I cleaned out the magazine rack. The next time I cleaned it I alphabetized the magazines so that **the old one could be pulled as soon as the current issue arrived.** Gulp—is this really me talking?"

and even the airport shops, once we're on the plane and six miles up and away from most of that stuff, there right in front of us, in the seat-back pouch, a half inch from our nose, is a gorgeous 130-page Airlines World of Gifts. 130 beautiful color pages of stuff, seven or eight examples on a page of "must haves"… like adjustable video game chairs, historical ball park replicas, solar-powered ventilated caps, pet water beds, heated towel racks, the best ever nose hair trimmer, foam phones, automatic paper folders, brass sun dials, water buffalo wallets, and nubuck leather boat shoes. How could life go on without these easy order, easy payment items?

❝ For the past three years I had been saving all the horse journals and sale catalogs I could get my grubby hands on. The stash amounted to three stacks each at least two feet high. I hid these behind an end table in the living room.

Before vacuuming, rearranging the furniture, or shampooing the carpet could be done, these heavy beasts (some over 400 pages) had to be moved. So I spent a couple of weekends searching each journal for valuable articles, vital to my success in the horse business. **I ended up with one file folder of articles, approximately one inch thick.** This excited me so much that I proceeded to clean out the file drawer where all my equestrian tidbits were housed. Approximately one third of the junk was removed."

Giddap and go for it!

CATALOGS

Seems as if we cannot win. If we escape the malls, the outlet stores,

❝ *A few thoughts on **catalogs**, from a woman who threw away another five or six hundred of them this week (wish I was exaggerating, but I'm not).*

*I found myself wondering how I could end up carting out hundreds of pounds of catalogs now again, when I just did a major catalog purge not less than a year ago. (Since the companies want to make their products look as magnificent as possible, most catalogs today are made of heavy coated paper, which weighs tons.) Then I stopped to think that the daily mail never has less than two or three new catalogs, and at some times of the year, such as early fall, it gets up to six to ten or more **a day.** So the mailman carted all those pounds in, and not so gradually!*

The mailorder companies who pioneered and encouraged others to adopt the practice of sending (I kid

you not) four or six or more catalogs a year—not counting special sale issues and flyers—have greatly aggravated this paper management problem. It was bad enough when everyone just sent a 'Spring' and then a 'Fall' catalog. There are now many who have an 'early spring,' before 'spring,' and then an 'early summer,' before the summer issue, an 'early fall' before fall, a special last minute gift-buying issue after the fall and winter ones, a 'snowbreak' issue for that lull in midwinter, etc., etc. This must cost a fortune to do, but must work, or so many of them wouldn't do it. These catalogs all have different, often lovely covers, too—so you feel inse-cure as to whether the one that just arrived might not have a few new items the last one didn't have, so you keep them all. Until you realize your 'Clothes Catalogs' box contains about a dozen 1994 'Lands End' catalogs, whereupon you begin to get a little more heartless. Who cares if the Midsummer edition of the Smith and Hawken garden catalog has a breath-taking photo of scarlet runner beans on the front. It's just a duplicate—out it goes! (Well, the scarlet runner bean issue is prettier than the late spring issue, with a beautiful set of aged garden tools posed against an old shed. Maybe dump late spring in-stead.) **The pretty covers on cata-logs threaten to pose a keeping problem edging up toward the custom of keeping old calendars for the pretty pictures.** The insides of catalogs can be pretty handsome, too, with all that delectable merchan-dise often photographed in beautiful or romantic settings.

After you force yourself to conclude that you are NOT going to devote a large part of your hard-won storage space to a historical museum of mailorder publications 1960-2000, **'disposal by date'** is at least one of the few really easy categories of paper decluttering. You can just go through all the catalogs and dump everything that isn't from the current year, or at least late last year (in case you have a sudden urgent need for some out-of-season item). Some catalogs have gotten crafty enough to leave the year off the cover, but you can usually tell by the copyright date or the 'sale good until' notice inside, or by the layer/stratum of catalogs it was found in."

❝ Re Catalogs: I get loads of them: Lillian Vernon, Smithsonian, Music Stand, Wireless, Signals, Walter Drake, Puzzles, Current, Domestications, etc., ad nauseam. What I did last year around November was to clip out hundreds of pictures from them and make a daily calendar for a little friend of mine, for her Christmas present. I used about 100 sheets of construction paper, cut in fourths. I dated each square with a big thick magic marker and pasted pictures on each day. I also photocopied pictures and captions out of books such as The French Cat, Everything I Needed to Know I Learned from My Cat (my friend loves cats) and ran themes around certain days and holidays, and custom-ized the calendar for the special days in her life (e.g. birthdays).

This did several things: 1) Put those catalogs to use; 2) Used up a lot of construction paper for which I had little other use; 3) Used up a lot of stickers I had sitting around; 4) The child loved it and each day could toss away a page so she could enjoy it for a year and not have clutter left over; 5) Gave me a great idea for her Christmas present this year— THE SAME THING!

(Her family appreciated all the time I put into it, too.)"

NEWSPAPERS

❝ *There I was, stooped over in the storage compartment, scanning an aged, flyspecked, yellowed, waterspotted magazine section, searching for the reason why I saved it.*❞

❝ While plowing through some of my own recently, I got to thinking that when you come across some of these **piles and stacks of newspapers-to-go-through-someday** (such as the last two years or whatever of unread local weeklies), you might be able to bring yourself to toss them by applying something like the following line of thinking: Ok, why do I feel I have to go through them? In the case of the papers just mentioned, because (if you ignore those highly evanescent latest news stories, which some of us can easily do) there might be some nugget of genuinely useful or interesting local information, or an ad or announcement that has a bearing on some real interest or need you have. Yes, it would be nice to pick up these little tidbits, but unless you're unemployed or otherwise have unlimited time at your disposal, the time spent to actually read or even to scan them (so many back issues) would simply not pay off, vs something else you might be doing. Anything of real importance (i.e., the World War that started earlier this week) you will probably learn through others anyway, and many of the little things you might have wanted to pursue, it will be too late to take advantage of. If you wanted to read these things just for the fun of it, you would have done so of your own free will, before now.

'Ought to reads' are a major mental burden of modern times. We ought to at least examine the underlying assumptions here before stashing tons of stuff indefinitely in honor of this 'obligation!'"

Gads, lady, the local paper recycling center just asked for your address!

No doubt about it, those newspapers pile up FAST (much faster than magazines or books)—a new supply arrives every day. Newspaper clutter is the undergrowth of every living room and kudzu vine of every kitchen table and counter. And if you look in the "magazine rack" you know what you'll find in there—it's crammed full of old newspapers, not magazines.

Let's review the possible reasons to save old papers:

• **For an article/coupon/recipe**: Don't save the whole section, clip or tear out what you want and file or circulate it **now**. If you wait, even if you do ever get around to it, you'll have forgotten why you saved this big hunk of paper, anyway.

- **To start fires**: You don't need all that large a supply for this, and if you keep too many it's not only unsightly, but may start fires you didn't intend.

- **To use as mulch**: Ditto, you don't need an endless number for this purpose, and not everyone likes to see "Highlights of This Year's Memorial Day Parade" peeking up from between the petunias, anyway.

- **To add to the compost:** When they're still sodden lumps after three years in the pile, you may be less enthusiastic about this. But if you are going to compost them, put them out on the pile (don't let a new one get started in the corner of the living room).

- **To clean windows with:** A bad idea, no matter what the hint and tipsters say. And all that ink will come off on your hands.

- **To make newspaper logs:** Have you ever done it? Are you actually going to do it any time this decade?

- **To make papier mâché**. If you don't come to your senses before then, you can always get some old papers the neighbors have saved.

- **To put down/spread around** when you're doing something messy. For most jobs of this kind, a dropcloth is better, it won't stick to your feet or let things seep through.

- **To line the bird cage**: The average bird can be thoroughly sanitized with a mere 1/60th of the weekly newspaper inflow.

- And now, the most time-honored excuse: **to catch up on reading them.** Saving a week's, or even a month's worth for this

purpose might be defensible (you might need to check back to find that article or ad everyone is talking about, that you missed).

But beyond a month—pitch! Remember, these things are called NEWSpapers, immediacy is the whole idea. Anything of more lasting importance is better learned from other sources than a necessarily shallow and possibly error-filled newspaper feature.

- Surely we should at least save those lovely color-picture filled **magazine supplements**, many of which are commemorative issues such as "Pope visits New York," or "Happy Birthday, Statue of Liberty."

If you subtract the ads, the entertainment, the stuff of strictly current interest (schedule of every minute of the 1982 Louisville World's Fair) from these, there isn't much left except those pictures, which won't age well in the storage compartment, I assure you.

- **But "I'm going to recycle them."** Well do it! Recycling, an entirely commendable cause, can easily become just one more excuse for clutter. Get those stacks out of the house, tie them up with some of that string I know you have, and get them out to the curb or down to the recycling center.

PAPER CLUTTER

❝ *Do you know of anyone needing invoices from a shop that folded in 1951?"*

❝ *It's amazing how many expired coupons one rubber band can secure."*

❝ **What's under all that paper? A typewriter I can't find and a computer I can't use."**

❝ I'm so sick of LOSING BILLS in the clutter!"

❝ Two years ago we moved from one part of Michigan to another. My husband moved two big boxes of scrap paper with us but he never uses it when he needs scrap paper."

❝ *I need help with paper junk. I have a four-drawer file cabinet which I can't find anything in, and boxes, envelopes, drawers, and so on filled with papers!* **I am always shuffling, moving, and sorting papers, and I end up right where I was.** *I can't get ahead!"*

❝ My file cabinet is 'unorganized' by weight and not by alphabet. The things that weigh more are at the bottom of the box and the lighter stuff at the top."

❝ **Going through some of my old 'to be filed' piles the other day, I realized the faucet wore out before I got the leaflet on it filed."**

❝ *I can't bear to part with coupons—just think of all the money I could save—so I stuff them in an envelope unobtrusively stored in a drawer. Every once in a while I go through the contents of the envelope and throw out the ones that expired. I rarely use any of them, but it's comforting to know I'm not throwing easy money away."*

❝ Help! I am a terrible clutterer! I have paper on the floors of each of my rooms (I have 3 1/2 rooms; one bedroom, a bathroom, and a living room where I don't have any furniture, but papers and boxes containing thousands of papers). From my childhood on up I have had too many papers—and now I have paper of all sorts on my bed, the bed I sleep on, on the bathroom floor, on top of the bathroom sink, and on the bedroom floor—paperwork. I even sleep with paperwork in bunches on my bed."

❝ My Mom had Russian newspapers from **1929** and also Russian calendars for each year except the few that my Dad burned in our kitchen coal stove when Mom went shopping.

In her later years she refused to leave the house for fear he'd burn some more of her 'precious papers.'

And yes, I now have my mom's Russian newspapers in plastic garbage bags in my basement, hoping to get a chance to browse them sometime to see what the news was back then."

❝ *One school our children attended had a contest for bringing Campbell's Soup labels into school (the school got supplies for them). So I began saving Campbell's Soup labels in case our children ever were in a school again having another Campbell Soup label contest. It's been years and no contest, but I keep saving those labels. I've got thousands—Someday?"*

Paper is obviously still one of the biggest clutter cul-de-sacs around. Paper junk has not only multiplied in recent years, it's somehow more demoralizing to deal with, more undermining to the ego, than any other kind. Maybe because the guilt content of paper clutter is so high. Papers record so many things we should have read, should have been aware of, should have attended to, should have done.

A lot of paper clutter, too, is **evidence junk.** Evidence of how much someone cared for us, how clever we were, or how magnificently (we think) we worded or handled something. Evidence junk is always hard to part with.

Paper is also high-density clutter. A single stack just three inches high can easily contain 100 or more different items to be dealt with, and if you multiply that by all the piles and stacks in a cluttered roomful....

My own best advice for shoveling your way out of the paper blizzard can be found: *in Chapter 8 of Clutter's Last Stand, pp. 111-120 of Not for Packrats Only and Chapters 5 and 9 of The Office Clutter Cure.*

Here's some insights and ideas from your fellow rats now.

❝ *Funny how we think we need to keep every piece of paper that enters our premises. It's probably the trickle-down fear theory from the IRS... YOU MUST SAVE YOUR RECORDS OR DIE. Of course,* **we all forget about the part that we only have to save records for five years...."**

Make that seven years, to be safe. If you write checks for everything deductible it cuts the stuff you have to save in half.

❝ Dispose of paper junk immediately, or as soon as possible."

Forget about ASAP when it comes to dejunking. It doesn't work. "Now" is better.

❝ Handle a piece of paper once. If you intend to answer it, answer it. Don't put it in a pile for later."

❝ I have begun to sort the mail into Check, Read, and Get rid of now. If I haven't opened something within one week or picked it up to read it, it goes."

❝ Use the computer to store important information: schedules, appointments, names, books to read, reports due. This saves shuffling though bits and pieces of paper."

❝ *Have a good filing system. Because if you can't find it you might as well not have it."*

❝ I was able to cut down to eight file drawers from twelve after I decided that I did not have to be librarian and researcher for the world. I keep articles and information that are of interest to me, and no longer keep duplicates and triplicates to loan out to people."

❝ *It takes a while to train yourself in this, but put papers that are worth keeping **where they belong right now**, don't just put them down. That's where all those disheartening stacks and mounds come from. With paper, especially, we're all too likely to say: 'I don't have time to put this away properly right now, but at least I'll keep it.'"*

When it comes to files, we have to remember that the passage of time, changes in course, the completion or termination of things, and forty other forces are at work every day in our lives and work, at home, in school, and at the office. This means that that which was saved or stored earlier, even though it was needed, important, or justifiable at the time, may now be mere garbage, taking up room and impeding our use of the information we DO still need.

Purging or cleaning the files is fun, finding all those old reminders. It's like shedding weight or pulling weeds from your garden of living and doing. Plus you do and will find good stuff you'd forgotten that can be repositioned and returned to usefulness.

DO IT!

❝ I personally found that the novelty of having a computer for storage of things like addresses, inventory, and so on, furnished the impetus for pitching out piles of paper records. Just think how much a floppy disk holds. It's easy to retrieve the information on it, and it only takes up a tiny space. Caution! Don't let the disks submerge in your clutter."

❝ A technique that seems to **help with the discouragement aspect** of paper clutter is to go through it all really fast, tossing all that can be tossed immediately and putting the rest into boxes or piles of things that do seem to need some kind of consideration, or at least a closer look. This helps because it immediately reduces the mass that must be 'gone through.' Taking a real look at three or even thirteen boxes of stuff is lot less demoralizing than a whole roomful. The older the paper stash, the better this works. We can see the idiocy of a lot of stashed paper more quickly and clearly when it's five or ten or even just a couple of years old."

❝ *If you like junk mail, you have to pay the price in clutter. But if you are one of the many who think junk mail is an intrusion into your mailbox, contact all of the companies who are deluging you with these items and ask to be removed from their mailing lists. Also ask the companies you do deal with to remove your name from any lists they might sell. This will gradually produce results and reduce your junk mail to a trickle.*"

❝ *Don't throw junk mail out immediately. Throw it in a junk mail box and review this once a year: It will enable you* **to see who is sending you what** *so that you can customize your junk mail reduction letter.*"

❝ *I've started to judge things by the amount of paper junk they generate (**some memberships, etc., are just not worth it**).*"

❝ **Watch those copies!** I know I've come a long way because the old me would've made several copies of this letter 'just in case' this one got lost. The new me feels confident this one will get there just fine."

❝ **Letters** are a problem. Some I still can't part with. I can easily envision my grandchildren reading about my cousin's business trip to Lexington in 1985. But I do have a **good system for business-related correspondence.** Whenever a letter comes in, I assign an arbitrary date after which I think it would not possibly serve any useful purpose. For example, letters saying I was turned down for a job usually get a year (just in case they change their minds about me!). Then I write in big letters across the top: 'Discard on January 1, 1996' or whatever the date is, and shove the offending document in a drawer. It may not seen like an ideal system, but dates roll around pretty quickly, and one fine day in 1996 I'll come across that paper and throw it out without a thought to its contents. Out it goes—**I don't even have to *look* at it.**"

❝ *Re letters, in case you don't know this timesaving trick I want to pass it on.*
*Nothing bugs me more than asking something in a letter and NOT getting an answer—so I'm careful not to be guilty of the same sin. What I do is this: When I get a letter I read the whole thing through first, FAST. Then I read it a second time with a red pen in my hand and **underline everything which requires an answer or comment**. When I've time to*

answer the letter all I have to do is glance at the parts I underlined, instead of having to read the whole thing again."

❝ I finally dejunked our desk drawer at home. I'd kept everything concerning the operation of our household there for several years. It was becoming so crowded with papers, receipts, bank statements, and warranties, that I couldn't find anything when I needed it. Even though I had folders to categorize this material, it was still cluttered. After reading your remark that 'files are one of the greatest repositories of invisible clutter going,' I realized I was hiding a lot of junk in the name of our file.

I really had a heyday with this one—**throwing papers that should have been discarded before they were ever filed**. Now we have a nice, neat, orderly desk drawer in which I can lay my hands quickly on any current information regarding household items."

❝ After I began working full time nearly three years ago, my husband and I had a battle over whose responsibility it was to sort through mail, pay bills, balance the checkbook, file important papers, and in general keep track of the necessities of modern life. While I had been totally willing to shoulder this burden as a housewife, after I started working full time, I didn't feel I could keep up with this **and** the cooking, laundry, housework, children, wood-chopping, gardening, garbage detail, car maintenance, snow shoveling… well, you get the idea. Needless to say, the physical necessities of life are taken care of first and the paper shuffle falls by the wayside.

For my dejunking project, therefore, I wanted to clean out my desk and its sister filing cabinet.

I started with the middle drawer of the cabinet because that was where the pile was most formidable. It was overflowing with last year's receipts and records, saved in the holy name of tax purposes. **I first organized these by category, threw out what I felt I would never need again, and filed the remaining with last year's bank statements in a large shoe box, labeled of course.**

By this time my endeavors had drawn the attentions of my husband, who was curious as to what treasures I was throwing away. He shuffled through the garbage for a few minutes, but eventually conceded that it was trash. He cautiously opened the next drawer and began to pull out things that I didn't know existed. These were all his treasures, of course, even though he prides himself on never accumulating junk. So I cleaned out my desk while he finished the cabinet.

There are some things I will never throw away, no matter how much space they take in my desk. Personal letters are a treasure to me in this time of automation, junk mail, and telephones. My desk is a constant reminder of my obsession to accumulate the handwritten word. I went through each item, often rereading letters and stacking them in the 'to save' pile. The junk mail and misc items that had somehow attached themselves to my mementos were trashed.

I was glad to finish the task. **It was a temptation to merely transfer the piles from cabinet to desk and back again in the guise of dejunking.** But I was glad in the end to have the file all well organized with inviting little labeled folders for insurance policies, receipts, bills, etc. And room on the desk to write a letter!"

There almost seems to be an unspoken feeling about paper clutter that **if you just age it enough**, then it will be "dead" and you can either bury it quietly in a forgotten box somewhere, or actually dispose of it. You can put this technique to conscious use by creating an "emotional withdrawal box" for paper, too. If you can't bring yourself to dispose of the iffy portion of the daily deluge (anything other than the small amount of first-class matter that really does matter) the minute it crosses your threshold, drop it in a "cooldown" container. A month later, when you ream through it, it'll be a lot easier to instantly trash all those junk mail packets and "respond by___" opportunities.

Disgrace by Place, Cont'd: PAPER

Junk likelihood by location, at home (the higher the number, the higher the junk quotient)
1. safe deposit box
2. in car
3. on desk
4. in desk
5. to be filed overflow
6. to be filed
7. in the file
8. top of file cabinet
9. stuck in a book
10. on bookcase
11. in kitchen or other drawer
12. on counter
13. on hall table
14. on or in end table
15. on coffee table
16. in boxes in attic
17. in boxes in cellar

❝ Right now I'm going to throw away the nice cardboard that this last sheet was torn from!"

COMPUTER CLUTTER

❝ *I saw you recently on a local cable TV show, and was quite interested in what you had to say. After reading* Clutter's Last Stand, *I was struck by how appropriate many of your concepts are to my industry... computer systems design.*

Your descriptions of junk in Clutter *have a direct parallel in the computer world,* namely junk data. The industry is constantly looking for 'bigger houses' (higher capacity disk drives) to store more and more **data that is rarely, if ever, used or needed.** Of course, beyond the purchase price, each disk drive must be 'backed up'—**instantly duplicated junk.** In fact, some software companies exist solely to create archival or storage programs that compress the size of this junk data and then more than make up for the size savings with catalogs and indices.

There is, however, an even more pervasive form of junk in the computer world—**poorly designed software.** I recently bought a program to create some presentations. It came in a forty-pound box, had over five hundred pages of manuals, and took me over three hours just to produce some relatively simple text slides. Needless to say, the program went back to the retailer and my slides now go to our art department.

I offer these examples to you to demonstrate that the fundamental principles of simplicity you expound are applicable in a variety of situations. And I believe that **we have an industry that's gradually beginning to suffocate under a terminal case of 'junkitis.'"**

❝ Another general area you might consider is computers and the stuff they generate. I'm not talking about printouts (although those can be cluttering). I'm talking about the miscellaneous backups and effluvia that accumulate. I have some five hundred diskettes of various kinds containing copies of source information. I actually trimmed this down by about one hundred disks not long ago, but I didn't realize how

much clutter and duplication had accumulated in the disk files until I scrutinized them. I also have extensive backups (about another five hundred disks worth) going back some four years now. I haven't sorted and purged them yet, but I'm going to shortly. I'll be keeping some of them, certainly, but **most of the material on them is worth throwing out or duplicated elsewhere.**

I also have lots and lots of miscellaneous bits of computer hardware and software lying around. **My solution to this is to (ta-da!) sell it.** I'll be going to a computer swap meet this weekend and trying to foist the lot off on otherwise unsuspecting patrons.

(Hee hee hee....)"

Computer clutter is going to be the national champion, you just watch! (Body building/exercise equipment will be the runner-up.)

CLOSETS

❝ *I thought I was doing great because I had all my clutter contained in closets. I didn't know how tense it made me.*"

Everything is coming out of the closet these days, except clutter. In an attempt to cure our closet congestion we are writing entire books and creating whole companies and catalogs of ways to pack more in. Forty-nine pair of unworn shoes are running out the door, down the hall, and into the creek but do we get rid of them? Nope, we search out a system, gadget, or organizer so we can hang them up and down the door. Most of us don't clean out our closets until we can see the strain on the hinges.

If you happen to be fighting with your closet contents, I can and will offer you two pointers:

1) Keep little or nothing on the floor.

2) Keep only active, not passive, items in there. Closets aren't idle storage, they're like the knife and fork drawer or the refrigerator—used all the time.

Just these two principles alone will do you more good than any number of closet stretchers.

" The first area I attacked was the master bedroom closet. There I found projects saved from my first year of teaching (twenty-six years ago). They must go. Also discovered there a pair of hand-knitted slippers dating from 1950 and half eaten by the family poodle. What insanity possesses us to save and cherish things like this?"

What's wrong with this picture?

(A walk through the typical handy hall storage closet.)

How many of the following can you find in your closet?

1. Faded curtains from the bedroom that's been redecorated
2. Shorted-out electric blanket
3. Worn out regular blanket
4 & 5. Pair of bedspreads from the bedroom that's been redecorated
6. Crushed rolls of leftover Christmas wrap
7. Halloween door decoration
8. Unruly rolls of Christmas ribbon
9. Empty Valentine candy box
10. Stack of sewing supply boxes
11. Picture frame, bizarre picture
12. Overstuffed bag of outdated mending
13. Abandoned ceramic project
14. Retired potty chair
15. Library book (two years overdue)
16. Nancy Drew novel, college zoology text
17. Missing tape measure
18. Stack of clean bed linen
19. Stack of clean towels
20. Sack of leftover gear from various craft projects (including the missing scissors)
21. 1978 phone book
22. Lace pillowcases and tablecloths
23. Dead flashlight

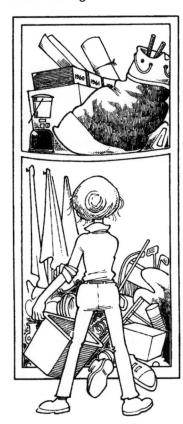

24. Obsolete correspondence
25. Plastic container of sundry worthless collectibles
26. Oily dustcloth
27. Puzzle with half the pieces missing
28. Games (some still functional)
29. Dilapidated box of crayon stubs
30. Assorted Easter baskets and tangle of Easter grass
31. Abused teddy bear
32. Surviving snow boot
33. Never-worn fancy apron
34. Grounded skateboard
35. Tennis racket with a nervous breakdown

❝ I have a closet that I keep all of my children's games, books, and unused clothing (too small, too large, and out of season) in. Together the kids and I and my husband began to dejunk it.

First, out came the games. Games I had as a child, new games, old games, pieces of games. We went through each one and asked:
> —**Are all the pieces here?**
> —**Did we like the game or would we use it? If not could someone else use it?**
> —**Was it in good shape, or could it be fixed (if needed)?**

We cut the number of games we had in half. Then we organized them by size and use and put them back on the lower shelves where the children could get to them easily.

Next, we went through the clothes. We kept only what we would really use and made a pile for a needy family. The family we gave the clothes to has worn them and appreciated them greatly. My girls loved the opportunity to give and to see unused items become useful again.

Last, we organized books. Books with missing pages were thrown away. Those we wouldn't use we gave away. The others we organized for use and better access.

The closet has become a fun and inviting place for my children and of peace of mind for me. My children use the things in the closet more often and are able to return each item to its proper place. What a GREAT feeling!"

❝ Now the plastic turntables in my cupboards actually turn, and you can see that nice shelf paper I put down a few years ago."

❝ *There are now two shelves in my cupboard that are BARE.*"

CLOTHES

❝ My clothes are so tight in the closet I don't need hangers. They're just suspended there by compression."

❝ *Now that the kids are grown and gone, my clothes have extended into their closets, too.*"

❝ I have had hanging in my closet most of the clothes I have ever owned for the past twenty years. My husband has been telling me for a long time I needed to go through and get rid of two-thirds of the clothes jamming up my closet. I have always replied with the statement, 'Things are going to get rough some time, and I'll be glad I have something to wear.' Or I figured I could recycle the material into something for the children to wear when things get really tough.

124

As I read through Chapter 9 of
Clutter's Last Stand, I almost ran to my
closet and couldn't wait to start whittling
down my wardrobe. I had accumulated
quite a collection through the years, and
as I tried some of the dresses on, I had
to chuckle as I realized I hadn't worn
some of them for five years, yet I had to
move them out of the way to get to my
current wardrobe.

You would not believe how nice my
closet looks now! **I can actually pull out
anything I want to wear and be able to
wear it without first having to drag out
the iron and ironing board because
that garment has been jammed in with
my accumulation of clothes from the
past century."**

❝ *I've always had a weakness for
keeping clothes. And I had plenty of
excuses as to why I had to keep
them:*

*…'What if I marry a poor man? I'll
need all the clothes I can get!'*

…'It might come back in style.'

…'What if there's another Depression?'

*…'I may decide to take up camping—these would be great for outdoor
living.'*

*I finally decided that I didn't marry
poor, it won't be back in style for
eons, I'll never like camping, and if
there is another Depression—what
I'm wearing will be the least of my
worries."*

Right on!

❝ Women have a particular problem with clothes. **I had a whole
storage closet full of clothes
one or two sizes too small.** I
thought I'd wear them when I got
thin again. Well, it hasn't happened. And every time I thought of
those clothes, I 'beat myself up'

about gaining weight. Those
clothes, inanimate objects, assaulted my self-esteem! And even if
I did lose weight again, those
clothes would be out of fashion, and
I'd want to reward myself with a
whole new wardrobe anyway."

❝ I began my dejunking with an easy
project—our closet. **I could not believe
what I found lurking in the back**—old
clothes I hadn't seen or used in over
fifteen years. (I know because they were
three sizes too small plus 'slightly' out of
style.) I found shoes—new ones I never
even had on my feet because they hurt!
Boy, were they ugly! Of course when I
bought them years ago they were the IN
thing. I found old suits of my husband's
that he had before we were married.
They would fit him even worse than the
one he wore to my daughter's graduation
a few years ago (the one someone told
him he looked like a stuffed polish
sausage in). I found old Levis he would
not even fit into, much less wear to
grease the car in. I also found old shoes
of his with the heels hanging off or the
insides all curled up."

❝ *I finally dumped those shoes I'd
been saving for when I appeared on
TV or before Congress. And any item
of clothing I didn't like. This left me
with nearly bare closets and drawers. Now I can start fresh. I love
having empty closets. And so much of
that stuff was worn out—now I
realize **I got my use out of it. I
don't have to keep on
owning it.**"*

❝ I was amazed at how small a
wardrobe I had after sorting out
all the no-wears. But it is big
enough. It will be fun to replace
things I wear out with something
I need to take their place."

❝ I finally gave away all my too-small clothes to charity. Good nylon nightgowns, for example, never wear out, but some of us change sizes over twenty years. I gave away several old but in excellent condition nightgowns to Goodwill, and replaced them with three nice new ones in the correct size."

Congratulations on rediscovering that condition called *comfort*!

❝ I am guilty of what *Clutter's Last Stand* talks about as **'Too Nice'** junk. I buy good clothes, then never wear them because they're too nice.

Oh, no! It's much too good to look at!

My biggest problem is the sale put on by our local up-scale men's store in January and February each year. I buy Pendleton shirts for as little as $12.00 apiece—not because I need them, but because they are a good buy and attractive. Living on a ranch as I do, they would be ideal for wear-ing outside to do chores and other work, but to me, they are too nice to get soiled. Consequently, even though my

wife encouraged me to do oth-erwise, I never wore them. I finally realized how ridic-ulous this really is, and de-cided to do something about it.

I went through all of my clothes and assembled those that I **would** utilize in the future. It surprised me what I did have. Of Pendleton shirts alone, I found eight (8) that I had never worn because they were so 'nice and attractive.' I have them hanging in our work clothes closet now, to be worn outside for work."

Wear will always beat stare!

A little success story from a clothes junkee

❝ Into the closet I went—**about a half inch**. The wall of clutter stopped me short. All I needed was a skirt hanger. What I got was a broken toe.

Time to face this. Even a 6' X 10' closet all to oneself is a finite space.

Day 1, the floor

Out went:
- four pair vintage aerobic shoes, shot
- broken lamp from college dorm room, 1970 issue
- full Hefty bag of bent wire hangers
- petrified corsage, Easter 1983
- a putter
- eleven pair of shoes appearing to have been worn to hoe potatoes
- Dick Tracy walkie-talkie with dead batteries
- six plastic dinosaurs
- a pipe cleaner spider (cat toy)
- twenty-seven empty shoe boxes (silverfish heaven)
- a pot of dirt/remains of a deceased fern

- a grocery sack full of shopping bags from vacation sites
- my gym suit circa 1964

Day 2, shelves
- fifteen boxes jewelry came in
- two broken exercise cassettes
- empty champagne bottle from my wedding toast—1983
- three forty-year-old teddy bears (mine)
- a stuffed chicken wearing a red hat
- three pair calf-length (shrunken) sweatpants
- one barn lantern (no idea where it came from)
- nine boxes teaching materials (quit teaching in 1976)
- twenty-two ties from 1982 Dress for Success
- sixty deteriorating, already-read paperbacks
- seven purses, one melted shut
- forty scarves that make me look like I'm a Boy Scout or injured
- 1950s jewelry relatives dumped on me from estates
- huge box glasses/ashtrays swiped in travel

Day 3, rods
- "Robie"—beloved white chenille bathrobe, in tatters
- eight bridesmaid's getups, farewell Bo Peep!
- red sweater emblazoned with black sheep from my Princess Di days
- all the clothing that didn't fit, was hopeless, hideous
- 1969 prom dress
- and a size 14 beaver coat (I wear a 6)—an inheritance also

All the awful stuff I threw in the trash. I sorted the functional items, took them to Goodwill, and said goodbye. What was left in the closet I actually had to wear. It was pathetic.

Examining my options, my clothing was too fragmented, too many colors requiring too much accessorizing, not easy to care for, and complicated. Something had to be done. So… I went shopping (I can hear you groan, but hold on).

[This letter went on here to tell how with the help of a fashion consultant she discovered and enacted the "5/4" plan—for more usable outfits with less clutter.]

Now I had nine pieces of clothing (five tops, four bottoms) that could be made into twenty different outfits—three weeks' worth of clothes, enough to get me through the entire fall/winter.

All nine pieces, seven accessories, shoes fit in one folding garment bag. Travel is lighter, clothes are appropriate.

Your cleaning books led me into the closet, which in turn led me to this new concept which I find invaluable. I am now hiring a contractor to try to figure out what to do with fifty-seven square feet of unused closet space. Who knows where that will lead?"

❝ *I've always had a fascination with clothing and think of it as an investment—much as wealthy people think of stocks and bonds. My first degree was in Fashion Merchandising, so I know a great deal about how clothing is made, how it is marketed, and how to take care of it. Unfortunately, if you were to look in my closet, there might be little evidence of this.*

I had a standard 3' x 8' closet with a shelf above it going wall to wall. I could barely open the doors. My shoes were in a miserable disarray on the floor. Clothing was smashed into the space, resulting in wrinkling problems. There were three wasted feet of space above the shelf area, and purses and sweaters that I tried to stack on the shelf were always toppling over and falling down. The closet was so poorly lighted that it was difficult to find what I needed without the aid of a flashlight. I had tried closet aids such as belt organizers, shoe racks, and telescoping hangers, but nothing seemed to help the situation. Something had to be done.

Because our bedroom was so small and cramped, we ripped out the closets to enlarge the room. We made a walk-in closet in an adjoining room. **I purchased inexpensive particle board storage modules and constructed organizer units similar to those sold by the closet remodeling firms. I painted the modules gloss white, wallpapered the interiors, and stacked them in place, bolting them to the wall studs. I put in an area of double rods to separate blouses and jackets from skirts and slacks.** There are cubicles just for shoes, and drawer units for scarves, belts, socks, and underwear. Sweaters could be stacked in special modules without fear of toppling over. **We even added a small wall-hung ironing board for convenient touch-up pressing. A laundry chute in the closet floor drops to the laundry room underneath.**

Before I put anything into the new closet, I followed your 'Whittle Down Your Wardrobe' advice in Clutter's Last Stand. I saved the things I wear constantly. Then I made two piles: one for repairs and one for charity. Nearly one-third of my wardrobe was disposed of.

It has been a month since the transition, and I have not missed anything I threw out. In fact, **it seems as though I have more clothes than before,** because I can see everything and I can wear items I had forgotten I had. It is easier to mix and match to create new outfits now. I have found that I am **saving time.** Because my clothes are no longer wrinkled from hanging, I spend less time at the ironing board. I also spend less time deciding what to wear each day. I am also taking better care of my clothing investment by storing appropriately.

Decluttering my clothes closet was one of the best things I've ever done for myself!"

DRAWERS

Does any of the following sound familiar?

The Junk Drawer

*Copyright 1991 by Sid Herron,
used by permission.*

I've got a broken pair of pliers and a half
    of a screwdriver in the junk drawer.
I've got an empty tape dispenser and
    some pieces from a blender in the
    junk drawer.
I've got four or five watch bands and a
    lock without a key,
I've got a dozen broken rubber bands
    and five dead batteries,
In the junk drawer.

I've got fifty loose staples and a caster
    for the table in the junk drawer.
I've got some rusty paper clips and a
    vinyl seat repair kit in the junk drawer.
I've got seven losing tickets from last
    month's lottery,
Got a Reader's Digest Sweepstakes
    form from 1963,
In the junk drawer.

I've got a used flea collar and a couple
    Disney Dollars in the junk drawer.
I've got some cards without no aces, I
    got three mismatched shoelaces in
    the junk drawer.
I've got thumbtacks and Phillips screws
    and picture hangers too,
Got Australian bottle openers in the

shape of kangaroos,
In the junk drawer.

Well I got jar lids and dental floss and
  pens that never write,
I got herbal teas and recipes and broken
  flashlights,
I got a package of petunia seeds from
  twenty years ago,
I got an old single earphone from a
  crystal radio…

Got some bolts that I found on the
  floorboard of my car in the junk
  drawer.
Got some widgets and some gadgets—
  no one knows just what they are—in
  the junk drawer.
I've got an old set of car keys from a '59
  Ford,
Got a Chinese finger puzzle I can use if I
  get bored,
In the junk drawer.

I've got some Doublemint wrappers
  someone made into a chain in the
  junk drawer.
I've got two or three lighters that no
  longer make a flame in the junk
  drawer.
I've got a tube of Super Glue that's
  gettin' pretty hard,
How come I didn't keep that Mickey
  Mantle rookie card?
In the junk drawer.

Well I got broken guitar finger picks and
  seven ten-cent stamps,
I got little glass things that came off the
  table lamps,
I got bent knitting needles, and scissors
  that don't cut,
I got three prescription bottles that are
  older than King Tut!
Well the junk drawer keeps growin', it
  gets bigger every day,
But it's full of priceless treasures I could
  never throw away!

May I look in your drawers?

A question I was advised not to ask again on BBC radio in Great Britain. Our drawers may be furnishings, but theirs are undergarments!

Those furniture drawers are pretty private, too, and that's a big plus for all you keepers out there. Here stuff is hidden and yet we still have instant access to it—the best of all possible worlds.

Unfortunately the word "cram" was invented only a few years after drawers were, and the all-too-well-established now tradition of filling drawers with utter junk and clutter is the defeat if not disgrace of a drawer. When there's a live person anywhere around, do you ever see an empty drawer? Never! We toss and pile stuff in, and drawers aren't choosy, they take the bad and the ugly right along with the good.

Yet drawers are one of the real secrets of good organization. They keep stuff handy and help it last and keep our working or "show" surfaces clean and uncluttered. And drawers can even be locked.

Hooray for drawers, you want all you can get. They can outclass and outperform shelves, closets, attics, trunks, and boxes. To work for and with you they only require one discipline: Fill them with active, useful, and in-use stuff—no passive, maybe, or "hope chesty" stuff (that's all clutter).

❝ I had a dresser drawer full of old eyeglasses that dated back to the seventh grade. The reason I kept them so long was because we were quite poor when I was growing up, and since I played basketball all the time I usually broke at least one pair a year. My father told me to save the broken parts in hopes that we could use them as replacements. The only problem was that I usually broke my glasses in the same place each time, and I got different frames each time I got glasses."

Easy clutter to see!

66 After we read your books (my daughter loves them, too) we decided to dejunk the house. It took over a week, but was much more fun than I'd expected. We found a good way to do drawers was to **put a clean old sheet on the floor, empty the drawer's contents onto it, put back the empty drawer, and then decide which things we liked enough to put back in.** We actually created two empty drawers this way (out of fourteen, desk and bureaus combined). I'm so proud of them!"

66 *An idea from my babysitter:* **empty a cluttered drawer into a plastic bag,** *and* **then carry it with you anywhere you may have some idle or waiting or 'fit in' time.** *Then dump it out and work through it, and only take back the best. (Yes, she brings bags like this of her clutter to my house and she and my son sift through it together. I'm sure he helps hasten the demise of many 'Maybe' items.)"*

It will go faster if the bag is transparent!

66 On page 67 of *Clutter's Last Stand* it says 'When you clutter your closets and drawers with things, you're cluttering your feelings and thinking. Freedom in your dwelling allows freedom to dwell in you.'

I need all the freedom I can get, so at this point I had to put the book down and do something. I started in the bathroom. I went through all my drawers and got rid of all kinds of things like old dried-out fingernail polish and little presents from students that I had been saving, with no intention of ever using them. I couldn't believe all the room I had in those drawers afterward!"

66 *I have always made a quarterly habit of dejunking the phone drawer—you know, the one in the kitchen nearest the phone where the phone book and who knows what else resides."*

66 In one drawer at the house, I put everything that I use only rarely in a small plastic grocery bag tied shut. It's still there, but not loose in the drawer where I have to reach around, through, and over it every time I need something from that drawer."

66 I never could find anything in my lingerie drawer. So I made different-sized bags out of fabric remnants—small ones with a zipper, larger ones with a drawstring. All my bras go in a medium bag, panties in a larger bag, slips folded in the largest bag, pantyhose in a medium bag, knee-highs in a small bag. I can find

anything fast, and tell when I am getting low and need to do a wash.

I decided how many nightgowns I would need, how many slips, etc. and weeded them out down to that number. Now when I get a new item, one of the old ones goes to Goodwill."

Now that's what I call sheer discipline!

There weren't as many drawer letters to print as I expected, it seems that somehow drawers are more commented on than written about. Drawers contain a big percentage of junk, in fact the bulk of our hidden junk, and they need to get a star billing on the dejunking project list for at least three good reasons:

1. As the letters we just read alluded, drawers are a prime if not the perfect catalyst for getting into the much-needed business of uncluttering. Drawers divide and break clutter down into little stand-alone sections offering us an assortment of piecemeal projects, easy starting and stopping places. Junk in a drawer is like a piece cut out of a pie, easier to dig into and digest.

2. Drawers offer a personal and private dejunking opportunity. Too often our dejunking enthusiasm is for someone else's junk, or to attack the public clutter (in our own home or the neighbor's). *The junk starting place is our very own drawers*—bedroom dresser, jewel box, tool box, jockey box, any place of containment for which we alone are responsible.

3. Portability—that one writer hit a productive note. You can take

a drawer or its contents with you almost anywhere. (Even fishing or to the ball game.)

JUNK BUNKERS

❝ When I came home yesterday a mailorder catalog had come FULL of what you call 'junk bunkers'—devices to store, hide, camouflage, disguise, beautify, etc., already existing junk. This sort of thing is what many 'organizers' advise using. They are into the business of organizing junk, not getting rid of it. Most of the stuff was outrageously overpriced. Enclosed is a page of such junk that encourages junking. I am proud to say that I refuse to put one of those tall 'storage' things (that come in lucite, brass, etc.) over my toilet for extra storage space. There is something definitely unwholesome about them. I wouldn't even accept one as a gift, much less spend money on it.

Even a junker like me is appalled by this stuff!"

All someone has to do these days is label something "organizational" and it seems to have instant appeal. Way back I remember that my grandmother had one butcher knife and one paring knife. Mother had a couple, my wife three or so. Many folks now who seldom need to cut more than the cellophane off a frozen pizza have at least a baker's dozen. Why? Because they have a lovely hardwood "knife block" with thirteen slots.

Many modern homemakers don't even know what about nine of these knives are even for. Beware of junk bunkers!

❝ I was very aware of junk bunkers from your book, so every time I emptied one I put it in a junk bunker pile. The few times I needed a junk bunker (or a smaller one as I dejunked and rearranged the residue), I picked one from the pile. When I was done, I used the remaining junk bunkers to replace plainer containers already in use (e.g., something has to hold the steel wool pad; a fancy dish replaced the plastic spray can top). The remaining junk bunkers went the way of the junk, easily, because I could now clearly see that I didn't need them.❞

If you'd like to look further into junk bunkers, see p. 72 of <u>Clutter's Last Stand</u> and 171 of <u>Not for Packrats Only</u>.

JUNK ROOM

Have you ever heard of anyone buying, designing, or building themselves a "junk room"? Never! Junk just takes over some room in your home and establishes a beachhead, and resists any efforts at eviction thereafter. In that room somewhere is the duplicate toaster you got for your wedding two divorces ago, right next to the toddler dress you wanted to return (bought for your now thirty-one-year-old daughter). It's scary, when you know in your heart that your

place ought to be listed as a 2 bath, 1 bedroom, 2 junk room home.

❝ You might call mine the case of Creeping Clutter, or the **whole-house junk room.**
First, clutter was stored in the small unused back bedroom. When that filled up, boxes were set by the door, waiting to go into the junk room. More boxes. Soon, the hall became 'one way' because of all the boxes. A box was set against the wall in the master bedroom, and then a box on top of it. Another on top of that. Traffic became 'one way' in the master bedroom. Then the condition spread to the living room and the study. Luckily, there is still room for boxes on the porch, next to the stacks of yellowed newspapers.❞

❝ *My apartment has two bedrooms—one for sleeping, the other for **opening the door, flinging, and then closing the door.** The junk room was heaped to the point that I needed a trail guide to cross the room.*
As I started cleaning and tossing, I felt as though at last I had control over my junk instead of it controlling me. Past conversations came back to me. Whenever the subject of dejunking came up, I would always say 'I have a room that really needs to be dejunked.' Whenever my landlord came I would say 'Don't go in there!' I felt embarrassed about the room.
In the past, I had just stacked the clutter in a neater pile. Now I was conquering it. I felt like a dieter who just lost a hundred pounds as I took out box after box of junk—put it in the burn barrel—and struck three matches to it. I felt cleaner and lighter as I watched the flames leap from the barrel.
When I dropped off the better clothes and books at the thrift store, I

felt as if I had just stepped off scales that registered a weight lower than my goal.

I hate to be nagged. **That room had been nagging me every time I opened the door. I now walk in and hear a welcome.**"

❝ My junk room was filled with paper. Having been in the field of public accounting for three decades, I have been educated, trained, and well practiced in the fine art of being a professional paper accumulator.

Having been hit repeatedly by your well-made points, I developed instant resolve when I read your statement: 'I hit the ground in the morning running and doing, and plan, so I don't get hung up hunting for information, tools, and help.' That seemed such a glorious idea that I immediately resolved to do so tomorrow. I'm rather good at planning, but junk does get in the way.

I started late tonight on my 'junk room,' and **spent only two and a half hours.** Here are the results:

I threw away five large wastebaskets-ful of junk which had been lying around and annoying me for longer than makes any sense. Being curious, I measured my wastebasket and did a few calculations. I threw away 15,394 cubic inches of junk. That translates to almost nine cubic feet or almost one cubic yard.

My 'junk room' can now properly be called a guest room. It was strewn with papers, no room for anything else. They are now all cleared out: many thrown away, and some stacked for future sort-

ing. (No, I did not, could not, and did not expect to do it all in one evening. We are talking about years of accumulation.) Last week I purchased a couch which converts to a bed, and put it in its home, the guest room.

The papers on my bedroom floor have been cleared away, as above, some tossed and some stacked for future sorting.

My office is in my home. The desks are cleared. Everything is cleared. Before retiring I will plan tomorrow. Tomorrow morning I will be in the delightful position of being able to hit the ground running and doing.

When guests and clients come, I will no longer have to keep the door to my 'junk room' closed. **Nor will I have to apologize for its appearance.**"

KIDDIE CLUTTER

Always raises the embarrassing question: Heredity or environment?

❝ My little girl, Alecia, turned one year old yesterday. She's our first baby, and after reading Clutter's Last Stand, I've decided we had better start dejunking her life, or there might not be room for baby #2."

❝ *I was raised by a couple of clutterholics. For years every time my parents came for a visit they would bring a box of junk for me to sort* *through. They saved **all** of our school papers, everything we ever made, even our broken toys—and now we have it all."*

Hopefully you aren't planning to do this favor for your kids!

❝ My son's bedroom is off limits and that knowledge is what gives me hope for the future. The room is so horrible that I do not allow his dog to stay in it long for fear her lungs will disintegrate. I strip the bed once a week after sprinkling holy water on my head. Breathing is a limited activity and I do not put the light on. I cannot afford a maniacal episode. But I sleep well knowing that no evil bacteria can breed in that 'room.'"

I'm glad to hear things are so normal at your house.

❝ I have two boys, ages five and nine, that not only have to be out of the house, but out of town for me to get into their room (the Bermuda Triangle) to get rid of junk.

I learned the hard way a long time ago, to never, ever stick my hands into, behind, or under anything in there. There is always an overabundance of hairy things like abandoned pizza, suckers, cookies, gooey candy, crackers, and chewing gum. Not to mention that half-eaten jar of peanut butter that couldn't be found a couple of weeks before. Did you know that when peanut butter begins to take on a life of its own, it looks a lot like some kind of furry little animal? Boys save a much different type of junk than girls. At least my girls don't save anything that looks like it would bite, spit, crawl, or slither."

❝ *My kitchen cupboard cleaning was so satisfying I went on to the next place that drove me nuts. My eight-year-old's room. She has a room of her own with hand-me-down clothes and toys from two cousins, a sister, and a brother. What a pile of things! We began with her closet. We had a great time sorting what to give to the neighbor girl and what to give to charity. **Her closet has never been easier to find things in and she LIKES it and now puts things away all the time.**"*

❝ I started by going through my kids' toys, and **threw away the broken ones, gave away the unused ones, and stored some in labeled boxes to rotate later.**
When I finished this project, it was so much easier to get the kids to pick up a few rather than a ton! It simplified my daily nagging routine and I felt much

better for yelling less and they felt better for being able to accomplish what I asked them to do!"

I've calculated that our kids have 75% more than they need (and guess who gave it to them?).

❝ My trick for getting my children to unload stuff when their lives begin to get too cluttered is to tell them a sad story about the poor little child who had too little. It works every time, even to the point of them wanting to give away their best."

❝ I was pleasantly surprised to find my daughter was able to rather calmly decide what to keep and what to sell, give away, or junk. **We left it to her** and I guess she had just spent long enough with certain items."

❝ To ease the junk syndrome, there are a few things my family does together.

Firstly, we've tried to get the children to recognize it. We have three (aged 6, 4 1/2, and 3) and they accumulate a whole heap! Periodically we have a **rubbish run** in which anything that qualifies get biffed. The kids get quite ruthless, especially as they earn points towards special things when they have a (fairly) tidy room.

Their school artwork gets clipped into a big bulldog clip and hangs on the wall and at the end of each term we go through it together and keep the best, which goes into a special file. The rest gets trashed."

❝ *My kids each have a toybox for their toys—if the lid doesn't shut, then some toys get moved out."*

❝ *Accomplishments are plentiful in our household, as both my son and daughter are achievers. My sixteen-year-old son has been active in sports since he was eight years old. He has won many trophies, medals, and certificates. My ten-year-old has been active in gymnastics and jazz dance. She has participated in dance competitions in which she has won many awards and trophies.*

*During these wonderful experiences many pictures were taken by a proud mom. I enjoyed it so much that I had two boxes of pictures in my bedroom closet. But who was enjoying them now? No one! So I **bought each child a 100-page album** and we spent a fun night going through the pictures. **Each child took their pictures and put them in their own album.***

They can now relive their accomplishments and enjoy them now and in years to come."

❝ Ever since my daughter was two, I had been saving art papers and school papers she did well on, awards, etc. This stack of papers had been sitting in the pantry for five years, unorganized, growing larger every week. After I read your advice to 'consider a scrapbook,' I faced that pile of papers. I bought a scrapbook and spent one hour a day for the next week weeding and organizing. Now all these things are neatly compiled into a logical sequence, and we can all sit down and enjoy the book. The new papers I save won't be hard to add and I no longer have to face that mess each week when I clean."

❝ Kids' school papers are a toughie to say the least. But I have found that almost every one of the 1.7 million pieces of paper brought home by the average schoolkid falls into one of these five categories: oooh and aaahhh for the moment; prize paper of the day/ week/month; holiday hanger; permanent/memory file; action notice. Here's a bit of further explanation:

Oooh, aaahhh for the moment: Is usually the bulk of the paper flow, all of the dittos, copies, colorings, cutouts, even art items belong here. You look hard at each and every page, of course, but you can't possibly keep every smiley face or dinosaur-sticker-bedecked one of them! So you savor the moment, give all the praise that's due (even some improvement pointers when indicated) and enjoy these. Now no six-year-old wants to see his hard day's work thrown in the garbage, but after you've made a proper fuss over it, that's where this kind of stuff goes! Nope, nope, nope you can't save them all and no they won't be meaningful to your great-grandchildren. Set this pile aside until the child in question's back is turned, then dump it. Wait out that sixty-second attention span and they'll be on to something else. Out of sight, out of mind, he/she will never miss it! But if you have a hovering student or artist, wait to do any disposals until they're in bed. You'll save a lot of tears if you don't sort school stuff right over the trash can.

Prize paper of the day/week/ month: There will float to the top that one special paper or project that your child is most proud of, loves best, worked hardest on, got the five stars or A++ on and this becomes the coveted paper of the day/week/month! This paper is hung in a place of honor (on the front of the fridge, framed in the living room, or on the bulletin board over the bed). The *choicest* of all of this category gets moved later to the permanent file.

Holiday hangers: These are those seasonal/holiday art pieces that arrive home at regular intervals—collages of fall leaves, peanut butter-and-birdseed-in-a-pinecone bird feeders, an assortment of cut and paste jack-o-lanterns, the ever present turkey made from a paper plate, right on through the heartrending Mother's Day soap dish made from a soup can. Expect, count on, and be prepared for them. Hang them up or otherwise display them during the season for which they were made and then dispose of them in one of two ways:

1. Trash
2. Permanent file

Here are some criteria to help

you determine the fate of the holiday hangers. Size, is it too big to save? Will the arms and legs stick out of your file, or your box, or your hope chest? How durable is it? Is it fragile and when all the glitter is gone will you end up with an unidentifiable cotton ball? And if it shatters, will you mind having chunks of it all over your memory bin? Will it draw insects or wee beasties? Choose the sturdiest, cutest, most dear to your (and your child's) heart to put away for posterity. Some smart (or dastardly depending on how you look at it) teachers incorporate a photo of the child in some of these masterpieces, knowing you'll hang on to them for life.

Permanent file: Includes report cards, certificates, awards and ribbons, programs from Christmas pageants and plays, special papers and letters, pressed flowers, name tags from momentous events, as well as other miscellaneous sacred items. Make a file for each member of the family and keep them close to your daily file so it's easy to sort to them. Then on a regular basis you can transfer the filed material to scrapbooks, boxes, trunks, chests, whatever you're using for the permanent archives."

❝ I was relieved to finally realize that a child's worth is not measured by how many greeting cards they have received (and their

mom kept) during his/her lifetime."

❝ *I got rid of a lot of toys, baby clothes, bottles, and baby food. But I just couldn't part with all those* cute baby things *we put so much time and effort into picking out.*"

If you're planning to have more babies, by all means save them. Otherwise see p. 158, Sentimental Clutter.

GROWN KID CLUTTER

❝ *What about all that stuff some of us have from our kids who are now raised and gone? Read us our rights here, Don.*"

❝ *My daughter lives in very small quarters, so guess where her junk lives?*"

❝ Today I thought of my two grown children and wondered how long I needed to store their old treasures and also all of these 'set-asides' that are intended to help them set up housekeeping some day."

❝ Your wonderful *Clutter's Last Stand* has become my bible since my daughter discovered (and talked me into buying) it at a local bookstore. It gets me right where I am and has inspired (in a month's time) two carloads of stuff to Goodwill, one truckload to the Cancer Society Thrift Shop, one-half truckload of 'good stuff' to the consignment store, and countless overfilled trash cans in the alley behind our house! Not to mention the **transference of one truckload of stuff to my son** who lives nearby (he has been married five years and this was the priceless stuff he left behind)."

❝ *I keep anything my kids have ever had that they didn't take with them when they went off to school or got married. Some of these things are real weird, but even if I can't hardly move in the rooms they used to use, I know that someday they may want these things again to show their children.*

So I just go around the things piled in chests of drawers or closets or under beds. So far nothing much has moved out of here. I have one whole wall full of athletic trophies."

THE MOTHER LOAD

It isn't organized yet, the GKLBJA (Grown Kid Left Behind Junk Association), but it will be, just hang on, all of you hundreds of thousands of parents who are housing your children's "I'll come and get it someday" clutter. Parents of old didn't suffer this plague of stuff. Kids today not only have MORE, much more than the kids of old, but are taking longer to "get their lives together"—all while you hold their things together, in storage in **your** already overcrowded space. And you never cease to be the interim storage: during college, Peace Corps service, divorce #1 and #2. And it isn't just a box or two in the back room, it goes from cars on down to clothes that take up entire closets (note plural).

This is the best deal going for clutter custody—while our offspring roam around and collect more, all their earlier collections are stashed here, rent and fee free. And when they visit their stuff or stop by to pick up a trinket or two they get a free bed and meal, too.

Millions of parents are suffering from GKLBJ, are restricted in their plans and activities because of 10-20 year old hoards left behind by 30-40 year old kids. Taking into account all the comments, wishes, frustrations, threats, and prayers over this "squatter storage," I came up with a Grown Kid Clutter code of ethics, see page 138.

JUMBO JUNK

❝ *Dear Don:*

If you can help me get rid of the old junk cars in the driveway, I'll give you my body.

Otherwise I'll give you my husband!"

❝ I'm the owner of a 325 lb. iron-frame roll-a-way bed. The mattress is old and torn and the bed is too heavy to carry up the stairs to use for guests. It's too crummy to give away and too heavy to haul to the dump, but it makes a good bed for

Official Dependent Departure List

1. I your parent will house your clutter through college or until you reach the age of 22, whichever comes first. (We're talking about what you left behind originally, not what you bring home between semesters.)

2. I cannot guarantee their absolute safety, but I agree to take reasonable care of your things and not to snoop through or attempt to dejunk them. And you understand that any complaints about nicks, rust, dust, roof leaks, paint drips, mouse nibbles, or cat scratches on your treasures can easily be resolved by moving them elsewhere.

3. When you find your first place, choose the space wisely, for this is the day your treasures will travel with you.

4. Stuff will be kept beyond point 3 above only in cases of special hardship or important public service, of which the sole judge shall be me. If and only if I have specifically agreed to further storage for such reasons, a small monthly stipend will be appreciated. (1/3 what you'd be paying for public storage will be fine.)

5. In the wake of natural disaster or divorce you can leave short term stuff—prelabeled ready-to-ship boxes, not a mountain of piled and strewn stuff.

6. None of your stuff will take up active space such as closets or shelves, only passive space like crawl spaces, sheds, barns, attics, or basement areas. It is understood that I have the right to relocate things until this requirement is met.

7. If your belongings legally stored under circumstance #4 above happen to fill an entire room or wing of the house, we may discuss adding, for a small additional fee, a sign over the doorway which identifies this as the "_____ Memorial" area.

8. Anything left over six months in violation of any of these terms, I your parent reserve the right to use or sell and keep the proceeds (or pack up and ship to you C.O.D.).

Signed_____ Date_____
Your loving ☐ parent ☐ guardian

the cats (where they can get up and away from the family dogs). So we leave it in a corner of the garage."

I think I'd put it to sleep.

❝ We sold the house next door to us and its three acres to a lovely couple. Unbeknownst to us, he was afflicted severely with junkitis. Being in the grading and excavating business, his vice is old equipment, and boy does he have it! What was once three acres of pretty farm field is now buried under the rusting carcasses of thirty or forty trucks, buses, trailers, bulldozers, loaders, and tractors—not to mention the 'support junk': the hundreds of balding tires, rusting plows, discarded frames, broken compressors, empty drums, etc., etc., etc. Hardly surprising that we discovered they were driven from their last place by angry neighbors anxious to do some dejunking!!!"

❝ *I realize I do have a tendency to pile anything oversize or that I'm not sure what to do with outside. I was at work one day and someone came over to fix something and evidently was at my house an inordinate amount of time. When I asked him what the problem was, his response: 'Well, I had to find the back door.'"*

❝ Our yard was a little untidy, but we knew things were getting bad when people started stopping to ask if we were the place that sells used doors and windows. (There is such a dealer down our way, but we were not it!)

We've been remodeling, so there has been a lot of stuff piled outside, but after the third such caller **we took a look at the outside of our home with new eyes,** and what we saw was not pretty: Parts lying about from the 'shade tree mechanic,' defunct lawn mowers, discarded spouting, extra siding and roofing ('in case we needed a piece later'), empty flower pots everywhere, fence posts leaning up against a tree, a roll of rusted fence, and the pièce de résistance, a junk auto, littered the premises.

We're working on our new image!"

Sheer weight too often seems to answer the question of whether to keep something or not. Look over those big things carefully—don't let the size or spread of something be the keeping factor ("if it's big, it must be valuable, plus it has more possible good parts to salvage… someday"). Things that take more than one person to move are the slowest to move out—big things take longer to die and a bigger disposal effort, so we keep big stuff indefinitely. But big stuff takes up a lot of room, and usually it's in some extra-inconvenient place because there was nowhere else it would fit.

Some of this stuff may be worthwhile, but not for us right now. And remember, one piece of clutter only attracts more. Like one empty pop can on a vacant lot, another will soon follow and then a couple, then a flood, then a trash site. Leave it and you'll have a landfill.

So get some well-muscled helpers and move out that jumbo junk now!

See page 168 of <u>Not for Packrats Only</u> if you need more detailed instruction.

Don't forget, there's plenty of jumbo junk indoors, too. Are any of these lurking in your life?

- excess or unused desks
- furniture full of nothing but clutter (i.e. china or whatnot cabinets)
- unused or not really needed appliances (or "the old one"—you already have a new and better one)
- outgrown kiddie accessories like high chairs, rocking horses, baby beds
  - unused organs or pianos
  - unused beds or dressers
  - big old monster sideboards
  - that antique rocking chair in four pieces
    - extra ironing boards
    - burned out water heaters
- the air conditioner that smoked the last time you used it, nine years ago
  - broken exercise bikes
- ancient, giant 4-H or science fair projects
  - the door that was removed from....

66 Before I read *Not for Packrats Only* I was anguishing over the removal from my basement of a perfectly good 250-gallon oil tank after I switched to gas heat. 'To heck with the building code—I want that tank,' I said, until I saw the nice space that now makes the basement two-thirds empty. And I have a photo that was taken once for inventory/insurance purposes to remind me. *Packrat* made the departure welcome. Good riddance! No one ever goes back to oil anyway. Dust collector only—out it goes!

I also got rid of a refrigerator that worked but we never even plugged it in once in five years."

66 *Your book* Clutter's Last Stand *saved me approximately $2,500.*

I'm writing to thank you and to explain briefly how this came about. When my wife and I finished reading we started dejunking. Of course we did all the easy things first and we pitched, hauled, and yard saled (to the tune of $500) until we had this place shaped up. I even got rid of my 1950's vintage Coke machine. We now have some EMPTY kitchen drawers.

But the shed was my most prized accomplishment. Our yard shed was getting old and needed replacing. I priced nice outdoor buildings to replace it and what I wanted was $2500. But then I remembered your book and said to myself 'Wait. Do I really need the shed?' It contained a rider mower, a hand mower, some garden tools, and JUNK. The mowers and tools fit very nicely in our oversized garage. That left me with a shed full of junk and with more junk leaning up in back of it. When we had our yard sale I offered the shed free to anyone who would take it AND ITS CONTENTS away. I scored almost immediately."

VEHICLE JUNK

66 *No one can ride as a passenger in her car; there's a cubicle for the driver and that's it!"*

66 **When I first dated my husband there was so much junk in his car I had to sit right next to him."**

(**R**omance has been advanced by stranger things.)

An apartment owner sharing his tenant selection process with me once said, "During our meeting and conversation, I always wander from the apartment out to their car. The condition of their car, no matter it's age, is a great indicator of how they will treat my apartment." Likewise, a manager of one of this country's prime and largest corporations told me that after the interview for a job, he always asked to look in the trunk of the interviewee's automobile. That would tell him all the rest he wanted to know.

❝ The chapter in *Clutter's Last Stand* called 'Junk on Wheels' helped me to decide that dejunking my car would be a worthwhile project. My car was a mess. I gave a friend a ride to class the other day and was embarrassed. She sat on the edge of the seat as if something were going to crawl out from underneath it.

I put a **trash can in the garage** by the car, to help keep the clutter from infiltrating. I put a **trash bag in the front seat of the car** to catch the junk before it hit the floor. I placed some **baby wipes in the glove box** to wash sticky hands. I got rid of the serious junk growing under the back seat. Toughest of all I washed the car, inside and out.

My car looks brand new, and this makes me very happy. And I feel more responsible because I'm taking better care of my investment. My friend seems to feel safer and more comfortable, too. This car is now a better reflection of my person."

A̲nd think of the improved gas mileage!

❝ I dejunked my van. I took everything out of it that wasn't necessary: old newspapers and school assignments, bottles, paper cups, out-of-date magazines, gum wrappers, broken crayons, old toothpicks, and a host of other such items.

I was hard to get rid of some things, such as worn-out road maps and partially good flashlight batteries. But I persisted to the point where many marginally needed items were eliminated. **In their place, I put together an emergency travel kit** containing first aid supplies, road flares, a flashlight with new three-year batteries, tire chains, a warm blanket, and several packages of army surplus rations.

These supplies, with the neat orderly interior of my van, should be capable of affording my passengers and myself safe, clutter-free journeys for the next few months (or until the kids mess it up again)."

66 My whole attitude (and personal artifact museum) has changed for the better and continues to improve each day since I read your book. A recent example is the difference in my relationship with my dad. He's in his fifties and moved to Minnesota three years ago and he and I could absolutely not live in a moment's peace. We got a 'divorce,' you might say. I am a Christian and this situation has been heartrending for me (and him).

So about a month ago, after reading the 'Junk on Wheels' chapter of Clutter's Last Stand, I realized that **my mother's '61 Chevy rusting away in the back yard wasn't doing me any good.** My father and I had several feuds over who would get the car when my mother passed away about ten years ago. As always, I had my way; I kept the car. My dad and I tried to correspond regularly, but found ourselves writing mostly about the weather if we even wrote at all. Then in a moment of dejunked sanity, I told him I would give him my mother's car if he would come down here and get it.

Don, honestly, I have been amazed at the change in my dad's writing. He is back to his old loving self. He tells

jokes in his letters. He writes more about interesting things concerning his job and of course, his plans for the car.

Before my revelation, he would write one page, about once a month. Now he's filling three or four pages this size most every week. I love it! I feel like I have a dad again!"

Now there's a sales point for a used car I've never heard before!

GARAGE CLUTTER

66 *You couldn't go into that garage without a hard hat.*"

66 I know a woman who would move in a second if she could ever find a new place. She's looking for a large garage with an attached house.

I know a lot of people are enlarging their garages today. But for a lot of people, I don't think this will work.

I only see one other hope for many families in the country today. They're going to have to move into the garage and use the house for storage."
—John Norberg in the Lafayette *Courier and Journal*

66 After we'd lived here for fifteen years, my wife made the request to be able to put at least one car in the garage."

66 There has NEVER been a car in my parents' garage. They even put a regular door in to replace the garage door but the place is a death trap."

❝ We moved into this house a year and half ago. My husband and I have been married for ten years but we never had a garage before. This house came with one of the biggest ones we had ever seen. It's not only a two-car garage, it's a **two-story** garage. Wouldn't you think that with all that space I would be able to park my little car in it? No way! It sits out in the driveway. Snow and all! I'm the most annoyed with him about it when I'm racing out the door or to work in the morning and I have to stop and take the time to scrape the car windows!!!"

❝ *You should see our garage. First, my husband fills his Explorer with junk—old magazines, newspapers, etc. Then he gets a box and clears out his truck... and guess where the box goes? Into the garage!"*

Gads, that garage!

Only those who have garage impaction need read this!

Garages are ten times more convenient than attics, and offer more stashing options than the rest of the house combined. So this spacious, sturdy-floored area de-signed to hold a vehicle or two is mainly used to keep junk out of the weather. Here you can hang things (on the walls or ceiling), lean them, lay them, box and shelve them, or in some of the most creative place-ment I've ever seen, rafter it. The garage has a nice big front door, too (it's no accident that the entrances to those deluxe jumbo self-storage units look just like garage doors).

The garage is everyone's show-room of intentions, the halfway house of maybes, kind of a clutter convalescence ward. Here all kinds of deceased debris is lying in wake.

Garage clutter is so common and generic that most of us could have our entire garage full of stuff switched with someone else's and it would be weeks before we real-ized the replacement.

Here's a little sample of some of your most commonly reported garage junk:

three milk cartons of unidentified stuck-together chemical pellets
big metal container with the bottom rusted out
old bed frames
old lamps and lampshades
part countertops
pieces of jacks
a camel saddle (from some relative who went to Arabia once)
hardened concrete in a broken bucket
two or three fans in some stage of dismantlement
unrechargeable empty fire extin-guisher
cat-clawed wooden blinds
third-rate fake bouquet
depressing framed pictures
never-used paint edgers
the little cardboard covers to the last forty-nine paintbrushes you bought
dry-rotted sponge brushes
toothless child-sized rake
lawn mower with bent shaft
dented mailbox
stopped-up cans of spray paint
four-foot section of old stovepipe
old furnace blower motor
1922 fertilizer spreader (with iron wheels)
six-foot archery target
incomplete croquet set
dart board so full of holes the bullseye is chewed out
replaced windshield wipers
ruined screens
aluminum lawn chairs that need re-webbing "someday"

spades/shovels with broken handles
1/2 hockey stick
Mexican-blanket-covered canteen with
    missing cap
aged paneling scraps and samples
the rims off the car you traded away in
    '54
the poles to long-gone tents
gunked-up portable barbecues with
    the grill missing
motorless mopeds
unreturned return bottles
disintegrating bags of charcoal
old chipped enamel bedpan
crutches that have been there so long
    the rubber tips and armrests have
    crumbled away
the replaced electric pole you begged
    off the utility workers
the old picture window someone
    remodeled out of their house, which
    is now resting against the back wall
    of your garage
punctured inflatable swimming pool
broken basketball hoop/backboard
battered furniture and burnt-out
    appliances

Garage clutter survives and
thrives because of three undisputed
factors:

1. Room, Room! ROOM! You can
even put BIG STUFF here.

2. Dejunking the garage is
everyone's Next Project.

3. The garage is public domain—
no specific person's, but **everyone's**
territory, and any place with
that questionable
distinction will
always be a transfer

station, the unofficial Lost and
Found department, and a great
place to put To Be Decided and To
Be Fixed stuff, as well as the odd
item we intend to sell.

There it all is, mixed and
unfixed, and as a good friend of
mine with a garage ready to deliver
any minute said:

"I built a shed out back to relieve
my garage, and gradually filled it
up, and now it's full and my garage
is still full."

"What's in there?" I asked. "Two
old soda fountains, some car hop
window trays, a broken deep freeze,
an old cash register, a stack of
storm windows, some construction
stuff, a few engine parts in mason
jars, a trunk, and some old sleds."

Sounds like home, doesn't it?
And recycling has added some
urgency to the situation. Now there
are nine categories of garbage
containers to be accommodated out
there too and gads, that is going to
crowd out those worn-out snow
tires, two of the old stoves, and at
least 37% of that inactive sports
stuff.

Yet degarbaging a garage is a
painless process, actually.

When you do it is your business—it's your garage, and only you know how badly you would like to regain garage function (and your self-respect). Here are the basics:

1. Convert garage content talking time into tossing time. This will go quick and easy. Just load up and haul off the obvious honest-to-goodness junk.

2. Leave nothing on the floor—hang it—shelve it—contain it—but get all that floor space clear. This will keep the floor easy to clean and help motivate you to go on and remove all the rest of the junk.

3. Prepare and seal the concrete floor with a penetrating sealer. You can get sealer at a paint or janitorial-supply store, and the directions are right on the can. Your garage floor will be shiny, protected, beautiful, and a lot easier to clean after that.

4. Brighten things up in there, finish the interior. Paint the walls a nice light color and upgrade the lighting. This will encourage you to keep the garage neat as well as make it safer and easier to see what you're doing in there.

" *People won't believe me when I say it takes me less than fifteen minutes once a month now to clean the garage—and I mean* **clean** *and that includes moving the car. Every tool in there is one we actually use—and garden tools are disposed of each fall if not working right, and replaced come spring. Papers to be recycled are tied up and toted out every other week. Small tools are hung, the hose hung in winter, and stuff banished to the garage stays there only until the next Thursday night, when the trash goes out.*"

Geronimo!

" My garage has always been a source of embarrassment to me. I have insisted that the car fit into the garage, but every other bit of space was filled with leftovers from every room in the house. My husband and I decided that it was time to organize this space in our home.

We began our project with a major cleanout. Several items were trashed or donated to local charity stores. Then the fun began. We **rewired** the garage and added outlets where we felt they were needed, We **insulated** the walls and then used some leftover **sheet rock to cover the walls and ceiling**. We taped and textured the walls also with leftover material. A trip to the local hardware store helped us obtain some excellent grade **paint** for a cheap price because it was 'mistake (mismixed) stock.' We were proud of the fact that our garage was shaping up and our storage pile was shrinking.

Our next project was to put **shelves** in the front of the garage and to hang a **pegboard** on one wall. The shelves hold

paint, lawn chemicals, and everything else that needs a place to rest. The pegboard holds garden tools, other small tools, sports equipment, and everything else that needs a place to hang. We then hung bicycle hooks in the ceiling to store the bikes during the winter.

We aren't finished with this project. We still intend to hang **fluorescent tube lights** and we would like to put doors on the shelves.

This project has been exciting for the entire family. We are all pleased with our accomplishment. Our 'new' garage makes our home seem twice as large. We have received numerous compliments and some of our neighbors have caught the dejunking spirit from us.

My husband is really proud. **The family Thanksgiving is being held at our house this year, and he wanted to hold the dinner in the garage."**

Congratulations. That's talking turkey!

CRAFT/HOBBY CLUTTER

❝ *Ironically, I'm writing this letter at a craft fair, surrounded by guess what?"*

I searched the scriptures for years to find what part of heaven is especially set apart for those of handcraft inclination. They are specially gifted and often required to maintain a fair amount of supplies, equipment, and inventory. Wonderful people, these, and I am sure their contribution to others' happiness through their crafts will earn them forgiveness in this life and the life to come for that incredible assemblage of stuff we might call craft/hobby clutter.

❝ I have about fifteen boxes in the attic that have moved with me, unopened, for years. They include things like a box of fleece (I haven't spun since Kansas City—five moves ago) and rug yarn for hooking projects at least six years old (colors all passé). On my last move I had 1800 lbs. of yarn...."

❝ *Recently a friend at work asked me for a pattern of a lamb made from paper plates. 'Sure,' I said, 'I have a whole folder full of paper plate animals.' I was positive I knew the exact spot I had put it, being the organized person that I am. To my dismay I found clutter. Patterns and art projects I don't use, patterns for November, October, and May in three and four different areas. Needless to say I never found the paper plate patterns. I decided that it was time to clean out my rat nest.*

My first objective was to **set aside time each day to go through one package a day**. *I started with my packet on August and* **sorted out patterns I never use, and gave them to someone who would. And I threw away excess copies of patterns that I use rarely.**

What I originally thought would take a week, took only three days. It's rewarding to finally finish a project I wanted to have done for years, and never started. It's good to know that next time someone asks for a pattern, I'll be able to say 'Sure, I know right where to look.'"

Sounds like Mary had a little clutter, too.

A reader who has obviously coped with more than her share of craft/hobby clutter sent the following in, and I couldn't resist sharing it with you. I wanted to include her address so you could send your protests (and additional nominees) directly to her, but she asked to remain anonymous.

Hobbies Rated by Junk Quotient

❝ Once you're hooked, you're hooked, but you might bear the following in mind before you take on any new hobbies.

The Rating Key here is 1 to 10, along the following lines: 1 = fairly neat and pure, 6 = a major clutter management problem, 8 = dangerously cluttered, 10 = clutter critical mass.

  ceramics—**10**
  collecting (rating depends on WHAT—knickknacks, for example, are **10**, butterflies **6**)
  decoupage—**9**
  fishing—**7**
  gardening—**8**
  gourmet cooking—**9**
  hunting—**7**
  macrame—**7**
  needlework: knitting, crocheting, embroidery, etc.—**5**
  painting, oil or watercolor—**6**

  pets (depends on type and number. Fish, birds, and horses, for example, are **8**, single cat or dog, **5**, multiple cats or dogs, **9**, single small reptile such as turtle, **3**)
  photography—**7**
  playing an instrument—**5**
  reading—**7**
  rock collecting—**9**
  sewing—**9**
  shopping—**11**
  show animals—**7**
  sports (depends on the which sport, and how good you are at it. Trophy status automatically ups the clutter quotient). Overall sports rating—**8**
  taxidermy—**9**
  weaving/basketweaving—**5**
  woodworking—**10**

CRAFT/HOBBY CLUTTER: SHOP

❝ Got to tell you about **tools**. Being an avid do-it-yourselfer and part time Mr. Fix-It, I had every tool imaginable, to repair anything—twice. Double everything. The old adage if one is good, two is better. Thirty-five years of accumulation. Had a hell of a yard sale. Made

enough to purchase my bride a long wanted gold chain, something we felt we could never afford. **1600 pounds of tools and misc exchanged for a six-ounce chain.** Good tradeoff."

Double appreciation is better than double clawhammers any day!

❝ The **shop** is a mess. I am slowly applying the principles of decluttering, but what was easy in the house ('who the heck needs a lemon zester, anyway?') is not so easy 'out there.'

I love tools and I love my shop. I love working with my hands, creating and fixing things, and the satisfaction I get from it. From little bits here and there in your book, I glean that you are a person who understands this phenomenon of tools and a 'shop.' Could you write a book sometime that deals in depth with this subject; maybe a whole book on how to declutter and organize not just a garage but a real shop? Detailed information what to do with what you keep, and logical layouts for efficiency and cleaning ease would be great.

P.S. Have you ever noticed how most woodworking magazines are **full of plans for utter junk?** Why must they encourage people to waste good wood constructing crude wooden candle holders and other yet-to-be-built clutter? As if the world doesn't have enough!"

I'm all for a book on shaping up the shop, and you sound like an excellent candidate to write it—**you** organize those tool and shop people!

Do-It-Yourself Clutter

Much of the clutter we have consists of the tools and equipment to DO something, from wallpaper hanging to car fixing to pressure testing. Just about all of this we could buy or hire done cheaper than we could ever tackle it as a private personal project.

A dentist, for example, stays home to paint a bedroom and it takes him all day. Had he stayed at work he would have made $472— and it would only have cost $140 to have the bedroom painted by a fast and expert pro.

Most of us haven't got around to admitting this yet, that there isn't really time any more in modern life to do many kinds of things that once may have made sense to do. Most people's time is unfortunately now more valuable than the "profit" or "savings" from many activities, unless you're doing them strictly for the fun, experience, or satisfaction of it. I'm talking about

everything from rag rug making to chair caning, window reglazing to walnut shelling. We get all the stuff we need to do these things, and seriously intend to do them, and then wonder why we never get around to it.

This is a tough call, determined solely by what value you place on self-reliance, what you want to use your saved time or money for, and what pleasure you get from the activity in question. I personally am very much a do-it-all-yourself person. I have and use all kinds of tools because I enjoy it and can save money doing it.

But if you really AREN'T going to do it yourself, maybe you should stop stashing the "makings," and give or sell the tools to someone who will.

A relative of the above is what we might call "Alleged or Former Hobby" clutter. Maybe just buying and owning the tools and trappings of something will do, make up for interest and application or even talent we don't have. So we accumulate all the gear and equipment for something it would be neat to do, or nice to be thought of as

doing. But we never do it, or do it for a little while and then drop it.

But we still have all that elaborate fishing, gardening, camping, hiking, rock climbing, or skeet shooting gear, taking up space in behalf of our "image."

As I said, it's a tough call , but you have to take a stand or someday you'll be buried with tools and accessories!

CRAFT/HOBBY CLUTTER: SEWING

❝ *I've been sewing for twenty-four years. My great-grandma started me out when I was eleven and I still love it. I am taking a whole week off to tackle my sewing room, because I know it's the worst, and **I'll suffer the most with it**."*

I know why, from what three excited women told me once at a wedding reception. "We have a fabric pact. We've sworn an oath with each other that if and when one of us dies, the other two (while the family is grieving) will slip in and remove all fabric on the premises, so none will be tossed or disgraced."

"Where will you take it?" I asked them. "Well... to our houses, of course."

❝ If you need additional examples of compulsive saving, I'd be glad to show you my blue jean collection. I started out intending to make a denim quilt. I began collecting at garage sales, auctions in Kansas, farm sales (great overalls!), cut-off legs—it progressed to going to thrift stores regularly to buy blue jeans. Relatives and friends saved for me. Now I have seven trunks full, plastic bags full in the attic, and the storage under the couch is also full. I have not made even one quilt. I am now too busy teaching, etc., to do any sewing. But when the millennium comes I'll have a supply of denim.

P.S. I am giving copies of all your books to my mom and all my sisters."

Did you get their denims yet?

(It's nice to know someone in a position to produce quilts by the acre.)

❝ I cleared out all my sewing fabric leftovers and gave them to the local elementary school for craft projects (except for one piece of wool for one of my daughters to use as a skirt). Then I bought a small bin to store neatly those patterns I plan to reuse and got rid of the rest."

Fabric is one of the most understandable stockpiles around. Fabric can not only be a real do-it-yourself moneysaver, but it stirs memories, feelings, and creativity, and is the source of some of the best gifts

going. I've seen saved fabric worth fifty cents make instant pajamas, doll clothes, Lone Ranger masks, drill team accessories, holiday table linens, skirts, scarfs, and shower gifts that were absolutely stunning—that saved the day and had a big impact on life quality. Fabric is a keeper for sure, **as long as you use it**.

Just two other things to keep in mind here:

1. Keep it dry!
2. Keep it drawered!

CRAFT/HOBBY CLUTTER: COOKBOOKS/RECIPES

❝ One of your books mentioned someone who had 184 cookbooks. I'm acquainted with two middle-aged sisters in the next town who have a collection of over 200. They buy every church cookbook that's published locally or else they get them from relatives for gifts. It's wild."

The record moved to 227 cookbooks not long ago, and then an Illinois woman claimed 243! Sorry about that.

Someone needs to invent, and offer the services of, a cookbook condenser. People could bring all their cookbooks and recipe folders and tear/pull out the few recipes they actually do use, and it will laminate them on the spot.

❝ *For years I have been a recipe collector. When they passed out recipes anywhere, I figured if one photocopy of a recipe was good, two copies were better. I saved all of the recipes and cooking sections from the local papers, too, plus recipes cut from magazines, etc. I had filled two drawers in my kitchen. Most I had never tried.*

What did I do? **I dejunked and discarded all extra copies, all newspaper sections, and all clipped recipes except specific recipes I use.** *Now all my recipes are contained in one small drawer, and that's a pleasant relief. Plus, my recipes are organized so I can find them readily. No more searching through lots of extra papers."*

❝ I went through my recipe card file and my cookbooks and typed out the ones I was interested in keeping and will make them into my own cookbook. I do not need the pictures in the books. I will keep one or two cookbooks that I use a lot but overall I type out what I want from the others and the books get sold."

❝ The need for more space to store placemats and hand towels and the like motivated me to dump a drawer stuffed full of unused recipes. I had accumulated the mass of them over the last twenty years at my present address. **This assortment of high-energy food ideas, however, was not my food choice or need presently, so why surrender space to them?**

I quickly put the drawer on the floor and first thumbed through them, sorting them into food groups. Next, I spent a few minutes reminiscing about the time in my life when I collected these recipes to fill up active teenagers. Then I remembered my desire for towel and placemat space, and again I was back to current events. I quickly dumped all the loose recipes in a garbage bag. I may be a bit of a packrat yet, as I salvaged two small cookbooks that were in the drawer and placed them with another favorite cookbook. Three small books are certainly a more organized way to locate favorite foods."

I'll bet your life is more appetizing now, too.

CRAFT/HOBBY CLUTTER: COLLECTIONS

❝ I am a collector (books, records, magazines, papers, etc.). Both my parents were collectors, so it definitely is in the genes. Sometimes I can't believe I have accumulated all this stuff. It's impossible to clean it anymore, so it's heave-ho for most of it. I need a Don Aslett Dumpster."

If it'll help move out a few hundred thousand tons of junk, I'll come up with one!

Hector the Collector

Hector the Collector
Collected bits of
  string,
Collected dolls
  with broken
  heads,
And rusty bells
  that would
  not ring.
Pieces out of
  picture
  puzzles,
Bent-up nails and ice-cream sticks,
Twists of wire, worn-out tires,
Paper bags and broken bricks.
Old chipped vases, half shoelaces,
Gatlin guns that wouldn't shoot,
Leaky boats that wouldn't float,
And stopped-up horns that wouldn't
  toot.
Butter knives that had no handles,
Copper keys that fit no locks,
Rings that were too small for fingers,
Dried-up leaves and patched-up
  socks.
Worn-out belts that had no buckles,
'Lectric trains that had no tracks,
Airplane models, broken bottles,
Three-legged chairs and cups with
  cracks.
Hector the Collector
Loved these things with all his soul—
Loved them more than shining
  diamonds,
Loved them more than glistenin'
  gold.
When Hector called to all the people,
"Come and share my treasure trunk!"
All the silly sightless people
Came and looked... and called it
  junk!

—Author unknown

❝ My friends get upset with me because I don't collect anything. They don't know what to buy me. The only collection I have these days is three books and two of them are yours.❞

❝ I travel all the time and for some reason, I can't resist bringing home the hotel soap and shampoo. My wife showed me that we now have all the drawers in three bathrooms filled with thousands of perfectly good bars of soap. In spite of that, the reason I couldn't find a pencil to write down your address when they gave it on the radio was that I was at the airport listening on a small portable and my briefcase was too full of soap bars which I hadn't emptied out at home. Do you think soap collecting is compulsive?❞

I don't know about that, but I think you could safely say it's time to stop!

The collector chronicled in the following article, which appeared in my hometown paper, really put his finger on the downside of collecting fever.

❝ OBSESSIVE COLLECTOR GOING COLD TURKEY

After 22 years as an obsessive collector, Peter P. Cecere is putting his Ecuadorian python skin, his Japanese kamikaze waistband, and his antique urinal from Holland—

and much, much more—on the auction block.

Crated and trucked away from his home in suburban Reston, VA, are scores of ceremonial masks and devil dolls from South America. He's blown his last oompah on the old brass tuba from Bohemia. He's bid adios to the Spanish butcher's shop sign, decorated with bull, goat, and ram's heads, 16 meat hooks, and 58 iron flowers with light sockets.

Frankly, he says, it's a huge relief.

'Your collection becomes your wife, your children, your mistress,' he said. 'It owns you and limits your options. In a certain benign way, it enslaves you.'

Cecere estimates that he spent $175,000 compulsively gobbling up folk art, antiques, outrageous gewgaws, and wondrous kitsch during his travels as a Foreign Service officer.

At one point, he was spending $1,400 a month on things like ostrich eggs, walrus tusks, octopus traps, and antique flatirons, tobacco tins, patent medicine bottles, hand-forged tools, and a 19th-century infant potty seat with original leather upholstery.

He couldn't resist those fantastic pinball machine panels, the antique wire 'turkey foot grabbers,' a set of Spanish sheep bells… Ditto for the antique horse hair clipper, the 1928 Buick radiator cap, the table lamp mounted on a Uruguayan

firefighter's helmet, and the tractor tire shoes with the words 'love' and 'peace' inscribed on the soles."
—Robert M. Andrews,
The Associated Press

❝ When I asked some of the neatniks how they do it, they could offer very few suggestions. Except my neighbor Sylvia. She said to **have NO COLLECTIONS of anything.** The end table was for a lamp. Period. And when I thought about it, it made sense. I went home and decided to give up collecting salt and pepper shakers. In the last few days I have been sorting them, keeping only the ones for special occasions like Thanksgiving and Christmas. I even gave up my collection of matches, even if it was an inexpensive way to have a memento. When I think about it, we almost never use salt and especially not pepper, and we don't smoke."

❝ This Christmas I received a beautiful Christmas mug. The very next day I gave away one of my other mugs as a white elephant. Your 'one in, one out' idea is very effective against the growth of collections."

All packrats know you have to be careful about buying or having more than two of anything. Anything from three on up is the start of a collection, and the acquisition rate from there is a geometric if not logarithmic progression.

When you stop getting real pleasure out of a collection, don't hesitate to pass it on—let someone else enjoy it for a while.

Some other good ways to cope with collection anxiety can be found on p. 106 of Not for Packrats Only.

CRAFT/HOBBY CLUTTER: PLANTS

66 Plants—every time I turned around we had a new plant somewhere, started from slips of older plants. Wife called them babies. We started giving them away—ran out of friends real quick. We put a little ad in the paper that said we were moving and plants were free. All gone! It's amazing what people will take if it's free."

66 *Did feel guilty depositing 'Fern' (twenty years together) in Hefty Bag. Now am glad she's gone. House-plants are 1) dirty; 2) leaky; 3) time-eating.*"

And like all clutter, they grow on you!

66 You'll be happy to know that we've even been dejunking the yard. We're leaving flower bushes that don't need constant trimming and eliminating ones that grow more leaves and branches than flowers. We're sticking to self-containing bushes that produce flowers for longer periods of time, like hydrangea, and annuals that don't need coddling, like marigold."

As all good gardeners know, there comes a time to prune the plants!

CRAFT/HOBBY CLUTTER: SPORTS

66 At a garage sale in Vancouver about four years ago, I bought a pair of wooden snowshoes made by native Canadian Indians. I thought they were great and that someday I would use them. Shortly after getting back to Southern California with my prized possession, I went to a closeout sale at a ski-rental store and purchased two more pair of aluminum-framed snowshoes (one pair to have 'just in case' the wooden one broke, and an extra pair for my partner).

Well, needless to say, they all sat in my garage for four years. All the bindings

disintegrated on the aluminum ones, so I gave them away to someone who said they would fix and use them when they moved to Colorado. I'll be selling the Canadian ones at our next garage sale. To be perfectly honest, I never liked winter sports in the first place!"

CRAFT/HOBBY CLUTTER: UNFINISHED PROJECTS

Guilt and "thrift" can really cloud our minds when it comes to this category. We either leave this stuff around forever, or are bound and determined (at least in theory) to go back and finish it. We rarely stop to think in terms of: is it really still worth finishing?

❝ Before long the charity bag was completely filled with clothes that my children had placed in the mending and then **outgrown before I mended them**."

❝ *I do have a concern regarding the construction junk mentioned on page 68 of* Clutter's Last Stand. *How long does this 'positive' mess remain positive' before it becomes just JUNK?"*

As I noted back on that very same page, "**the big question is whether it is active or inactive**." Live projects can be interrupted or set down or aside for a day or week or even more. But once something has been sitting untouched for three months or longer, if you haven't been prevented from proceeding by outside forces beyond your control, it's edging toward limbo, if not already there. For large and really ambitious projects, we might up this cutoff to six months or even a year.

Once the materials for something have started deteriorating, you can be pretty darn sure it's evolved to plain old MESS.

❝ After sorting, the unfinished projects bag will be saved for six months. Anything that is not finished then will be thrown or given away. I tried **to dispose of any unfinished projects that would only be finished junk**."

❝ I gave away to a thrift shop: dress unfinished except for hem. It was the wrong cut for me, anyway. Rather than finish it and wear an unflattering style, felt it was better for someone else. Also tossed the leftover fabric and pattern."

I'd say this woman is on a roll:

❝ *I had literally a whole chest of drawers full of remnants of cloth and yarn. I decided that **I couldn't buy any more until I used up what I had, or gave it away**. I had eight needlework projects unfinished as of last spring. I decided that I couldn't start another until I finished them. I finished five last summer, including a tablecloth I had started to embroider as a teenager!*
Because I finished all the knitting projects, I allowed myself to buy yarn for another project to knit. Not falling off the wagon takes self-discipline and control."

CONTAINER CLUTTER

❝ *I never put things away*
I might need them again
I even have 10 empty bags
In an onion bin."
    —Ginny Kent

❝ Our former neighbor had a drawer full of plastic bottle lids, in case she lost one to a bottle which still had contents."

❝ I have always helped to do the dishes. One day a jam jar appeared in the sink, and I promptly threw it in the trash can.

A few days later it appeared again. After about four more sessions of the same I took the jar right out to the front yard for the trash collectors to pick up. It reappeared in the sink the next day.

Flabbergasted, I asked my wife how the darn thing kept coming back. She said that just before the garbage truck came she took something out and found the jam jar. We still have it."

Hold it! Hold it!

I know that many of you are professional "boxers"—heavyweight, middleweight, or at least lightweight.

I'm not talking about punching and feinting in a ring, of course, but those all too compelling boxes and containers we can't help collecting.

If you're just an average (middleweight) boxer you have 60+ unneeded containers at hand. Heavyweight packrats have over 120. Even you purists have 30+ kicking around somewhere, totally useless, taking up room and causing anxiety. You have them, for sure, by the cupboard and skidful!

Why, we might ask?

Boxes are among the sneakiest and most seductive forms of accumulation... maybe it's all that luscious space we know is inside them. They do project a promise of portability, storage, padding, serving as a ladder or a chair, or even fuel in a pinch. Why during the next depression, you could even live in boxes.

Packaging, believe it or not, even has some pull on the emotions. Boxes and containers are the mother of all that arrives in our modern life—whether it comes from the store, the UPS truck, or the post office, almost everything arrives in a box or package these days. Boxes record the instructions, the "unique features," where the item came from, and often fond memories of the former contents.

And should those former contents be lost, consumed, or compromised there is often a lovely unblemished picture of it in its original glory, right there on the container.

> Manufacturers of new forms of packaging should be required to do a study of the environmental impact of people saving tons of it.

90% of you are hooked on empty container collecting, be it bread bags or cute and clever bottles, and these husks and wrappings hold you more firmly than whatever they held before. I'll bet right now you can find two dozen useless boxes faster and easier than your life insurance policy. There are more memorable excuses for keeping boxes than any other kind of junk around!

Not too many years ago there *were* some boxes out there—real boxes such as dynamite and cheese and cigar boxes, sturdy structures of wood or metal—honestly worthy of saving and reuse. Boxes and containers of all kinds are much flimsier and more ephemeral now, but there are lots more of them, and in a matter of months they can mount up to fill the back room, or even the back forty!

The container population was once kept in check by natural perils and enemies like fire, flood, rodent wreckage, and wear. With the help of Rubbermaid and others it is now entrenching in plastic, which will last forever in even the darkest or dampest basement or attic.

Boxes are lying to you, folks:

Six FALSE Promises of Boxes

1. Boxes might help me organize things/myself.
2. If and when I move, I'll have all the boxes I need.
3. If I need to mail something, I'll have all the boxes I need.
4. If I need to return it (or give it someone else as a gift) I'll still have the original box.
5. Especially those strong old ones will get more valuable with age.
6. People are impressed with my box net worth.

What is the bitter truth about these six statements now?

1: Boxes and containers are more likely to end up just another thing to organize.

2, 3, 4: When you need one, you won't be able to find the one you want, or none will exactly fit your requirements. Or you won't be willing to part with "just the right one," even if you do unearth it. So you'll end up going out and getting another box anyway.

5: Boxes get shabby, beat up, dirty, and dog-eared. They also draw moisture and attract termites and one way or another get to the point where it would be embarrassing to use to them. Or the bottom will fall out after you fill them up.

Boxes are also wonderful apartments for insects (turning quickly into insect ghettos). Other critters are similarly attracted to the housing possibilities of boxes. Unless you're planning to go into mouse or rat farming, don't provide the nest boxes!

6: Right now your neighbors are trying to decide whether to call in the fire inspector or the funny farm.

I can tell you boxers right now, this is one fight that is fixed, you are going to go down for the count someday soon. When they go—all those boxes that aren't boxing anything, those bags that aren't bagging anything, those containers that don't contain anything, those bottles that will never again be filled—so will much of your "space shortage."

You paid nothing for 99.9% of those containers, so keep a few and turn the rest loose—trash them, compost them, or give them to someone who **will** use them. Or use them yourself to haul some clutter out to the dumpster.

Once the boxes go, a lot of fantasy space for more clutter and junk is gone, lowering the yearning as well as the inventory.

SENTIMENTAL CLUTTER

❝ *History begins at home.*❞
—Christian Sanderson, a world-class packrat whose small rented home contained no less than two tons of sentimental debris.

❝ I considered myself pretty dejunked until I read your book. I finally threw away the keys to my parents' house. (They were divorced and sold the house ten years ago.) I'd kept the keys 'just in case they got back together and bought the house back.'❞

❝ I kept my first slice of wedding cake for twenty-eight years. When it turned brown I sprayed it white.❞

Anyone this bad should get married more often, so they can get some fresher cake!

❝ *I saved the wishbone from the turkey at our wedding dinner, now forty-four years ago.*❞

❝ *After thirty years I finally trashed the ribbons from the wedding gifts.*❞

❝ We knew a family who saved 'Grandma's last fruitcake' forever, passing it reverently from freezer to freezer, until someone dropped it and it broke his toe.❞

❝ When my sister-in-law's mother died it took the family (15-20 people) a full week to go through a barn and house and garage to prepare some things that were valuable for an auction, and we kept a bonfire going for **three days straight** behind the house.

Two of the most memorable items we found were:

1) A small jelly jar sealed and labeled 'Sand from my shoes Arizona trip 1951.'

2) A very large box approximately four feet tall and about two feet square filled with souvenir matchbooks.❞

❝ We found some strange stuff when we were dejunking, and the most bizarre was the 100 yellowed wedding napkins and 50 little wedding favors (almonds wrapped in netting). This box was over nine years old, and we found it in the attic. No, we didn't taste the almonds, we just tossed.❞

❝ *Speaking of clutter, back when I was a marriage counselor, I had a couple in my office who were in bad shape. It was the fourth marriage for each of them, and the thing that really got the husband's dander up was his wife's photo albums of her previous husbands, including nude pictures of them! She contended that they were part of her past that she wanted to remember. He insisted that he did not want naked pictures of previous husbands in the house, and besides, if they were so great and their memories so fond, why did she divorce them, anyway?"*

❝ In my dejunking session earlier this year, scanning the piles and stacks and barrels and boxes and trunks still left to do in the moldy silence of Shed #1 alone, I found myself wondering: **why do we feel that this stuff—our main stash, not necessarily the stuff we picked up in the last year or whatever—is owed such care and effort and reverence?** Why do we assume that we must sift with full attention and solemnity through each ancient drawer of furniture that hasn't been used for decades, each box moved from storage area at one address to another and another, before we dare chuck anything, can be released from our 'obligation' to it? It's such a deep sensation I can't help but feel it must be related to the terrifying idea that by throwing anything away here, we are throwing some part of ourselves away.

It is true, that when you are sifting through this stuff, seeing the cocktail napkins you and some past deathless love exchanged phone numbers on, or that faded high school graduation tassel, or some little childhood relic, or the chest of drawers you stained and varnished yourself, however imperfectly, when you were fourteen— you do get a keener evocation, realization of your previous lives and selves than from just thinking back on it. We rarely think back consciously on such things, and many things—at least on the surface—we just plain forget, over time, once enough new layers have been added on top of the old. Going through stuff like this, we get little shock waves of re-remembering and even amazement that this was really us.

Is it all bad to have such back-flashes of memory and insight? What is the answer here—stripping it down, at least, to the core stuff that does keenly (and happily) evoke these former, earlier versions of yourself?"

Don't you dare call sentimental stuff clutter!

Sentiment—the feelings we have about the good and not-so-good things that happen to us—is the underlying force in all our lives. Recording the important happenings over the years in the form of little mementos or souvenirs is like having a three-dimensional diary— the best! Something you can see, feel, smell, or hear beats just reading about something any old day. The fact that you were prompted to **keep** some trace of it in the first place is proof that a thing or event had real meaning for you. Sentiment feeds the soul as surely as supper feeds the body. Pity those without it, or who have failed to store up some sentimental stuff.

But are you actually savoring these savings? When you have to dig for something dear, hunt to hug, rummage for a realization, search for a sensation from your sentimental stuff, then even the choicest keepsake isn't doing you any good. Stashed sentiment is scarcely sentiment at all, it's just deceased debris. Having something just entombed somewhere is like having a bank account you can't withdraw from.

Here lies the problem with sentimental clutter, not in having it, but in **not having it handy to do its job**. You have it for a purpose, remember—it holds treasures of influence and history, triggers deep and important emotion, not only for you but for your family and friends. If you can't find it when you need to feel it, forget it, it's not worthy of its room and board.

Your goal here isn't keeping it all, as most of us are doing. What you want to do is weed it down to what really matters and then work it—make it bless, enrich, warm, and strengthen your life. Engage it, don't enclose it. Possession alone is of no value. Put it in a position to be seen and enjoyed, to cast its spell. Buried sentiments are dead, so dig 'em up and put them on a daily duty roster, or dump them.

Dive into that sentimental stuff today. Some stuff saved for sentiment does lose its allure, so give what isn't still giving away. Divide the doers from the duds and then move those doers to your front line

of living. And you'll live in a more loving, fulfilled way.

> One in the hand is worth twelve in the attic!

In _Not for Packrats Only (pp. 99-100)_ I gave a wide range of suggestions for coping with sentimental clutter constructively. Let's look at some reader solutions to that heart-clutching clutter now.

Weed It Down

❝ My father died a month before I was born, and my mother saved everything of his in a cedar chest. When I was about twenty-five I 'inherited' it. And I kept it around for years. When I finally decided to go through it, I discovered that most of it was, in fact, junk. Now I have thrown a lot of it away. Such as: A collection of about one billion (a conservative estimate) pop bottle caps with inner seals to be saved for some prize, a stack of papers at least a mile high, a single beach sandal, etc. None of which really brought me fond thoughts of my father, which was the alleged reason for keeping those things. **Now I have only a few items of his… but these REALLY make me think of him fondly.**❞

❝ *My husband found four copies of his senior yearbook from high school, and we were able to toss three of them.*❞

❝ *Your suggestion to cut out special messages from cards and letters received was great. I did that and pasted portions of them into a scrapbook, saved a few special cards, and eliminated the huge box of cards and letters I'd been saving since the sixties. I love writing to people (I'm one of the last of the almost extinct species known as pen pals), but I also realized that I didn't have to hoard every letter I receive in return."*

❝ Personal mementoes. That stuff that means something to you alone. It is helpful, when weeding these items out of closets and drawers, to imagine your heirs wading through your shrine/s to who-knows-what after your demise, speculating on your deteriorating mental condition near the end, and then shoveling your all-encompassing collection into a rented dumpster in the course of one afternoon. Save them the trouble."
—Regina W. Merwin
in the *Los Angeles Times*

Let It Go

❝ I've found that **when I try to (and succeed) in holding onto every little knickknack that reminds me of an experience or thought, there is no room for new experiences or thoughts.** Just like you said. It's fun to just let it go and forget about some of the junk I've remembered for its fair share of time."

❝ I'm thirty-one and recently threw away a greeting card for the first time in my life. I was surprised at how lighthearted

that made me feel. By not saving the card for the future so I could reflect on the past, I had a true sense of **living for the moment**."

Keep a Journal Instead

❝ *I have kept every letter and card I ever received since I was six years old, as well as scraps of wrapping paper, and ribbons. The only organized memories I have are my photo albums. I guess I am afraid that if I were to toss any of it, I would throw away the memories too.* **I sure wish I would have kept a journal during those years instead.**"

Save a Picture Instead

❝ Now it wasn't easy to get rid of stuff even though my sense of panic (my husband was transferred and we had to move within a month) compelled me to do it. Especially when it came to my four-year-old son's baby clothes, toddler clothes, outgrown toys, and baby equipment. 'Sentimental value' they screamed to me. I'll be sorry if I don't keep it, I thought. Then it occurred to me—**the objects themselves weren't important. It was the memories they invoked and the warm, sentimental feeling I got whenever I looked at them.**

So I got out my camera and arranged groupings of these objects and outfits on the floor to photograph. After the photos were developed, I realized they gave me the same warm fuzzy feeling that the actual stuff did. Suddenly the stuff became clutter. I bagged it up and gave some to friends with infants and toddlers, and the rest to the Salvation Army.

The photos are in an album measuring about 10" x 12" x 3". The album has many years worth of space left to fill and it takes up very little room on the bookshelf. The nice thing is, when I want a sentimental journey, **I can sit in a chair and travel the years without getting dusty and dirty or pawing through boxes.** I will confess that I kept the little outfit in which my son came home from the hospital. That's it.

The photo taking has worked well with other objects that I kept mainly for sentimental value, too. I have yet to regret getting rid of anything. I don't miss it, and frankly, I don't even remember now more than half of what I threw out or gave away.

No regrets, but a lot of pleasure and joy at being streamlined and free of junk!"

You're hired!

Make a Scrapbook or Memory File

❝ Another 'miracle': I organized a **personal scrapbook** seven inches thick containing printed dance programs and mementos of other things I have taken part in dating back to 1956."

Binding of odd size pieces (local print shops can direct you to a bindery) can be done for a reasonable price and it's even better!

❝ After reading *Clutter's Last Stand* I was motivated to clean up several boxes of 'precious' papers.

I did several things:

a) bought two **inexpensive storage folders**

b) burned (!) all but a select few of my first grader son's first grade and kindergarten papers

c) burned (!) all but a select few of my preschooler's preschool papers

d) put the selected items in the proper folder and PUT THE FOLDERS AWAY

e) burned(!) three empty boxes.

Yes, I finished junking the boxes, and I also go through each day's papers with my children and then immediately burn them. Because I burned those boxes we no longer store school papers. I might keep an occasional paper, but it will be put away in the proper folder.

I feel WONDERFUL and I'm no longer tripping over boxes of paper."

Frame and Hang It

❝ Tip re sentimental stuff: If you want to keep it, hang it on a wall. If you can't hang it on a wall, pitch it! (I spend a lot of money on framing!)"

Get Someone Else to Help

❝ One way to dispose of something of great sentimental value that is otherwise worthless is to **get someone else to do it for you.** I enlisted a friend, who lived several miles away, to put the straw Moses basket my first three babies slept in out with her trash, because I didn't have the heart to do it. (#4 slept in a plastic clothes basket, which reverted to its original purpose and was thrown out with no regrets once it fell apart.)

Stern, no-nonsense, non-junker friends are best for this chore."

SENTIMENTAL CLUTTER: DECEASED PEOPLE'S

We might call this "heaven or hell clutter," and I devoted an entire chapter *(Chapter 16) to it in Not for Packrats Only*.

❝ Please, more about memorabilia and possessions of people who have died that we cared a great deal about. We need more ammo for the fight!! How difficult it is to trash those little things (I'm personally committed to trying not to ever leave this burden behind)."

❝ *We inherited part of an estate which left an entire family divided over the way things were divided up. Some of them still don't speak to one another and EVERY one of the families involved now has a too-full overcluttered home as well as a storage unit rented to contain the runover."*

❝ *Dealing with deceased people's junk? It's a real pain and can take*

*years. I watched my aunt deal with three estates. She **had everything appraised first. She sold the good things she didn't want, kept what she wanted, gave the rest away.** When she brought stuff to us, I couldn't say 'no' but just got rid of it myself. It is really hard to get rid of stuff with sentimental significance, and sometimes someone else needs to do it for you."*

❝ Your book arrived at exactly the right time. I had just returned from clearing up the family home so that my mother could move into sheltered accommodation, and was feeling rather low.

It took over three weeks of solid work to get everything cleared and sorted, and **it made me vow to leave everything easier for my own children when the time comes.** As you say, it all becomes clutter.

We sold everything that could be sold, gave an enormous amount to charity (Cancer Research, bless their hearts, came and collected vansful on a regular basis!). We mopped up provisions, pictures, and odds and ends of sentimental value—very little in terms of what there was, but too much for our space here, alas—but I am working on it. As we loaded up the car, I could hear you saying 'You can take it all with you, but don't....'"

❝ ...my overwhelming emotion at having to help my great-aunt and sister go through my grandmother's house after her death was RAGE! Traumatized by the Depression, I guess, she spent the next fifty years buying duplicate sets of anything that caught her fancy or was on sale. The sheer volume of the stuff she accumulated made you discouraged before you even started, and the fact that I had to leave my husband and kids in the next city, and take a three-month-old baby with me to sort through all this stuff **made me so mad that I know I made some bad decisions about what to keep**. (My mother, her daughter-in-law, warned me that's what I was doing, but I was too put out to listen to her, either.) And I didn't even have the brunt of the job, either. My poor great-aunt had already been sorting through it for months before Grandma died. I did get some furniture that I wanted and lots of the books that were mine as a child. But it was **so** frustrating to try to make a reasonable decision about all these mounds of *things* without having the time to do it properly, that I passed up some things I shouldn't have.

So please keep reminding everyone that their memory can really be tarnished by JUNK."

❝ *Dear Mr. Aslett:*

I just finished your book Not for Packrats Only *and it brought my life as a confirmed packrat to an end. I found it not in a bookstore but in the home of a dear aunt. The aunt lived to the age of seventy and lived in a two-story, twenty-room house with an-other woman. The duty of cleaning out the house after she passed away fell to me. Your book was on top of a pile of old clothes and newspapers that filled the bathtub in the bath-room, and under all this was a small child's coffin. Upon seeing this I ran out of the house. I went back with my dad and he opened the coffin and there in a state of decomposition was the body (or what remained of it) of my aunt's poodle.*

I got through your book in a rather short time (and to think I found it in my aunt's bathroom on top of a pile of

junk!) I like to think that my aunt in all honesty wanted to change as I will now, too.

Thank you for taking the time to write this book and for getting me through a hard time."

❝ *Before I read your book I did keep belongings of dead family members because I felt guilty if I discarded these items. Your book made me see that keeping their memory was all that was needed."*

❝ After loved ones pass away, their belongings must be gone through, sorted, and disposed of. Be practical, and **do this as soon as possible.** Things of real value, such as jewelry, might have to go into the estate, depending on circumstances.

After the heirs have squabbled over the sentimental things, and useful things have gone to the family members who most need or want them, the rest of the clothing, furniture, etc., must be disposed of. Sort it and box it all up, and call a charitable organization, who will likely be delighted to come and haul most of the remaining away. Anything else can be put out with the garbage.

Don't get bogged down in/allow yourself to be disabled by nostalgia—just grit your teeth and move it all out. **Let someone else get the use of it; that's the best way to honor the memory of a loved one."**

What Do I Do with My Child's Things?

❝ This is a problem that faces all bereaved parents. We discuss it from time to time at our [parent support group] meetings.

Some of us keep the child's room just as it was before the death. We don't want anything touched or moved.

Some of us find solace in giving things away to close friends or relatives. Knowing that someone we love is wearing our child's clothes or playing with his or her toys brings us comfort.

Some of us find we can only deal with a few items at a time: clothes, one month; books, another; perhaps toys, a few months later.

Some of us find that as time goes on and we would have gotten rid of the things anyway, it becomes easier. For instance, after awhile we realize that if the child were still alive, he/she would have outgrown the clothes. Then it's easier to give them away. Or he would have graduated from college this year and therefore would no longer use the study desk or the clock radio. We can give these things away in the normal time sequence.

The important thing is not to let others rush us into doing something before we are ready and not to let ourselves feel guilty about the amount of time it takes us to make decisions.

When the time is right and the decision is right for us, we'll know what to do."

Just think of how hard it is to deal with our own junk. No wonder it's even harder to deal with someone else's. And then there's the jealousy and envy aspect of it, when other "heirs" are involved.

Simple math can separate stuff, but no system or authority can handle emotion. One poor old mother in a little Nebraska town left a houseful of stuff behind when she passed on, its total value generously estimated at about $3,000. That was six years ago and the family still meets every summer to fight over it. One brother anxious to make peace offered to pay $5000 cash for it so that he could junk the stuff itself and then all could divide the cash evenly—no one went for it. Emotion!

One of my kids not long ago asked me for something "eventually" (when I die, in other words). It sure triggered a thought as to how older people feel when all the family members start plugging for their inheritance. "I'd sure like this when... a... you... ah... ...don't need it anymore." (They can't quite bring themselves to say "die.") It's kind of like hatching a bunch of baby vultures. And don't count on anyone forgetting anything—the question will be asked thirty times in the next twenty years: "What happened to that _____ Dad had?"

I'm 59, and hope to be good for another 30 years or so, so I sure don't want people speaking for my stuff—I hope to be using it for quite a while yet. It makes you want to see all your equity and holdings reduced to zero the day you die, but no man knoweth the hour.

All of this is incentive if not impetus to deal with your own stuff **now**. While you're alive, so it won't live on to loosen the bond of love between your loved ones.

One thing that will help with the objects you leave behind:

166

Make a "who gets what" list addendum to your will, and keep it current. I keep an envelope in my desk with a list of who gets my personal things like pocket knives, collections, cameras. There's always something new to add here and updating this is great clutter inventory discipline.

GIFTS

❝ *I am still recommending* Clutter's Last Stand *to anyone who will listen to me. Recently, I had a group of women madly grabbing paper and pencil to write down the name of your book. The final convincing remark when recommending your book is 'He tells you how to get rid of gifts and not feel guilty doing it.'"*

❝ *I was finally able to tackle the kitchen cabinets. Practically all the items not in use had been gifts, and they were filling the back of every cupboard."*

Read the above again and let it sink in!

❝ My eleven-year-old son was recently invited to a birthday party. As we walked up and down the aisles of K Mart trying to find a gift, I found myself becoming impatient and saying 'Hurry up and decide—you have to take something to the party.' No sooner had I spoken the words when I remembered reading them the day before. Yes, those exact words were on page 13 of *Clutter's Last Stand*—another excuse for obtaining more junk.

Suddenly an idea came to mind. I suggested to Cameron that **instead of buying a toy that would soon become part of his friend's junk, we could take his friend on an activity.** Cameron thought that might be fun. So on the day of the party he took his friend a coupon 'Good for swimming and picnicking at Green Canyon.' Cameron came home from the party very excited because everyone had liked the gift he took.

I was able to take Cameron and his friend to Green Canyon two days later, and they had a fun afternoon. And Mark's mother commented on how nice it was to have a gift that didn't add to the clutter in their home."

❝ You must be a real gentleman. I'm almost through reading *Clutter's Last Stand* and I have yet to find mention of 'Gifts from people who don't like you particularly, gifts which you detest on sight.' I salute the loving kindness which presupposes all gifts are given in affection.

Anyhow, after forty years of running across gifts I hated but couldn't throw away, and of feeling a pang of annoyance each time, I finally found a solution. In the window of my apartment is **a sill six feet long and about seven inches wide, perfect for displaying all the garbage I haven't yet had the courage to throw away.** There's a pedestal dish, handpainted by a brother-in-law, that's too small to hold anything but decorative soap (which I won't have in the house), and a soup mug with 8 'MOTHER'S,' 6 'MA'S, AND 5 'MOM'S' printed in black on a hideous grey. Three chipped miniature houses (a Wells Fargo station bank and two Indonesian houses on stilts). A drinking glass with a barn on it (I'm sure my friend wasn't wearing her glasses when she bought it) and a mug with blue roses and ribbons on it for which there is no room in my cupboard since I already have four mugs with little houses on them.

Ugliest of all is a birdhouse planter, carefully modelled in clay by a dear friend. The roof looks like a pancake and sits on the house so precariously I'm afraid to touch it.

You won't believe what a comfort it is to have all this stuff away from the things I cherish. I look at it and giggle.

Someday I'll be ready, I know, to toss it out, along with the birdhouses, lighthouses, barns, schoolhouses, outhouses, and doghouses that don't belong in my collection anymore."

❝ *One particularly burdensome gift which has often come my way is the unmounted, unframed picture. In the old days, I felt obliged to spend vast sums framing and mounting the various offerings which artistic relatives passed my way—not to mention those old pictures with tatty frames and moldy mounts!* **Not any more do I spend on such things!**

For one silver wedding my mother-in-law gave us a family mirror which would have cost a fortune to repair if my father had not been a glass craftsman and agreed to do it for us! I tried to tactfully refuse this present, but was overruled!

I do feel strongly that gifts should be given to please the recipient, not the giver, or have I got it wrong?"

Presents bought to delight **us**, rather than the person we're giving them to, are undoubtedly one big reason the junk quotient of gifts is so high. Try focussing relentlessly on the giftee next time, even if it means giving that "cold, impersonal" gift of cash—it's less likely to result in something that molders in the storage bin.

❝ When someone offers me something, and I am not sure I want to keep it, I ask, **'Do you mind if I give it to Goodwill when I don't want it anymore?'** If they reply 'That's fine with me' I'll take it. But if they say 'Yes, I mind' then I don't take it because I don't want to be burdened with a lot of stuff that I have to keep for someone else. When people give me things, I want no strings attached."

You have real guts, Ma'am—good!

66 When you start to feel guilty about not using and/or throwing out a gift, **ask yourself what were the last five gifts you gave to that person?** If you can't remember, then it is ok to throw out without guilt."

66 *At least a quarter of our cluttered storeroom is taken up with all those great hand-me-downs from my mother-in-law: including a foot bather and three facial saunas (I gave these away to three friends who had sinus headaches)."*

66 **Your book has taken away a lot of guilt about dejunking. After all, I inherited those fancy un-used glasses from my mother-in-law** *because she dejunked by giving them to me."*

I'll bet 60% of hand-me-downs are junk, at least to the first people they're handed down to.

66 Your books have helped relieve me of the guilt that always made me afraid to get rid of something that was given me. **I take a photo of it** and then donate it to our church yard sale. I also try to be more careful about what I give."

Who could help noticing how often the word "guilt" comes up in relation to gifts? "Guilt gifts" will be a major junk category of the future. All of us today are trying to motivate and reward our children (and other relatives and friends) now with gifts to cover or compensate for any nurturing lacks. "I'm not home enough with the kids/don't keep in touch with my sister as I should, so I'll make up for my nonpresence with some presents."

66 What I have found most helpful is my **new attitude toward buying;** for myself and for others. When I buy for myself now, I ask myself a series of questions. It helps prevent impulse buys. For others, I buy practical items only. If they have requested an item, I get that specific item (trying hard to get the brand/color/type they want). If not, I buy or make food or drinks in disposable containers."

66 *Tumblers (glasses) make ideal gifts. They tumble and within six months all are broken and disposed of."*

I'll drink to that!

66 As far as gifts are concerned, I tell my grown children that cards or letters with personal messages are the best gifts they can give me (and truly, they have been). Having been a massage therapist for twenty years, I like to give friends or family members a massage for their birthdays—they usually say it's the best gift they've ever received. As a gift to my mother, my partner and I have helped her unclutter her closets and drawers because she said she couldn't do it herself. So was so appreciative and couldn't thank us enough. It felt great to us, too, to have been able to help her."

❝ *On the subject of gifts: for the past several years we have given the older members of our family **gifts for others**. The Salvation Army had a Christmas tree at one of the shopping centers with 'want' and 'need' cards on it. We took several of these, filled the needs, and then sent a card to my parents detailing what had been given in their name.*

When my brother lived in the mountains of Colorado, there was a devastating forest fire in his residential area. His house was saved, but many others were lost. He talked so much about all the help the Red Cross had given that we made his Christmas gift that year a contribution to his local chapter. He was so impressed that he matched it, thus doubling the benefit, and creating no clutter for anyone!

We had an exceedingly cold winter here two years ago, and the Salvation Army was begging for blankets, so a new blanket became my gift for a friend on the east coast. She teaches in college and one of her students had been homeless for a year or two, so although I was not aware of it at the time, the gift took on a special meaning for her.

Another much appreciated gift was a box of children's coloring and activity books for an 'abused adults' center. Contributions to public television and adopting an animal at the zoo are nice ideas, too."

❝ The real test came this Christmas when we decided not to exchange presents. My mom and I ventured out to a Christmas tree farm to cut down our own tree. We had a very special day putting up the tree and decorating it with old-fashioned ornaments. It was a pioneer Christmas.

Christmas afternoon we went to my sister's house. No presents to load in the car, just ourselves. We had a delicious dinner and spent the rest of the day talking and laughing. The real thing I discovered about Christmas, Don, is that people need not necessarily Santa Claus, but an event to bring them back to their childhood. Not gifts. When people asked me what I got for Christmas, I just said 'a lot of nice things.'"

DECLUTTERING OTHERS

❝ Mine is no doubt a common story for you, but I wanted you to know that you have probably prevented a divorce—perhaps even a murder. It's likely the latter, though I can't tell you which of us would have been the victim. I have a sneaking hunch it would have been my husband."

❝ *Since our seven children have married and left our home, my husband has taken over two bedrooms, in addition to his own room built originally for his model airplanes. He also has drawers in the other two bedrooms, plus the overflowing papers and magazines he keeps in our bedroom."*

❝ My mother, a real packrat, had storm damage at her house. Workers everywhere, a big mess. 90% of the soggy stuff was junk—a perfect chance to unload! NOPE—so now wrinkly magazines, etc., are sitting around everywhere. This is depressing as I am the only soul in line to inherit this stuff. I offered to help clean out. I got adamant refusals to toss even **one** dead book entitled *Travel South: 1963.* Surely this is useless!"

(**I** guess you'll have to hope that you go before she does!)

❝ Last month, I filled the nineteenth eighteen-cubic-yard dumpster from my father's accumulations. (19 X 18 = 342 cubic yards of clutter.) He was raised in near poverty and couldn't bear to throw things away if they could possibly be repaired, but he rarely took the time to repair something unless it was already in use. He would not even throw away broken bricks from the 1989 earthquake. I estimate the weight of his accumulations at **twenty tons.** Eat your heart out, Christian Sanderson!"

❝ *When I was growing up I was always embarrassed to have friends over to play, because our house was a disaster. Recently my mother purchased your books and it is now a pleasure to go home and visit a dejunked house and not have to worry about what my children are going to find!*

Now if only my mother-in-law would read Clutter's Last Stand. *She has a two-story home, and there is a door and a staircase, but you can't get up the stairs because of the junk. My husband knew she had candy bars stashed in there somewhere, and he proceeded to find them. They were no longer there, just a bag of weevils and crumbs. She also has six cabins (which used to be a bed and breakfast) full of junk. None of the doors can be opened, because of her 'collections.' I would say this lady has a problem, wouldn't you?"*

Any of you who felt a ripple of envy when you read "six cabins" has an equal problem!

❝ After I read *Clutter's Last Stand*, I knew it was all right to throw away what I didn't need or want. I figured if I could throw out the box my Mom kept her teeth in before she died, anybody else living in the same house with me could get rid of some of the junk that was almost to the point of taking over. Well, getting my family to throw away any kind of junk would almost take an act of Congress!

I sent my two daughters, ages twelve and fifteen, to clean out their closet. They came out of their bedroom almost two hours later with less than a grocery bag full, saying 'It's all the closet would let us have.' I'm thinking 'Well, ok, another possessed closet. No big deal.' I go to do the job myself, armed, of course, with my usual garlic necklace and silver cross. By the time I'm through, the closet has been dejunked and de-spirited. To keep it that way, however, I'd have to padlock the thing.

I have an 86-year-old grandmother who lives with us. I honestly believe she is a packrat in a little old lady's body. This woman saves everything, even her used napkins from fast food restaurants. She says she might need to use them for something later, and she does. She stuffs them into all those old pork and bean cans she is well known for scavenging from the garbage to spit that nasty snuff of hers into. At her age, nobody around here has the guts to tell her that she can't do exactly what she wants to do.

She has her own mini-landfill that she calls her bedroom. When she passes away I'm not real sure how to begin to clean that room, but I believe the best way would be to just back a two-ton truck up to the window and use a shovel. Right now nobody is allowed into her domain (which she protects like a she-wolf). If we were to intrude on or touch any of her stuff, she would kill us in our sleep. So for the time being, we wait, hoping there's nothing hairy, ugly, and mean growing in there.

Husbands are in a class all by themselves. Actually, I think it must be men in general. Of course they never save junk—it's always priceless goods. Well, color me stupid, but why would anyone with an ounce of common sense want to save the kind of stuff I found in my husband's closet and in the attic? I mean, don't he realize that a 25-pound workout weight ain't no good any more if at least 22 pounds of its guts are scattered all over the bottom of the closet? And even if it could be patched up, didn't I see the bar it goes on hanging across 2 x 4s in the attic with god only knows what hanging over it?

On second glance, I believe I recognized the mud flaps that came off his dad's old 1958 Mercury hanging up there. Now you tell me, what possible use could he have in mind for those relics? Maybe he's gonna' melt down that 5,000 miles of copper tubing and wiring that he's been saving since birth, and dip those flaps and all the rest of his precious goodies in it. That way when he starts feeling bored, he can go dust his new copper toys (instead of helping me throw all the mess away like he should have from the start).

I truly believe I have enough trouble trying to keep my own household junk from rising up and taking over. So I really don't need anybody else contributing anything.

I know for a fact that sanitation workers keep a big box on the back of the garbage truck, specifically for the purpose of stuffing all those goodies they come across into. That's one of the hazards of being the wife of a sanitation worker. They get all the junk from about every other house in the city. The wife can't throw it back into the garbage can, because her husband will only find it there later that very day and haul it right back. What to do? You make that man understand that his home is not the city dump, no matter what his coworkers believe, or have brainwashed him into thinking. Either he stops bringing home everybody and their brother's junk, or somebody from the morgue will be digging out, sorting, and matching back together the body parts of what once belonged to him, a man who refused to listen to the common sense warning you gave him. This usually works, but if it don't, well after they let you out of prison, marry a professional house cleaner instead of just another garbage collector."

Yes, that letter is printed just as it came in!

" A big part of my clutter problem is my husband. He works at a grocery store. If spaghetti goes on

sale he'll buy a whole case even though we don't have room for it. If something gets discontinued and marked down, he'll bring it home, even if I don't need or want it. I really get annoyed. He writes phone numbers and other information on thousands of pieces of paper and leaves them on the dresser. He gets mad when I try to organize his clutter, but if I throw it away while he's at work he doesn't even miss it."

❝ *My father and I are at our wits' end over my mother. My parents moved from a suburb of a large city up to a small town to retire. It was my grandmother's house, and my mom deposited some of the furniture at the house, but she took just about everything else with her in the move. Since they are retired, the only entertainment in a town of 1600 is the Friday night football game and garage sailing on weekends.*

As a result, my mom has got piles of stuff all over her house with paths between it. Some of it is old and some of it is new garage sale acquisitions. It got so bad that I can't go visit my parents on weekends because of the dust. I have sinus and allergy problems and an electrostatic air filter in my house, and if I go see them, I come home and get bronchitis and a sinus infection and it costs $150 in doctor visits and antibiotics to get over it.

Mother says she keeps sorting out, but Father says she never throws anything away. She is seventy-one and doesn't want to do anything except eat, sleep, and watch TV. Her mantra is 'someday I'll use it' but she never finishes anything. She has enough patterns and piece goods to

start a fabric store! In fact, she's gotten so possessive and childish that if I tell her I want to use some of her stuff, she won't let me and wants me to pay her original retail for it. When I was younger, if I borrowed her stuff and used it, she didn't mind. It breaks my heart to see lots of nice stuff entombed in a plastic sack, never to see the light of day again.

If we throw out things like old magazines or cooking sections from the paper she panics, gets hostile, and tells me to 'shut my mouth,' and takes tranquilizers to cope and turns into a zombie. Apparently all her junk acts as a security blanket. Maybe it's from being a Depression child.
Help! Aaaagghh!!!!"

This represents at least 100,000 unwritten letters, from people faced with similar problems.

❝ We cannot comfortably go visit my mother with our kids for fear they'll ruin some of her things, besides the fact that there is no room to play.

We are a family of nine kids and eight of the nine of us live out of town and she and Dad have come into the habit of rotating weekends at each of our houses in what I believe is an effort to keep us from seeing her house and/or escaping from her house herself.

At Christmas, two of my brothers announced they weren't coming to Mom's house for the holiday until she got rid of some junk because there simply wasn't enough room for everyone to sit. Her solution was to rent a hall for Christmas. I was very disappointed when I heard this, but through some costly phone calls and some effort on Mom's part we did have a (cramped) Christmas at home. It was not enjoyable, however. Mom was so proud of how much room we had, yet we were all literally closing in on each other as the gifts were being opened and stacked behind us and we had to keep moving toward the center of the room."

A Happy New Year will never come, until the dejunking is all done.

" Dear Don:

When I heard you on 'Prime Time America' you asked for a clutter story, so here is mine, about my grandmother, and it is all true.

My grandma collects everything from *National Enquirers* to dead ducks. She lives in a two-bedroom house, and both bedrooms are cram packed. One is full of old newspapers and magazines, and when I say CRAM PACKED I mean clear to the ceiling, you can't even hardly open the door. The other bedroom is full of junk such as old clothes she found on the highway and got out of dumpsters. She even had to move her bed out of the bedroom because she couldn't get to it anymore. Her bed is now in the living room covered with more junk. Her living room is full of knickknacks, newspapers, and many other sorts of junk, most of it being things she has found along the highway. She also has tons of dead plants in her living room, she collects them for the pots and planters. Her living room is unbelievable—and as for her bedroom, she has to move the junk off her bed every night so she can sleep in it. Then in the morning she puts it all back on the bed, making a small walkway to the kitchen.

Her kitchen is also very cluttered.

She doesn't eat at home because she has no room to cook or eat. The kitchen counters are covered with bottles and containers, and lots of old food that would break your teeth to try and eat. She has two cars that are full of junk, so full that you can't even open the door without things falling out. She has a third car also, and she is working on filling it up too.

She picks up everything she sees along the road, things like old ropes and strings, cans and bottles, old clothes and shoes, even old dead animals. She brought home two dead ducks once, and her car stunk for a week. When she got home she put the ducks on her front porch, and they are still there to this day.

Her porch is piled high with many other sorts of junk—an old bird cage, a broken baby stroller, an old broken chair, and more bottles and cans—it is a big mess. She has a small log shed that is full of more junk.

Another thing she saves is wood ticks—she has little jars for them and each year she starts a new jar. She has some that are very old.

Oh, I almost forgot the basement full of boxes and boxes of junk. There is also a large herd of mice, rats, and squirrels living in her basement. Her toilet leaks in the back, and she has a bucket under there to catch the water. Well mice must come to get drinks and fall in because it's always full of dead mice, and the worst part is that she takes them out and saves them. She has a bucket of them sitting in her basement stairway.

There is no end to the clutter in and around her house, and she has another shed across the street—it is so cluttered it is terrible. I have never known anyone worse than her—help!"

Your grandma needs help, for sure, but it sounds as though she needs more than what can be gained from this or any self-help book. Cluttering that has reached this point probably calls for professional psychological counseling.

❝ Dear Mr. Aslett:

I would like to get your input on an issue. It is the classic case of opposites attracting, as I, a 'tosser,' married the Arch Packrat.

Our marriage three years ago started out great. However before long I realized he isn't willing to part with anything, not even dead, broken, or obsolete junk. So when he went out of town on business I rented a storage unit to put all the excess in. The house looked wonderful for a couple of months until his father's house sold. (My brother-in-law, who has power of attorney over my ailing father-in-law, decided suddenly to break up the latter's estate. Pappy lived in a 3,000-square-foot house.)

Needless to say, all the junk in that house was loaded on a truck, a LARGE truck, and it was deposited here in this house. All kinds of stuff, including furniture we don't need and (I kid you not) a lawn mower, is now sitting in our living room. Every horizontal surface is covered with junk.

I have read your decluttering books and understand the concepts. However my husband doesn't and he is petrified that he will throw out something important.

Short of divorce, which we don't believe in, what can I do? I want to empty the storage unit (it's a drain on our finances), but I don't know where to put the stuff, when I do.

Before I got married, my house was clean and organized. I entertained guests regularly. The house now has so much clutter throughout that I am embarrassed to invite anyone over.

Can you offer advice or suggestions. 95% of this stuff is my husband's, granted, but I'm surprised we haven't committed 'junkicide.'"

Thanks for the letter—changing the junk behavior of a mate is a long, long, and sometimes discouraging process, generally because inside they don't really want to be changed. It really boils down to two things… education and example. It sounds like the example you're giving is great, so keep it up.

Room isn't a problem for a confirmed junker, they can find it everywhere and stack it deeper and higher. Don't nag, but do keep the heat on as far as his stuff infringes into your life. I'm a believer in dedicating certain space as hers and his (he gets only half the garage, etc.) and refuse to let him encroach on your neat and dejunked space. Most men love their wife and family enough that eventually they will see the light and change.

I don't believe in getting into someone else's things, but when he is away you could dispose of some of the really cruddy stuff, or something that poses a safety hazard to the household. This will get across the message that you might throw some good stuff out too sometime and they will often start straightening up some of their stashes strictly as a matter of salvation.

Dejunking Others— The Big Dilemma

As is clear in these letters, "our junk" seldom remains a personal problem—our mounds, like measles or mumps, spread to those we touch. We wouldn't think of invading their personal life, but our junk can and will do it. Junk that may be a comfort to us can be a curse to a companion, a company, or the cause at hand… another BIG reason to control our junk.

What to do about someone else's impending junkicide is probably THE hardest case in decluttering. Our own immersion in stuff we can cure as soon as we come up with the will and gumption to do it. Other people's junking is both easier to see and harder to cure. Someone else's excess possessions, like the excess pounds on someone else's body, is an exceedingly touchy subject. I can just about guarantee that any frontal attack will only escalate the problem. Notice when you downgrade or criticize others' junk, they double the lock size on it.

I devoted an entire chapter (Chapter 14) of Not for Packrats Only *to artful ways of aiding other clutterholics.*

Here are a few ideas from readers now:

Give Them a Good Book to Read

❝ I reminded my husband that when I was single I never had piles of junk so it was clear he was the root of the problem. I had ordered your book on clutter and it arrived the next day. I placed it on the table where he couldn't miss seeing it. He read the whole book that night and the next morning he told me how much he enjoyed and agreed with everything that was said. It's funny, **I had said the same thing for years, but when you said it he listened.**"

❝ After I dejunked my life about two years ago, I became a disciple. I have talked to many people about the freedom and happiness available away from junk. I purchased your book for my mother last March, and the only thing that inspired her at first was the idea of dejunking her friends. She quit a women's church group she dreaded going to. Thinking about it still makes her happy. It relieved a lot of stress.

Then this past summer an additional motivator occurred and Mom has been going like wildfire. My parents have lived in the same house for thirty years. They have two attics, a garage with rafters, umpteen million bookshelves, and tons of 'storage' areas.

She has already hauled away 100 plus boxes of 'stuff' and thrown away an equal amount of garbage. I went to visit in the end of September and helped her for three days. She is doing an incredible job, and knows she has a long way to go. I realized at that point how extreme her case was. But she is excited about the process and her progress."

What a woman—we all applaud!

Give Them Some Good Example

❝ Do I know of anything that works well to help others decide to dejunk?

Setting an example. I mentioned my dejunking frequently to my coworkers, who look upon this act with awe. They view me as ultra-organized and not a clutterer (as I myself thought prior to amassing the evidence)."

❝ What to do if your domestic partner has a tendency to be a packrat? I believe the best way is to set a good example. I never touch any of her things. I just keep lightening my own load and occasionally make remarks such as 'Are you sure you need that?' or 'Don't you think we should either give or sell that to someone who will use and enjoy it?' As a result my partner is now making a concerted effort to pare down."

❝ As for getting my husband to dejunk, when he sees what a nice person I become after doing some, he realizes it's in his own interest to do it too, and then he's off and running."

Help Them

❝ *How to get others to dejunk? Have them read your book!* Then offer to help them. *Sometimes the prospect of doing it all alone is just too discouraging."*

❝ *For a long time, my brother and I have been concerned about our parents' things. They have a two-story house with an attic and basement, have been there forty years, and were young adults during the Depression. Need I say more? The problem is compounded by the fact that they live on the east coast and the rest of the family is scattered all over the country. During the spring, we spent a couple of weeks trying to help them dispose of a few things. I think lack of energy and physical strength is more of a factor here than unwillingness to let go of things. Reaching and bending are difficult, and if something is not more or less at eye level, it goes unnoticed. If some-*one helps with the lifting and moving and is willing to box things up and take them wherever they are going, the task doesn't seem quite so overwhelming. *The emotional drain isn't quite as great either when they are mainly supervising. I gave my mother a copy of* Not for Packrats Only *for her birthday, and by follow-ing some of your suggestions they have been able to do some further sorting on their own."*

" I have packrat genes on both sides of the family way back, but with your help I discovered I may also have an organizing gene.

My mother's house was so full that there were just pathways in some rooms, and rooms one could not walk into. There was a full double garage and two 10' x 10' storage sheds in the back yard. She literally spent hours every week looking for her keys, for bills in the avalanche on the desk, for anything she needed.

With my mother's permission I dejunked her house for her and it is now easy to live in. I sold a lot of valuable things like the 12' x 15' oriental rug underneath everything in a completely (look into only, not walk into) full room. I had industrial carpeting laid in there when I was done and put in tables and work space items to turn it into a workroom for her hobby, dolls. I made another room into a doll display room. I have worked on every room, closet, and almost every drawer. She feels renewed, and everyone who sees what I did has two reactions: First question: How many dump trucks did it take? Second question: Can you do it for me?

My mother still has everything she values, including a vast collection of extra doll clothes, and crazy things like probably 300 spools of thread when she won't even sew on a button. All of her collections are intact—no matter how little I thought of them, I knew that she wanted them. But now they are organized so she can find things. We found things she hadn't seen in twenty years. Her keys are never lost, her bills are paid on time, and she can find almost anything because I seldom moved things more than six feet and left Post-its everywhere. She feels like she has **more** things, not less, because she can see them and admire them. And life is easier for her. She can even park her car in the garage!"

Nudge Them and Help Them

" *When thinking about dejunking, my first thought was my husband's video room. We have a small video business downstairs and occasionally people will go down there for video work. There were tape splices, pieces of cellophane from video tapes, and tapes scattered to and fro, and electric cords and electronic gadgets all over the place.*

My problem was how was I going to get my beloved to go through all those boxes of junk and actually throw things away? **I waited until the day before a big family party was to be held at our home.**

I took everything out of the video room and put it in the family room on the floor. I then vacuumed and dusted the whole video room, and put some things back in there that I knew he needed to keep.

Now the family room was a disaster, but remember that junk had to be out of there by the following day for our party. In other words, he couldn't say 'I'll do it later.'

Even though I'd told him I was going to do this, I think he wasn't too excited about it, but he had to do it

178

anyway. He made it clear I was not to throw things away; he would do that.

He started going through things and actually throwing some things away. I didn't leave him to do it on his own. I put video tapes away and put things back into the video room. A few times he became very upset with me because there was so much to go through. We finally finished and had a good load for the junkyard and a box for the thrift store. If it was my choice, I would have thrown much more away, but we did throw a lot of junk away.

I love to just walk in there now and look at how nice it looks. It took at least eight hours to clean up, but when we finished I had such a sense of accomplishment that it was all worth it. I even went and bought a new rug to put in there!"

Whatever you do— don't try to do it for them!

❝ Some years ago when my parents were moving from a twelve- to a seven-room house I was on site to lend a hand. Mother was confined to bed following a surgery and I was having a delightful time sorting and throwing—but more often than not, discards reappeared. Unknown to me, Mother conspired with a much younger sister to check the trash barrels and report to her. Consequently, certain items were retrieved. Ah well!"

No doubt she was masterminding this from the hospital's "recovery room"!

MENTAL CLUTTER

❝ I have been a compulsive collector of all kinds of weird things, and my possessions have possessed me. The care and feeding of those THINGS has overwhelmed, depressed, and frustrated me. No time to do the things I enjoy doing. But **even more depressing was the junk I was carrying around inside**. Things that did nothing to contribute to the quality of life—just clutter! Clutter that was ruining my relationships, health, and life in general."

❝ *I am, by profession, a marriage and family counselor. I work with people every day who have given their lives over to emotional clutter: **lack of forgiveness, low self-esteem, broken loves and friendships, etc.** Others are carrying around physical clutter: chemical dependencies (everything from chocolate to cocaine), obesity (if we could just lose this weight, I'm sure we would feel better about each other), and the great emotion killer, tobacco.*

My clients don't know it yet, but they are going to be strongly encouraged to declutter their lives."

There are at least a hundred little "holder backers" like this that we harbor inside, and they're just as burdensome as those piles of clutter in the house, garage, and granary. So sit down on a rock or dock somewhere and take a little inventory of the mental clutter you're carrying—anything from disappointments, dishonesties, or unkindnesses of the past, to jealousies and prejudices of the present. Then either do something—take some action—to set them to right, or decide now, today, that you're going to clear them from your mind and mode of operation.

❝ Right before the end of school in May, I received an anonymous letter in the mail. It was vicious and mean, attacking my family and me and my performance as a mother and a teacher. I was devastated. My family and my school principal were very supportive and encouraged me to forget it… and I tried. However it began to have a serious influence on my self-esteem and my performance. I carried the letter with me and reread it often. Part of me understood the negative signal this was giving, but part of me also believed perhaps it was true. It perpetuated the pain and sadness and I began to doubt myself and my abilities. It cluttered my mind and had a crippling effect.

During a class I was attending then I shared this experience and a lively discussion followed. At the encouragement of the class members I brought the letter in the following day and we held a 'burning.' I lit this piece of paper on fire and someone turned out the lights and everyone cheered. These great people, who didn't know me, weren't related to me, cheered. All the sadness and hurt that had so crippled me went up in smoke. I was finally free and will be forever grateful to this wonderful group of strangers who believed in me."

One more kind of mental clutter is something that many of us fall into after the age of forty: **Physical ailment anxiety**. We're aware that we've reached the age beyond which going to the doctor isn't just an affirmation of how great we are (our secret attitude when we're younger). We realize that things can start to go wrong anytime now, and they could be serious, or the beginning of some chronic nuisance. So when we develop little aches and pains, or more serious symptoms, we spend lots of time brooding and worrying about it. We read up on what we imagine we have, and discreetly question others we assume share the same misfortune. We may even start sampling folk remedies and others' medication for it. But we put off going to the doctor and finding out what it might actually be, for as long as possible.

Make that overdue doctor's appointment today and get relieved or get cured!

MENTAL CLUTTER: "JUNK ON THE HOOF"

In my two earlier books *(Chapter 18 of Clutter's Last Stand and p. 91 of Not for Packrats Only)* I was bold enough to suggest that the idea of decluttering could extend even to the live two-legged clutter known as "people we'd just as well not be spending time with."

Let me say a little more in behalf of this "uncharitable" concept now.

Have you noticed how time seems to go faster and faster, since those wonderful endless days and weeks when we were kids? Well the years as they slip by from here will pick up speed like you'll never believe. Years will seem like mere months, and this will happen right when your talents, opportunities, and ideas are at their peak. You'll have more choices than you've ever had before, and more ways and means to take advantage of them—but less time.

So how, where, and with whom you use that time will become the most crucial issue of your life. You'll come to resent any burden or barrier to "quality time," you'll drop friends, habits, activities, schedules, meetings, anything not fully worthwhile that threatens to gobble up any of that tiny time you suddenly realize you have left.

And the idea of using up time just to tend stuff will make you nauseous, just you wait and see.

> 66 *You sure are right about the 'carryover' of dejunking. As I tolerate less crap in my house, I tolerate less crap from people.*"

66 I was really impressed by the idea of not putting up with people who waste your time and money—such as **phone sales people.** You know, the ones who call at least once a day, Monday through Saturday, selling everything from insurance to water softeners. Since I don't have the money to spend on things that 1) I don't need 2) Take up space 3) Make me feel stupid or 4) Make me worry, I made the decision that my decluttering project would be to say 'NO' to every phone sales call within the first thirty seconds, thereby not wasting my time or theirs.

WHAT I DID: Well, I stuck to my guns and have, within just one week, successfully said 'NO' to the following (without being rude).

Caller	Item	Cost
MCI	Long-distance service	?
American Handicapped	Light bulbs	$35.00
Olan Mills	1 free 8" x 10" plus four sittings	$18.00
Local boy	Neighborhood directory	$3.50
J.C. Penney	Accident insurance	$144/yr.
Sears	Appliance maintenance contract	$20.00
TOTAL SAVED...		At least **$220.50**

How do I feel about it? GREAT! I am happy with AT&T, still have the five light bulbs bought last year, never used the sittings I bought the time before, don't care who the other 299 homeowners in my neighborhood are, have plenty of insurance, and don't need the maintenance contract.

These are things I would probably have said 'Yes' to before. They would have ended up sitting around my home taking up space and causing unneeded worry, and I would have been hard pressed to pay for them. So now there are six less things cluttering up my mind AND I saved at least $220.50."

66 I am working now to eliminate the clutter of nonconstructive friendships. I just dejunked my boyfriend of many years. He was habitually irresponsible and incredibly draining both emotionally and financially."

66 Yes, I agree that we should AVOID JUNK PEOPLE as much as possible. They are almost invariably ill-tempered, ill-mannered, and incompetent. They'll make you lose your temper and forget your own manners— even with people you love. Furthermore, it is highly unlikely that you will teach these 'junkees' anything. Their mouths are usually open wider than their minds. Your manners will be taken as elitism. Your patience will be taken as wimpishness. Your expertise will be taken to be showing off. Just stay away from them!"

66 If I was satisfied with myself, my home, my relationships, and my career, what could I dejunk that would enhance my life? The thing that infringed on my well-being, I decided, was **the time I spent trapped with people whose company I did not initiate or enjoy.** Although the solution to this problem in *Clutter's Last Stand* was humorous (take a hike through the sagebrush or move away), these methods were unacceptable in my situation. Therefore I resolved to place a higher priority on my time spent listening to people who talked for the sake of hearing themselves talk. I decided that if I was not enjoying a conversation, or if the conversation was not serving my interests or a positive purpose, I

would politely excuse myself from the situation and leave.

Not only did this work out well in several situations at work, but I also became courageous enough to refuse several jobs and assignments that would infringe on my time and the time of my family. When asked to conduct a club meeting that I rarely went to regularly, for example, I politely declined."

MENTAL CLUTTER: TV

A topic that obviously struck a chord in you up-and-coming declutterers!

❝ Many friends have told me they've heard you speak on television, but unfortunately I won't be able to catch you on the tube. I recently gave away my TV set—one of the most pernicious pieces of clutter I had (and this is a whole subject in itself).

Sorry if I seem a bit fanatic, but the credit is all yours."

❝ *Last year we turned off the TV for three weeks as part of an experiment so that I could present a talk on TV and kids for my nursery school (based on the book* Unplugging the Plug-in Drug). *When we turned the TV on again, I was amazed at how much clutter it represented in both time lost and material presented. I don't want to be a zealot; we haven't kept the set off entirely, but it is watched rarely and usually only for programs we've pre-selected."*

❝ I wonder why clutter is such a problem today... or was it always? Is it the society in which we live, or just greed? I think TV with all its enticements to get more and more, is partly to blame. We haven't had a TV for eight years now, and I bless the day we got rid of it! I guess that was one of the first things we threw out, that prepared the way for future dejunking. I honestly have never missed it, and wonder when I'd find the time to watch it if we had one!"

❝ **We threw the TV set in the trash can four years ago and haven't had one since—talk about freedom!"**

❝ Now I'm dejunked—yes, me!
I am all neat and tidy.
But I don't know what's on TV—
I tossed the 'TV Guidey!'"

—Anne Wolflick

Chapter 7

Preventing Re-Junking

In the previous pages you've read all kinds of cures for clutter, from your friends, neighbors, and fellow packrats. There are lots of good ideas there—remedies, antidotes, counteractants, correctives. But this chapter is devoted to those who dug deeper and found the #1 junk stopper—**prevent** it! Don't get a deeper drawer, a thicker curtain, or bigger and better garbage cans. Head off that clutter before it ever enters your premises.

❝ I really would like to see you say more about **staying dejunked**. We have worked hard for four years to get to this point and we don't want to regress."

❝ I have decided that being a junker is like being an alcoholic—once you're afflicted, you may bring it under control, but unless you diligently work at staving it off, it will always creep back into your life."

❝ Junking is a lot like alcoholism, gambling, or overeating in that overcoming it is **a step-by-step, day-by-day commitment** you must make with yourself. It requires self-discipline and the ability to resist temptation."

❝ Four years later, I am still in the war against clutter, losing a few minor (and major) battles along the way. After all I am in enemy territory, but I do manage to recruit a soldier every now and then."

❝ The other day I was thinking about the various areas of my life in which demon clutter had begun to creep back in again. Then I began to ruthlessly attack my night table, which is

a very obvious indication of clutter in my life. Books and articles waiting to be read had begun to pile up, notes stuck here and there…. I thought too about how junk food had begun to creep into my diet again, a little bit here and there, starting sometime around Thanksgiving, so innocently at first.

Well, after getting this area in order again, and filing most of my papers under 'G' (Garbage), I proceeded to eat a healthy oat bran muffin for breakfast, and start dejunking the mail."

Just how do my readers suggest we cut back that creeping clutter now?

RE-READ A DECLUTTERING BOOK

❝ Dear Don,

Do you realize you are like a daily dose of vitamins? A daily dose of decluttering philosophy is needed to keep inveterate junkers like me on the straight and narrow.

I just stopped dead in my tracks and caught myself at it red-handed: neatly organizing my junk into piles, corners, and boxes. Again! And I'd slipped back into the mindless habit of saving coupons for products I won't run out of for months yet (I wouldn't find the coupons when I did, anyway).

And I thought I was permanently cured, stopped at the pass in my cluttering. No way!!!"

It struck me rudely, forcefully: we need that fellow again. To relearn the basics of NOT succumbing to the momentary temptation to snatch up just one irresistible memento we're certain we'll cherish until death do us part, then agonizing about assuring its eternal life long after ours is over. It can't be heard too often.

What's the answer? RE-reading the fat green book, that's what.

Out came *Clutter's Last Stand,* your trusty bible of cajolery, threats carefully veiled in gentle logic, explaining as though to a slow child the pitfalls of being trapped EVER in the too-easy-to-embrace habits of casual accumulation. It's now reinstated in my kitchen, sitting there as an admonishment, silently at times, clangingly at others. I detoured around it yesterday, but not without its tentaclelike reach affecting me. Result: one stripped-down closet, another on the agenda this morning."

PRE-DEJUNK

(**O**r think ahead and nip the junking impulse in the bud.)

❝ *As for pre-dejunking, I've practiced that for a long time. I love to walk around the midways at fairs—the jostling of the crowds, the calls of the barkers—but you can't pay me to participate in any of the games and contests. Why? Because I'm afraid I'll win something. The last thing I need in my life is a four-foot stuffed Garfield.* **Pre-dejunking is like recycling; it takes a little practice at first, but the righteous feeling one has when one is not filling the garbage can frequently is well worth it.**"

❝ I've begun **to think in a new and energetic way**. For instance, instead of building new cabinets to house more kitchen items, I think I can reorganize the existing cabinets and take the few canned items from the kitchen 'Misc' shelf and fit them in, in about an hour.

Also, we were about to buy the biggest new refrigerator we could find, to house more food. Now I don't think so, it will just mean a bigger food collection and more spoiled and wasted food. Instead we're going to store fresh only what will fit our old-time fridge downstairs and can and dry the rest for the rest of the year. (I enjoy doing it, too.)"

❝ *I thought I needed a new, larger filing cabinet, but all I really needed was some creative self-discipline."*

A key advisor of one of the country's major corporations whom I met with once summed it up well. "Our main problem these days is, we are OVER OFFERED."

That was pretty profound, I thought. We are blessed, or perhaps cursed by choices these days. Everything has at least twenty options or variations, everywhere we go—whether we're going off to college or out for the evening, whether we're buying clothes or tickets, a car or a VCR. Those choices for the most part are all good ones, too. The trouble is we can only use one thing at a time and be in one place at a time. Most of us have the money and the means, and

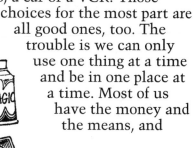

even the space left to tuck in a few extra items, more than we really want or need. "Just in case" has filled many a suitcase and split level to the stress point.

The big bottom line of all this?

We are ending up with no space (mental or physical) to live.

STOP SHOPPING

“ I saw a woman in a local discount supermarket going around with a cart collecting the cans and boxes people abandon here, there, and everywhere in a supermarket because they changed their mind or discovered they don't have quite enough cash or whatever. I asked her what she was doing and she said 'unshopping.' In a sense much of dejunking is unshopping."

“ I stuffed my treasures and I treasured my stuff, I shopped till I dropped and still couldn't get enough. Ignoring a 'Blue Light Special' became increasingly tough, Because I was a Clutter Collector."

“ I knew it was getting bad when I was out shopping and found myself looking for something (anything) the right size and shape to fit the one space left in the trunk of my car!"

“ *This month the store I was working at closed. We had a Going Out of Business Sale. On the very last day we had a $5.00 a cart sale. Stuff your cart for just $5.00, plus tax. I wish you could have been there, Don, to see people picking up merchandise— **just anything**—in armfuls and cramming their shopping carts. One man bought thirty bottles of cat shampoo. He proudly said: 'I don't even have a cat.' If you had been there to observe it would have fueled you to write a whole new book."*

“ *I did a speech a couple years ago on recycling and it started out, 'Reduce, reuse, recycle, and refuse to buy REFUSE.' I guess the bottom line of it was declutter!"*

“ Flea markets are to junkers what all-you-can-eat dinners are to a Weight Watcher. You say 'you'll be good,' but it's **just asking** for trouble. And you can't easily stop once you start. So you just have to stay away."

“ **'Not buying more, using what we have, and seeing how long we can go before replenishing the stockade' is my motto now."**

“ We are no longer buyaholics. We can pass a sale without stopping. **If the urge occurs, we buy an ice cream cone.** Ever try to keep an ice cream cone for longer than ten minutes?"

“ *Buying less 'stuff' allows my husband and me more money to travel, which is the thing that* gives us the most pleasure anyway. Our souvenirs are the pictures we take. I always joke that my secret way of saving money is to not go to the store. Credit cards are a definite no-no."

❝ As I continue to rid my home and life of clutter my days become easier. Also, I can pass by a garage full of antiques or a store sale and not get that nervous feeling of 'I'm missing something.' Instead, I feel sorry for those people junking up their lives with more things. You are right... less **is** more!"

An overheard bit of conversation that rather nicely sums up the dangers of "antique and collectible" shops: "This store is so wonderful, it has everything in it we ever threw away!"

❝ When I am shopping, usually at the thrift store, I am tempted to buy something just because it is a bargain. **I stop and ask myself if I really like the thing, or am I buying it because it is cheap? I also ask myself how I am eventually going to get rid of it.** I don't buy anything unless I know where I am going to store it and how I am going to get rid of it later."

"Gasp... this is a good price!"

"...but we don't need it."

"Yes, it is a **real** good price."

"But we don't need it..."

(Who do you think will win?)

❝ I have saved a lot of money because I ask myself this question whenever I am tempted to buy 'something.' 'Will this become clutter, **how much time will be spent enjoying this item**?'

Most of the time I don't buy it, thereby saving money."

❝ I save money. I don't buy bric-a-brac. **I think seven times over before I make a purchase** and I don't take photos or carry a camera when on vacation. I feel so free."

❝ I have long given up the bad habits of 'cutesy spending,' 'gotta have it,' garage sales, flea sales, craft sales, any Rubbermaid storage sections in stores—**NO MORE SHOPPING unless necessary**!

I actually become ill now at the sight of gropers in a yard sale. It sure is a disease."

❝ I just don't buy anymore. And I was finally able to afford a trip to California to visit a dear friend after I hadn't been able to go out there for seven years. In fact, she was the one who talked me into buying your book! Hmmmm...."

❝ I was one who was **very** attached to things. I like to shop, display, collect. But now **I'll write an article or story or do something more constructive than loiter in the stores.** I'll stop and think before I buy, as to where I'll keep it and why and I'll even do some thinking before I enter a store at all."

> ❝ The less I see, the less I'll bring home. If we never had it or knew it existed, it wouldn't be a problem. Once it enters the home it does tend to enter the heart.❞

❝ When it comes to those clutter multipliers called **mailorder catalogs**, an extra-dangerous category here is the special sale flyer or section of any catalog and there are many that we know always has a lot of neat stuff. If you open that thing or scan the 'special sale pages,' I can just about guarantee that you will succumb to something. The allure of the neat stuff (which we might be able to resist, if we get on a thrift or de-junking kick) combined with a big savings ('40% off!' 'Half price!' 'Closeout!') will be irresistible. **The only way out is not to look.**❞

Someone called in during one of my radio show appearances bragging about what he bought at "Post 4th of July sale." Sparklers were on sale 1000 for a dollar, and he got $6.00 worth... 6000 sparklers. Man did you get a deal, the rest of us are really envious.

❝ ...a pet peeve of mine is **clutter parties**—Tupperware et al—in which clutter is pushed in the guise of friendship. These are clutter orgies which nickel and dime one's friends to death.❞

❝ **You helped me realize that even 'free' came with a price tag**—where to store it? And would this free thing ever be used, etc. I had socks I got for free from Hydrox cookies, for instance—white socks with a cookie motif. They were so 'cute,' but didn't match any outfit I owned, so they never even moved out of the sock drawer."

While we're on the subject of free, a bona fide clutterer I know was attending a large book industry convention, and she stepped into the autograph hall where frenzied lines were forming to get free books complete with author signature. While waiting in a line moving rather slowly toward the prize, she noticed another, smaller line that seemed to produce a quicker reward so she jumped into that line. She ended up telling me an embarrassing story later. "I didn't know what it was, but the line was shorter." When she reached the end, she received an autographed calendar—of photographs of nude men!

❝ I've often thought about the terrible gripping addiction that is responsible for so much junk: **The something-new-for-its-own-sake high**. What is the real allure, I wonder? The novelty of having something at least a little different from everything else you have? The 'hunting' of going out and finding something new, getting it/or receiving in the mail, the opening of the package, the new smell, or...??? Gads, as garage sale popularity would indicate, even *used* new stuff is thrilling.

As in when you're attempting to diet, cut back on food, it helps to remember that the incredibly brief time something is on your lips/in your mouth, is nothing to how long that extra fat will be on your body. (Or in the case of bought-to-have-something-new clutter, to how long you'll be working or scrounging to pay it off).

I've discovered, to my horror, that you can get almost as much of a thrill out of buying something and then shortly thereafter taking or sending it back, and getting your money back. Scary indeed. And not as good as a true cure of the impulse, because it does take time and money to take things back."

My vote for the root of all this is that good old "hunting and gathering" instinct from our distant ancestors, right along with having a "trophy" to show for it.

People will peruse dumps and come away proudly with a pair of Levis with knee holes as if they'd unearthed some wonderful treasure. Or they'll find something at a garage sale with a $19.95 price tag still on it, and snap it up because they can get "something new" for $2.00. So what if it's new, or a bargain, if you have no use for it, or don't even know what it really is or how it works? In the moment of purchasing passion, few really

think of what or why, they just know it's NEW!

SO?

Remember when saying "So...?" to every statement or question was the big fad? Someone would make one of those remarks meant to settle things and someone else would say "So...?" It did have a way of making us think beyond our first impulse or judgment. Let's take all those trigger "taker" words in the junker's vocabulary and ask that "so":

But it's...

"New!"	SO?
"...old!"	SO?
"Well made!"	SO?
"A miniature!"	SO?
"It's so heavy"	SO?
"So light"	SO?
"On sale"	SO?
"One owner"	SO?
"Within my budget!"	SO?
"One of a kind"	SO?
"A first edition"	SO?
"The last one!"	SO?
"A collector's item"	SO?
"It matches"	SO?
"It's imported"	SO?
"It's handmade"	SO?
"It's automatic"	SO?
"It's manual"	SO?
"It can be fixed"	SO?

Let's take this appraisal process a step farther and apply a couple more questions: "Will this enhance my life and the lives of others? What will all the costs of collecting and containing it be?"

Watch those "Always Wanteds"

❝ I was about to get some goats which I have 'always wanted.' However, to do that, I need to fence the yard—$700 to $1500 or more in materials, plus my time (I've never done it before). Then after I got the goats, I'd be tied down to milking them (babysitters for my chickens are easy to find). Well your book has made me think it may suit me better to buy goat milk elsewhere for quite a few years, instead of spending the money on fencing. Or do the whole project more gradually. After all, since I had a baby in March I haven't even had a chance to plant a garden (though I have all the seeds). And the goats would eat the orchard and grapes I did plant—that would mean even more fencing."

Those Winsome Always Wanteds

If we had a dollar for every time we've sighted something and sighed "I've always wanted one of those," we'd be able to buy it for sure. We're a ground-gaining and greedy bunch, aren't we? The minute we have "it," then we've always wanted a better one.

Always Wanted clutter is older than any of us, inspiring I'm sure that "Thou shalt not covet" in the Ten Commandments. No doubt the greatest punishment that could be dished out to mankind would be to grant us all of our Always Wanteds. We generally get and have what we need, but it's the Always Wanteds that haunt us, those "have to haves." Yet we often don't have a real use for them or even a place to keep them. And we usually haven't considered all the costs and requirements of owning and having our current obsession, which may go way beyond the price tag on it.

❝ I always wanted a deluxe set of matching luggage. Then I got it and I still use my old one now so the nice set won't get beat up."

Most Always Wanteds are spare or image stuff, not front line necessities. And Always Wanteds are heavy on tax, insurance, upkeep, and storage expense. I can see a couple of nice pieces of Always Wanted clutter chatting now:

"Hey BMW, this is baby grand calling. I've always wanted to be owned by someone who doesn't even play the piano. I think I'll look extra attractive today and get a home where I'll be polished, patted, protected, insured, pointed to, admired, and never pounded on or played once."

"Yeah, piano, that family with four good cars already is dreaming about adding me to their vehicle collection. I hope they do it. Then I can rest in that air conditioned garage and hardly ever be driven."

The underlying motivation for most Always Wanteds is "if I have it, it will change me." That's a big lie—it won't. The majority of those who always wanted an exercise bike, for example, discover after they own one that the most exercise it gives them is moving it to clean under it.

Once you get it, then the always wanted urge will be to get rid of it!

Are you sure you "Gotta Have" it?

Some stuff we "gotta have" or that we get with all good intentions fools even the veteran collector in the end. I think you'll find the following "wish I'd never bought it" list interesting.

• **Expensive exercise equipment**—You could just dump a cheap one when you discover how little you use it.

• **Camera extras**—"They only helped give me a shoulder callous and a big Mastercard balance."

• **A guitar/organ/saxophone, etc.**—The idea of owning and playing one of these is so neat, if only you didn't have to do all that practicing.

• **Expensive jewelry**—The few times you get to wear it never compensate for all the worries over it, including the possibility of getting mugged or killed for it.

• **A juicer, food dryer, smoker, meat grinder, ice cream, yogurt, or pasta maker, etc.**—We just have to have one, it would be so healthful, helpful, or thrifty. After the novelty wears off, it just takes up cupboard and counter space.

• **A boat**—You have to transport it, store it (in season and out), dock it, scrape it, paint it, and license it. All for something most of us can only use about four months a year.

• **An in-ground swimming pool**—After all the kids have completed drownproofing lessons, you've added that expensive privacy/safety fence, and got your M.S. in pool cleaning and chlorine chemistry, you'll discover that everyone would rather go to the pool downtown.

• **A motor home**—By the time you finish packing it with (and realize that later, you're going to have to unpack) half the contents of your home—bedding, food, clothes, pots and pans and dishes, microwave, TV, a/c, lawn chairs—you're too tired to take a trip.

• **A second or vacation home**—You'll spend all the rest of the year worrying about it and paying for it back in home #1.

• **A motorcycle**—If you can afford the insurance and manage to protect it from thieves, you can take advantage of this opportunity to spend as much time in a hospital ward as you do on the open road

• **A parrot, cockatoo, etc.**—Yes, you can get tired of vacuuming up seeds, scraping up bird bombs, and listening to screeching.

- **A horse**—Must be housed, fenced, fed (big time!), mucked, groomed and trained. Then you'll have to buy all that tack for it, and special clothes for you. Then all the neighbor kids will want a ride, until one of them finally falls off and sues you.

- **Exotic animals, from ocelots to miniature potbellied pigs**—After you've remodeled your entire home and grounds and schedule to accommodate it, you'll realize you've fallen out of love with it.

- **Aquariums**—Aren't as appealing after you find out how hard it is to keep those little rascals alive and healthy, and the tank looking as good as the one in the doctor's office.

- **Oversize houseplants/indoor trees**—Look wonderful for at least a week after delivery, or while maintained by a professional landscaping service.

- **Pool table**—Hard to find an alternate use for, once the billiards buff has moved on.

- **Fountains**—Lose some of their fascination after you've removed the five thousandth dead leaf, and performed or paid for the fiftieth unclogging

- **Fancy china set**—Nothing but anxiety from the minute you lift it out of the china closet, till it's tucked back in there again.

- **Satin sheets**—Too slick to sleep on!

- **A sauna**—The minute it falls out of favor, it's just a damp overheated room with rustic paneling.

- **Ham radio equipment**—Once you tire of listening to static and "space emissions," and talking to other boring hams, even plain old AM will be a welcome treat.

- **Observatory-grade telescope**—If you could have back all the $ you sank in this, you'd be perfectly happy just squinting at the stars again.

- **A greenhouse**—The light and space, at last, to start plants from seed, coddle out-of-season vegetables, and nurture exotic ornamentals is only half of it. The will and energy to keep on doing it is the other half.

- **Season tickets (to anything from the opera to your favorite hockey team)**—Once "have to" or "ought to" enter the picture, even fun things aren't fun.

- **Rental freezer locker** If you'd just taken up elk hunting as you'd planned, this would have been a great idea.

- **A farm or ranch**—Great as long as you have an independent income large enough to support all the new ways to spend money you will discover here.

- **A baby**—"Everyone else was doing it, and I always wanted to know if I could, too" (but there's no returns policy on this little item).

- **A husband/or wife**—You'll no longer have to wonder about the meaning of those expressions "ball and chain," "wings clipped," or "grounded."

BEWARE OF BUZZARDHOOD

(Another big creator of junk piles.) The brotherhood of

buzzardhood is the simple belief that what has been discarded is surely only partially discardable. Somewhere in the heap, along that curb or in that pile of rejects, there is something that deserves rescue. Some of that stuff is surely perfectly good!

This inner flood of moral conviction is what drives us to retrieving old worn-out sinks from dumpsters, to scabbing lumber scraps from construction sites, to wastebasket sorting and robbing. By renaming this swooping through the sweepings/digging through the ditched "salvage," we feel fully justified in picking through garbage, stripping parts off old junk cars, and snipping belts and zippers off old clothes.

Buzzarding is great if you are a professional salvager or have a definite use for the recovered loot. But buzzarding for the mights and maybes (or the rush it gives you) is bad news. When you see something like this, do what is right—"turn the other beak"!

PRACTICE "UPKEEP DEJUNKING"

66 *It always amazes me* **how fast clutter can accumulate** *even for us clutter-conscious people. It seems like I am always cleaning out and throwing out and sorting out."*

66 I find that once I do a big dejunking, **a once-a-year going over** is helpful (**like a room or area a month, or every other month**).

But things do slip by, and if in five years things are still around, I realize it's time for another overhaul."

66 *Some things that have worked for me to help keep clutter down:*

1. Announce to the kids that I'm sending some stuff to the D.I.

2. Keep a box handy for usable junk and as soon as it is full, drop it off at the charity collection box on my way to town.

3. Dispose of paper junk immediately, or as soon as possible."

66 My main concern at this point isn't dejunking, but staying dejunked! I have three habits that help me:

1) This one dejunks **the refrigerator**. One day each week for dinner we have oven-heated leftovers. I take all the odds and ends of previous dinners for the week, put them into separate foil containers, put them all on a cookie sheet in the oven at 350 degrees for twenty minutes. Then we have a hot smorgasbord of goodies, with nothing left to rot on the bottom shelf of the fridge. We waste a lot less food this way.

2) This one dejunks **our closets**. In our family, we put clothes we no longer want into boxes in the basement and once every six months or so, we donate them to charity. The time those clothes

spend in the basement gives the donor a chance to change his or her mind and reclaim a garment. If it isn't missed, we don't need it and someone else does.

3) Finally, to dejunk **the whole house** once a year, I have a yard sale with my sister. Throughout the year and especially in the spring, the whole family contributes things to those ubiquitous boxes in the basement, and in May, we price and sell everything. What amazes me is the sheer amount of stuff we always have to sell. This is a noncluttered house, and year after year I go over each shelf, each cupboard with the question: Did I use this item this year? Do I really need it? And year after year we manage to cull ten or twelve boxes of stuff from an already clean house. I guess that's not really surprising when you consider the amount of goods that come into a house each year, through shopping and gifts, etc."

66 *My personal quest for dejunking continues and will be a lifelong project. I've put out the word that I no longer want sacks of baby clothes (my baby is going on eight years old!), or stacks of material scraps (polyester has never been a favorite 'blend' for me), or cartons of 'raw materials' that always come with helpful suggestions as to what to make into!"*

66 A couple of things I do to cut down clutter:

1) Whenever I buy any clothes at all, I always give away at least as many pieces as I buy (and usually more). I take them over to the local Shelter and my closets never overflow.

2) I've gotten to the point where I'd just as well **rent** something I might use every year or two, rather than 'own' it and have it clutter our home or garage the rest of the time. This makes sense, especially when you stop to think, on a philosophical level, that we never really **own** anything, we just *use* it while we're residing here on this planet."

66 One of the things that's been most effective for us in staying on the dejunking wagon is to **continually be giving stuff away**. We discovered that it's important to have a 'staging' area for this: someplace that's clear enough to dump things or accumulate them for removal. We've created a couple of staging areas in the house that are permanently assigned to outgoing clutter. There is a **basement staging area for rummage** (with a box especially for books we've outgrown). Friends of ours make bimonthly trips to a bookstore in Portland called Powell's (about an acre of books used and new) and they often ask us if we need anything. We give them the box of old books and say 'Get whatever you can out of them,' and bingo, the books go away.

We also have an **'outgoing' area right next to the front door** for things that we borrowed and are returning, things to drop off, things to mail, and things to get rid of. By placing everything to be returned in the same spot, we can remember to give it back when the lender comes over and it's always **right there**.

It's gotten to be something of a joke among us and a few of our more observant friends that you can't get out of our house without us giving you something. Not completely true, but say, why don't you take this book with you, you'll enjoy it. No, don't bother to bring it back. If you like it, keep it; if not, pass it on. No, don't thank me, you're quite welcome. Glad to do it.

(Hee hee hee....)"

❝ *How to stay on the dejunking wagon?*

*Objectively look at each room of the house and **pinpoint the junk collecting areas in each**—for instance, at my house:*

1. Bathroom—medicine chest

2. Living room—magazine rack and drawer in the end table next to where I sit to read

3. Bedroom—bottom shelf of the closet

4. Kitchen—top, lefthand drawer of the cabinet

5. Family room—desk

6. And so forth, for each room.

Once a month, dejunk one of these areas. *It will take less than an hour and your home will stay in good shape.*

Once a year, dispose of things that you can now let go of."

Those clutter collection depots

Any flat surface will gradually (or not so gradually) be drifted full, so constant vigilance is needed at those clutter collection depots, such as:

> top of fridge
> windowsills
> counters
> dressertops
> desktops
> mantels
> hall or foyer tables
> end tables
> coffee tables
> pianos
> top of TV
> top of washer/dryer
> top of toilet tank

These are the places that catch everything anyone is too lazy to dispose of or put where it belongs.

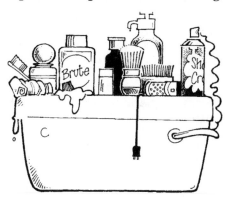

SAY "NO THANKS"

❝ My favorite way of refusing junk is to say 'No thanks... have you read this great book on de-cluttering? You haven't? Hold on, I'll get it for you....' They never offer anything ever again!"

66 I try not to slip from the dejunking wagon, and it's a constant vigil. When my anxiety level rises, then I go to work and throw out, throw out.

My 'quickie comeback' is a blood-curdling shriek, glazed eyes, and electrified hair which discourages anybody from saying cute phrases such as 'Can I bring the kitty home?'

What works for me? It's knowing the sense of relief I feel when the clutter level has been decreased."

GET ORGANIZED

66 I do have a suggestion for a topic you might want to include in one of your books in the future. As I've dejunked, I find I still have a lot of everyday useful things which I have trouble organizing. These things, such as shoes, toys, clothes, etc., are often thrown all over the house—they're being there is proof they are used. I've taken it on as a project to learn from people who are naturally organized and have begun to analyze and figure out systems. For example, books are a major problem so I'm buying an adequate bookshelf instead of the several flimsy ones I have. I've also finally realized that I never learned to fold things properly and that's why my closets have always been messy.

Don, it seems that if we weren't raised in an organized family, we need to learn a lot of basic skills and ideas to become organized. Until recently, I didn't want to learn because the only 'neat' people I saw were compulsive. Your books showed me that we could simplify our lives and be organized without it being a full-time job. I believe this concept would be the next step after dejunking and a big service to we who wish to control our own lives instead of 'things' controlling us."

66 *Immersed in the (hot, ugly, bug-infested) piles and stacks, you can't help asking yourself: how did things get this bad? And the answer is simple.* **I kept too much... and in a jumbled up way.** *A very real part of the oppression—and junkiness—of junk is that everything is stored and stacked in such a hopelessly confused and mixed up way. Anything of value in there is impossible to find, or you've forgotten you have it."*

People keep asking me about that big "O" word in clutter control, most being under the impression that the big "O" is *organizing* (everything you own). Funny how people seem to either have an organizing fixation or fear of organizing. But in fact most of you are good organizers already, it's one of those survival skills that just comes with living. Most of you with a big family, for example, if it came down to a contest, could out-organize most business "executives" or university professors of efficiency. I will write my own organizing primer someday, to help you deal with the "good stuff" that's left. Meanwhile don't forget that the real big "O" secret when it comes to dealing efficiently with clutter is OUT—not organize. When the excess goes, what's left almost organizes itself!

FUTURE JUNK

In case you need one last thought here to help you cut down your accumulations—think of this, all you folks out there in Saving City. Most of the stuff you have hidden away for "another day" has serious competition, because that day will be one of accelerated automation and evolution. Which means things will only go obsolete faster and easier.

Today there are available (neater, prettier, and now electrified or electronic, not manual) at least a dozen times the devices and machines there were ten and twenty years ago. On every side, where once we had one or two items from one or two companies, now fifty companies, local and foreign, make them and in dozens of models. And updating is done yearly instead of once every few years. There are five times the magazines there once were and they're slicker and thicker. Catalogs (no longer suitable for honest use in the outhouse) are now in gorgeous color, and so plentiful that every one of us gets more of them than the entire block got a few years back. And mail is not the sole medium. Now TV has hundreds of shopping channels displaying super-enhanced images of every imaginable kind of merchandise. And it's so easy to buy, you don't even have to write out or mail in anything. Just call that free 800 number, read off a couple of credit card digits, and before you know it—whatever happened to catch your fancy is delivered to your door.

So now we can, in the blink of an eye, without even thinking about it, collect all kinds of things that are just about instantly obsolete. Consider "sound systems," for example:

In

The 1920s—Any sound was great
1948—FM sound was better
1961—Hi-fi was the sky
The mid-60's—8-track tapes took the lead
1966—Stereo was the way to go
1967—Quadraphonic systems added that extra dimension
The mid-70's—Cassette tapes were the only kind worth considering
1983—Compact discs demonstrated their superiority
1987—Digital audio tape made the scene
1990—Surround sound now a must
1991—DCCA outdoes compact discs
1995—Who would be without a Full Modular Inner Ear unit?
2000—Your guess, but it will come

It's all sound, and the improvements between some of these stages may be minute. The hi-fi, the stereo, surround sound still work, but updating and upgrading is our whole mission and destiny. So we get new, but what do we do with the "old" now?

We have this problem already on every side. Fancy brand, extra special function phones, radios, TVs, clocks, computers, gauges, and gadgets, mini, midi, and maxi appliances of all kinds are everywhere. Look around—need I say more?

So far clutter collection has just been in its incubation stages. The door may still close on our junk today, but we're going to be pushed right out that door with what's coming.

If you can't handle what's there now—bad news, Virginia, in another decade you're dead! It's **part with or perish,** the future!

Chapter 8

Success Report:
"Yes, Fellow Rats, I did it!"

How would it feel, folks:
to hear an echo in one of your closets or drawers?
to say "I'll get it"… instead of "I'll try to find it."
to open the garage door in daylight without fear
to slam the refrigerator door and not have to pick things up off the floor
to have everything fit where it's supposed to, all the time.
to have someone ask you… "Wow, how did you do it?!"

These are just a few of the symptoms of successful clutter conquering.
We could end here by going back through the book and counting up all the "It made me feel betters" of one kind or another. That's what this book is really about, personal freedom… feeling better, that's all that needs to be said, and that's all there is—feeling better. I challenge you to find anything more rewarding than feeling better, or a more dependable source of it than dejunking. Before we look at a few last success reports let me remind you one last time of what junk does to you.

❝ Our life seems to be used up just buying all this, trying to digest it, and then trying to excrete the leftovers."

❝ What I notice everywhere I go is not how new or expensive things are, but how over-junked everyone's places seem! They scream chaos, disorder, 'don't care' at me."

❝ *I suppose most people carry their junk and clutter to their dream home and that 'stuff' that comes with them stresses them and turns it into a nightmare home."*

Don't wait until it's too late and you have too much—until your life has been used up by things you can't use up. Clutter keeps you weighted down and running on a rat wheel. This is surer than death and taxes (and clutter has been known to cause both). The smart thing is to get it now, before it gets you later. Isn't that what your fellow rats are telling you?

66 I started dejunking with the 1987 calendar hanging behind the current one, and the rest is history."

66 I've derived great joy from dejunking—I wouldn't have believed anything could be so exhilarating!"

66 As I began tossing out things right and left from our closet floors and overburdened shelves, I began to feel lighter. May I even say more clear-minded."

66 There is a spiritual change with the physical changes I've made in my dejunking. Many friends have commented on how much more peaceful and joyous (and mentally organized) I am."

66 I now know what you mean when you say 'Life truly begins when you discover how flexible and free you are without clutter.' IT'S TERRIFIC!!!"

66 After years of an impossible basement, I am feeling that great sensation you describe of FREEDOM AND CONTROL."

66 I can travel to Arizona now with all my stuff packed into an 8' x 10' U-Haul, and be free. I hope your book made you a million dollars. It made me wealthy. My wealth being freedom—freedom from stuff!"

66 I never would have believed I would look forward to dejunking, but I look for a new place to hit every day. It is great to have an empty drawer and not feel obligated to fill it!"

66 I quit my second job when I realized I no longer needed 'extra' money. Combined income for us is 92K a year and we have no children. Besides rebuilding this house, my money was wasted on junk.

I now spend Saturdays in the yard or sewing instead of packing and sorting junk!"

66 Even though I am still in the process of dejunking my life, I already feel better, lighter, freer than I have in years. Your book is underlined and highlighted for quick review and reminder of my goals. I take it with me everywhere (in my cleared and organized attache case—very little else in there.) As I look forward, I am regaining my positive attitude and appreciation of life and living with enthusiasm. Decluttering is much less expensive than a shrink and probably more beneficial."

66 I never realized how much time I spent on our things. No wonder I never had time for what I really wanted to do, or for other people. Now at the age of forty-four I can start living. When I think of what I will accomplish over the next year—dejunking my life—tears of joy come to my eyes. It's like being freed from a prison. Thank you from the bottom of my heart."

66 I'm going to keep on trying to 'find the bottom and keep it visible'! Thanks again!"

" *My desk is always neat and I get a 'rush' when I deep-six junk into the wastebasket. All around me there is clutter on desks—not mine!"*

" I have been decluttering not just my junk but also me. You helped me find my priorities—to realize that all this stuff is just material and doesn't really matter. It's living and enjoying each day! I guess the biggest thing I don't miss is the arguing with my husband about (cleaning, fixing, sorting, etc.) stuff we don't use. We give your book as wedding gifts."

" What I love about dejunking is that it puts me in control. When you think about it, there's a lot we can't control: We have to work, spend on necessities, do this and that…. But we alone control our junk."

" *If people ask if it's worth it—Yes! People who come to my house (one person in a 1180 sq. ft. house plus garage and yard) always remark how clean it is. I do love to clean, but even when the house is dusty or there are things on the stove or wash being put away, it looks clean because there is no junk/accessories, etc., all over. Even my collections are neatly shelved in a den, in order—they're a snap to clean too, because they're controlled."*

" *The dejunking continues! Dejunking as a lifestyle is so much fun.*
The best part is the empty drawers and shelves. Is there a greater luxury than UNUSED SPACE?"

" *Less clutter to me means more room for walking, more room for being spiritual. More time for my family. Freedom to have company over. Freedom to buy those few extra groceries when they go on sale."*

" My husband, John, is wondering why we didn't do this sooner. My home is cleaner, my attitude brighter because I don't have to look at the clutter anymore or search through piles of boxes to find my treasures. He can't believe how excited I can get about 'cleaning things up.' I also have his things organized in his own drawer, his favorite part of the adventure. He can now go directly to 'his drawer' and find things without asking me 'Where did you put…?'"

" *As I put your ideas into practice, I find myself spending less time tending junk, and more time involved in creative endeavors such the fine arts, and helping those in less fortunate situations. I now realize that changing oneself for the better is the first step in changing the world!"*

" You inspired me to go through this apartment and pitch out nearly one hundred pounds of stuff that I'd dragged across the country in six moves. There's still more to be dealt with, but at least the truly scary stuff is gone."

❝ I wondered at your bold guarantee that I would lose 100 pounds without dieting. I probably threw away 300 or more within a day of reading your delightful book."

❝ I started with the biggie. The house itself. Put it on the market—priced it realistically, and sold the sucker (energy sucker) the following week. An eleven-room Victorian can hold a lot of stuff. So now we were faced with moving, and the fun began.

During the two-and-a-half-month closing period, I dejunked myself. Three tons to the landfill. Doors, screens, short pieces of lumber, bricks, piles of newspapers, magazines. Cans of What If I Need It Some Day.

The good stuff went to a yard sale. Made a couple of hundred dollars. Dressed a janitor with eight silk suits size 38. Now I wear a 42. As if I would shrink back to that size.

Three closets full of clothes, wall to wall, just went—bingo! Crazy, it's over today and I don't miss a single thing."

❝ *I started with the obvious—things I was shocked to find: posters to concerts I'd forgotten about, a cracked souvenir ceramic pig from Mexico, tons of old textbooks. Two months later, I attacked again! Things I thought I loved I now no longer liked. Most of my treasures were sentimental, childhood clutter. Throwing them out was exhilarating! The freedom of being dejunked is indescribable. No clutter under the bed or on my*

shelves. There is room in my closet! Objects that were treasures hours before, now were junk."

Another born again dejunker!

❝ *You asked what was the hardest thing about dejunking? All of it was easier than I expected."*

❝ I looked around. Perhaps there were a few things I could part with. I was finally motivated to look.

I did not throw away my complete collection of *The Ensign* magazine from 1969 on. And I kept the *Homeowner* magazines, because, after all, someday I'm going to get those bookcases and cupboards built, and my husband is going to have to have the directions. I did, however, manage to part with all but the last two issues of *Boy's Life, Sports Illustrated, Time,* and *Personal Computing.* I was surprised that I had two large garbage sacks full of unnecessary items.

I was so exhilarated by this project that I felt motivated to move on to one or two others. My office desk is clear; my junk mail hits the garbage can either before it leaves the post office, or shortly after it enters my house; and the entire family now has a sock drawer containing only wearable, matching socks.

Then I went on to those drawers and cupboards that hadn't been sorted in two or three years. I found three items I haven't been able to find for months, and when my son asked me where his scout scarf and slide were, I was able to say, smiling, with pride, 'Right here, son,' as I pulled them from the bottom of the tablecloth drawer."

Less stuff usually does equal more self-esteem.

❝ When I bought *Clutter's Last Stand* my husband, myself, and our only child—a six-year-old—were living in a 2,000-square-foot home on four acres with a double garage that could not be walked through.

I spent the better part of my time cleaning my large home that never looked clean, and arranging and rearranging all of my 'collections' (clutter). Most of these were antiques. I never passed up yard sales—I looked for them! While our home was full of whatnots, knickknacks, and bric-a-brac, we all had inadequate furnishings, no dressers or chests of drawers of any size or in good condition, no desks, no good mattress sets. There was wall-to-wall furniture, though!

It took a year, but I successfully dejunked our home. I sold more than forty pieces of furniture, numerous boxes of 'decor,' and transformed our home. We've moved to a 1000-square-foot duplex to save money to build a house (we've always leased). Our home is clean, cute, cozy, and clutter-free! We have replaced worn pieces with nice new totally functional and adequate pieces, and only own 26 pieces of furniture IN ALL!

I truly feel like a co-ed again and am in fact returning to school for my degree. I am 31 years old and finally free from the burdens and bondage of consumerism! It amazes me how many people do not examine their motives and the results before becoming so attached to possessions and the acquisition of them."

❝ *Several things I've noticed since dejunking:*

1) It's much easier to clean a sparsely decorated house.

2) Amazing how little 'junk' we need to exist day to day. Jewel-stitched kleenex box covers don't help us live longer, increase our productivity, or stay sane. One can live with very few 'doo-dads.'

3) Important stuff is easier to find when you don't have to rifle through piles of worthless tripe.

4) The beauty of an older home is more apparent when wall-to-wall hangings, furniture, and the like don't hide the woodwork, wallpaper, or floors."

❝ Last night I looked in a large cookie tin that hadn't been opened in years, and in it was a tangled mass of thread, rickrack, etc., etc., even a plastic musical note. I also found bobbins to a long-gone sewing machine, enough needles to last if I should live to be 125, and buttons galore. There were even things that I no longer knew what they were! I also opened and sorted and/or discarded a large box of food company cookbooks and clipped recipes that hadn't seen the light of day in four or five years. These are in addition to all the cookbooks on the shelves that are never used. Anyhow, I'm sure you get the picture.

Oh yes—the night before last I finally threw away two pair of contact lenses I hadn't worn in over twenty years! Nevertheless, even after all of this, I still find myself setting aside too much 'to think about.' So I am going to review *Not for Packrats Only* and *Clutter's Last Stand* frequently until my junkpile is finally depleted, and I'm 'free at last!'"

Gasp! You could have used those contact lenses for Barbie Doll car headlight covers!

66 After reading your book, I was motivated to dejunk several long put off cubbyholes:
1) My sewing closet—I straightened all the fabric, put laces on cards, and gave way all the fabric scraps that I was saving to make quilts with (I'll let my mother-in-law do that).
2) The window seat—I threw out all my old magazines and put the ones I did keep in order.
3) Storage area under the stairs—I gave all the old clothes I was storing under there to charity, filled the shelves with canning bottles, and threw out the other things I had been saving there that I will never use."

66 The day we moved, we hired a moving company, and the men were shocked when they arrived at our home. They were flabbergasted when they saw the amount of stuff we had, and had to make two trips with the enormous moving truck. We 'savers' can really pack it away. It was so humbling. I vowed 'never again' and decided I had some major changes to make.

I made some little stabs at liquidating after we moved; garage sales, Amvets, and the local mission took some of the things. Other stuff got picked out of the trash at our curb, but I didn't mind. I was feeling lighter and lighter.

I began to find such freedom and joy in simplicity that I felt our entire lives were being recreated right before our eyes. What a pleasure to have space, true space in our new home. I just wasn't sure I wanted to eliminate that beauty by filling it up with all sorts of things. I was amazed at how much we did **not** need.

It's been almost four months, and we're not finished with the saga, but I can proudly say that only essentials are within the walls of our home. The boxes and things that remain are out in the garage and I process them as I am able... letting go, letting go. Soon even the garage will be clutterless! Then we'll be able to drive our vehicles into it!!

The clean, light, uncomplicated and unshackled feeling is too glorious to believe."

Another sinner "unsaved" from stuff!

66 My husband and I got rid of three-quarters of the contents of our attic and over half the clothes in our closets. We had a neighbor who did weekly yard sales and her husband had a pickup, so we gave her everything and she was thrilled. I've never gone back to my old way of thinking. So I have a lot to thank you for."

❝ *In the past week, after and while reading your book, I achieved the following:*

1. Liberated half the garage.

2. Cleaned out my purse.

3. Sent fourteen bags of baby clothes to the Salvation Army.

4. Sent away eight bags of off-size ladies' clothes.

5. Twenty bags (two pickup trucks full) of garbage went to the landfill.

6. Fixed up shelves for the boys.

7. Threw out their missing-piece puzzles.

8. Cleaned out my van.

*9. Stored away my Christmas decorations **neatly.***

10. Freed up a complete storage room.

11. Found a family room downstairs for the boys to play in, also found a guest room and study.

I plan to spend every Friday evening continuing to dejunk!"

The best weekend date going!

❝ Dear Don:

I feel I can call you by your first name because you have been part of our family for over five years now. You're more of a mentor than just an author to us. We bought your last book this spring and it took a few months to haunt us into action. This Labor Day we did a four-day toss-a-thon. We have been dejunking for at least four years—it's the onion effect, layer by layer, tossing, tossing all the way. Each layer seems harder because it gets down to the emotional stuff—the last areas to conquer. The attic. My pantry (the place where you put stuff that doesn't have a home). And my husband's workshop—lots of old paint cans and half-finished projects that he had no intention of finishing. And of course the garage, the continuous dumping place. We had four days of emotional dumping, it was a very soul-searching experience, and **it felt great afterward**. Our pile was huge—five feet high, twelve feet long, and about four feet wide. (We are sending our trash collectors a Christmas bonus this year!)"

❝ Reading your book was an incredible relief. You were able to put into words what I've always felt about the tremendous amount of junk we Americans accumulate and tote around with us. I'm dedicating the rest of the year to decluttering my home. Once that is done, I intend to keep it that way. I can't wait to see what my apartment will look like at the end of the year."

❝ *This dejunking business has really boosted my morale. To date, I've hit 20% of the house in my junk war and have carted off eleven large boxes plus six bulging Hefty bags of miscellaneous items to charity. What a relief to be rid of the pasta maker (**who** makes pasta?), the waffle iron with the broken plug, the 62 empty jars, odds and ends of glasses left from roommates in 1974—you name it."*

Wow, think of the superb shape you'll be in after carting the other 80% worth of boxes and bulging Hefty bags away!

❝ My own decluttering included two 33-gallon bags of miscellaneous trash, two unused and thirty-two unusable ex-kitchen chairs, my excess toilet plunger and broom supply, and a huge ladder unused since my dad died twenty-four years ago. Plus a trio of useless knickknacks received for Christmas (I kept'm a week, enjoyed the thought, thanked the givers, and gently disposed)."

❝ You motivated me to reduce the amount of clutter in my classroom.

As I prepare lesson plans and projects for my fourth graders now, I try to be more selective in the choice of teaching techniques and practice materials.

I have thus been able to **free myself** of many unused and less effective teaching supplies. It has become easier to me to recognize things that I will never use. There are now two shelves of my cupboard that are BARE.

Even my lesson plans have become less cluttered. The students can quickly identify the concept they need to master and see how their independent practice drill will help them achieve the goal. The objective is clear and not hidden behind a lot of meaningless clutter.

Just cleaning off a couple of shelves made me feel more organized. But the real reward is finding that it's better for both teacher and student to unclutter teaching and learning."

❝ Clutter's Last Stand *went with my husband, twelve-year-old twin daughters, and I on vacation this summer, and life will never be the same.*

Amidst a great deal of laughter and help from each other, we took the 'Junkee Entrance Exam.' Nora, who ranked with me as 'The End is Near,' declared, 'I'm not getting rid of my junk! I love my junk!' (It turned out that she had a sock hanger collection as well as a candle wax collection. We won't discuss my plastic container collection. My family has already done that at great length.) Norm and Sarah weren't as bad, but nothing to brag about.

After four rainy days in Idaho and eight sunny days hiking at Mt. Rainier, we decided to go home and start dejunking. Somewhere along the line Nora became a convert. She was too busy dejunking her room to help unload the car. We awoke at six a.m. the next morning to the sound of her sorting and throwing. We gave up sleeping or trying to air sleeping bags and joined her.

*For the next week I would look up from my sorting to find Nora looking at me with this '**Do you really need that?**' look on her face, but not saying a word. When one of us would try to get someone else to decide about our treasure we'd hear: 'It's yours—you decide.' We had some good laughs on ourselves and each other.*

A breath of fresh air has blown into our lives. We didn't bring one souvenir home from our trip. The girls can clean their rooms in twenty minutes, instead of two hours. The house is easier to clean and we're enjoying it more. In short this is a happier, more productive household."

❝ ***Thanks to you, I got rid of a load of junk including:***
- ***one spare hairbrush***
- ***approx. 100 spare pens and pencils***

- *a few metal clips off pens (honest!)*
- *my collection of the plastic clips that come on new clothes*
- *three pair of headphones that didn't work*
- *a lot of clothes I hated*
- *a huge headache."*

❝ My life would have undoubtedly been buried—in all senses of the word—if it had not been for the timely arrival of your book.

I read it just before circumstances caused us to 'inherit' a spacious old farm house with **four large barns**. The previous owner, a dear relative, moved to a warmer climate. Since he was a frugal Dutchman with thirty years and lots of space to accumulate, you can only imagine the nightmare that confronted us! Not only did we have our own junk, but now a whole farmful was added to it.

Fortunately, I was freshly fortified with the principles of a dejunking master.

After our dear relative was safely away, we ordered a twenty-yard dumpster. We began emptying one barn—and filled that dumpster in two days! We hadn't even put a real dent in the mess, so we ordered another, this time a thirty-yarder. That took us another three days to fill. Since then I've hauled twenty 200-cubic-foot trailer loads to the landfill. I filled a three-foot-deep space underneath half of one of the barns with hundreds of bags of colored sand that were left behind.

We've had enormous rummage sales for the last three springs. (The relative came home recently for a visit—and never even noticed that any of this stuff was gone!)"

❝ *I cleaned out closets and hauled clothes to the thrift store. I cleaned out cabinets and threw away empty prescription bottles and games with missing parts. I cleaned drawers and threw away treasures that aren't treasured any more. I felt tired but good and was proud of my accomplishments. However, all this work didn't make for very relaxed weekends. My husband said Don Aslett would give me an A, but he was concerned that with all my throwing away I might dejunk him too."*

❝ I read your book during an eight-hour trip to Montana. It must have motivated me, because when we pulled into the driveway after our trip I was in a White Tornado mode. I started with completely unloading the vehicle (unlike the two weeks it normally takes to get out all the bags of fast-food garbage and coffee mugs and other food debris, all the baby toys and used wet wipes). Then I got the vacuum and completely cleaned the inside of the car, and even scrubbed the dirty carpet and car mats. Then I washed the exterior of the car and parked my spotless vehicle in the garage. It felt so good, I kept going.

Next, I went in to take a bath, but instead I noticed how junky my medicine cabinet was, as well as my vanity. I cleared them both out, cleaned the shelves, and then only put the bare necessities back. I decided I really didn't need all the bottles and tubes of stuff that I moved with me from North Dakota. It's been four years since I hauled it all here to Idaho. I guess if I hadn't used any of it for that long I really didn't need to hang onto it anymore. **I felt great** after I hauled out two garbage sacks full of junk. I couldn't believe how much space I actually had.

I've always complained about how little storage space my little 1930's house had, and how I wished I had so much more. Well, I think I'll have plenty of space as soon as I complete my dejunking!"

❝ I find that decluttering is a continuous process, since my tastes and needs are constantly changing. But strangely enough, I LOVE IT! **Some of my happiest, most exhilarating and freeing hours are those spent detecting and**

pitching out clutter. What I'm left with is a home containing only the things that bring pleasure, utility, and beauty.

This constant simplifying has even changed my taste in interior design. I now aspire to create a home that reflects the Japanese value of 'shibui'—the peace and calm that is reflected in elegant simplicity.

I can't tell you how many friends, relatives, and coworkers I've converted to decluttering. It seems that virtually everyone longs to exercise dominion over his environment, but doesn't realize he can give himself the permission to take charge of it. That's what decluttering did for me: **It gave me the permission to take control of my environment—without guilt and without fear.**"

Chapter 9

Don Aslett
PO Box 700
Pocatello ID 83204

Write to Me

Help me recognize the deserving in the upcoming Clutter wing of my world-famous Cleaning Museum.

DO YOU HAVE SOME PRIZE POSSESSIONS?

I know that all packrats secretly pride themselves in their caches and stashes, so here's a chance to assure yourself a place in the Junker's Hall of Infamy, earn your page in the Aslett Book of Junk Records.

We all have more than we should of the following, but I'm looking for those (if you're willing to admit to it) who have the MOST!

If you think you have enough of any of the following to at least place or show, photocopy this page, fill in the appropriate blanks, and send it to:

Don Aslett
PO Box 700
Pocatello ID 83204

Champions will be announced in my Clean Report Newsletter, and suitably enshrined in the wing of my Cleaning Museum devoted to the Grand Jewels of Junk!

If you have what you suspect is a record amount of anything not listed here, I'd like to know about that too. (Numbers in parentheses are those for which a starter number has been established.)

- [ ] dried-up bottles of correction fluid (59) _____
- [ ] extra combs and hairbrushes _____
- [ ] magazines more than one year old _____
- [ ] newspaper clippings a) articles b) cartoons c) recipes _____
- [ ] cookbooks (243) _____
- [ ] aged bottles of perfume _____
- [ ] old toothbrushes (137) _____
- [ ] nonworking ballpoint pens _____
- [ ] broken clocks and watches _____
- [ ] vases, sound, cracked/broken (100) _____
- [ ] old eyeglasses/sunglasses _____

- [ ] belts to clothes you no longer have (187) _____
- [ ] odd coffee cups or mugs (with or without advertising on them) _____
- [ ] empty medicine bottles _____
- [ ] blouses (217) _____
- [ ] pairs of pantyhose, run and unrun _____
- [ ] hand cultivators _____
- [ ] empty paper/plastic bags _____
- [ ] extra blankets/afghans/throws _____
- [ ] empty cardboard boxes _____
- [ ] rusty paper clips _____
- [ ] undecipherable telephone messages and numbers _____

WHAT'S THE JUNKIEST PROFESSION?

Now's your chance to nominate the deserving. I've put together a starter list here to help jog your recollections, and put asterisks on a few of my own "honorable mentions." For my money, farmers, schoolteachers, and mechanics—in that order—lead the (rat) pack.

Cast your votes here for the top three junkiest professions, and send them to: Don Aslett, PO Box 700, Pocatello, ID 83204. Results will be published in my "Clean Report."

- [ ] *accountant
- [ ] architect
- [ ] *artist
- [ ] beautician/barber
- [ ] banker
- [ ] builder/ contractor
- [ ] butcher
- [ ] carpenter
- [ ] clergyperson
- [ ] computer programmer
- [ ] deliveryperson
- [ ] dentist
- [ ] doctor
- [ ] *editor
- [ ] electrician
- [ ] exterminator
- [ ] *farmer
- [ ] florist
- [ ] *government worker
- [ ] jeweler
- [ ] junkyard owner/operator
- [ ] law officer
- [ ] lawyer
- [ ] *mechanic
- [ ] mover
- [ ] musician
- [ ] nurse
- [ ] pharmacist
- [ ] photographer
- [ ] plumber
- [ ] psychologist/psychiatrist
- [ ] real estate agent
- [ ] salesperson
- [ ] seamstress/tailor
- [ ] secretary
- [ ] *teacher
- [ ] *trash collector
- [ ] truck/cab driver
- [ ] undertaker
- [ ] veterinarian
- [ ] welder
- [ ] *writer
- [ ] _____
- [ ] _____
- [ ] _____
- [ ] _____
- [ ] _____

(add yours/others)

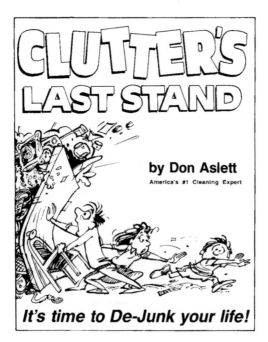

by Don Aslett
America's #1 Cleaning Expert

It's time to De-Junk your life!

CLUTTER'S LAST STAND

The book people say belongs on the shelf right beside the Bible, the one they read over and over, and give to their friends—CLUTTER'S LAST STAND. This is the bold, unique volume that first put the finger on one of the major causes of depression and inefficiency in modern life—junk and clutter! With good reason has CLUTTER'S LAST STAND been called "the book that convinces you to declutter." With a nonstop sense of humor and hundreds of hilarious illustrations, it lays out the case for dejunking, dramatically demonstrating how clutter invades and affects every area of our homes and lives. Among the many delightful features you will find here in "the big green book": The Junkee Entrance Exam (the self-test that's launched many a resolve to reform), very funny (but true) accounts of the origin of junk, 101 Feeble Excuses for Hanging onto Clutter (they'll have you rolling on the floor), a chapter called the Economy of Clutter that makes the many costs of clutter chillingly clear, and an expert guided tour through all the Junk Danger Zones from garage sales to mailorder catalogs to souvenir shops. Plus full chapters on dejunking your clothes closet, your vehicles, and your paper accumulation, and even how to rid your life of junk associates, junk food, and mental clutter!
286 pages; 220 illustrations; $10.95.

NOT FOR PACKRATS ONLY

The book Don wrote in response to all those requests: "But can you tell us more about HOW to do it, Don?" Here he guides you through the process of dejunking every step of the way. It begins with Your Personal Clutter Checkup Exam (to see just how bad off you are), and why—in case you had any doubt—you need to dejunk NOW. Then you will learn how to make your own personalized dejunking plan, where to find the time to put it in action, and Don's 4-step program for lowering your clutter count. In the chapter "Finding and facing the clutter hotspots" he leads you through every room of the house and all through the yard and grounds in a hunt for clutter. The chapter "Easy places to start" unmasks 25 pages of junk so ridiculous it'll be easy to part with it once you read this, and "How to deal with the dirty dozen" gives expert advice on coming to terms with the types of junk that derail many a dejunker. There are good solid chapters on the Basic Technique of Dejunking and identifying junk, too, as well as how to make sure you actually dispose of all that stuff that's been weeded out (and where). Plus in-depth guidance on helping others to declutter, coping with deceased people's clutter, kiddie clutter, do you need a pro organizer?, and how to stay on the wagon once you're dejunked!
224 pages; 134 illustrations; $10.00.

THE OFFICE CLUTTER CURE

If you're surrounded by piles and stacks of paper, haven't seen the top of your desk in years, or you're afraid to even look into your file cabinets, this is the book for you! It takes a hard (but hilarious) look at the state of our offices and cubicles, and serves up at least two dozen convincing reasons to clear all that clutter out (vividly details all the obvious and hidden ways office clutter is hurting us.) Then it outlines the cure, including how to deal with those big bad backlogs of paper, how to clear out filing cabinet clutter and turn "the files" from graveyard into a genuinely useful tool, how to set up paper processing systems that aren't just dead ends, how to get control of the mail, how to reclaim your desk, how to make better use of briefcases, and bulletin boards, how to halt the flow of clutter into your office, how to cope with office common area clutter, some easy places to start your office decluttering, even a look at that insidious mental clutter hovering over the office, how to keep your office looking sharp, and how to design clutter out!

192 pages; 186 illustrations; $9.99.

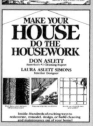

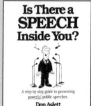

New edition in '94!

ORDER FORM

		QTY	AMT
Clean In A Minute	$5.00		
Is There Life After Housework?	$10.95		
Not For Packrats Only	$10.00		
Clutter's Last Stand	$10.95		
Special see p 48			
Personally autographed, clearly print name Only Both of the two books above	$20.00		
The Cleaning Encyclopedia	$14.95		
Make Your House Do the...	$12.95		
Pet Clean-Up Made Easy	$8.95		
How Do I Clean the Moosehead?	$10.00		
Do I Dust or Vacuum First?	$9.95		
Who Says It's A Woman's Job	$5.95		
Video Is There Life After Housework	$19.95		
Cleaning Up For a Living	$12.95		
Upgrade & Motivate Your Crew	$10.00		
Stainbuster's Bible	$10.95		
Is There A Speech Inside You?	$9.95		
Everything I Needed to Know About Business… Barnyard	$9.95		
How to Be #1 With Your Boss	$5.95		
Painting Without Fainting	$5.00		
The Pro. Cleaner's Handbook	$10.00		
The Office Clutter Cure	$9.99		
Clutter Free! Finally & Forever	$12.99		

Shipping:
$2 for first item
plus
50¢ for each
additional item.

Subtotal	
Idaho res. add 5% Sales Tax	
Shipping	
TOTAL	

☐ Enclosed ☐ Visa ☐ MasterCard ☐ Discover ☐ American Express

Card No. _____

Exp Date _____

Signature X _____

Ship to:
Your Name _____

Street Address _____

_____

City ST Zip _____

Phone _____

Mail To: Don Aslett • PO Box 700 • Pocatello ID 83204
Phone orders call 208-232-3535

Don:

Please put my name and the following friends of mine on your mailing list for the **Clean Report** bulletin and catalog:

Name_____

Street Address_____

City ST Zip_____

Name_____

Street Address_____

City ST Zip_____

Name_____

Street Address_____

City ST Zip_____

Name_____

Street Address_____

City ST Zip_____

What would I like to see in Your Future Books?

Here's something I'd really like to see you do a book on:

Here's my own cleaning or clutter question, headache, heartache, or story, which I hope you'll mention in your next book:

_____

_____

_____

_____

_____

_____

_____

_____

_____

_____

_____

Don:

Please put my name and the following friends of mine on your mailing list for the *Clean Report* bulletin and catalog:

Name_____

Street Address_____

City ST Zip_____

Name_____

Street Address_____

City ST Zip_____

Name_____

Street Address_____

City ST Zip_____

Name_____

Street Address_____

City ST Zip_____

What would I like to see in Your Future Books?

Here's something I'd really like to see you do a book on:

Here's my own cleaning or clutter question, headache, heartache, or story, which I hope you'll mention in your next book:

_____

_____

_____

_____

_____

_____

_____

_____

_____

_____

_____

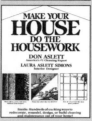

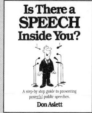

Don:
    Please put my name and the following
friends of mine on your mailing list for the
Clean Report bulletin and catalog:

Name_____   Name_____

Street Address_____   Street Address_____

City ST Zip_____   City ST Zip_____

Name_____   Name_____

Street Address_____   Street Address_____

City ST Zip_____   City ST Zip_____

What would I like to see in Your Future Books?

Here's something I'd really like to see you do a book on:

Here's my own cleaning or clutter question, headache, heartache, or story, which I
hope you'll mention in your next book:

_____

_____

_____

_____

_____

_____

_____

_____

_____

_____

_____